W9-BCY-889

LEARNING C.O.D.

CAN THE SCHOOLS BUY SUCCESS?

EDITED BY

J. A. Mecklenburger,

J. A. Wilson,

and R. W. Hostrop

LINNET BOOKS

1972

Library of Congress Cataloging in Publication Data

Mecklenburger, James, comp.
Learning C.O.D.

Includes bibliographical references.
1. Performance contracts in education. I. Wilson, John Alfred, 1938- joint comp. II. Hostrop, Richard W., joint comp. III. Title.
LB2806.2.M38 371.1 72-8345
ISBN 0-208-01291-5

Published 1972 as a Linnet Book
by The Shoe String Press, Inc.
Hamden, Connecticut 06514

Printed in the United States of America

CONTENTS

FOREWORD

Performance contracts emphasize *results* of education. By entering a performance contract, a school district agrees to spend tax dollars to purchase learning results; that is, the district pays according to how well students learn.

The focus on results makes performance contracts exciting, controversial, dramatic and important. For, conventionally, people judge schools by measures of process: we say a school provides "good education" when it has "good" teachers, libraries, buildings, tax base, curriculum and reputation. Performance contracts require that schools be judged on the quality of their product—student learning.

Performance contracting provokes vehement emotional reactions, both for and against. Measured in dollars, or in number of projects, performance contracting is a small phenomenon, but measured in emotional impact, it rivals desegregation or merit pay. It has come to symbolize many "new" directions in education—directions sometimes called "systems analysis" or "educational technology" or "applying the scientific method to learning." It has also come to symbolize educational "evils" such as "dehumanizing instruction", "Madison Avenue techniques" and "making a profit, at the expense of kids."

The contractor may be a private corporation, or it may be a group of teachers; in theory, it could be anybody. Whoever it is, since the first contract in Texarkana, in 1969, contractors have not avoided controversy. The same heated arguments are repeated, it seems, whether the contract is in Texas or Maine, Oregon or Florida, small towns or large cities, poverty areas or wealthy suburbs.

"Performance contracts are dehumanizing!" say some. "Nothing is more dehumanizing than schools that don't teach students to read!" comes the rejoinder. "You can't use tests that way!" say some critics of these contracts. "All schools use tests that way," comes the reply. "How DARE they bring in OUTSIDERS to run our schools!" some say. "All teachers should be put on performance contracts!" say others. "We could do these things without performance contracts!" many educators claim. "But you haven't!" is the response.

In this book, the reader can relive and examine these controversies and others. The title essay, "Learning C.O.D.: Can The Schools Buy Success?" presents an overview of performance contracting. After that, the reader returns to 1969-1970 to visit Texarkana, to become embroiled in the debates and excitement and scandal that enveloped that project, and to meet the men and ideas that established it.

Then he visits many other performance contract sites, including some that attempted to imitate Texarkana's project and many that did not.

Next he dwells on the extraordinary project in Gary, Indiana, where a private company contracted to operate an entire elementary school for four years.

Later he meets some of the men and corporations involved in performance contracts. Testing and "contingency management", two crucial issues in the debate over performance contracting, receive special scrutiny.

Two chapters survey reactions, analyses and opinions, and the final chapter explores the ways and means of entering into performance contracts.

Throughout this book, one finds references to "accountability", a kind of banner, slogan, and policy that grew from the same roots as performance contracts and which continually draws upon the example of performance contracts for sustenance. Leon Lessinger, who was instrumental in the Texarkana project, appears very briefly in the first article in this book, contributes to the first chapter, and his influence is evident throughout; he popularized "accountability" and urges performance contracts as a method for achieving accountability. Because accountability is such a broad topic, ranging philosophically and methodologically far beyond performance contracting, the editors of this book have compiled a companion volume entitled *Accountability for Educational Results,* also published by Linnet Books.

A second threat throughout this book is the subject of management. Contracts, including performance contracts, are techniques for managing human affairs—including education. Charles Blaschke, a management consultant to school systems, designed the Texarkana project and then many others. If Lessinger is the "father of accountability," Blaschke is the prime mover of performance contracting, which he calls a management technique for change.

A third thread throughout this book is the question of the role of teachers. Teachers, as a profession, have been the most vehement critics of performance contracts. Teachers surface at the center of every argument. Performance contracts, because they shift emphasis from process (i.e., teaching) to results (i.e., learning), because they stress accountability, and because they require management reform, challenge basic assumptions about teaching—how it is done, by whom, and for what reasons.

In sum, performance contracts have many facets. They are a new idea; a new way of thinking about schools; a way to challenge teachers, management, and organization of schools; they stir controversy, and they raise a legion of fundamental questions about the purposes and methods of public education. Performance contracts are a phenomenon, a "movement", an event of lasting significance for education as a whole in such diverse locations as Texarkana and Gary.

This book depicts performance contracts in all these guises.

James A. Mecklenburger
John A. Wilson
Richard W. Hostrop

Introduction

LEARNING C.O.D.: CAN THE SCHOOLS BUY SUCCESS?

by James A. Mecklenburger and John A. Wilson

"Advocates of performance contracts hail the dawning of new school-government-business cooperations; critics denounce the beginning of an 'educational-industrial complex.' "

One of the newest, most controversial, and, perhaps, least understood phrases in the contemporary lexicon of education is "performance contracting." A performance contract, strictly speaking, is a variety of legal contract. The contractor is rewarded according to his measured performance at a specified task. Evelyn Wood Reading Dynamics, for example, has offered such a contract for years: Triple your reading rate, or your money back. Aircraft corporations frequently sign performance contracts. But performance contracting for instructional programs–*paying according to how much children learn*–is new to public schools. There have been fifty performance contracts in education since they began in 1969; there may be fifty again this year.

Performance contracting has a Pandora's Box quality; applying business-military-government procedures to education unlocks debate over a whole series of educational issues.

"Hucksters in the schools!" is the cry of the American Federation of Teachers (AFT). Many educators concur. In contrast, two polls by the National School Board Association during 1970-71 show two-thirds of its members sympathetic to or favoring performance contracting. "Performance contracting does what [teachers] won't do–it rises or falls on *results,* not on schedules and seniority and protected mediocrity," said one school board member. Some performance contract advocates hail the dawning of new school-government-business cooperation; some critics denounce the beginning of an "educational-industrial complex."

The sharpest controversy emerges from the tense alliance that performance contracts create between school people and industry-government people. For example, such tensions nearly wrecked a project in Gary, Indiana, during its first semester in 1970. Don Kendrick, "center manager" of the project, arrived in Gary with experience as a systems analyst in the Air Force and at Lockheed. He considered schooling comparable to aircraft production—each was a system producing a product, whether airplanes or learning—and made no secret of the comparison.

"I'm a systems analyst," he told one visitor. "I view things analytically. Keep out emotions. . . . Industry says we want a job done. This is the difference [between industry and schools]. You don't have to love the guy next to you on the assembly line to make the product. He puts in the nuts, you put in the bolts, and the product comes out. Teachers can hate me and still get children to learn." As one Gary teacher remarked, "There's no way a man with that attitude can succeed in a school. No way."

The fault was not Kendrick's but was inherent in the situation. Because business and school allies are people with vastly different experience, ideas, expectations, and jargon, merely talking together is sometimes difficult. People who talk of management, cost-effectiveness, needs assessment, and *product* emphasis rouse hostility in people who talk of the whole child, individual differences, *my* classroom, or the learning *process.* Much of the public debate over performance contracting (and over accountability, which is frequently associated with it) has foundered on this rocky language dilemma.

Performance contracts have taken a number of different forms, and the variety is likely to increase in the future. The first such contract between the schools of the twin cities of Texarkana, on the Arkansas-Texas border, and Dorsett Educational Systems stipulated that Dorsett would be paid a certain amount for each child in grades six to eight whose performance in English and mathematics was raised by at least one grade level. In 1970, under a more daring agreement, the Behavioral Research Laboratories (BRL) of Palo Alto, California, contracted to take over completely the organization and administration of one elementary school in

Gary, Indiana, for four years—with payment to be based on student achievement. And the most ambitious program, funded by the Office of Economic Opportunity at $6.5-million, resulted in contracts similar to that in Texarkana being negotiated between the schools in eighteen cities and six different performance contractors, involving more than 27,000 children.

Companies with performance contracts in schools presume that schools ought to be "learning systems." The systems idea is not new; it has been applied with varied sophistication and success to military, engineering, city planning, and other enterprises The most prominent example is the space effort, and one hears the argument *"If we get men to the moon, why can't we teach kids to read?"* Or, *"If industry had forty per cent rejects in its system, it would revise the system; therefore schools too should revise their system."* Some apostles suggest that schools, like the Apollo missions should try to be "zero-defect systems."

The jargon surrounding systems ideas is nearly impenetrable. In effect, a system is a goal-oriented enterprise. It is characterized by formal procedures for defining goals, for identifying the tasks necessary to the achievement of these goals, for organizing to accomplish the tasks, for measuring one's success, and for revising the process as experience (data) dictates.

Applied to schools, the goal or product of a system is usually said to be student learning—measurable, observable student learning.

This demand for observable outcomes, for specificity of goals, coincides with pressures within education (associated with B. F. Skinner's behavioral psychology) to define teaching-learning in terms of "behavioral objectives"—that is, precise and observable student behavior. Some contractors now call these "performance objectives." One product of the behavioral objectives movemen has been programed instruction in which a student proceeds step by step through a preordained learning sequence until he achieves an objective, as demonstrated on a test. Because such instruction is inexpensive, individual, and above all produces measurable results, programed instruction is integral to virtually all performance contractors' learning systems.

Since materials provide the instruction, teachers' roles change; adults now coordinate the learning system, making certain that each child has the right materials at the right time. Teachers "teach" only when a child needs assistance. Appropriately, in many projects, teachers are now "learning directors" or "instructional managers" and classrooms have become "learning centers."

Several learning systems employ only a few certified teachers, replacing them with paraprofessionals or "assistant learning directors" who are usually local parents. A few systems have replaced teachers entirely—a fact not lost on teacher unions and associations.

The result of these innovations is often praised as "individualized instruction." Advocates of such learning systems assert that children learn at different rates so that group instruction is neither efficient nor effective. Confusion surrounds the term "individualized," however, because many educators use it synonymously with "personalized" or "humanized"—thinking that "individualized" implies regard for each student as a unique human being, capable of freedom of choice in the learning process. A few learning systems foster a personal touch; others pay little heed; most are highly structured, individualizing only the *rate* of instruction.

Neither the systems approach nor individualized instruction is the unique province of performance contractors, however. Other educational technology companies, university and government research laboratories, publishers, and teachers also have experimented with systems approaches. As a Michigan Education Association position paper summarized the situation, "What the performance contractor sells is not new ideas per se, but the way in which new ideas are put together to produce a result. The primary reason for [his] success lies in the fact that he brings to the school a *well thought-out system* and operates the system free and *unencumbered by the school administration of the district.*" (Emphasis theirs.)

Within each school or school system where contracting has occurred and in the larger state and national programs, performance contracting has created pressure toward systems for learning. And some educators have gotten the message. For example, in Grand Rapids, Michigan, Elmer Vruggink, the assistant superintendent for instruction, says that performance contracts have taught him that "sometimes we scatter our efforts too widely; teachers must become more systematic. It is not so much *the* system, but merely being systematic, that will succeed." (Grand Rapids will have twice the number of contracted projects this year as it had last year.)

Within a learning center, terminology is pseudomedical: Learning managers "diagnose" what the student needs to learn and then "prescribe" the learning sequence each student will follow.

Testing has been the sticky wicket for learning systems, but particularly for performance contractors, whose payment is usually based upon test scores. Most contracts employ individual student scores on standardized achievement tests as the basis for paying the contractor. A number of the nation's leading testing experts have heaped scorn on this procedure, calling performance contracting a gimmick, highly questionable and invalid.

The culprit is the so-called grade-equivalent score. This score implies that a student is above or below grade level. The assumption is that tests provide precise yardsticks of student progress, and educators have allowed parents and school boards to believe in these scores. But these tests are not precise. As measuring devices for individual learning, they have the accuracy more of a fist than a micrometer. Henry Dyer, vice president of Educational Testing Service, called grade-equivalent scores "statistical monstrosities." The tests yield scores that can be treated as precise data, but these numbers are actually very imprecise. So many factors can influence these scores that they become virtually meaningless. Maturation, testing conditions, the timing of tests, student attitude, and pure chance can create statistical increases that would fulfill a performance contract without the student's learning anything.

In recent months, some performance contracts have moved in more defensible directions—either using different kinds of tests, or employing more statistically reliable applications of standardized tests (which more adequately measure group performance than individual performance), or setting goals not requiring testing.

Nevertheless, scratch almost any performance contract and a defensive scream emerges over testing. Said one superintendent, "For better or worse or right or wrong, that's the way we do it! We let kids into college based on the SAT, and we let them into graduate school based on the Miller Analogy, and we let them into industry based on all kinds of standardized tests." No doubt, the testing and measurement of performance are the Achilles' heel of performance contracting.

How a student should be motivated to proceed through a

learning system—especially a student who habitually performs poorly in school—is a question about which contractors differ. Some assert that learning is its own reward. Some presume a bribe—by any other name—at the right moment helps; they use dolls, radios, Green Stamps, hamburgers, and trinkets as rewards or incentives. Some contractors emphasize praise and motivation. Others presume comfortable surroundings will motivate students, so they create colorful, carpeted, air-conditioned learning centers.

Some contractors have adopted the practice of "contingency management," which assumes that if the classroom environment contains appropriate rewards for desirable behavior, undesirable behavior will disappear. A few contractors take this theory seriously and train their staffs to use varied techniques of positive reinforcement.

The most intricate incentive system we witnessed was in Grand Rapids. It was conducted by Alpha Learning Systems, and teachers reinforced both good behavior and good academic work by distributing tokens (rubber washers in elementary school, paper money called "skins" in junior high). For a portion of the school day, youngsters go to a Reinforcing Events Room where they use tokens to purchase goods and activities they enjoy—for example, jump ropes, puzzles, soft drinks, candy, and toys for elementary children; pinball, billiards, soft drinks, candy, and dance music for adolescents. John Cline, the program director for Alpha, justifies the system in this way:

> When you put kids who are two or three years behind into that social studies class down the hall, and this kid is fifteen years old and reading at a third-grade level, and you say to him, "Read pages fourteen to twenty-one and answer the twelve questions at the end," what you're doing to that kid is saying, "Hey, loser! We want to reassert that you are a dummy! A loser! You have no inherent value!"
>
> And we do this to him time after time, day after day, year after year. Sure the kid believes he's a loser! He doesn't like himself. He doesn't like school. He doesn't like anything.
>
> And to expect that that kid is going to be intrinsically motivated to do anything in school is stupid! The way we justify extrinsic motivation is to say, "We've got to get him motivated. And since it is stupid to assume that he has any inner motivation, let's give him outward motivation to get him started."
>
> We hear from people that the kid should *want* to succeed. Well, goddamn yeah, he should. But he doesn't.

In the Alpha program, the teachers we met favored

contingency management. We were impressed also and agree with Melvin Leasure, president of the Michigan Education Association, who says: "At first it was very hard to accept the extrinsic motivation. When we were able to see how it was used in Grand Rapids, however, we saw that the kids were motivated and that after a while the extrinsic motivation became less and less important. Apparently, it was doing the job without any possibility of permanent damage."

Implicit in the learning systems we have discussed is a mechanical conception of learning: Learning (of certain kinds) can be divided into discrete units; units can be labeled (with objectives) and tested. Students must acquire learnings—as many as possible. The system succeeds when the child tests 100 per cent. Learnings are things; since contractors are paid for student learning, learning, by implication, is a commodity to be bought and sold. Most performance contracting so far has tied simple, perhaps ill-conceived, goals to crudely designed monetary rewards for the successful contractor. Perhaps most performance contracts exemplify what Ivan Illich characterized [*SR*, June 19] as the school mentality: "Knowledge can be defined as a commodity" since "it is viewed as the result of institutional enterprise [and] the fulfillment of institutional objectives."

However, not all performance contracts have displayed this mentality; and they need not do so. "Performance" can be far more widely construed than it has been. Teaching methods can differ entirely from today's practices. And the use of incentives can be applied to others than private corporations.

We are encouraged by an extraordinary performance-contracted project in Cherry Creek, Colorado, in which teachers, not a corporation, contracted with the school district to try a new idea. "I-team" was a dedicated effort to create within the public school a very personalized program to provide potential dropouts with a meaningful, responsive educational program tailored to them—virtually a "free school" within the public schools. The contract calls for a salary bonus to the teachers if the program succeeds in achieving its original objectives. There are ten objectives ranging from changes in attendance patterns to change in academic work, from changes in attitude to change in social behavior.

Outside evaluators, using several different tests, unobtrusive measures, and personal observation, ruled on the program's success (and expressed their own amazement of how successful I-team had been). In the judgment of the evaluators, the performance contract provided a useful incentive for excellent teachers to perform at their best.

Performance contracts, then, need not necessarily purchase rigid learning systems for teaching reading or mathematics. They are one device for making changes in schools, and many kinds of programs could develop under them. John Loughlin, Indiana's new state Superintendent of Public Instruction, asserted recently that "the principles inherent in performance contracting are applicable to teachers, universities, and schools. Performance contracts are a process, not a solution within themselves. They take the untried ways out of the ivory tower and put them into the classroom. I see no reason why performance-contracted projects cannot be developed on the campus, in the halls of the state Teachers Association, the National Education Association, or the American Federation of Teachers."

Change is the keynote in talk of performance contracting, and with some justification. In at least some cases, parents see clear proof that kids learn; school boards find a new way to share responsibility and to seek federal funds; superintendents gain prestige as innovators; testing experts acquire some long-awaited attention; work and salary patterns for teachers begin to change; new professions in education begin to emerge; an opening has been made for entrepreneurs; and whole school systems seriously address fundamental educational issues.

There are modest changes, such as better ways to teach reading, to squeeze the tax dollar, or to sell more textbooks; and major changes, such as paying children to learn, ending the autonomy of the classroom teacher, shifting power away from old vested interests, even redefining what school is and what learning is.

It is also claimed that performance contracting stimulates change in the schools generally through the innovative example it gives, through the posibility it provides for school boards to experiment without high risk—they can claim credit for successes and blame the contractor for failures—through the provision of system design and management skills not usually available to the schools, and through simply shaking up the system so that it is easier to get change started and keep it going.

The most elaborate and most formal answer to the question of how performance contracting changes schools has been advanced by Charles Blaschke and Leon Lessinger. Blaschke, drawing upon defense industry procurement procedures, planned the Texarkana project. Lessinger, then an Associate U. S. Commissioner of Education, funded it. Lessinger now invokes Texarkana as the best example of what he calls "educational engineering." This formal and complex process systematically links planning, teaching, and evaluation. Planning is in two parts. All interested parties are consulted until an entire educational project is outlined, based on specified needs—a process called "needs assessments." Then a Request For Proposals (RFP) is issued to competing companies, asking them to bid on the project.

After a contract is agreed upon, an outside evaluator to do the testing and final report and an "educational auditor" to superintend and attest to everyone's honesty (similar to a certified public accountant) are hired. Presumably, everything is the focus of community attention, open, and scrupulously honest. At the end of the year, a project will have had every opportunity to prove itself.

Blaschke has adapted the term "turnkey" from the building trades, where a contractor may accept full responsibility for construction of a building, then turn the keys over to the new owner. Similarly, an educational contractor may run a project for a year or more, then turn it over to the school system. This has occurred in some cities, including Texarkana, where in the third year, beginning this fall, the school system will run the program begun by the contractor.

Some contracts have followed the Lessinger-Blaschke model, from needs assessment to turnkey; but in many contracts, such as the one set up in Gary, the contractor was selected without competitive bidding. Most companies prefer to negotiate performance contracts without competitive bidding. Some contracts dispense with the evaluator, with the school board assuming responsibility for evaluation. Some contracts dispense with the auditor. Similarly, at the end of a project the school may accept the entire program, adopt part of it, or drop the whole thing.

Some experts assert that turnkey is a device for avoiding legal problems. If the contract specifies the school board's intention to turnkey a project, then, it is claimed, it abdicates no responsibility to the contractor. But the question of control of the schools remains one of the most difficult of all those raised by performance contracting.

The Gary contract, calling for the turning over of an entire elementary school, Banneker School, to BRL, was the boldest challenge to date, not only to tradition but also to the education establishment. George Stern, then president of BRL, rejoiced that through the contract BRL had "gained the clout to implement all our ideas." But the reality wasn't as simple as merely signing a contract. Nowhere has the power struggle inherent in performance contracts been more explosive.

In the first skirmish, a summer ago, Indiana Attorney General Theodore Sendak, at the request of the state Department of Public Instruction, expressed his informal opinion that contracting for the operation of a public school by a private corporation would be illegal. School City of Gary (which is the name given to the city's public schools) and BRL felt compelled to modify their contract to reduce somewhat the school board's delegation of authority to the company. In late summer, state Superintendent of Public Instruction Richard D. Wells asked School City to consider planning for one year before beginning the project or, failing that, to hire BRL as consultant only; he offered Gary $20,000 to pay for BRL's consultant services. Not to be co-opted, School City chose to continue in its own direction.

When it became clear that neither Sendak's opinion nor Wells's advice had deterred the contract, the Gary Teacher's Union voted to strike over involuntary teacher transfers and other contract violations. School City countered by seeking a judicial restraining order, after which the union felt constrained to use its own grievance procedures. The results are still being argued.

After extensive investigation, the state Department of Public Instruction in January challenged the legality and quality of the project: Classes were too large; state-adopted textbooks were being ignored; some staff were uncertified; only reading and mathematics had been taught. Some community elements in Gary and some school administrators joined with the state in insisting that subjects other than reading and mathematics be taught. BRL is paid only for reading and math test score gains, although the company contracted to operate the entire school; BRL argued that it had planned from the beginning to phase in a broader curriculum. It was phased in quickly.

"There is nothing uniquely innovative about the Banneker program," asserted a state investigatory report in February, "except the abdication of professional responsibility on the part of School City of Gary and the placement of primary emphasis upon building and maintaining a systems model instead of upon the children and their needs and interests." The State Board of Education decommissioned Banneker School in February, a move which threatened to cost Gary $200,000 in state aid and resulted in adverse national publicity.

Some changes in the program resulted quickly; a change also occurred in the political climate—Governor Edgar D. Whitcomb visited Banneker School just before the March state Board of Education meeting, calling the school a "worthy experiment." The board recommissioned Banneker School.

Finally, under School City's prodding BRL consented to run a 1971 summer program, using Banneker's teachers under BRL guidance, to produce an expanded curriculum that would be suitable for the wide range of academic ability found among the children in the school. Perhaps coincidentally, several BRL and Gary administrators connected with the project will not return this second year.

Similarly, performance contracting upset the national power structure in education. After a series of blistering resolutions at their August convention, the AFT established "listening posts" East, Central, and West to monitor performance contracting; its publications were filled with accusations, many of them embarrassingly accurate. And its *Non-coloring Book on Performance Contracting* is a vicious piece of political cartooning that has been reprinted widely.

The National Education Association (NEA) seemed to want, at first, to respond in the same manner as the AFT, but two of its locals signed contracts with the Office of Economic Opportunity (OEO), forcing the national organization to bite its tongue. The NEA was hardly solid on the issue, in any case. Its Michigan affiliate wrote and spoke very highly of the benefits caused by performance contracts in Michigan, and NEA locals elsewhere were at least respectful of projects in their jurisdiction.

Clearly, the final verdict on performance contracting is far from in. Some contracts have shattered complacency, inspired creativity, improved learning, and turned the spotlight of public attention on the quality of classroom instruction. But others have inspired greed and chicanery, created poor environments for children, and fomented unhealthy dissension.

Performance contracting has as its kernel a powerful idea: Someone other than children must bear the responsibility for whether children learn successfully. Who bears that responsibility, and to what measure, are questions loaded with dynamite. Surround these questions with money, risk, publicity, new teaching strategies, new people, new rhetoric, systems analysis, contingency management, and more, and it is no wonder that this recent, and thus far minuscule, phenomenon has raised such a ruckus in public education.

To date, most performance contracts have been primitive in design, method, and evaluation, their high-flown rhetoric notwithstanding. Results are beginning to be reported. Some projects undoubtedly will appear to do very well; others will be instructive as failures. All should be regarded with the kind of hopeful skepticism that greets the first trial of any new invention.

However, there are signs of emerging sophistication. Here and there, creative and knowledgeable people are questioning the narrow definitions of performance that have bred mostly mechanical teaching of basic skills; they are questioning the evaluation that places wholesale reliance on inappropriate tests; and they are sharpening their contracting skills so that projects of more than publicity value emerge.

If this sophistication grows and triumphs over the hucksters and panacea hounds who also flock to inventions, the performance contracts of the early 1970s could well be the first ripple of a new wave in education. □

James A. Mecklenburger and John A. Wilson began their research on performance contracting in the schools a year ago as EPDA fellows in instructional systems technology at Indiana University. They are completing doctoral dissertations on various aspects of performance contracting and have published several articles on the subject in professional journals. Mr. Mecklenburger is currently a research assistant at Phi Delta Kappa International. Mr. Wilson is an administrative assistant in the Indiana State Department of Public Instruction.

Chapter One

TEXARKANA

I

THE AGE OF ACCOUNTABILITY DAWNS IN TEXARKANA

by Stanley Elam

"There's no question about it now. The Texarkana experiment in performance contracting with private industry for rapid improvement in pupil achievement has started a nationwide trend. Large systems in particular, looking for quick, low-cost dropout prevention, are going stark, raving Texarkana. Here's the first detailed account of what is going on in Texarkana, U.S.A. For good measure: some analysis and a few cautions.

On April Fool's Day, Mrs. Elam and I headed southwest for Arkansas, where teachers say, "Thank God for Mississippi."

Without Mississippi, Arkansas would rank lowest among the states on several traditional indicators of educational potential: teacher salary levels[1] , per capita personal income; percent of educationally deprived children eligible under Title I, ESEA; etc.

The goal of our pilgrimage was to find answers to such questions as this: Why is Texarkana, a small city (50,000) with a precarious economy (now bolstered by nearby defense plants) currently the center of attention for alert school policy makers? What are the unique features of the Texarkana schools' performance contract with private industry? How successful is the Texarkana project in raising achievement levels of potential dropouts in reading and math? What are its strengths and weaknesses? Can the plan be successfully adopted and adapted elsewhere? How?

We must confess that our short visit with the courteous, helpful, and intelligent people who run the Texarkana Project did not answer the key question about achievement boosts. No one will

---

know the full answer, we suspect, until much later. As has been widely publicized already, preliminary tests are "encouraging." However, the private contractor, Loyd Dorsett of Dorsett Educational Systems, Norman, Oklahoma, won't even know whether he is a financial winner or loser until the first year's testing is analyzed sometime this month.

Unfortunately, an "evaluation" report completed in late March by a third party who tried to compare the Texarkana experimental and control groups is seriously flawed. Its basic flaw was a failure, because of the late start, to match the control group properly with the treatment group.

One of our early disappointments in Texarkana was the discovery that the schools' contract with Dorsett does not include a clause, discussed at the negotiations stage, which would have provided penalties should initial gains disappear after six months. Thus temporary achievement spurts so familiar to educational researchers—usually due to all those factors we lump together as the Hawthorne effect—may fade away without anybody noticing.

If all this is true, why have an estimated 25 U.S. school systems, including those in major cities like Detroit, Dallas, San Diego, and Portland (Ore.), already jumped on the performance contract-accountability bandwagon? Why is an entire state, Virginia, about to contract with private industry for public school instruction? Obviously, it is because of the hope Texarkana holds for demonstrating what the economists call low labor-intensive production, and it may be a chimera. As we look back on our investigation of the Texarkana phenomenon, this appears to be *the* major question, and perhaps an answer, or at least a warning against over-optimism, will emerge from what follows.

It soon became apparent to us, upon examining the most up-to-date materials on performance contracting, that there is one towering figure among the many individuals and companies[2] who would like to see this new educational panacea sweep the country. He is not Leon Lessinger, although the movement probably would not have begun when it did without Lessinger's influence. As associate commissioner of education at the USOE for a year, Lessinger pushed hard for the principle of accountability.[3] He said, "The fact that many results of education are not subject to audit should not deter us from dealing precisely with those aspects that lend themselves to precise definition and assessment."

But Lessinger left the USOE last January for the relative obscurity of the university (Georgia State). Before he did he had met a young man who was thinking on similar lines but emphasizing the notion of performance contracts. The result was the funding of the Texarkana Project in April, 1969.

Today this young man is the real leader of the performance contracting-accountability movement. He is Charles L. Blaschke, president of Education Turnkey Systems, Inc., of Washington, D.C.[4] He represents a special breed, a scholar with the drive and persuasiveness for entrepreneurship. Only three years ago, Blaschke was finishing doctoral requirements at Harvard with a case study of the educational technology industry. At the same time, he was on active duty in the Army with the rank of lieutenant and was teaching graduate courses in political economy and educational technology at Catholic University. (We don't know how he did it all either.)

The question that bothered Blaschke most at that time was, "Can we create the political innovations to effectively develop, evaluate, and utilize the technology which is capable of being produced for public education?"[5] It still bothers him, but he now thinks he has many of the answers. A number of them appear in Volume I, Number 1, of *Education Turnkey News,* dated April, 1970. It is published by his company. Interested educators may secure a copy by writing Education Turnkey Systems, Inc., 1660 L St., N.W., Washington, D.C. 20036 – which is only a few doors from National Education Association Headquarters, where the outlook is generally quite different from Blaschke's.

Blaschke had an early hand in the Texarkana Project. Texarkana's city government had secured Model Cities Demonstration Agency money from the Department of Housing and Urban Development late in 1968. The project included a small education component for dropout prevention, and this is where Blaschke came in.

At the time–early spring, 1969–the Nixon Administration had just added Title VIII (dropout prevention) to the Elementary and Secondary Education Act. It provided money for exactly the kind of project Blaschke had in mind, and he was instrumental in getting a five-year $5 million dropout prevention proposal approved by the U.S. Office of Education. The Texarkana Project was in business, and Blaschke went about developing a program plan, evaluation procedures, and a request for proposals.

In the first *Education Turnkey News* there is a special interim report on "Texarkana–First." What follows immediately is taken primarily from this report, with some added facts secured from Loyd Dorsett's representative in Texarkana, C. J. Donnelly; from Martin Filogamo, the local school system representative; and from Ed Trice, superintendent of Arkansas District 7.

On September 9, 1969, the boards of Arkansas District 7 and the Liberty-Eylau District of Texas selected Dorsett Educational Systems from a group of 10 companies–including RCA, QED (Quality Education Development of Washington, D.C.), and McGraw-Hill–to operate Rapid Learning Centers (RLC's) on a guaranteed performance basis. Their major goal was to prevent dropouts, primarily by raising achievement levels in reading and mathematics.

The RLC's were opened on October 15. By November 1, four were fully operational, with over 100 students enrolled. Centers were established in mobile 900-square-foot classrooms adjacent to junior and senior high schools and, in two cases, were put into vacant classrooms in junior highs. Between October 15 and March 2, over 300 students enrolled in the RLC's, for an average of two hours per day, while participating in extracurricular activities and other school studies during the rest of the school day. All participants were diagnosed as potential dropouts. At the ninth-grade level, Texarkana's black students on the average were 70 percentiles below the white students in reading and math.[6] About 30 percent of the junior high children in the two districts are black; about 50 percent of the RLC children are black.

A letter of intent was agreed upon and signed by Dorsett and the local education agency (Arkansas District 7) on September 15. The actual subcontract, based on the letter of intent, was submitted in late November to the USOE for final approval.[7] USOE contract officials recommended the deletion of several conditions agreed upon by the school and Dorsett in the letter of intent. These included a clause specifying that students culd be re-tested some six months after "graduation" from the RLC's to determine whether retention rates were equal to those of the average student within the system. Less than average retention rates would have been the basis of contract renegotiation.

At present 20 local teachers and administrators have been

hired as "expert consultants" working part-time (on their own time) to assist the contractor in refining his program. At the same time, these people are being exposed to the RLC instructional system in order to facilitate adoption by the schools during the turnkey phase, which will begin this fall. Training sessions will be held during the summer, once individuals have realized their need for training.

The typical RLC has one paraprofessional and one professional working with 15-25 students each hour. (The goal is 25 students next year.) All of the instructional personnel were hired by Donnelly, who as Dorsett's director in Texarkana has all the duties of a principal without some of the restraints. For example, he fired one teacher a few months after she was employed because the performance of students under her tutelage was not up to expectations. The reason for this? "She just didn't like children."

(Arkansas has no tenure law, and anyway, the State Department of Education has suspended certification and certain other requirements in the interest of promoting Texarkana's "innovations." Nevertheless, Donnelly was careful to hire only certifiable people as teachers, most of them applicants who had not gotten jobs in the city before. All are paid the same as teachers hired by the school board, except for bonuses paid to compensate for their longer day.)[8]

The RLC instructional program consists of programmed reading and math materials presented largely (about 90 percent) through the Dorsett AVTM-86.[9] A $200 film strip and record teaching machine, relatively simple to operate, it uses mostly Dorsett-developed software. Students log in their time on their punch cards, move through the material at their own rate, and record test results on a punch test card which is later processed to determine progress and branching needs. Science Research Associates reading labs, Portal Press (John Wiley) "Springboards," Job Corps reading programs, Grolier reading labs, and other programmed materials are used in various branching patterns on an as-needed basis. Through student feedback indicated on tests, critical learning points are determined and programs are modified.

These procedures are old hat to educators familiar with school-operated dropout programs. One feature of the RLC programs is not old hat, however. This is a special motivation technique employed by Dorsett. It is frankly extrinsic, but it seems to work. For each lesson successfully completed (100 percent correct) by an RLC pupil, 10 Green Stamps are awarded, at least in one of the centers. For one grade-level advancement in math or reading, the pupil gets a small transistor radio. ("Some of the kids think they're worth \$10. Actually, we get them in quantity for \$2.98 each. Since by contract we get \$80 per grade-level advance, it's a paying proposition to spend \$6 on rewards," one teacher told me.) And this is not all. The youngster who makes the greatest advance in grade levels, as measured by the Iowa Tests of Educational Achievement, wins a portable television set. One winner advanced 8.3 subject grade levels—5.1 in math, 3.2 in reading—in just three months of instruction.

There are still other forms of reward. Games, puzzles, popular magazines, and free time to "rap" with friends are part of the RLC philosophy of motivation. When a child has successfully completed a day's assignment, he can employ his spare time in any way he likes. Often the teacher or paraprofessional will play a game of checkers or chess with an early finisher. Superintendent Trice says this procedure may actually bring students and teachers into personal contact for greater lengths of time than traditional group instruction permits, despite the emphasis on technology.[10]

Trice's description of what happens in RLC's is graphic and makes sense: "The role of the teacher in the RLC is altogether different from the role of the teacher in the traditional classroom. She could be called an instructional manager. She programs each individual's assignment. At the end of her school day she goes to the main center and picks up her material for the next day—that is, the film, records, and other software she needs. She takes this back to the school, where each child has his assignment in a folder. He knows exactly where he finished the day before and where he needs to start today. And so when the child comes into the room he doesn't take a seat and wait for roll call or the tardy bell. He goes directly to his folder, picks up his material, gets his record and film, goes to his machine, and threads it himself (unless he runs into some difficulty, when the teacher will help). Then he puts his headset on and he's in business.

"He couldn't care less about what others are doing; he can't even see or hear them, for one thing. Then he starts his program. If he makes a mistake, there's no one to laugh at him. Most of these people have come out of a classroom with group instruction where first of all they've been timid about reciting because they realize by now that they don't know the answers. They've been completely frustrated and humiliated. If they make a wrong answer, then the whole class will laugh at them. Children are just that way. And usually the teacher will not call on them because she too knows they can't answer. But here in the lab they're working at their own level, and if they make a mistake only the machine knows about it.

"As you know, there are incentives built into the process. We have found out that tangible incentives have real value until the youngsters begin to achieve. After a while, according to Mr. Filogamo, and it makes sense to me, achievement is itself an incentive. Children enjoy actually achieving and they forget about the material incentives. But until they enjoy achievement, the incentives are built in."

Trice takes little credit for planning the RLC's, but is proud of one, contribution. It was his recommendation that the phrase "dropout prevention" be eliminated from the project vocabulary and that the units where children are taught be called "rapid learning centers." This change has had much to do with the apparent lack of any stigma attached to attendance at the RLC's. As Trice says, "No one is opposed to 'rapid learning.' "

Students were selected for the program, for the most part, on the basis of grade-level deficiencies. However, because of the larger number of volunteers (57 students volunteered last summer for the program, and a waiting list of 200 existed by March), a third of the target population was chosen from the volunteers, so long as they were two grade levels behind. Another third (many of whom were much more than two grade levels behind and came from deprived—often broken—homes) were selected by teachers and counselors. The remainder of the students were selected on a random basis, if they met the entry level criterion of two grade levels behind in math and reading. No children with measured I.Q.'s lower than 70 (in one system) or 75 (in the other) were to be admitted. But some got in anyway, usually at the request of counselors.

It was not until January that the local education agency contracted with the Magnolia (Arkansas) Education Service Center, operated by Dean C. Andrew, to perform the "internal evaluation," using funds from Title III, USOE. In developing the evaluation design, ESC undertook to test and report monthly.

On February 2, 51 students were post-tested with the Iowa Tests of Educational Achievement (which the schools had used in pre-testing) to determine extent of progress. Results indicated that in a total of 89 hours of instruction, the average student had achieved an increase of .99 grade levels in math and 1.50 in reading. In vocabulary subtests even better results were realized.

A second post-test, involving 59 students, was conducted on March 2. Results indicated that in a total of 120 hours, equally distributed between reading and math instruction, students were achieving, on the average, 2.2 grade-level increases in reading and 1.4 in math.

These, remember, are averages. It was somewhat surprising to note that as many as 32 percent of the pupils had made *no* progress–had even slipped back by from .1 to between three and four grade levels in one or another subject. This was true even after 60 hours of instruction in a given subject. For example, of 51 pupils taking the March 2 test of reading comprehension, 13 had slipped from .1 to one grade level and four had slipped between one and two grade levels.

Donnelly had several explanations for this phenomenon. For one thing, several of the poorest performers were not members of the original target population but were less than a grade level behind to begin with. Then there is testing error, both pre-rest and post-test. Donnelly also points to the unexpected unreliability of Form I of the Iowa tests (admitted by Houghton Mifflin, the publisher, who pleads that the tests were never intended to determine whether a contractor is paid for instruction). Finally, there is the desire of some youngsters to remain in the program and the fact that the teaching machines just may not suit the learning style of some children.

Blaschke reports that there have been significant behavioral changes as a result of the project: Only one of the 301 participants has voluntarily dropped out of school. Meanwhile, the dropout rate among other high school students, especially in grades 11-12, has increased.

Only five percent of the teachers and administrators have indicated slight or no interest in the RLC program or an unwillingness to use it in the schools. Teachers from two of the junior highs have already requested that the RLC equipment be integrated into their classes immediately. (There is money in the government contract to pay for substitute teachers while regular teachers visit and learn about the RLC program. One teacher who was taking advantage of this opportunity while we visited cheerfully reported that she had learned the Pythagorean Theorem from helping one of the youngsters with his slide-tape math program.)

Vandalism in the cooperating schools has been cut in half. Cost of window replacement is down by one-third. Only one of the Rapid Learning Centers has been burglarized.

Community support and participation is reportedly good. As an early illustration, to save the program, voters who elected four "freedom of choice" proponents to the Texas Independent District District board in April, 1969, went back to the polls in a referendum the next month and voted against this segregation-saving device. The issue had been put to them as follows: In order to insure the district's participation in a program which "guaranteed" to raise performance in deficient children, so that upon full-time integration these children could compete educationally without lowering the overall quality of instruction, it would be necessary to vote down freedom of choice. Despite the fact that Texarkana is the home of Freedom, Inc., the national advocate of the so-called freedom of choice plan, the margin was 7-1 against it.

On March 12, 1970, another school board election was held for Arkansas District 7. Even in light of an apparent reversal of federal policy with respect to freedom of choice at that time, and despite growing opposition to busing to achieve desegregation, no board member was replaced by a freedom of choice advocate.

In early February, 1970, the Texarkana schools entered into a contract with Blaschke's organization to conduct program planning and analysis for turnkey operations. ETS, Inc., is now working with the Texarkana Education Service Center and the project management staff to analyze the relative cost-effectiveness of the RLC Program and the existing math and reading programs within the school systems. Filogamo believes that the RLC Program will work out to be about $100 a year cheaper per pupil than the others, on a time-equated basis. But no official figures are yet available.

Once cost-effectiveness has been analyzed, the next step will be to determine the changes required within the existing school system for it to adopt the RLC math and reading programs "to realize a large percentage of the actual potential efficiency demonstrated during the year," to use Blaschke's words. Cost will include actual purchase of equipment required, staff development, implementation of performance budgeting and accounting systems, etc. Administrative changes will probably include a movement to individualize scheduling, computer-based student monitoring, and the like. Preliminary analyses indicate that cost savings may be realized, especially in the math area, through a doubling or tripling of students throughout, by better use of facilities, and by hiring paraprofessionals.

These analyses, plus others, will be part of Phase II of the five-year Texarkana Dropout Prevention Program. It is presently expected that, in addition to the turnkey operation, RLC's will be established for grades 4-6 and grades 7-12, especially for those students who will require maintenance as well as accelerated learning due to the vast difference between their present grade level achievement and that of their peers. An integral part of Phase II will be a special project funded through the local Model Cities Demonstration Agency for grades K-3. At present, ETS, Inc., is helping develop a list of bidders and a request for proposals to be sent to various firms, including, of course, Dorsett.

The implications of performance contracting do not seem to disturb the teachers in Texarkana, although they have disturbed teachers elsewhere. I talked with Mrs. Norma Shaddox on this subject. She is executive secretary of the Arkansas Dist. 7 Classroom Teachers Association which recently became one of the five such associations in Arkansas (which has no collective negotiation law) to negotiate a written contract with the local Board of Education. Mrs. Shaddox said Texarkana teachers, on the whole, view the RLC's very favorably, certainly not as a threat. "The consensus has been, 'If I had 10 students and 10 machines, I could do this too!'

"A few teachers are afraid the machines will take their jobs; I'm not," Mrs. Shaddox said.

She doesn't agree with the Dorsett reward system, however. "I would stand on my head if that would make them learn, but I wonder if the children are *really* learning or just storing a little knowledge for long enough to get the reward."

We discovered later that Mrs. Shaddox is one of the 20 paid consultants employed to advise the district with respect to the RLC's.

What can one say in summing up the Texarkana experiment? First, it must be reemphasized that it is still an experiment. Only a few of the original objectives have been reached, if one insists on definitive proof. Mr. Donnelly, a scientist who has an engineering degree and not one hour of academic credit in education (although he has been working for 17 years with learning materials, including several years in educational publishing) expressed impatience with some of the accolades already showered on the Texarkana Project. Though by no means poor-mouthing the project, he squirms when people like Jim Wright, associate editor of the *Dallas Morning News,* say "Private organizations, business or otherwise, are far more capable of experimenting to find the best methods to solve the problems than our public agencies [are]. That's because they can abandon an experiment that fails and try another approach—remember the Edsel?—while government tends to perpetuate its failures."

Donnelly is sophisticated enough to recognize and admit that private organizations can cover up their mistakes too. What about Ralph Nader's revelations, Mr. Wright?

Donnelly believes that the performance contract and the Dorsett techniques constitute a very powerful instructional program. But he is disturbed by at least two aspects of the RLC Program in Texarkana. He talked freely about the faults of the instruments that now must be used to measure pupil progress. He is aware that they don't accurately reflect the school's instructional program. He also knows that articulation of RLC programs with the school curriculum is poor. Although an effort is made to avoid conflicts, it is inevitable that a student will sometimes miss a regular math, English, or other class in order to fit into the RLC Program. When he goes back to the traditional program next term, the student may find he has missed important concepts. "So he succeeds in the Dorsett program, but his math teacher doesn't see much transfer. He gives the youngster a D."

Donnelly regards the essential purpose of the project as

demonstration of a low labor-intensive system; he believes this goal is being realized, but he is aware of the problems involved in achieving some of the other goals of instruction.

It may yet turn out that Texarkana-style multi-media projects are suited best for exactly what they are doing: boosting achievement of potential dropouts on nationally normed reading and arithmetic achievement tests. Wholesale acceptance of the procedures for other purposes, at least in the present state of our ignorance, will not serve American education well. To the extent that Texarkana-style programs do not meet the instructional objectives of a school, we will continue to have problems with them. Loyd Dorsett himself says, "Broad-scale contracting with private industry for the exclusive operation of schools, like the Job Corps contracts, would probably be unwise. But to contract with business firms on a performance basis to install educational innovations in educational procedures now appears to be useful."

Certainly the power of the performance contracting-accountability concept is real. It must be explored further—carefully. □

---

[1]Actually, at $6,155 Arkansas ranked 45th in 1968-69, ahead of North Dakota, Alabama, South Carolina, South Dakota, and Mississippi, in the estimated average salaries of all teachers in public schools. The national average was $7,908. (Half of Texarkana is in Texas, which ranked 38th in teacher salary averages at $6,619.)

[2]Texarkana's request for proposals was sent to 113 potential bidders and Superintendent Ed Trice says he missed several.

[3]See Leon M. Lessinger and Dwight H. Allen, "Performance Proposals for Educational Funding ' PHI DELTA KAPPAN, November, 1969, pp. 136-37.

[4]ETS is, in Blaschke's own words, a management support group providing program planning and development services in the area of contracting and turnkey operations. "Turnkey" is a word borrowed from the housing industry. As a process, turnkey gained favor with government when local public housing authorities developed performance specifications for bids by private firms. After building the homes, contractors "turned the keys ' over to the local government. As Blaschke notes, "the private firms enjoyed a flexibility which public housing authorities did not, in terms of dealing with local on-site construction labor unions, as well as building codes." The parallel with "inflexible" education institutions and outdated state school codes is obvious.

[5]As phrased in "The DOD: Catalyst in Educational Technoloyg," his article for the January, 1967, KAPPAN on "Big Business Discovers the Education Market."

[6]By and large, Texarkana's participating schools were not desegregated until last September, when the all black high school was closed. Token efforts had been made at the ninth grade level during the previous two years.

[7]Terms of the contract are fairly complex, but the essentials can be summarized. Prior to contracting, the Texarkana, Ark. District was made the administrative unit for the $270,000 five year project funded by the USOE, with the Liberty-Eylau School District in Texas a program participant. The Dorsett contract provides for a base payment of approximately $80 per student per grade level increase in math or reading in no

more than 80 hours of instruction, or $1 for one hour of instruction. If the increase is achieved sooner, there is a bonus. If a child fails to reach the specified grade level in the designated time, the company will suffer penalties. If it takes as many as 160 hours to do the job contracted for there is no payment at all. But if Dorsett does as well as he expects, he will receive a total of $125 to $135 thousand for the year's work. No one expects him to net a large profit from the Texarkana effort, but the experience should give his company an edge in competition for instructional services in other larger districts later on. He is convinced that it is possible to produce a grade-level increase in achievement in reading or math at approximately $80 per student and do it profitably. "We're not trying to 'fair trade' the education market," Donnelly says, "but it's the truth."

[8]I found out later that this is not the whole story. If Dorsett's "learning managers" and "associate managers" produce high achievement among the children in their charge, they will be rewarded with stock and stock options in Dorsett's company. Donnelly revealed in a phone conversation that at the end of the project "some kind of efficiency formula will be applied for making differential awards." (At Christmas time all RLC managers received equal stock bonuses.)

Will Texarkana's public school teachers accept the public school counterpart of bonuses: merit rating? We'll have to wait and see.

[9]Although simple in appearance, the AVTM has 50 transistors and a computer-style shift register. It took Dorsett 13 years and $2 million to develop it.

[10]One of the outcomes of the reward program is a tendency of some shrewd pupils to fail miserably at the final hurdle in order to qualify for another month in the RLC and a short at more rewards.

II

PERFORMANCE CONTRACTING

by Richard Bumstead

The performance contract. No increase in achievement level, no fee. For a greater than anticipated increase, a higher fee. A businessman's profit is hitched by the school directly to student achievement, which motivated a businessman to do his best in language he understands. The first contract motivated too far. Will $100 million more rectify the errors of the past?

For the past school year, Texarkana, Arkansas, has been the Mecca of the educational world.

Administrators, government officials, publishers, vice-presidents of educational firms, journalists—all made a pilgrimage to Texarkana (a city as dry, dusty, and hard to get to as Mecca itself), there to observe and wonder at the good things resulting from a new arrangement between a school district and an educational business firm looking for a profit.

The new arrangement is the performance contract; the expected results are increases in the achievement levels of 13-, 14-, and 15-year-olds, students on the verge of dropping out of school because they function two or more grade levels below their peers in reading and math.

What has fired everyone's imagination, however, and set them trekking off to Texarkana, is the risk the educational business firm—Dorsett Educational Systems Inc.—accepted under the performance contract. No increase in achievement levels, no fee. But the reverse is also true: for a greater than anticipated increase, a higher fee. The firm's profit is hitched directly to student achievement, which motivates a businessman to do his best in language he understands.

The word from Texarkana has spread throughout the land in a fashion any prophet would envy. School superintendents and vice-presidents of educational business firms and some publishing houses, plus whatever consultants each side could muster, have been hammering out performance contracts these last few months, so programs could start in September. The Education Commission of the States estimates that 150 such contracts have been signed so far.

Most of the money for this surge of performance contracts has come from the Federal government. Texarkana got $250,000 for the first year of its project under Title VIII of ESEA, which established a nation-wide program for dropout prevention. Recently the U.S. Office of Education (USOE) has permitted proposals for performance contracts to be submitted under Title I of ESEA.

Charles Blaschke, the Washington-based consultant who organized the Texarkana project, told a group of educators in Chicago this summer that, as he reads the Washington scene, a good deal of money will go into performance contracts. "Out of fiscal year 1971 funds," he said, "I estimate that close to $50 million will be expended on performance contract projects during the school year 1970-71. It is conceivable that as much as $100 million will be expended under the fiscal year 1971 budget."

Federal support also comes in other forms. USOE hired Rand Corporation to analyze performance contracting as it occurs in the real world with its reactions on budget, time, and expertise, and write a guide book that would aid school administrators in negotiating contracts. One official estimated this guide book would be ready in November, 1971. This fall the Office of Economic Opportunity (OEO) launched a $5.6-million experiment in 18 school districts involving 20,000 students, to test the effectiveness of instructional methods brought to these schools by performance contracts.

Any movement commanding such funds and educational attention that performance-contracting has been receiving inevitably stirs up a host of critics, and some of these are now beginning to speak up, alarmed, perhaps, at the fervor of the advocates of performance-contracting. Officials of NEA and AFT, for example, are calling performance-contracting an abdication of the school's responsibilities, and not really necessary, if only the regular staff had the resources to do the job right in the first place. As for examining the assumptions of performance-contracting, William Ellena, deputy secretary of the American Association of School Administrators, said that AASA, in conjunction with the American Educational Research Association, is organizing a task force of distinguished educators, psychologists, educational researchers, and other experts to take "a hard look" at performance contracting. "This group will particularly focus on the role of the independent auditor," Dr. Ellena said. "We are really concerned about safeguards that must be necessary so that an honest assessment or evaluation can take place." A report should be forthcoming next spring.

Few people, however, would have paid much attention to educational researchers arguing seemingly esoteric issues of measurement and evaluation. And that is precisely what critics would have been forced to do with only a year's history on one project and the ink barely dry on 150 contracts. But it turns out they have a great peg to hand their discussion on. The Texarkana project—the wellspring of all this ferment in educational circles—was badly botched.

Specifically, Dorsett Educational Systems, Inc., was found to have been "teaching the test." Items were taken verbatim from the standardized achievement tests and inserted in programs, or lessons, that were taught over the Dorsett teaching machine. Each student ran through these programs a week or two before he took the exit test. The independent evaluators hired to assess the effectiveness of the Texarkana project said this practice invalidated *any* measure of achievement gains. Their conclusion destroyed the rationale for Texarkana's having paid Dorsett Inc. $105,000 in monthly installments over the year. These payments were based on estimated grade level gains. The firm's final payment is also jeopardized. Dorsett Inc. could have earned an additional $25,000, depending upon the results of the final tests. But, as of mid-September the Texarkana school board was still arguing what course to take, and payments to Dorsett Inc. had been suspended.

In light of the Texarkana experience, one can ask a number of questions. Will performance-contracting survive this heresy committed on the site of its first, bright moments? Will it be subjected to a fair test? As a technique, does performance-contracting rest upon fundamental misconceptions about tests and measurements?

What really happened in Texarkana

The press has reported that the blame for committing the cardinal educational sin—teaching the test—has been assigned Rosella Scott, the director of programming for Dorsett Educational Systems, Inc., and sister of Loyd Dorsett, founder and president of the firm. It was she, it is said, who authorized the firm's staff of programers to prepare programs for the Dorsett teaching machine, M-86, that included items from all forms of the SRA and the ITBS, the nationally-standardized tests used to measure achievement gains of students in the program. It was she who ordered the managers of the Rapid Learning Centers to assign students these programs a week or two before they took the final test.

She did this, Mr. Dorsett is reported as saying, because she was possibly motivated by pressure to show good results. Seemingly in the next breath, he also reported that she resigned in April, leaving the implication that the firm was purged of the kind of over-zealousness and misjudgment that fed to this situation. Acting upon the theory that the sin had been expiated, Dorsett Educational Systems, Inc., submitted a bid for the 2nd year of the Texarkana Project.

(Mrs. Scott, on the other hand, said she intended to resign all along and establish her own educational company, which she did. Her firm is under contract to supply Dorsett Inc. with programs, Mrs. Scott said, in addition to conducting field tests on a new phonics program.)

Dorsett Educational Systems, Inc., after winning a public bid, entered into a contract with Texarkana, Arkansas, and Liberty-Eylau, Texas, to provide remedial instruction in reading and math for at least 200 students from grades seven to 12. The company set up six Rapid Learning Centers (four in trailers parked outside schools, two in classrooms) where these students reported for two hours a day, instead of going to their regular math and English classes.

At the RLCs, students worked through reading and math programs displayed over the Dorsett Teaching Machine. This is an AV device that synchronizes a filmstrip with a record player. A student listens while he reads. At certain points in the program, he is asked to answer questions on what he has read. If he punches the correct button of the three before him, the program continues. If he doesn't, he hears a buzzing sound signifying "wrong!" Nothing happens until he hits the correct button. There is no branching based on incorrect responses. Occasionally, students worked with paper and pencil programed materials, but the teaching machine was the primary instrument of instruction. Managers of these centers, and their aides, assigned programs, administered progress checks, and tutored anybody who seemed to be having trouble. They did not teach in the accepted sense of the word.

Dorsett, Inc. designed the RLCs so students felt they had stepped from classrooms, where they knew failure, into a place where they could relax and work without pressure. The RLCs were carpeted; paintings hung on the wall. Draperies, couches, a rack of magazines, games stored in the corner—these softened the atmosphere. Students who completed their work early could play checkers or listen to a phonograph as a reward. They also earned S&H green stamps, for completed lessons, and transistor radios for a grade level increase. For the student with the greatest increase in each RLC, the biggest prize of all—a portable TV set.

The contract called for Dorsett to be paid $80.00 for each grade level increase, in either reading or math, occuring in 80 hours of instruction. The formula adjusted up or down proportionately. Dorsett could earn as much as $106.67 for one grade level increase, if a child achieved this, in 60 hours of instruction, or as little as $58.18 if it took her 110 hours of instruction.

The U.S. Office of Education (USOE) funded this program for $270,000 under Title VIII of the Elementary and Secondary Education Act (a title establishing a dropout prevention program).

Texarkana Project Audited

This title required that there be some objective measurement of the effectiveness of the programs funded under it. Thus, the Texarkana project was subjected to an "educational audit," as USOE called it, which is a procedure to give some substance to the notion of educational accountability.

For the Texarkana project, this meant that the results of the instructional program would be "evaluated" by an independent evaluation team—in this case, Dr. Dean Andrew and Dr. Lawrence

Roberts. They are staff members of an Education Service Center established under Title III of ESEA, and located in Magnolia, Arkansas. They had the responsibility of setting up an evaluation design so that the impact of the Dorsett instruction system could be measured at the end of the year. Their fee: $11,500.

In addition to the team of internal evaluators, as Andrew and Roberts were called, an auditor was engaged to look over their shoulders and render judgment on their work, much as a CPA would check the accounting system developed by a firm's accounting staff. Dr. Robert Kramer of the EPIC Evaluation Center in Tucson, Arizona, took on this assignment for a fee of $5,400. Both the evaluators and the auditor were under contract to Texarkana, not to USOE, although USOE approved their contracts, as it did all the subcontracts.

Achievement gains reported

Early newspaper reports on the Texarkana project suggested "startling gains" in reading and math skills. These reports were based on tests given in December and again in February to students who had worked through the most programs and seemed, in the judgment of Dorsett, Inc., likely to score at or near grade level. (If they did, back they would go to class, Dorsett, Inc. would collect its fee, and more students would be assigned to the RLCs to take their places. The firm was in a sense, creaming off the top.)

Stories about Texarkana continued to appear in the national and educational press as reporters visited Texarkana to see for themselves. While critical in some respects, the stories filed by these reporters enhanced the general perception that things were going quite well.

The *N. Y. Times,* for example, published a story that highlighted the achievement gains of a ninth grade student. She rose from a third grade reading and math level to seventh grade in math and a little under ninth grade in reading, as measured by standardized tests. Dorsett earned more than $900 on her alone, the highest fee they received on any student. Senator George Murphy, (R-Cal), author of Title VIII of ESEA, and a supporter of the Texarkana project, inserted the *Times* story in the Congressional Record of June 24.

Reporters write what they hear, checking out whatever claims that deadlines allow them to. But the internal evaluators had time and expertise to take a hard look at the Texarkana project and report accordingly. They joined the rising chorus of acclaim. On April 5, 1970, Texarkana released a summary of an interim report prepared by Drs. Andrew and Roberts. They said students in the RLCs showed a significant gain at the .01 level of confidence in tests of vocabulary, reading comprehension, and arithmetic as compared to students in a matched—or to use their label—an "equated" control group.

Here was the stamp of approval by professional researchers. Employing tests of statistical significance, they said, in effect, that the Dorsett educational program was responsible for improving the achievement level of RLC students.

Andrew and Roberts had no business employing tests of statistical significance and reaching the conclusions they did. When they entered the project sometime in February, almost 5 months after it started, the found no bona fide control group. They spent a good deal of time trying to establish one by matching students with those in the RLCs in terms of pre-test scores, race, sex, grade level, and school of attendance. Not only can one quarrel about the factors they chose for matching, but the very fact they used a machine technique for establishing a control group would prompt most knowledgeable readers of research reports to send it the way of mail-order advertisements.

In their final report, Andrew and Roberts maintained they worked under unfavorable conditions because they started their research so late in the life of the project, and had little opportunity to influence the original evaluation design. They were stuck, in effect, with what they found. This is true, and it points up a flaw in the educational auditing concept, that is, hiring the auditors after the experiment has been irrevocably set and then asking them to make scientific statements about the results. But, despite these obstacles, Andrew and Roberts still issued an interim report confirming statistically significant gains. The mischief was done.

Teaching the test discovered

In the last week of May, 1970, Marty Filagamo, Texarkana's project director for the RLCs, and his assistant, Mary Lisle, toured the RLCs to see how the testing program was coming along. As Filagamo reported later, one young fellow volunteered the information that he had seen the paragraph about a visit to a

THE OEO EXPERIMENT ON PERFORMANCE-CONTRACTING: WHO AND WHERE

Site	*Company*
	Alpha Learning Systems
Hartford, Conn. Taft, Texas Grand Rapids, Michigan	This company minimizes the use of teaching machines. Its instructional system rests on programed texts, a reorganizing of existing curricula, and an intensive incentive system for both teachers and students. Its program will be conducted in an informal, relaxed learning environment.
	Singer/Graflex Inc.
Portland, Maine McComb, Mississippi Seattle, Washington	This company will combine teaching machines, AV materials, and the use of para-professionals with an incentive system that rewards students, teachers, parents, and schools.
	Westinghouse Learning Corporation
Philadelphia, Pennsylvania Fresno, California Las Vegas, Nevada	WLC will use teaching machines, tape cassettes and other AV materials, as well as programed texts. A unique feature of WLC's program is the use of a computer to prescribe an individualized program for each student. Incentives will be employed, and the learning environment modified to reflect a more relaxed atmosphere.
	Quality Educational Development
Rockland, Maine Dallas, Texas Anchorage, Alaska	This contractor relies heavily on AV teaching machines, tape cassettes, and programed texts. Performance of both students and teachers will be rewarded by incentives.
	Learning Foundations, Inc.
Duval County, Florida Hammond, Indiana New York, N.Y. (Bronx)	This company's approach involves an extremely heavy use of teaching machines. Para-professionals rather than certified teachers will monitor student performance. Incentives given to students and teachers will gradually change from extrinsic and tangible to intrinsic and attitudinal in nature. Computerized managed instruction will also be used.
	Plan Education Centers
McNairy County, Tennessee Clarke County, Georgia Wichita, Kansas	This approach employs very little hardware and few extrinsic incentives to students. The contractor will use programed texts and existing instructional materials, and will place much emphasis on diagnostic testing and placement of each student.

submarine (an item in one of the SRA sub-tests) in one of Dorsett's programs. Filagamo said, "Well, I'm sure you thought you saw it, but you probably saw something different." The boy would not budge. "No," he insisted, "I saw that same story." Filagamo decided to check it out. The student was right.

On May 27, Trice (Superintendent of Schools for Texarkana Ark., and fiscal agent for the project), Filagamo, Andrew and Roberts confronted Loyd Dorsett and C. J. Donnelly with evidence that Dorsett had included test items in its programs. According to a report of that meeting written by Andrew and Roberts, and included in their final report on the project, Dorsett admitted that was so. He said in effect that Mrs. Scott was responsible for this happening and she had resigned. He stressed the fact that the percentage of test items made up a very small part of all the Dorsett instructional programs, although it was concentrated in a few programs. Otherwise, he said, it would have had little effect on achievement.

Next day, the group met again. Dorsett was asked to provide whatever information Andrew and Roberts requested so they could find out how "contaminated" the exit tests were. Dorsett promised his cooperation.

At stake here was Dorsett, Inc.'s entire fee of up to $135,000, of which $105,000 had already been paid in monthly installments on the assumption that children had been learning. If the tests had been taught directly, if the eight percent of the items were concentrated in a few programs, then increases in test scores did not represent achievement generalizable to other situations and Dorsett, Inc. would have been paid under false assumptions. It was up to Andrew and Roberts to find out how extensively the tests were compromised.

After working during the summer, and calling in some experts from the Educational Testing Service, they concluded, first, that test items had been taught prior to all exit tests (Feb. 2, Mar. 2, April 7, and the last week of May), although fewer programs with test items were available for the earlier tests. (Ironically, Dorsett said that students tested in May, who had extensive training of the test items, did less well than those tested earlier. Perhaps the kids who were still in the program in May were the slower kids, the others having left the program after getting good scores on the earlier tests.)

Secondly, after trying to measure achievement by disregarding compromised test items, they concluded: "The teaching of test items, or closely related test items, has invalidated the test results to the extent they cannot be used as a valid measure of achievement." Dr. Kramer, in his final report, concurred in their judgment.

By mid-September the question of Dorsett Inc.'s fee remained unresolved. The board did decide, however, to award the second year's contract to Educational Development Laboratories, Inc., a division of McGraw-Hill. EDL also bid on the first year's program although Dorsett Inc. submitted a bid for the second year, the firm was not invited to discuss it before the board—a polite brushoff.

Thus ends Dorsett Inc.'s risk-taking venture in Texarkana. Loyd Dorsett told a conference on performance contracting early in June that he had spent $10 for every $1 he earned in Texarkana on development and supportive costs incurred back at headquarters in Norman, Oklahoma. The payoff for such investment was to have been new contracts. Now he can't get the ears of school board members in Texarkana, even though they own $20,000 worth of Dorsett teaching machines.

The fault is not entirely Mrs. Scott's; it must be shared, beginning with those people—Blaschke, Trice, Filagamo, the USOE project officer, Lew Walker, and anybody else who influenced the selection of Dorsett Educational Systems, Inc. over other bidders for this project. Dorsett had a teaching machine and the abiding faith, shared by his sister, that the machine could teach anything displayed over it. Dorsett Educational Systems, Inc., had no reading program to speak of when they bid on the project (the JOBS CORPS reading program they acquired when they bought EVCO, a software company, could not easily be adapted to the teaching machine), and little notion of a theory of reading that would guide them in constructing a remedial reading program. Mrs. Scott began her assignment as the director of programing by interviewing reading experts throughout the country. She told me that she found they didn't know what worked either except for tutoring students, so she returned to Norman, Oklahoma, with the job of developing an instructional package from scratch. Hence, Dorsett Educational Systems, Inc. built their machine, won the contract, and began developing a reading program—in that order. It was a weakness in the bid that should have been detected.

On her own behalf, Mrs. Scott maintains that she, and Dorsett, Inc. were forced into teaching the test because Texarkana assigned a type of student to the RLCs that she was unprepared to cope with.

In a telephone interview, she said, "We were supposed to have normal IQs. Out of all the students in Texarkana-Arkansas, we had only one or two sho had IQs of 100 or better. Most were under 80.

"The lesson we had originally scheduled for Texarkana-Arkansas for normal IQs just did not work. We found that out definitely. You need different kinds of lessons for students with IQs under 80."

She has a point about being assigned slower students than she had anticipated. The original Request for Proposal (RFP) to which Dorsett, Inc. and the other bidders responded stated that students selected for the RLCs would possess average or above average IQ. This was whittled down in contract negotiations. It was agreed that any student could be admitted who exceeded the IQ level at which he would be labelled educationally retarded—70 in Texas, 75 in Arkansas. Mrs. Scott said the Liberty Eylau people chose their students accordingly, but the Texarkana-Arkansas people selected students for the RLCs, then gave them IQ tests. "We had several students assigned who had IQs in the 50's and 60's," she said. Other sources confirmed Mrs. Scott's complaint that the students sent to the RLCs in too many cases were kids everybody had given up on.

One can almost feel the pressure building on Mrs. Scott. Early in the project, she and her staff of programers took reading material from encyclopedias, magazines, textbooks—wherever they could find something they thought would interest these students. Once the stories were shaped to the format of the teaching machine, she shipped them from Norman, Oklahoma, where she and her staff worked, to Texarkana. Early tests showed that the students were working through the programs and increasing their achievement levels. They should have. The kids were enthusiastic about this new way of learning and the informality of the RLCs—with prizes for good work yet! Also, the first students tested were those considered the top students in the RLCs.

As time went on, Mrs. Scott must have begun to realize her programs were simply not getting through to those kids who remained in the RLCs after the brighter ones were sent back to class, and the final exit tests were not too far off. In the meantime, the educational community was hearing favorable reports about what was being accomplished in Texarkana, of all places, by a heretofore unknown educational firm. Although this does not excuse her actions, you can sympathize with the position she found herself in. While everybody else connected with the project was off making speeches or showing people around the place, Mrs. Scott had to produce results. Why did she do it? She said simply, "We needed to exist as a profit-making company."

Mrs. Scott maintains that she told the Texarkana people what she intended to do. "We had memos to the effect that if we were coming too close to teaching actual test items, then they were to call our attention to it. So unless we got a halt to the materials we were sending down, we would presume they were acceptable. Nobody took the trouble to look at anything and tell us if we were doing anything wrong."

Nobody was watching

What about this—sour grapes? Whether memos were sent, received, and noted we shall perhaps never find out (The Texarkana people deny it), and it really isn't that important. *Somebody* should have been guarding against this obvious temptation of teaching test items. Filagamo manfully takes the blame himself. "I looked at the programs, but I just didn't catch it," he said. "I wasn't looking for things like this anyhow. I was looking for the pertinency of the instructional material."

There's no doubt he should have looked more closely, but what is disturbing is that internal evaluators were paid $11,500 to evaluate the program, and they didn't bother to check out this possibility. If it hadn't been for a chance visit to an RLC and a boy talking up (I wonder if he realizes the stir he caused?), we might well be reading a final report describing the success of the Texarkana project, with accompanying statistical evidence, all impressive and thoroughly convincing.

The U.S. Office of Education does not come off entirely unscathed from the turn of events in Texarkana either. According to several sources, the contract-reviewing officials deleted some provisions, agreed to by Dorsett, Inc. and Texarkana, that would have strengthened the contract. For example, the contractor was originally required to post a performance bond. This was deleted by USOE. A vocabulary test was to have been developed locally to include some 3,000 to 4,000 words of usefulness to young people living in Arkansas. If Dorsett could have taught all 4,000 words—fine! This was deleted. The RFP proposed a retention test six months after the program finished. Contractor fees would have been adjusted downwards if the retention rates of RLC students did not hold up to those of average students. This was deleted. (Albert Myerhoffer, an aid to Dr. Lessinger in USOE, argued for this deletion. He believed it would have been highly inequitable to hold the contractor liable for any erosion of achievement after students returned to the same classrooms in which they had failed before and were expected to fail—the reverse on the Pgymation effect.)

But overshadowing the deletion of any of these provisions was the reduction in the funding available to the Texarkana Project. Blaschke and his group, the Texarkana people, were counting on, and planning for a budget of $750,000. This was cut at the last moment to $250,000, requiring a reduction in concept and staffing and, quite possibly, the quality control checks that would have been made otherwise.

Finally, although the tests were named specifically in the contract, nobody—Blaschke and his staff, the Texarkana people, USOE officials—insisted upon a provision in the contract prohibiting the teaching of test items. It's implicit all right, but whether a court of law will recognize the implied prohibition is quite another thing. Maybe, just maybe the Dorsett people read the contract more closely than anyone else.

(Joe Connor, information officer for the Bureau of Elementary and Secondary Education, USOE, said the final report—in its entirety—would be available through ERIC by December 1.)

The other point, of course, is that the Texarkana project has prompted a national look at the technique of performance-contracting. It did not get a fair test in Texarkana; it will under a $5.6 million experiment being conducted by a Federal agency, the Office of Economic Opportunity.

The OEO experiment

Some 18 school districts, 6 educational companies and 28,000 students, grades 1-3 and 7-9 are participating in the year-long experiment. (Only 11,880 students will take the special instructional programs; the remainder are controls.) Students assigned to the experimental groups will receive one hour of instruction daily in both reading and math for the entire school year.

This experiment is being conducted, by and large, by two young men in their early thirties, Jeffry Schiller, the project director for OEO, and Charles Blaschke, president of Educational Turnkey Systems, Inc., and the man who organized the Texarkana project. In a $525,000 contract with OEO, Blaschke's firm will conduct a cost effectiveness analysis of each program, study the change process in the school triggered by the new instruction program (if any), explore the policy implications of each program, and otherwise provide management support to OEO.

Achievement tests kept secret

To do away with the temptation of teaching test items, few people know, and certainly not the contractors, which standardized tests will be given students for determining gains in achievement levels. Actually students in each class will be randomly assigned one of three standardized tests as a pre-test. At the end of the year, they will take an alternate form of the same test. All identifying information on the tests themselves will be blanked out.

Contractors will receive *no* payment for any gain less than 1 full grade level, not even cost. At 1.0, a contractor gets $110-115 approximately, and this amount increased proportionately as the grade level gain increase, until the maximum is reached—approximately $215 for a 2.2 grade level increase. The contractor is paid for gains in reading and math, computed separately. There is no time factor in this formula because students remain in the program the entire year, unlike the Texarkana students who were sent back to class as soon as they tested out at or near grade level (a practice many observers thought traumatic for children who were just beginning to develop some confidence in their ability to learn.)

In another departure from the Texarkana project, 75% of the contractors' payments will be computed on raw gain scores from standardized tests, 25% will be based on students' performance on criterion-referenced tests. These tests measure attainment of specific objectives in instructional programs. For example, if an aim of an instructional program is teaching skill in alphabetizing, then a pertinent criterion-referenced test item might be this: Locate Victor C. Jankowski in the Hartford telephone directory.

Schiller also insisted on a test of retention for half of all the groups at the beginning and end of the academic year following the experiment. Payment to contractors will not be affected by the results, however.

Contractors were required to put up a performance bond.

The contract to evaluate the program has been let to Battelle Memorial Institute, Columbus, Ohio, for $610,000. They will administer the tests and analyze the results. The final report should be completed by July 31, 1972, with quarterly reports during the interim.

Educators are not waiting for the final report on the OEO experiment, however, before plunging into performance contracting. It is a technique with great political appeal, because of the precision of the arrangement. Educational companies promise a product—gains in achievement levels—for X number of dollars or money back. That is how it is understood popularly. Members of Congress certainly look upon performance contracting favorably, with the exception of Representative Edith Greene, who has cast everybody connected with it into what she calls derisively the industrial-educational complex. But other Congressmen know the frustrations of trying to measure the impact of the billions of dollars spent under ESEA and other educational acts, so performance contracting speaks to them.

One would expect that where performance contracting has been tried with little success, as in Texarkana, everybody from the grass roots up would raise quite a howl. Interestingly enough, Texarkana citizens whose children went to the RLCs failed to understand what the fuss was all about. An official of the Model Cities program said parents generally were pleased the school had scheduled something special for their children.

In its proposal for a performance contract in San Diego, Educational Development Laboratories (EDL) suggested that it be paid on its ability to raise the mean achievement level of all selected children in target schools to city-wide norms in three year's time. The goals per year were 25% reduction of the gap between target schools and city-wide achievement levels in the first year, 50% in the second, and 100% in the third. This proposal, contrary to many reports, has not been funded. No money available.

Behavioral Research Laboratories has taken the ultimate step in performance contracting. It will run the entire instructional program of an 800 pupil elementary school in Gary, Indiana, for 3 years. It will organize and staff the school, provide all materials, develop non-graded individualized learning programs for each child, and launch a parent-community participation program. At the end of its contract, it will refund the annual fee for any child ($800) who is not at or above the national norms in all basic curriculum areas.

Critics speak up

While Gary, Indiana, was turning a school over to private industry, a noted psychologist, Dr. Kenneth Clark, was calling performance contracting a "cop-out." He and his Metropolitan Applied Research Center, Inc., had studied performance contracts as part of their review of innovative educational programs prior to their submitting a plan for revamping the school system in Washington, D.C. While noting some advantages to performance contracts—especially its assumption that normal children *can* learn, despite a disadvantaged background—he suggests that the Hawthorne effect produces dramatic short run gains, and therefore companies might run programs for brief periods and fail to engage in longitudinal contracts.

Generally, teacher opposition presents two arguments. NEA's legislative head, John M. Lumley, developed one before a Senate subcommittee recently. His theme was this: "It is our contention that the schools themselves would be quite capable of producing the results sought in Texarkana—if the schools had the same amount of money to spend per pupil in the project."

The second argument as voiced by Donald Wilson, president of the Association of Classroom Teachers, NEA, complements the first. In a telephone interview, he said that a teacher should not be held accountable for results if she has had no hand in developing the instructional materials she is to use in her classroom. (Mr. Wilson is anticipating the turn-key aspect of performance contracting. As Blaschke saw it in Texarkana, once Dorsett, Inc. had shown how children could learn on his machines, the regular staff could take over the RLCs or incorporate his equipment and programs in their classrooms—in either case, with the same effectiveness as the Dorsett people.)

I reminded him that industry spends millions of dollars developing instructional programs, sizeable consultant fees to educators with years of classroom experience. Why then ask a teacher in Puducah, Kentucky, to put together her own reading program? She can hardly command the resources of Westinghouse Learning Corporation.

"Because you are holding the teacher accountable. It is that simple," he replied.

Suppose she chose one of many reading programs available to meet the needs of her class which, granted, she knows better than anyone else. Wouldn't that preserve her professional role?

"How about letting the teacher have the resources to develop the instruments according to her professional training and competence," he said.

"You see, if a teacher has the major part of developing a system herself, utilizing her expertise, having the knowledge of her students and the situation from which they come, then I would say there is some validity in holding a teacher responsible.

"But when industry has not used the teacher in developing its process, then I have some real doubts about her being held accountable."

Most of the criticism so far has assumed the rationale for performance contracts: that it is possible to measure gains in achievement according to the current state of the art of tests and measurements. But is this so? Especially when measuring the gains of individual students rather than a population group numbering in the thousands?

Roger Farr, director of the reading clinic at Indiana University, recently completed a survey on measurement of reading under a USOE grant. In his book, *Reading: What Can Be Measured,* the chapter "Assessing Growth in Reading," Dr. Farr states simply "Research in assessing growth has been sparse, and this in itself has been a major obstacle to improving evaluation procedures." Sparse? With volumes of tests and measurements in educational libraries? An entire industry built on testing? But so he concluded after reading the research literature. And he points out some difficulties in assessing growth that have arisen in studies conducted by the few researchers in the field.

Are tests accurate enough?

One of the more common errors, he says, is for people to test for skills not taught in the instructional program. For example, often student, take timed tests, when speed is not a goal of the instructional program. They tend to score higher on the post test because they know they are being evaluated on the difference between the results on this test and their pre-tests.

One researcher (Fisher, 1961) suggested that tests pegged to a particular grade level may not be valid for either advanced or retarded readers in that grade—certainly an issue to be reckoned with in selecting tests for measuring change in remedial students.

Dotson and Bliesmer (1955) and Coates (1968) conducted correlation studies. Dr. Farr reports, that suggest alternate test forms of the same test are *not* as comparable as users might assume. OEO rests its entire payment schedule on the concept of comparability between the various forms of the same test.

Dr. Farr also points out that the regression effect (regression towards the mean) seriously complicates the problem of assessing growth of students who are found at the extreme ends of a distribution of test scores. Regression towards the mean is a statistical phenomenon. It reflects the high probability that a student who scores at, say, the lowest percentile in a distribution of scores will tend to score nearer the mean on later tests. Why? Most likely the factors which influenced him in the pretest and produced the extreme low score, including such mundane things as an upset stomach, a quarrel with mother, no money in his pocket, will not be repeated at the post test. So he should score higher, regardless of the instruction he receives in the interim.

And when it comes to assessing growth in retarded readers with standardized tests a whole host of problems arise. Dr. Farr sums it up by saying, "Retarded readers from an atypical population and comparing their growth with that of a normed typical population is completely inappropriate. It is questionable that standardized tests should be used for them in the first place."

I asked Dr. Farr if he thought the technology of testing was up to the demands put upon it by performance contracting.

"I don't think we know enought about the processes involved in teaching and learning to measure everything to the fine degree that people want us to measure them in order to do performance-contracting," he said.

"Sometimes a gain on a test can be statistically significant," he pointed out, "but the question is—is that educationally significant? Can a student now do something he couldn't do before, like reading and understand the front page of the N.Y. *Times?*

Dr. Farr thinks that developing criterion-referenced tests, as OEO is requiring its contractors to do in order to earn 25% of their payment, will overcome objections about the transferability of gains in achievement to the classroom.

Anybody contemplating a performance contract should read Dr. Farr's book, especially the chapter on assessing growth. It might generate some interesting discussion around the negotiating table. The book is available in paperback from the International Reading Association, Six Tyre Avenue, Newark, Delaware, 19711. ($3.25 to members of IRA; $4.95 to others.) Also, see *Measurement and Evaluation of Reading,* edited by Dr. Farr, available from Harcourt, Brace, and World, Inc., (1970), in paperback. And if you plan to attend the IRA convention in Atlantic City in May, 1971, catch his micro-workshop on assessing growth in reading, given along with a colleague Dr. Fred Davis, who has done considerable work in this field with standardized tests.

It is somehow ironic that the technologically minded, behaviorist types who advocate performance contracting might be brought up short by assuming too readily that gains in achievement scores necessarily reflects changes in behavior, either in the testing situation itself, or outside of it, in the classroom, or in life.

Still, performance contracting poses the right questions. Where large sums of money are being spent, and school superintendents begin to wonder just what they have bought, some funds surely will be siphoned off to researchers so they can examine the assumptions underlying the technique.

Out of this clash between researchers and operations-minded executives in both education and industry may well come a modus operandi (if researchers manage to get themselves heard) that suits everybody and produces "educationally significant" results. We still have a ways to go.

C. J. Donnelly, project director for Dorsett Educational Systems, Inc., in Texarkana, explains the difference between teaching to the test and teaching the test.

The problem of teaching the test has arisen in Texarkana with the discovery that a considerable number of the contractor's programs contain actual test items.

The contractor has been on record, dating back to their basic proposal, as intending to teach to the test, that is, teach the skills tested for on SRA and Iowa Tests of Basic Skills.

In the case of arithmetic, it was believed that this meant teaching the concept tested for, but changing the numbers used in the test item to some other number. This would be acceptable.

In the case of vocabulary, it was believed that the contractor intended to teach a 3,000-word vocabulary which would include words tested for on the SRA and ITBS instruments, but would not emphasize these words or concentrate them in any particular lesson segment. This would be acceptable.

In the case of reading comprehension, it was believed the contractor intended to give strategics for and practice in taking the paragraph comprehension type of test typical of the SRA and ITBS instruments. To the extent that the stories and excerpts used are not identical to those in this test, this would be acceptable.

We now find that all the vocabulary words of the five ITBS and SRA forms in use in the project are packed together in five programs, making them susceptible to intense review just prior to the time of an exit test, which in fact has happened.

We also find that there are numerous programs in both arithmetic and reading comprehension that are lifted verbatim from the test instruments and that staff and students have been instructed to concentrate on these programs. . . .

III

ENGINEERING ACCOUNTABILITY FOR RESULTS IN PUBLIC EDUCATION

by Leon Lessinger

"Performance contracting is one *process for which accountability is the product."*

An important change has taken place in what Americans expect of their public schools. The optimism about the value of education is still there and continues to be strong, but serious doubts have arisen about the public school system's ability to actually deliver on its promises.

The shift in attitude becomes apparent through analysis of the questions being asked at hearings by elected officials of both parties at every level of government, from Congress to state legislatures and local city councils. The same line of questioning can be heard among businessmen, at school board conventions, at various citizen group meetings, and in the highest circles of the executive branches of government. Seekers of educational funds have always talked in terms of books, staff, materials, equipment, and space to be acquired or used, together with students to be served and programs to be offered. Questioners in the past were content to listen to accounts of resources allocated. This has changed. Today the questions focus on results obtained for resources used. The questions are pointed, insistent, and abrasive. The public school system is being held accountable for results. Accountability is the coming sine qua non for education in the 1970's. How to engineer accountability for results in public education is the central problem for the education profession.

Reprinted with permission from *Phi Delta KAPPAN,* December, 1970. ©Phi Delta Kappa, Inc.

It would be interesting to speculate about the reasons for the growing demand to link dollars spent for education to results achieved from students. Increased and accelerating costs, poor academic performance of minority children, and inconclusive results of federal compensatory education projects (totaling, since 1965, in the billions of dollars) are probably important casual factors.

Accountability is the product of a process. At its most basic level, it means that an agent, public or private, entering into a contractual agreement to perform a service will be held answerable for performing according to agreed-upon terms, within an established time period, and with a stipulated use of resources and performance standards. This definition of accountability requires that the parties to the contract keep clear and complete records and that this information be available for outside review. It also suggests penalties and rewards; accountability without redress or incentive is mere rhetoric.

Performance contracting is *one* process for which accountability is the product. The idea of contracting is older than free enterprise. Its appeal to both liberals and conservatives revolves around its attention to two things that leaders agree are desperately needed in education – quality assurance and knowledge of results.

At its most primitive level the process works like this: A public authority grants money to a local education agency to contract with private enterprise[1] to achieve specific goals within specific perios for specific costs. The money is targeted at pressing needs which are not being adequately met, such as dropout prevention among disadvantaged groups or bringing the underprivileged and undereducated up to competitive educational levels.

Seen from this vantage point, accountability appears to be merely the utilization by education of private enterprise for getting things done. Of course, such utilization is not per se a new development. For example, any superintendent of schools can show that performance contracts have long been used in school operation and maintenance. The use of performance contracts to achieve accountability is, therefore, not new to education. It is the extension of this idea into the realm of learning through a particular process, called in this paper educational engineering, which represents what some are calling the "coming revolution in American education."

Educational Engineering

Since World War II several fields have been developed to enable managers of very complex enterprises to operate efficiently and effectively. These emerging fields of knowledge and practice are commonly known as systems analysis, management by objectives, contract engineering (including bids, warranties, penalties, and incentives), logistics, quality assurance, value engineering, and human factors engineering, to name a few of the more important. If to these are added instructional technology and modern educational management theory, a new and valuable interdisciplinary field emerges. This body of knowledge, skill, and procedure can be called educational engineering. It is the insights from educational engineering that makes it possible for performance contracting to achieve accountability for results in education.

Why couple the term "engineering" with education? Why more apparent dehumanization? It is not appropriate here to treat this question at great length. But I note that engineering has traditionally been a problem-solving activity and a profession dedicated to the application of technology to the resolution of real world difficulties and opportunities. While the teaching-learning environment differs from the world of business and industry, some rationalization of the two subcultures may be beneficial. A major objective of educational engineering may very well be to arm educational practitioners with both the technological competence of essential engineering generalizations, strategies, and tools and the professional practice of a successful instructor or educational manager. From this point of view, educational engineering can be a symbiotic art – a marriage of humanism and technology. It is this possible symbiosis that makes performance contracting for learning accomplishment feasible.

Accountability in Operation

The application of one educational engineering process to achieve results in the basic academic skills can be used to illustrate the concept of accountability in operation. This accountability process can be engineered as follows:

1. The local education agency (LEA) employs a management support group (MSG), whose members have competency to assist them in political, social, economic, managerial, and educational matters. The relationship between the management support group

and the local school leadership group resembles that of long-term consultants on a retainer account.

2. The MSG works with staff and community (or other groups as required by a particular local situation) to produce a request for proposal (RFP), which is a set of specifications indicating as clearly as possible the service to be performed, the approximate amount of money to be invested, the constraints to be observed, the standards acceptable, and related matters. The RFP is the local education agency's blueprint for action to meet pressing priorities.

3. The next stage of the educational engineering process occurs when the RFP is set out to bid. The pre-bidding conference becomes the forum for educational exchange. Here a rich and varied communication through competition occurs between elements of the private and public sector. The bidding process is flexible to the extent that allowance is made by LEA officials for new insights and better elements to be incorporated into a revised RFP.

4. Following the bidding conference, a revised RFP is issued and actual bids are entertained. The MSG assists the LEA in operating the conference and reviewing the bids. The local board "hears" the top bids in a manner similar to the process used in the employment of an architect.

5. The local school board selects what it considers to be the best bid and enters into negotiation for a performance contract with the successful bidder. The MSG assists at this stage.

6. Concurrently with the signing of the performance contract, an independent educational accomplishment audit team is employed by the LEA both to monitor execution of the performance contract and to provide feedback to the LEA to certify results for purposes of payment.

It may now be helpful to analyze the structural elements of this process in more detail.

The *performance contract* is the managerial tool to assure the achievement of results, while encouraging responsible innovation. The approach is simple in concept although complex in actualization. With technical assistance, the learning problem is analyzed, and a delineation of achievement outcomes to be expected is specified. An RFP is developed and sent by the LEA to potential contractors who have demonstrated competent and creative activity in the specific and related fields. The RFP does not prescribe how the job must be done but does establish the performance, financial, administrative, and legal parameters of the operation. The RFP requires that the bidder guarantee specific results for specific costs. The confidence that the bidder has in his approach is reflected in the level of the guarantee, the social practicability, the time, and the costs indicated in the bid he presents.

The program to be bid, including the specified number of students, is described in the contract. Incentives are provided for the contractor to bring each child up to specified levels of performance, at the lowest cost. Provision is made in the performance contract to develop a program for which the contractor will guarantee results.

After the demonstration period is completed and all relevant costs, procedures, achievements, and performance data have been validated, the contract requires that the contractor guarantee an effective, fiscally responsible program. Then, on a "turnkey" basis, the LEA incorporates the instructional program into the school. Thus performance contracting is a capability-creating resource for public education.

The *management support group* is the catalytic and buffer agency which provides not only technical assistance to the district, but a communication link between those who determine priorities, such as a federal agency, and the school system that is developing program proposals. The group has access to new developments in the field, especially in industrial and governmental sectors, and assists the LEA in developing the RFP to assure that conditions and constraints in the RFP do not preclude but actually encourage the opportunity for these new developments to be demonstrated. The MSG also plays the role of a buffer between the LEA and community groups, as well as between the LEA and potential bidders. It provides assistance to the LEA during the proposal evaluation and operational stages on an "as needed" basis.

As operational results during the initial stages are determined, the group provides program planning assistance to the LEA so that the instructional programs are effectively and efficiently "turnkeyed" into the school. In this way, the school can achieve the potential benefits which have been demonstrated. Too often school systems either adopt programs not proven or acquire techniques proven in pilot programs only. Later they sometimes discover that the results erode over time. The MSG can provide critical technical assistance to the school officials during the adoption or turnkey process, ranging from projecting administrative costs required within the system to the implementation of performance budgeting techniques that will insure continuing quality assurance.

The *independent education accomplishment audit* (IEAA) is a managerial tool to assist quality control of the program. By reporting on results, this procedure encourages responsibility, creating a need for clearly stated performance objectives and an accounting for the costs incurred in achieving results. Just as the performance contract allows the school to monitor the contractor, the IEAA is designed to assure the lay board and the community it represents that the school leaders and the contractors are doing their work. The independent accomplishment audit, first introduced through ESEA Title VIII by the U.S. Office of Education, is a practical recognition that education is an important investment in human capital. Just as fiscal audits certify that public school resources and expenditures are (or are not) in balance, the IEAA certifies that investments in human beings are (or are not) successful according to stated goals and demonstrated accomplishment.

Patterns of funding the educational engineering process are critical. The flow of federal, state, and local funds must encourage the creation and responsible control of process components. Budgeting must be based on clearly defined criteria for "go" or "no go" decisions to be made at the end of each discrete stage. Three-stage funding as a facilitating device consists of resources and the timely freeing of previously earmarked funds for other new starts or operational programs.

The Texarkana Model

The Texarkana Dropout Prevention Program, under ESEA Title VIII, was the first to use performance contracting with private enterprise in instruction. A number of new ventures have since been started, including those in Dallas, Texas, and Gary, Indiana, as well as the 18 centers funded by the Office of Economic Opportunity. These "second generation" approaches make use of performance contracts that are independently audited. They are built on the Texarkana approach and have employed techniques and strategies to overcome difficulties exposed during the first year of operation of the Texarkana experiment.

The assumption behind the Texarkana program and those of the second generation is that a private contractor will have greater freedom to innovate and thus be more successful in motivating students than the regular school system has been. A direct instructional service and a self-renewal function are the dual objectives of the projects.

Let me turn next to some of the wider implications of engineering accountability into public education.

Advantages of Performance Contracts

The advantages of performance contracts are inherent in the nature of the serious problems that confront education today.

First, contracting facilitates the targeting and evaluation of educational programs. Many good instructional programs have not been given the opportunity to demonstrate their potential due to the lack of an effective delivery system at the school level. Recent critical evaluations of Title I of ESEA note this operational inadequacy. The performance contract approach, which utilizes a separately managed and operated center with separate accounting procedures, fosters the objective evaluation of educational results and also the managerial processes by which these results were achieved.

Second, performance contracting for instructional services could introduce more resources and greater variability into the public school sector. Now, new programs are being offered to the public outside the school system; the process of fragmentation and competition has begun. Several large corporations are establishing franchised learning centers across the country. One company, for example, has at least 40 centers operating in the major cities of this country; 10 others are establishing centers in other cities. Performance-type contracts to improve student achievement in compensatory education are usually enacted between the parents and the franchisee. As a result, the parents pay for the schools' operations. As these franchised centers expand, parents may refuse to pay property taxes by defeating tax and bond issues. On the other hand, the performance contract approach would allow the school system to utilize the services and products of a particular firm or firms so that the public schools could be renewed through a turnkey process. Performance contracting can be looked upon as a means to foster and catalyze institutional reform within a school system, allowing systems to continue operations and to become competitive with private schools and franchised learning centers.

Third, the performance contract approach allows a school system to experiment in a responsible manner with low costs and low political and social risks. Both school officials and critics have expressed the need to determine the relative cost effectiveness of various instructional methods in contractor-operated centers, as well as upon incorporation into the particular schools. The performance contract approach not only allows for determination of these costs and benefits but also provides the bases for projecting initial adoption as well as operating costs when the system is introduced into the schools. In this way, the approach allows policy makers to make rational choices when choosing new techniques for extension into standard classroom practice.

Fourth, the new "bill of rights in education," proclaiming the right of every child to read at his grade level, will undoubtedly generate great pressures upon school resources. If our schools are to make this right a reality, they might want to consider using performance contracting for the development and validation of new reading programs. Upon successful demonstration, districts can then adopt the program or portions thereof. The success of these programs will in large measure depend upon the ability of the school to skillfully design and execute performance contracts and then effectively incorporate the projects into its normal operation.

Fifth, performance contracting can play a significant role in school desegregation. One of the major fears of the white community (rightly or wrongly) is that black children, upon integration, will hold back the progress of white children. Through the performance contract approach, many of the previously segregated black children will have their academic deficiencies, if any, removed on a guaranteed achievement basis while they are attending the newly integrated schools. From this point of view, performance contracting would allow communities to desegregate in a nondisruptive, educationally effective, and politically palatable manner.

Finally, the approach creates dynamic tension and responsible institutional change within the public school system through competition. Leaders will now have alternatives to the traditional instructional methods when negotiating salary increases; performance contracting and its variant, performance budgeting, permit the authorities to couple part of a salary increase to increase in effectiveness.

Probable Trends

Whatever may be the merits of performance contracting, dramatic increases in its use are virtually certain in the immediate future.

Proper guidance, in the form of descriptive material as well as guidelines for implementing performance contracting and/or performance budgeting, is essential to avoid a potential backfire. For example, certain firms which develop tests and sell curricula might bid on performance contracts; other firms might develop specific reading and math curricula around specific tests. Franchised learning centers are bidding on performance contracts with schools in order to force state agencies to accredit their programs. Certain schools facing desegregation problems are considering very seriously the establishment of performance contract projects without a capability or an in-depth knowledge of the concept.

Two actions on the part of public policy officials would be helpful. First, additional operational proposals and planning grants should be funded, not only to legitimize the concept of performance contracting in education, but also to develop a "learning curve" on the "do's and don'ts" of developing RFP's for large urban schools. Because of the Texarkana project, those associated with its development have amassed a stockpile of knowledge; yet the applicability to diverse urban school systems is limited. Second, concurrently with the development of additional planning exercises and based on the experience of Texarkana, a booklet describing performance contracting and a procedures manual that could be made available to schools across the country should be written. The demand for such documents will increase dramatically over the next few months.

The Management Support Group

The concept of the management support group is new to education. Its precedent was established in the defense-aerospace area when, in the mid-Fifties, the Aerospace Corporation was created to act as a buffer and technical assistance team between the Air Force and weapons systems suppliers for the Air Force. The Aerospace Corporation's major functions were to develop programs, design requests for proposals based on performance specifications, assist in evaluating proposals, and provide management services to contractors. The major functions of the MSG in education under the concept of educational engineering would be in the following areas:

1. *Program planning and development assistance.* School systems generally lack such a management capability, or, if such is available, "day to day" operations prevent effective utilization of that resource. Moreover, an outside group provides new insights and a different perspective in analyzing educational and other problems and in developing alternative solutions. For these and other reasons, it is advantageous for the school to have an MSG develop the RFP. The MSG could assist in the following ways during the program development and planning:

a. analyze and determine the community's educational needs and the desired levels of student performance;
b. conduct program definition phase studies and determine sources of funding;
c. develop the RFP and experimental design to be used for turnkey purposes as well as national dissemination;
d. develop and recommend "program change proposals" on a continuing basis during the initial stages;
e. develop means for gathering and maintaining political and community support for the program during all phases;
f. contact potential bidders in the education industry and R & D laboratories to insure that the latest innovative techniques are considered and are encouraged for application by the direction and flexibility allowed in the RFP;
g. determine the qualified bidders and send them the RFP.

2. *Project management assistance.* Too often, proposals are developed by outside groups who curtail relationships with the school once the contract has been awarded. The management support group has to provide extended and sustained services in the areas ranging from establishing the project management office to developing evaluation techniques. The project management services would be in the following areas:

a. develop a multi-year management plan for the conduct of the demonstration and turnkey effort, including an administrative system for the LEA's project management office;

b. conduct, when appropriate, pre-proposal development and bidders' conferences with all interested parties;
c. establish a proposal evaluation procedure and assist in the evaluation by presenting strengths and weaknesses to the LEA;
d. continually evaluate the contractor's progress and assist in contract renegotiations as required;
f. manage pilot programs when specifically requested to do so by the LEA;
g. analyze the administrative and managerial changes required when the techniques proven in pilot programs are integrated into the school systems. This turnkey phase is critical to overall success and requires careful analysis and program planning and budgeting.

3. *Communications link.* Because many firms of unknown or questionable reliability will be entering this newly created multi-billion-dollar market, the MSG is a necessary mediator and "honest broker" between the firms and the school systems. At the community level, the vested interests of powerful groups and important decision makers must be determined. Here, the MSG, acting as a buffer between the LEA and these interest groups, both inside and outside the school system, can obtain such information in an effective and politically advantageous manner. (For example, the superintendent could point to the MSG as a scapegoat if specific ideas or recommendations are not accepted by the board.) The MSG can provide an on-call, as-needed manpower pool during planning and implementation. It can hire potential school employees in order to allow officials to see them in action. Moreover, the MSG has access to consultants around the country; on short notice it can provide their services while bypassing combersome district procedures.

In short, the politics of experimentation where private industry, local schools, and the federal government are all involved creates the need for unofficial advocates and buffer mechanisms to protect politically all parties concerned, while insuring that the project does in fact become a reality.

Probable Trends

The concept of the management support group was made legitimate by the Title VII and Title VIII ESEA grant guidelines.

Only a few firms have the capability to perform this function on their own, although many individuals do have this capability and could form a fertile cadre to advise and train others. The concept of catalytic buffers was included in the enabling legislation for ESEA Title III, presented to Congress in 1965-66; however, it was deleted in final legislation. Many people attribute the failures of Title III projects to the lack of a mechanism that would have provided the necessary political and technical skills to insure effective planning implementation and eventual adoption by LEA's of successful projects. A strategy for developing this capability within school systems across the country would reap enormous cost savings, reduce time wastage, and effect early adoption of new programs.

Independent Accomplishment Audit

Similar to the earlier demand for fiscal audits is the public's present demand for an accounting of student accomplishment. Just as the independent fiscal audit of schools had eliminated most fiscal illegality and has forced fiscal management changes, the IEAA group can also be used to create a demand for necessary instructional reforms. The concern for results in education among the electorate is a recent development, but it is gaining momentum. "Equal opportunity" in education no longer mollifies the majority: some "equity of results" is demanded. This is especially true of the educational benefits conventionally called the "basic skills." Even though Title I language reflects a traditional concern over inputs such as equipment, teachers, space, and books, the subsequent questions raised by Congress have moved beyond how the money was spent to whether the students have learned, have secured jobs, or are falling behind. This is the political soil from which the independent accomplishment audit has grown.

The independent education accomplishment audit is a process similar to that used in a fiscal audit. The emphasis, however, is on student performance as a result of financial outlays. The IEAA relys upon outside independent judgment and has six essential parts: the pre-audit, the translation of local goals into demonstrable data, the adoption or creation of instrumentation and methodology, the establishment of a review calendar, the assessment process, and the public report.

1. *The pre-audit:* The auditor selected by the school system starts the IEAA process by discussing with the staff, students, and community the objectives and plans of the particular program to be reviewed. This phase produces a list of local objectives and a clear description of the programs in some order of priority. In performance contracts, he reviews the project's "procedures" manual.

2. *The translation:* In concert with local people, the auditor determines what evidence will be used to indicate whether the objectives have been met and decides what methods will be used to gather the evidence. This phase produces a set of specifications indicating what the student will be able to do as a result of the educational experience, the manner in which the evidence will be secured, and the standards which will be applied in evaluating the success of the program in helping students to achieve the objectives.

3. *Instrumentation:* Along with the translation, the auditor, working with the LEA, determines the audit instruments, such as tests, questionnaires, interview protocols, and unobtrusive measures, which will be used to gather the evidence. The product of this activity is a set of defined techniques and procedures for data gathering.

4. *Review calendar:* An agreement is secured in writing which indicates the nature of the reviews, where they will be held, how long they will take, when they will occur, who is responsible for arrangements, the nature of the arrangements, and other logistical considerations. It is essential that the calendar be determined in advance and that all concerned be party to, and have the authority to honor, the agreement.

5. *The audit process:* This is a responsibility of the auditor. In this phase, the auditor carries out the procedures agreed upon in the pre-audit, translation, and instrumentation phases as codified in the review calendar.

6. *The public report:* The auditor files a report at a public meeting giving commendations and recommendations as they relate to the local objectives. The report is designed to indicate in specific terms both accomplishments and ways in which the program may be made more effective.

Advantages of the IEAA

The IEAA is a new technique designed to put local school

personnel and the clients they serve in a problem-solving mode of thinking. It is built around a financial core, since money is a common denominator for the heterogeneous elements of input, but its focus is upon student attitudes, skills, and knowledge. From the IEAA, a whole range of useful by-products is anticipated. First, it may lead to a knowledge of optimum relationships between outputs and inputs – for example, the "critical mass" in funding different types of compensatory programs. Second, it can form a basis for the discovery and improvement of good practice in education. Third, the IEAA creates the need for performance-type contracting and/or budgeting in the basic academic and vocational skill areas. Finally, it can renew credibility in the educational process by effecting more responsiveness to the needs of children and supplying the understanding necessary to produce change. The power of the electorate over public education must be politically, not administratively, derived. If techniques can be developed to convince the community of the benefits of responsible leadership through accountability for results, those interested in furthering education can better support the educational enterprise.

Probable Trends

The IEAA concept is now a reality. Over 20 groups or individual auditors across the country are receiving special training and guidance at USOE-sponsored audit institutes. Most of these groups will serve as auditors in Title VII and VIII of ESEA. However, if Title I and Title III funds were made available in a way that would allow LEA's to use performance contracting, and a large number (say 500) decided to do so, the existing resources for training and conducting professional educational audits would probably be inadequate. A superficial survey of existing USOE resources (Title III service centers, the regional laboratories, and resources of private firms) indicates that the auditing capability is limited. A full-scale inquiry should be undertaken. At the same time, university-based graduate studies on educational engineering with heavy emphasis on educational audits should be instituted in a select number of qualified universities. Such curricula must be developed in light of the political and social milieu in which the audit must take place and must be conducted by qualified individuals who understand the concept from a theoretical as well as operational point of view.

Developmental Capital

For too long a period of time, the public schools have been funded and operated in such a manner that educators and administrators have been discouraged from providing efficient and effective instructional services. Federal funding – despite a plethora of regulations and guidelines, proposals and reports – actually supports and, in some cases, encourages inefficiencies and inequities in public schools. At all levels of financial support, money has bee been directed toward specific problems as they emerge, rather than being systematically used to reform the institution. Hence, taxpayers and legislators find themselves in the tragic position of throwing "good money after bad"; while school costs have never been greater, the problems emerging from public education have never been more numerous.

The hard lesson to be learned from the past five years of major federal funding of educational programs is that the way in which the money is delivered is as important as the amount. If the cycle of more money and ever greater problems is to be broken, political authorities should realize that discretionary money must be used not only for successful programs, but also for system renewal. Writing in the Fall, 1969, issue of *The Public Interest,* Daniel Moynihan admonished: "The federal government must develop and put into practice far more effective incentive systems than now exist whereby state and local governments, and private interests, too, can be led to achieve the goals of federal programs." Properly conceptualized, therefore, federal aid to education should be viewed as capital, which, when made available in a predictable and systematic manner, will provide the energy for educational engineering. The basic purpose of developmental capital is to provide a financial resource to stimulate and sustain reexamination and modernization of the educational system. The investment of "risk" capital can generate new educational traditions by applying the developmental aspects of business success to the public sector.

Effecting necessary change requires discretionary funds which are not now available to local school leaders. In the absence of an infusion of new monies for development, dissemination, and installation of new products and practices, the gap between the demand for higher quality education and performance is likely to widen even further.

With developmental capital set-asides, renewal can be directed through federal, state, and local channels, and activity can be aimed at improving management leadership capabilities. All three sectors of government can work in conjunction with each other to attract the best minds and resources to the renewal of the system. Funds at the federal level can be applied to "high risk" investments, for this is the only governmental level that can commit the necessary amount of money and manpower to accomplish research and development.

Using Developmental Capital

Developmental capital, available in a three-stage process, is the means of responsibly fostering change and renewal. If educational engineering is ultimately to have any impact, it must receive its "energy" from a pattern of funding.

Three-stage funding of projects is one way to maximize the effectiveness of this developmental capital. In this process, the first step is to provide small amounts of money to the agency so that a management support group or technical assistance can be used in the planning process. These planning grants accomplish two purposes: First, schools can afford to attract the resources necessary for good planning. Second, they equalize opportunities among schools that are competing for project approval. No longer will wealthy schools have an unfair advantage over poor schools in the competition for developmental dollars, as happened in the Title III and Title I ESEA application process.

Program operation and management funds are then made available to schools that have demonstrated the best use of the planning grants. There are two major criteria for awarding this money: First, the schools should demonstrate skill in the assessment of system needs and imagination in relating expected program outcomes to the identified needs. Second, the request for proposal should be a clear and comprehensive document. The heart of the RFP is in the clear statement of outcomes, not only for the program but also for the renewal of the school system. The art is in setting parameters in such a way that the bidder is able to make his best response to this statement of need. The third stage of the funding would automatically follow the money for program operation and would be for the independent educational audit. There must be no chance for the auditor to be involved in either program planning or operation; rather, the accomplishment audit group must be independent.

Grants management, funded by a risk capital account at the local level, must also follow this three-phase process if sustained innovation is to be accomplished. Risk capital can be used by an administrator to build an in-house innovative capability or at least to utilize that which exists on the outside under contract as a management support function. If the administrator could make this risk capital available in three stages, talented and ambitious teachers would be encouraged and would have the resources to bid on requests for proposals. This process could take on a myriad of forms.

Probable Trends

The need for new patterns of funding in education is receiving wide-spread attention. Congress has already taken limited action by requiring planning grants and educational accomplishment audits in the provisions of ESEA Title VII and Title VIII. The expansion of this new pattern of fudning to ESEA Titles I and III should be given high priority if these programs are to achieve their original objectives.

While these new directions at the federal level support the concept of educational engineering for accountability, action is also required, and is already occurring in some instances, at the state and local levels along the lines previously mentioned. The trend for states to assume an increasingly greater role in educational financing will provide an opportunity for a more cohesive and systematic approach to school funding. Even with total state responsibility for financing education, this three-stage funding process would prove to be just as important as the proposed equitable redistribution of education resources.

At the local level, a developmental capital approach to grants management would foster a responsible strategy of educational innovation. LEA's are caught in a fiscal crunch; since most school budgets can be altered only slightly, any sudden increase in discretionary money would probably have an insignificant impact upon the system, because the money would be treated as an "add-on" under the current lump-sum dispersal of program money. If promising innovations are to have a marked impact, money must be programmed so that innovations are comprehensively planned and implemented, objectively evaluated, and then effectively turn-keyed back to the schools when appropriate.

This sort of approach will lead ultimately to modernizing reforms, such as program budgeting and performance evaluations. School decision makers have not enjoyed the freedom of choosing among alternatives. If a developmental capital approach to program funding were adopted, responsible innovation could begin to produce relatively unambiguous results. As alternatives are generated through developmental capital and performance contracting, the way will have been prepared for the installation of PPBS and other necessary reforms.

Summary

The educational engineering process described above is consciously directed toward increasing the capability of the schools. Thus it is that a turnkey arrangement is called for in every RFP and is incorporated into every performance contract. With costs underwritten by the local education agency, provision for adaptation, adoption, and installation of a successfully completed performance contract is assisted by using school personnel as consultants and as trainees in the process successfully bid by the contractor. The turnkey, or turnaround, feature is potentially a bodkin's point to pierce the armor of resistance to change and innovation that is so permanent a feature of school life. The objective of the standard turnkey feature of all performance contracts with private enterprise is simple and clear: to arm the school with the know-how of better instructional practice and to see that validated practice is adopted.

In general, educational organizations are influenced by three basic factors: the cultural or belief system, which sets policy in the form of goals and creates the mind-set by which activities are accepted; the technology, which determines the means available for reaching these goals; and the social structure of the organization in which the technology is embedded. An educational engineering process to produce accountability for results in the public schools attends constructively to these three basic factors. □

Leon Lessinger is Callaway Professor of Ecucation and Urban Life, Georgia State University. He wishes to acknowledge Charles Blaschke of Educational

Turnkey Systems and Peter Briggs, Albert Mayrhofer, Tom Burns, Karl Hereford, and B. Alden Lillywhite of the Bureau of Elementary and Secondary Education for their invaluable insights and assitance. This paper is the product of many minds.

---

[1]Performance contracting need not be limited to private enterprise. The principles are applicable for arrangements with teachers, universities, and nonprofit organizations.

IV

EDUCATION TURNKEY NEWS

"Everyone keeps asking for more money for more inputs: more classrooms, more equipment, more money for teacher, and more teachers to lower the teacher-pupil ratios. None of these demands is necessarily relevant to what should be the focus of education—whether students are learning."

ANALYSIS

Federal Education Policy

Before leaving the U.S. Office of Education, Associate Commissione Leon Lessinger commissioned *Education Turnkey* to develop a report on his concept of "educational engineering". Entitled "Educational Engineering: Managing Environmental and Institutional Change to Increase Educational Productivity," it was the first descriptive report on performance contracting, turnkey operations, accountability, and management support groups. Lessinger presented recommendations to White House advisors in late December, based partly on conclusions and recommendations of the Education Engineering Report.

On March 3rd, President Nixon sent his long awaited Education Message to Congress. It was a clear statement of a new and creative federal policy toward elementary and secondary education. Unfortunately, little of the discussion that followed the statement centered on its more positive aspects, for it was almost immediately attacked on political grounds. Critics focused on what they considered to be a typically Republican approach: to cut back on funding in general and to spend those fewer dollars on studying problems, rather than doing something about them. On March 24th, the President issued a second major statement

---

Reprinted with permission by *Education Turnkey News,* May, 1970.

affecting our public schools, his Message to the Nation on Desegregation. It was attacked as a thinly veiled slowdown of federally assisted integration as part of a general "Southern strategy".

To those informed about new trends and possibilities in education management, there was much in both of those statements which could lead toward a new strengthening of public education. An analysis of the Education Engineering Report prepared as this Administration was developing its education policy, should help to highlight some significant features of those two Presidential messages.

The Report cites the current low status of performance of our public education system and the problems that have been mounting over the past few years. Costs have increased astronomically while performance levels have remained the same, or in some cases, declined. Taxpayers are removing their support through bond issue defeats. Parents who can afford to are taking their children's educational future out of the hands of the public schools. Experimental programs do not seem to work, or, at least, the success of demonstration projects seems to disappear as they are spread throughout the system. New educational programs from Washington are often not economically, socially, or politically feasible or palatable at the local level, and thus do not succeed. Those in charge do not seem to be able to help themselves and community pressure is rising to put someone else, anyone else, in charge. The system is truly sinking under its own organizational weight.

No one seems to know how individual students are performing but minority students, getting less and less out of each year of school, are dropping out at an increasing rate. No one is willing to be held accountable for what is happening in public education. There is no quality control over programs. Equal opportunity is often a sham, for even if opportunities are equal, results differ greatly between races. Everyone keeps asking for more money for more inputs: more classrooms, more equipment, more money for teachers, and more teachers to lower the teacher-pupil ratios. None of those demands is necessarily relevant to what should be the focus of education—whether students are learning.

The Education Engineering Report suggested an heretical thought, similar to a point for which the President was criticized: That there should be less concern with more money and more concern with how money is being spent. Lessinger had been developing the concept of "accountability" through the practice of independent education accomplishment audits. For half a century, state audits have certified that education dollars were spent legally, but no one has ever certified that they were spent responsibly or effectively. Amendments to ESEA Titles VII and VIII made funds available for a similar educational audit. A logical consequence of this is that until accomplishment in experimental projects is audited and certified, more dollars should not be called for, and where they are, they should be spent on certified successes and not on proven failures. As President Nixon phrased it in his later speech, we should find out what works and then ask for money.

A second point advanced in the Report is that schools should be measured on the basis of performance. Indices such as pupil expenditure, pupil-teacher ratios, average teacher salaries, experience of teaching staff, students per classroom, racial composition, and so forth have their place, but the first indication must be student performance levels. In President Nixon's words: "There is only one important question to be asked about education; what do the children learn?" The usual input measurements have to do with school keeping and administrative chores. Now we must have measurements of outputs based on productivity. In addition to average per pupil expenditure, we need cost per grade level increase; along with average days of attendance, we should have hours of instruction per grade level increase. Nixon summed it up: "The corresponding need in the school systems of the Nation is to begin the responsible, open measurement of how well the educational process is working. It matters very little how much a school building costs; it matters a great deal how much a child in that building learns . . . We have, as a Nation, too long avoided thinking of the *productivity* of schools."

The third basic argument of the Report is that relevant educational personnel must be held accountable for student performance. A major symptom of the current educational malaise is the lack of incentives for anyone to try to do better. Teachers have no reward for trying different approaches to raise student performance; officials have no incentive to adopt management reforms. If persons are held accountable, there is such an incentive. Some teachers and teacher unions have understandably argued that teachers cannot now be held accountable because they are not responsible, i.e.—they cannot make choices and cause changes. It would be unfair and almost capricious simply to hold teachers and others accountable today, under the present system. But once alternatives are available, accountability is an essential ingredient to cause choices among those alternatives to be made on the basis of effectiveness in increasing student performance.

Teachers have also argued that they should not be held responsible if they happen to have a slow class. Avoiding the argument over whether there is such a thing, the Report suggests that judgments about performance will be based on specific local situations, with an information system sufficient to enable a student's progress to be contrasted against comparable groups. Or, as President Nixon suggested: "Success should be measured not by some fixed national norm, but rather by the results achieved in relation to the actual situation of the particular school and the particular set of pupils." This accountability concept would require a management information system much more sophisticated than now exists in any school. The Report suggests how this crucial system can best be developed as part of a performance-based contracting approach, which is what is really required in this whole concept of accountability for increased performance.

The fourth area treated in the Report is the concept of "equity of results". Equal educational opportunity is a goal we must strive for, but it alone does not guarantee that equal results will be obtained. The struggle for equal educational opportunity takes one along the road of inputs such as racial balance, comparability of resources, and supplemental funds. It only implicitly addresses student performance and what is learned. The Education Engineering Report calls for "equity of results" as a national policy for the 70's. The Texarkana Project, using a private contractor to guarantee student performance, has shown that an equity of results in realizing potential among students is possible. Simply giving deficient students a better share of the present system may do little good. As President Nixon predicted in his March 24th Desegregation Statement: "If our schools fail to educate, then whatever they may achieve in integrating the races will turn out to be only a Pyrrhic victory."

That statement also suggests an administration posture that has troubled many citizens—that integration is too heavy a load for the already overburdened public schools. Vice President

Agnew, in two recent speeches, has opposed open admissions policies at the higher education level because universities should not serve a social goal. Nixon's statements on desegregation, administration guidelines, policies on busing, and Justice Department activity in regard to Southern schools all indicate that schools at any level are considered an improper vehicle for fighting civil rights battles, presumably because it jeopardizes the educational priority. The Report suggests that an equity of results approach can increase educational performance levels while lessening the emotionalism surrounding desegregation. The potentially most disruptive force in desegregation, and the force toward which the White House is accused of catering, is the fear of the white community that upon integration, deficient minority students coming from the poorer half of a dual system will lessen the already threatened quality of instruction. If deficient students are raised at an accelerated pace to be on a par with their peers, then the Nation's goals will be doubly served: deficient students will be brought up to equitable levels of performance; and a major force threatening to disrupt desegregation will be removed. This approach won the approval of 71% of those voting in a public referendum in Texarkana, the home of the "freedom of choice" movement.

The March 24th Desegregation Statement pledged: "We shall launch a concerted, sustained and honest effort to assemble and evaluate the lessons of experience: to determine what methods of school desegregation have worked, in what situations, and why." Equity of results, as it is explained and proposed in the Educational Engineering Report, is the most effective way both to increase deficient student performance and to hasten the process of desegregation. It is a logical component of the overall framework which the Administration seems to have adopted: judging schools in terms of student performance; judging expenditures in terms of results achieved; and holding personnel accountable. And it is logical to assume it will become part of the Administration's approach.

The President has indicated he will divert $1.5 billion in the next two years to fund whatever desegregation approaches seem best. Three priorities for funding mentioned in the desegregation statement were: areas where "immediate infusions of money can make a real difference in terms of educational effectiveness;"

special needs of those needing "to catch up educationally with the rest of the nation;" and "innovative techniques for providing educationally sound inter-racial experiences." Rapid Learning Centers such as the facility in Texarkana can affect educational effectiveness, aid deficient students to catch up educationally with their peers at an accelerated pace and provide an inter-racial experience for those in transition from a dual to a unitary system. If funding is made available for programs of accelerated learning aimed toward equity of results, the Nixon policy, currently being attacked by liberals, would produce a faster and surer process of politically palatable yet educationally effective integration than has any previous administration.

The fifth general theme of the Report was the need for better application of technology in our public schools. The technology has been, or is being, created to meet virtually every education need, from pre-school to adult basic education. This effort will be stimulated by the Administration's call for a higher percentage of the education budget to go toward research and specifically, the creation of a National Institute of Education to conduct research. As technology has developed, a second need arises to introduce it successfully into schools. The usual problem is that the school is not equipped to manage the technology, so results achieved in demonstrations quickly erode, and machines are eventually abandoned to gather dust. The Education Engineering approach suggests: a performance contract to tailor instructional development to local school situations and needs; an administrative management system to realize the greatest benefits possible from the new technology while it is being demonstrated; and a turnkey phase to guarantee that a demonstrated level of benefits will continue as the approach is spread system-wide. As technology is coupled with the guaranteed performance approach, it will mean more education for each dollar spent and will thus meet the requirement for funding stated by the President: "As we get more education for the dollar, we will ask the Congress to supply many more dollars for education."

The final theme of the Report is that better funding patterns are needed. The hard lesson to be learned from the past five years of major federal funding of educational programs is that the way in which the money is delivered is as important as the amount. Federal funding, despite a plethora of regulations and guidelines, proposals, and reports, actually supports, and in some cases encourages inefficiencies and inequities in public schools. As President Nixon observed: "The present system of federal grants frequently creates inefficiency. There are now about 40 different federal categorical grant programs in elementary and secondary education. This system of carving up federal aid to education into a series of distinct programs may have adverse educational effects. Federal pieces do not add up to the whole of education, and they may distract the attention of educators away from the big picture and into a constant scramble for special purpose grants."

Those grants, to a major extent, have not been effectively evaluated, and they are treated by many local recipients as "add-on's" to the budget, which slowly grows each year. The problem, once again, is a lack of incentives to conduct educational business any differently. Daniel Moynihan, writing in the Fall, 1969 issue of the *Public Interest* stated that: "The federal government must develop and put into practice far more effective incentive systems than now exist, whereby state and local governments, and private interests, too, can be led to achieve the goals of federal programs."

The incentive system suggested by Lessinger to the White House was a process of applying developmental capital to education in a three-stage funding of projects to maximize their effectiveness. The first step would be small amounts of money to the local education agency so that a management support group or other technical assistance could be used in the planning process, thus attracting resources needed for good planning and equalizing opportunities among schools competing for project approval. Second, program operation funds would be made available to schools which demonstrate skill in the assessment of system needs and imagination in relating expected program outcomes to those identified needs. The third stage of funding would be for the independent educational accomplishment audit. This three-stage incentive funding is needed for the Nixon Administration to be able to effectuate its policy of discovering what works at the local level with the least initial expenditure of federal funds.

Despite the fact that Administration education spokesmen are still receiving very rough treatment at the hands of education audiences, there is much in the Administration's approach to education which, if implemented, will bring praise from those same audiences in the years to come. One possible impediment to full implementation of this policy lies in the newly issued ESEA Title I guidelines on "comparability".

The success of Title I projects has long been in question. A recent critique by a former HEW official lays the blame for program ineffectiveness to the use by some localities of Title I funds to supplant state and local funds for regular programs in Title I project schools. Thus, federal funds did not go toward special compensatory efforts, but simply to regular operating expenses. To rectify this, USOE issued new guidelines for Title I on February 26th. They required that state and local funds must be spent to provide comparable services among all schools, whether eligible for Title I projects or not. Only then can federal funds be added to provide supplementary services in project schools.

Questions have been raised with regard to how performance contracting, or even the President's Education Messages, comply with these guidelines. Under a performance contract operable in Texarkana, a rapid learning center has been established. It has a higher pupil-teacher ratio, more expenditures for hardware, a higher paraprofessional to pupil ratio, longer hours of facility utilization, and so forth, than other schools in the district. If state and local funds were being spent there, which must be the case when federal funds are eventually phased out, then they will not be spent in a way to provide comparable services among all schools. Does this mean the system will not be eligible for any Title I funds? HEW Assistant Secretary, Lewis Butler, was asked after his speech at the National Committee for the Support of Public Schools about this conflict, and he stated it was not his understanding that "comparability" would conflict with the special circumstances of performance contracts. One might predict a policy in which States are allowed to certify that guidelines are met and OE has a diminished role in State plan approval.

The problem which OE is trying to deal with concerns minority students not obtaining a competent education. The traditionally attempted solution has been to ensure equal educational opportunities, and the concept of comparable resources is aimed at that. A surer form of compensatory education can be gained through attention to equity of results. A Title I guideline requiring comparability of results, rather than comparability of resources, would seem to be more to the point.

The comparability guidelines seem to be in conflict with the tone of the President's March 3rd Education Message as well. In that speech, the President seemed less interested in the actual resources among schools than in the results produced. "It is simply not possible to make any confident deduction from school characteristics as to what will be happening to the children in any particular school. Fine new buildings alone do not predict high achievement. Pupil-teacher ratios may not make as much difference as we used to think. Expensive equipment may not make as much difference as its salesmen would have us believe." Thus effort expended to make these resources comparable may not actually make any difference in educational achievement.

The President's speech suggested an even deeper reason why these guidelines may be in jeopardy. Federal funding is about 8% of the total spent on elementary and secondary education. State and local funds account for 92%. In order to get a piece of that federal 8%, local agencies must obey federal guidelines in spending their own 92%. This flies in the face of the "New Federalism", which promises more local control. The trend is becoming clear: the President has stated that de facto segregation is a local matter and that he favors federal aid through revenue sharing as the system "most consistent with local control of education". In his March 3rd speech, Nixon said: "I am determined to see to it that the flow of power in education goes toward, and not away from, the local community. The diversity and freedom of education in this nation, founded on local administration and state responsibility, must prevail."

Thus, the new "comparability" guidelines are susceptible to criticism by those within the bureaucracy, as well as those at the local level. They may become of little consequence as the Nixon federal education policy continues to develop with concern for results, rather than inputs, and moves from federal initiative to local control and its complement–local accountability.

FORECAST

Performance Contracting Market Expanding

Performance contracting is creating a new market for small or new instructional management system firms. The qualitative nature of the market is being changed overnight as schools buy results, rather than inputs such as textbooks on a piecemeal basis. To the extent that state adoption boards approve total learning systems and school systems are able to adopt proven programs on a turnkey basis without having to go through the performance contract first phase, the market will expand geometrically.

Large equipment manufacturers and suppliers in the education field with high markups and high inventory stand a chance to lose a major portion of their market because of their inability to compete in terms of costs. Properly planned, a performance contract turnkey project will not allow a firm to "buy into" the contract. Nor can a large firm afford to sell equipment to one school at a reduced cost without expecting similar requests from others. Recognizing this trend, certain large firms are entering into agreements with independent instructional management firms or newly acquired subsidiaries to provide equipment on a reduced markup basis. This action has already created internal disruption, especially between the state sales representatives and the parent equipment suppliers

Within the next six months, a number of creative and productive education technicians, as well as program managers, will be leaving major corporations to form their own firms and enter the performance contract industry. They have received intensive training in the emerging instructional management field in large scale projects funded in part by federal support, but mainly by internally financed research and development of large corporations, such as Project PLAN, Naval Academy CAI and University of Texas CAI projects. Their opportunity for quick equity growth will be greater in small independent corporations because most of the education subsidiaries of major corporations have little impact on the overall stock of their parent corporation.

The Great Cities Research Council, presided over by Nolan Estes, Superintendent in Dallas, where *Education Turnkey* is now planning a major performance contract (See Volume I, Number 1), can be expected to enter the market to provide planning and management support group functions. Great Cities will bid on the HEW procedures manual and hopes to place staff in projects being planned for Fall operation in order to train them. Once they gain the necessary experience, they can then be expected to offer planning services to member schools.

Seasoned education budget analysts suggest that Nixon will

not ask for new legislative programs on which to spend the $1.5 billion he will take from domestic sources to commit to desegregation in the next two years. Rather, it is expected that he will spread it across current programs which are relevant to desegregation, raising the funding of those programs nearer to their authorization levels. Thus, ESEA Titles peculiarly susceptible to performance contracts and particularly effective in desegregation efforts, such as Dropout Prevention, may get a new boost in funding.

State Support for Performance Contracts will Grow

California will be the first State legislature to consider performance contracting. State Assemblyman and Democratic gubernatorial candidate, Jesse Unruh, recently introduced "The Guaranteed Learning Achievement Act of 1970", which would earmark federal funds for performance contracting projects. The legislation would authorize selected school districts, with the approval of the State Advisory Compensatory Education Commission (ACEC), to contract with private contractors to provide experimental special programs in fields of reading and mathematics for pre-school and primary level pupils. It specifies terms and conditions of such contracts, including performance standards for pupils enrolled and penalty and incentive provisions with respect to attainment of such standards. The legislation would authorize funding by allocation to the State under ESEA. It further authorizes school districts to include such programs in their budgets and authorizes partial support for such programs in the State budget for FY 71-72.

Bipartisan support for the measure will increase. In at least three Senate speeches during debates on the HEW Appropriations Bill, Senator George Murphy (R-Cal.) lauded both the Texarkana project, funded under his Dropout Prevention ammendments, and the possibility of a San Diego performance contract. □

Education Turnkey News, published by Charles Blaschke's management consultant firm Education Turnkey Systems, was a low-circulation insiders' newsletter which, during 1970 and 1971, helped keep the "movement" intact and provide it direction. It ceased publication in 1971, replaced by a monthly column written by Blaschke in the influential *Nation's Schools* magazine. ETS announced in 1971 the availability of a new computer-based cost-ED model which it claims precludes the need for school systems to go through the time-consuming and costly performance contract stage, thereby entering into turnkey projects immediately.

Chapter Two

OTHER PERFORMANCE CONTRACTS

Background: The Office of Economic Opportunity (OEO) Experiment

I. Performance Contracting–An Experiment in Accountability
John Oliver Wilson
(The director of the OEO experiment describes it.)

II. Performance Contracting Comes to Seattle
John DeYounge, Warren Henderson
(An uncomplimentary report on OEO's Seattle site.)

III. Performance Contracting–One Experience
Suzanne S. Taylor
(A spokesman for the Connecticut Education Association reports on the rather bitter remarks of the project director in Hartford, Connecticut.)

IV. Incentives Only: Mesa, Arizona
Instructor
(Teachers, under OEO funding, try their hand at performance contracting.)

V. Performance Contracting: The Dallas Experiment
Donald R. Waldrip, Nolan Estes
(Success and failure, Texas style.)

Background:

THE OFFICE OF ECONOMIC OPPORTUNITY (OEO) EXPERIMENT

The Office of Economic Opportunity awarded performance contracts to six education companies for projects in 18 school districts during the 1970-1971 academic year. The companies varied in their emphases on the three primary innovative teaching methods: student and teacher incentives, teaching machines and reorganized texts, and workbooks.

Quality Educational Development, Inc., with projects in Rockland, Maine, Anchorage, Alaska, and Dallas, Texas, was the only firm not to rely more heavily on one technique, subordinating the other two. QED used all three methods in moderation.

Learning Foundations, Inc., with projects in New York City, Jacksonville, Florida, and Hammond, Indiana, placed more emphasis on audiovisual aids and other teaching machines than any other contractor. It also utilized incentive rewards to a large extent, but placed little emphasis on programmed text materials.

Singer/Graflex, Inc., with projects in McComb, Mississippi, Portland, Maine, and Seattle, Washington, also relied primarily on programmed material. It used some audiovisual equipment and a few incentive rewards.

Plan Education Centers, with projects in Athens, Georgia, Selmer, Tennessee, and Wichita, Kansas, relied almost entirely on programmed materials, with minimal emphasis on machines and none on incentives.

Alpha Learning Systems, with projects in Grand Rapids, Michigan,

Hartford, Connecticut, and Taft, Texas, depended almost entirely on a system of teacher and student incentives, using some programmed material, but few teaching machines.

Westinghouse Learning Corporation, with projects in Fresno, California, Las Vegas, Nevada, and Philadelphia, Pennsylvania, used a wide variety of programmed workbook type materials, as well as a number of instructional machines. It gave incentive rewards to students only in moderation.

In addition, OEO financed two contracts between school districts and local education associations, one in Mesa, Arizona, and one in Stockton, California.

To evaluate and compare all these projects, OEO subcontracted with Battelle Memorial Institute to conduct the evaluation. It also subcontracted with Charles Blaschke's firm, Education Turnkey Systems, to help design and later help manage the program.

The program had many problems, some logistical, some political. The announcement of results was postponed several times. Competent observers both inside and outside the project suggested that the final evaluations would be statistically questionable.

However, the project did provide great visibility for the concept of performance contracting and, in addition, created some worthwhile models to examine.

In these pages the reader will find descriptions of the overall project, the sites in Seattle, Hartford, Rockland, and Mesa. In addition, the later articles in this book on Dallas and Grand Rapids include some discussion of the OEO projects in those cities. (These cities had other performance contracts as well.) □

I

PERFORMANCE CONTRACTING
AN EXPERIMENT IN ACCOUNTABILITY

by John Oliver Wilson

"The Office of Economic Opportunity decided to mount a nationwide experiment to provide the information that school boards should have before deciding whether to enter into performance contracting."

Over the years there have been many efforts to improve the education of underachievers. These efforts have emphasized the provision of more funds, additional books and tutors, summer study programs, smaller class sizes, and counseling, with the hope that a greater flow of resources into the schools would guarantee better education. Recent evaluations, in particular the now famous report of Dr. James Coleman, have indicated that per pupil expenditures are not the primary factor in determining the child's progress in school. In spite of this, we have continued to pour millions upon millions of dollars into our public schools while underachievers continue to lag behind their successful classmates.

Thus, there was excitement in the winter of 1970 when educators and government officials heard rumors that a new project in Texarkana was doubling previous achievement levels of some children.

Apparently this result was being achieved through something called performance contracting. Its elements are relatively simple:

- A contractor signs an agreement to improve students' performance in certain basic skills by set amounts.
- The contractor is paid according to his success in bringing

---

students' performance up to prespecified levels. If he succeeds, he makes a profit. If he fails he isn't paid.

Within guidelines established by the school board, the contractor is free to use whatever instructional techniques, incentive systems, and aids he feels can be most effective.

The Texarkana project, funded under Title VIII of the Elementary and Secondary Education Act, was intended primarily as a program for preventing dropouts. The contractor, a private firm, removed students from their normal classrooms and conducted the program in mobile units. Teachers were aided by paraprofessionals and a broad range of teaching machines and other audiovisual devices. The curriculum was highly individualized. These features in themselves were not revolutionary. What was more unusual about Texarkana was the contractor's use of material rewards to trigger the children's learning process and the teachers' instructional efforts. It was hoped these material rewards later could be replaced with intrinsic incentives.

The children were offered such rewards as trading stamps (which they could use for gifts) and free time during the class period (which they could use to read magazines, listen to records, or engage in other recreational activities). Incentives to teachers included stock in the company.

The contractor was paid only to the extent that he was successful in improving students' scores on standardized reading and math tests.

Staff members from the Office of Economic Opportunity who visited Texarkana saw great promise in performance contracting as a means to help children achieve satisfactory results. But they also realized that results of this one program did not prove its value. A much broader, clearly defined, and carefully evaluated experience was necessary before it could be confidently stated that performance contracting could help children learn. Thus the Office of Economic Opportunity decided to mount a nationwide experiment to provide the information that school boards should have before deciding whether to enter into performance contracting.

The Experiment

The experiment was launched in August and September, 1970, in 18 school districts with six private firms—Singer/Graflex,

Quality Education Development, Westinghouse, Plan Education Centers, Alpha Learning Systems, and Learning Foundations. Every major geographical area and every major racial and ethnic minority are included. Students in the experiment are Puerto Rican, Mexican-American, black, white, Eskimo, and Indian. All were carefully selected; the majority were at least two grade levels below norm.

In each location, two sets of levels are involved—first through third, seventh through ninth. About one hundred students per grade per sit have been receiving instruction for about an hour daily each in reading and in math for the school year.

Because the primary purpose of the experiment is to compare the impact of performance-contracting education with the impact of normal education received by underachieving children, a similar group of students in traditional classrooms was selected and tested. These children, who attend nearby schools, are matched closely with the children in the experimental program. Since students in the experimental schools but not in the experimental program are exposed to rub-off or transfer effects, they were felt to be a less than ideal control group. However, they have been included as a special comparison group to provide an opportunity to examine the transfer effect itself.

In addition, several of the selected schools already had some type of remedial reading or math program—specialized teachers, tutors, or teaching machines. Students in these classes make up a special program group, and their performance, whenever possible, will be compared to that of students in all other groups.

Altogether, more than 27,000 children are participating in the experiment. About 10,800 are in the programs offered by the private firms; 11,880 in the control group; 2,700 in the comparison group; and 1,000 in special programs. An additional 1,030 pupils are part of a contract between two districts and their teachers' groups.

One contractor, Education Turnkey Systems, Inc., is providing management support for the schools. This support is necessary because of the newness of performance contracting and the rigorous reporting and program documentation needed for evaluation. Another contractor, the Battelle Memorial Institute, independent of all other experiment participants, is administering pre- and post-tests to experimental and control students, analyzing the differences between the scores of the two groups and collecting and analyzing other data needed for a thorough evaluation.

The six private firms were selected for the variety of their approaches to performance contracting. For example: Plan Education Centers uses few audiovisual aids and offers few incentives to students or teachers. This contractor relies heavily on programmed texts and existing instructional materials, believing that incentives are intrinsic to the system. Learning Foundations, on the other hand, relies strongly on teaching machines and other devices, and, for both students and teachers, emphasizes incentives that gradually change from extrinsic and tangible to intrinsic and attitudinal.

To gauge the extent and nature of performance contracting capabilities and to avoid "teaching to the tests," an elaborate evaluation structure has been devised. First, the test of reading and math achievement being used to determine the contractors' pay is randomly selected from three standardized tests. Part of the payment is also determined by the performance of students on criterion-referenced tests, used to measure the attainment of interim performance objectives. Finally, a separate and broad standardized test is being used for OEO's evaluation purposes.

To guarantee the reliability of the test scores, four safeguards have been incorporated in the evaluation:

- Companies do not know which form of the standardized test is being used. Company personnel are not involved in administering or scoring the tests.
- Because companies might inadvertently use material that contains test items, however, the management-support contractor is conducting a curriculum audit on a spot basis to remove any test items from the classroom curriculum.
- Retention tests will be given during the 1971-72 school year to determine whether gains have been made because of "cramming" or "teaching to the tests," or whether the students have actually learned under the firm's instruction.
- The final safeguard is the strict penalty for "teaching to the tests." If it is determined that this has occurred, the Office of Economic Opportunity has the authority to terminate the contract and require the contractor to return all funds paid so far.

As a result of this careful design, the Office of Economic Opportunity hopes to learn what kind of results can be expected from a variety of students from a variety of backgrounds. It is hoped that the results of this experiment will be replicable across the country. Because of the use of a variety of control and comparison groups, the Office of Economic Opportunity may discover what levels of skill improvement can be credited to performance contracting and which might have occurred during the traditional learning process. Rigorous accounting procedures will give reliable estimates of cost/effectiveness ratios. And, finally, a great deal will have been learned about the problems of administering, implementing, and negotiating performance contracts.

If OEO learns that performance contracting does not produce significant gains in achievement levels, that it is impossible to administer, or that its cost/effectiveness ratios make it impractical, obviously it will have to attempt to devise different methods. If performance contracting proves successful, educators and government officials will have important knowledge on how to educate disadvantaged children. □

Dr. Wilson is Director, Office of Planning, Research and Evaluation, Office of Economic Opportunity.

II

PERFORMANCE CONTRACTING COMES TO SEATTLE

A VIEW FROM THE PRESS **by John DeYonge**

"To whom are these people accountable?" Henderson (president of the Seattle Teachers Association) asks. "Whom does the citizen complain to–Rochester, N.Y.?"

She bent over the section of cartoons in her reading book and whispered out the difference between "pin" and "thin"–not always an easy thing when you're eight years old.

Other youngsters, here and in a neighboring class, worked their own ways–at their own speeds–through the programmed text.

Read a section, answer the question, check your answer. If it's right, go on. If not, try another section like the last one. Or go to the alcove and try the little machine that pronounces the word printed on a card you insert. Helps you remember.

Two classes at Van Asselt Elementary seem like second and third grade classes anywhere in the city, except:

- They are experimental and are being put on by a private firm which has bet its potential pay that it can offer a better program for disadvantaged children than is now being offered in most ordinary classrooms.
- They are controversial, because the logic that set them up upsets teacher organizations here and nationally.

One local teacher representative called the program a "gimmick" and another referred to its sponsors as "hucksters from out of town."

Probably the youngsters in the Van Asselt classes don't realize the significance of what they do for two hours a day under the

---

direction of teachers hired and directed by the Singer-Graflex Corp. of Rochester, N. Y.

Nor do youngsters in Singer-Graflex classes in other Seattle schools—Brighton and Cooper Elementaries and Boren Junior High.

At Van Asselt, the children, all identified as behind average in reading and math, were in their second week of testing and of working in programmed math and reading books, of practicing pronunciation with the machine that speaks back to them, of learning words by following a funny filmstrip on a hand-operated viewer.

In each room, two teachers—or a teacher and an assistant—worked with the pupils, no more than 25 to a room.

That ratio of instructors to pupils immediately marked off the classrooms as being special in Seattle. The usual ratio—and the ratio being maintained in a number of "control" ordinary classrooms across the city—is about one teacher to 25 students.

All this is being paid for through a $343,800 contract the Seattle School District received from the U. S. Office of Economic Opportunity as part of a $5.65 million OEO experiment nationwide to see whether private companies can beat professional public educators at their own game.

In turn, through agreement with OEO, Seattle has subcontracted Singer-Graflex Corp., for the "performance" program here.

Singer-Graflex has promised to produce or go payless. It will receive no pay at all if by the end of the school year there is no significant improvement beyond what the students normally would have achieved in ordinary classes.

The company, which has designed the program, hired the teachers and trained them, can receive a maximum of $263.50 for each student who gains two years' achievement in reading and math at the end of one year. In all, 600 students are involved.

According to Dean L. Dalby, project administrator here for Singer-Graflex, "at the heart of all we do is the child. That's what's important."

Dalby, a former teacher, said Singer-Graflex is not doing anything extraordinary in its program—except bringing together all kinds of special teaching materials and techniques used individually here and elsewhere so that all bears on helping an individual student advance rapidly in learning what has been difficult for him.

To avoid criticism springing up from teacher organizations that the private firms are "teaching to the test"—that is, giving a child a test and then drilling him so that he can do better in the same test the next time—all the Seattle children were tested by an independent firm, Battelle Memorial Institute of Columbus, Ohio, before they entered the Singer-Graflex classes.

Dalby said Battelle selected the children to be in the program, tested them "blind"—that is, with unmarked, mixed standardized tests.

When the experiment is over, Battelle, under a separate OEO contract, will test the children again to see how well Singer-Graflex has taught them.

Dalby is confident. "We try to have a tailor-made program for each child . . . and each week his progress is checked. Through our own tests, we plug the student in where he is in achievement and go from there."

Dalby and Dr. Randall Rockey of Singer-Graflex's Training Division said the firm worked up its program through its experience as a contractor running a Job Corps camp but said that the particular program has not been tried before on elementary or junior-high age children.

Rockey, like Dalby a bit non-plussed by the fuss the program's presence is stirring up, said:

"We're not saying we can do better than what's being done . . . but it's apparent that certain segments of the school population aren't making it in regular classes.

"We're saying, give us those and we'll try to correct their problems."

The fuss arising locally mirrors criticism from the National Education Association and the American Federation of Teachers, AFL-CIO—the organized teacher establishment.

Dallas Shockley, executive secretary of the Seattle Teachers Association, early last week said every parent here should be upset by "hucksters who come from out of town and take over the educational program for a profit."

Stanton Bloom, organizational director of the Seattle Federation of Teachers, classified the Singer-Graflex program as a "gimmick" blinding the public to the need for more teachers and more money for schools.

Warren Henderson, president of the Seattle Teachers Association and main officer of the Seattle Alliance of Educators, representing all Seattle teachers and administrators, offers perhaps a more reasoned critique.

There's no doubt Henderson and his organization are bothered by the notion a private firm can teach students better than ordinary teachers. Hurt pride is an element.

First, Henderson points out that Singer-Graflex should do better because where it has two teachers for every 25 students, the ordinary Seattle teacher faces 25 or more students routinely and thus has but half the time available to devote to an individual child.

And, he adds, the firm is using materials in abundance that an ordinary teacher would like to use but often cannot get.

Henderson said: "Beyond that, the experimental design is really rather poor. There are no real control classes to compare the results with."

Henderson touches on a critical point. Battelle Memorial Institute, according to Robert Wuflestad of Seattle Schools, has set up "control" classes at Gatzert and Adams elementaries and Hamilton junior high—all schools with disadvantaged children in them by federal definition.

Wuflestad, who oversees the Singer-Graflex program for Seattle Schools, said Seattle Schools have nothing to do with how Battelle will compare the results of the Singer-Graflex classes with those from the control classrooms.

There seem to be comparison problems.

The controls all have 25 or more children in a class, use ordinary school materials and are taught by teachers of varying experience.

The Singer-Graflex classes, with a spate of new materials and two teachers to 25 students, are being taught by instructors with very little classroom instruction.

Most are recent graduates, just certificated to teach. Only one has had a year of ordinary classroom experience.

Henderson criticizes the short training period the Singer-Graflex teachers received—nine six-hour days of training in the program before they entered program classrooms.

"Some of them are so naive," he said, "that they think they are using teaching materials and methods new under the sun, when many of the things they do are being done elsewhere in the city."

Critical to the battle shaping up is that Singer-Graflex walked into the midst of a local and statewide battle between teachers and school districts over how much power teachers have in influencing school decisions.

Thus Henderson and his organization have invoked formal negotiations with the Seattle School District about some parts of the experimental program.

Singer-Graflex teachers are not hired by the district but by the company and thus do not fall within the bargaining representation of the Seattle Alliance of Educators.

"To whom are these people accountable?" Henderson asks, "Whom does the citizen complain to–Rochester, N. Y.?"

There are slight differences in pay scales and working hours and Henderson sees the contracting out of teaching as a way for school districts to get around legitimate negotiations over curriculum, materials, teacher working conditions.

"We're not being obstructionists to innovative programs," Henderson said. "But we want to be involved in them.

"Our concern is the implied undercutting of normal staff and what this kind of contracting does to the Professional Negotiations Act by removing segments of the teacher corps from the negotiations process."

He and other STA officers have met with the STA's attorney and with attorneys for the STA's parent group, the Washington Education Association. Court action by teachers against the Seattle School District and Singer-Graflex is a possibility, Henderson vows.

Dalby and Rockey say that they and Singer-Graflex don't understand what the hassle is about.

They point out that by agreement, any teacher or Seattle school can study their program, copy it, duplicate it, use it.

They add that if their experiment is successful it will show that what local teachers want–low class sizes, concentrated teaching materials–is what the school district should institute.

And they ask, "If we can help a child learn to catch up and go forward in his reading and math, what is the complaint? We've helped the child."

Seattle School District officials, knowing that the negotiation struggle with teachers never ends, simply say that the Singer-Graflex agreement is not negotiable under the law and that's that.

And Henderson says it's not the program but the principle of turning education over to companies seeking a profit.

"It erodes teacher rights and the rights of the public."

Meanwhile, below the debate, in classrooms innovative or otherwise, the youngsters work at their lessons . . . not knowing that how well they do today may determine the quality of their lives 20 years from now. □

"Classroom Experiment Under Criticism", the *Seattle P-I* headlined this story in its October 11 editions by John DeYonge, *P-I* education writer. Reprinted with permission.

A VIEW FROM TEACHERS

by Warren Henderson,
president, Seattle Teachers Association

A performance contract has been introduced experimentally into four schools in Seattle by the Singer-Graflex corporation. Brighton, Cooper, Van Asselt elementary schools and Boren junior high have specialized classes in reading and mathematics for underachieving youngsters. Teachers have been hired by the corporation. They are not controlled by the school board. Individualized programmed learning for youngsters in classes with a 12.5 to 1 pupil-teacher ratio has been in operation for more than a month. Classes are closed and doors are locked to parents and concerned citizens. Visitation hours have been promised at some future date.

SAE has been attempting to get answers to some fundamental questions regarding the Singer-Graflex program. These answers have not been forthcoming. The district has thus far refused to allow SAE to examine the contract between the district, the federal Office of Economic Opportunity, and the Singer-Graflex corporation. *If there is nothing to hide, why the mystery?*

The apprehension felt toward the program primarily revolves around educational issues. Quality evaluation is a must in any experimental design. The pre-testing program was done so poorly that conclusions are practically meaningless. Frustration levels became so high among first-grade youngsters during the pre-test that many began to cry. In one school a child ran home. Interestingly, the district found itself *powerless to call off the testing to force the corporation to guarantee more adequate planning and proper administration of the tests.*

Control groups that match pupil-teacher ratios of Singer-Graflex classes have not been set up. Good experimental design requires only one variable, with all other aspects of the program similar. Otherwise the results have no validity. Materials, techniques, equipment, methods, and class size are all variables in the present situation. What has one measured at the conclusion of such an experiment? Yet the results of these procedures presumably will be the basis for determining the extent of Singer-Graflex's performance and payment of thousands of dollars to the corporation, for fulfillment of its contract.

Underachieving and poorly motivated youngsters deserve the very best a district is able to provide. In the Singer-Graflex program, inexperienced teachers are asked to instruct poorly motivated and underachieving youngsters in an untried program. The "sparkle" of rapport between the teacher and student, which is so badly needed, is a missing ingredient and evident to any visitor to these classes.

Why cannot the district listen to its own teachers? Teachers who have developed innovative programs designed to reach poorly motivated and underachieving youngsters here in Seattle have never received significant funding. □

III

PERFORMANCE CONTRACTING–ONE EXPERIENCE

by Suzanne S. Taylor, Ph.D.

"Does a profit seeking company have the right to direct the manipulation of students?"

A Connecticut Education Association spokesman reports the rather bitter remarks of the school system's Project Director in Hartford, Connecticut. They make an intriguing contrast to the comments of the Project Director in Grand Rapids, Michigan (see "The Performance Contracts in Grand Rapids", (p. 121-31), which also had an Alpha project under the OEO experiment. (See also the remarks of John Cline, Alpha's project director in Grand Rapids, pp. 129.)

The advantage of Performance Contracting was summed up recently by Hartford's Project Director, Ernest Cermola, in one word, "Change." Change was improvement. Change occurred primarily because of what is known as the "Hawthorne effect", the good will and spirit that ensues with the institution of any innovative process into a system. Nonetheless, Cermola's appraisal emphasized that good teaching was the key to achieving the goal of effecting student learning, thus implying that the change brought about by performance contracting provided the impetus for teachers to improve their performance in teaching.

Specific changes occurred in several areas. The learning environment was improved as classrooms were reorganized and refurbished. Teachers received extra assistance in their teaching with counsel from professional consultants, a variety of teaching materials, classroom aides and encouragement from the community. The voluntary nature of the program meant that teachers

---

Reprinted with permission of *Connecticut Teacher,* November-December, 1971.

wanted to be where they were and therefore morale increased. Moreover, if a teacher had volunteered for the project, this usually indicated the flexible nature of the teacher and his or her receptivity to change. Money could be accrued by a teacher for exceptional performance up to $700. This money, by vote of the teachers, did not go directly to the teacher, but to the schools where the teacher practiced. Also contributing to the good morale was the extraordinary attention devoted to the entire program.

Major Accomplishments

In summing up the positive factors of the program, Cermola cited four major areas of accomplishment. (1) Teachers were helped to look at their teaching and to make modifications. (2) The schools were forced to analyze their administrative policies and procedures with a view to finding ways of producing results similar to the positive benefits of the project. (3) Performance Contracting provided practical training experience in the art of teaching with incentives. (Comments on this aspect appear later in the article.) (4) Teachers were inspired to be good teachers by accepting a challenge. An interesting paradox occurred, however, in the ninth grade. Cermola cited these students as the most successful participants and attributed this to outstanding teaching. The paradox lies in the fact that ninth grade students housed in the High School Annex were seldom visited by the Project staff, which meant that the teachers were self-directed rather than project directed. Morale was high and cooperation excellent as the teachers modified the Alpha techniques and materials to suit the needs of the students.

If these are the major benefits and change is viewed as the net result of the program, many more questions remain to be asked. If change occurred, how can it continue? How can the good things that ahppened in the ninth grade and in the other grades be made to happen in the future on the basis of this experiment? The opportunity to benefit from the Alpha program and adopt some of its benefits was supposed to be part of the original contract known as a turnkey provision; certain aspects of the performance contract were to be turned over to the school officials for continuation. As yet there appears to be no decision as to how this may come about. Provision for future implementation should come from the management support rendered by Education Turnkey Systems (ETS) to the Hartford Board.

Other questions which need more answers relate to supplemental funding of the basic OEO project.

Management Support Contract

Education Turnkey Systems, Inc. was to provide 40 days of management consulting to each of the 18 OEO projects for a fee. Yet there appeared to be few occasions when Hartford's particular needs for assistance could be met by ETS. In fact the Education Turnkey Systems, Inc. representatives visited Hartford only about 10 out of the 40 days, performing services their firm desired, such as materials inventory and setting up a system to collect data. The significance of ETS's connection to OEO should be clarified since the Principal Investigator for the OEO projects is Charles Blaschke who is also chief executive officer of Education Turnkey Systems, Inc.

Alpha Learning Systems, Inc. Project Administration

It appears that Alpha's project Administrator didn't have sufficient time to administer the program or an adequate educational background to provide counsel. Commuting daily from another state to supervise the subcontract for Alpha, he was unable to spend a complete school day in Hartford. His efforts seemed to be concentrated on working with the paraprofessionals whom he hired and fired. He was not accessible to teachers and seldom visited the ninth grade in the High School Annex, where the program worked well. Moreover, conflicts in the administration of the contracts within the school were created, as it was unclear who had which responsibility for what aspect of the instructional program. Because of the project administrator's business background and his limited educational experience he had difficulty comprehending instructional problems. Sometimes, therefore, the teachers could not get satisfactory answers for most of their questions and turned to Hartford's Project Director for advice rather than to Alpha.

From Consultant to Monitor

As the program developed the project director for the Hartford Schools functioned as a consultant. He felt compelled to work for the best interests of the students and to that end he offered constructive criticism aimed at modifying the program and improving the learning process. One of the earliest problems was the scheduling of math and reading. At first math was taught on Tuesdays and Thursdays for 80 minutes and reading on Monday, Wednesday and Friday for 40 minute intervals. Believing this was poor use of timing, Cermola opted successfully for the restoration of balance by rescheduling the time spent on math and reading, thus giving 40 minute periods for each five days a week. In January the project director assumed the role of an observer and monitor instead of that of a consultant.

Insufficient Planning

Implementation of the program less than a month before the opening of school meant that there was insufficient pre-planning time. Moreover, there was little time in the program for inservice training. Recruited in late summer, the teachers were instructed in a two week planning session. Difficulties arose during the two week session as most of the time was spent by Alpha personnel in discussing the psychological principles behind incentive teaching. It was only near the end of the two week period that the teachers convinced the Alpha personnel of their need for some practical directions as a result of role playing. Nonetheless, since the program had not been put into practice, it was difficult for Alpha to give many explicit directions. These would have to come as the program was put into practice.

Testing

The testing procedures described by Cermola raise several questions. The procedure for testing was awkward. The system used its own cumbersome compilation system. Battelle Memorial Institute of Columbus, Ohio, who had the independent testing contract, appeared frustrated in their attempts to secure valid test results. Planning to test a large number of students in one location, they were surprised at diffident students who refused to take the tests and walked out. With these brief indications of testing chaos the obvious conclusion is to question in some detail the reliability of the testing procedure. It is also difficult to obtain reliability with the high drop-out rate in the program. Turnover was about 50 per cent. Moreover, it has been leanred from OEO that the final test results will not be released to the public until mid-December.

Retesting

A sample is to be selected and by the terms of the contract should be tested four months after June, but not earlier than two weeks after the start of school in the fall. What about retesting a year later to see if there is regression?

Payment Terms

It is also of note that the Hartford contract provided for Alpha to receive up to 80 per cent of the $180,000 before the end of the year; a refund would be made if it was later found Alpha didn't come up to par. Should pre-payment prevail? In August, according to other reliable sources, Alpha requested that it be paid on a different basis than that previously agreed upon.

Constant Negotiations

Hartford, like the other 18 cities, had no choice in who was to be the contractor. They were assigned Alpha and then negotiated details. These negotiations seem to have been in a state of constant renegotiation. As the year progressed extensive modifications to the contract became routine. Modifications which came about as a result of practical problems were numerous.

Paraprofessionals

Paraprofessionals were recruited from the community and consisted of mostly blacks with some Spaniards and Puerto Ricans mixed into the group. In this way community involvement resulted in enthusiastic community support of the project. Some problems of responsibility did occur as the paraprofessionals felt they were responsible to the Alpha Project Administrator rather than the teachers or school administration. To what extent the contribution of the paraprofessionals helped or hindered the program is a matter for further study.

Administrative Oversupply

A glance at the organizational chart will show how the lines of responsibility are duplicated and unclear. Could it be that too much of the contract expense was paid to a top heavy administration for Project Alpha? Could it be that too many administrative representatives were involved in conducting the project even though this was not a direct expense for the Performance Contract?

Although teachers received no additional pay, they did benefit from assistance provided by paraprofessionals. Suppose instead of more administrators, more teachers had been hired, reducing the pupil teacher ratio from 25 or 30 to 1 to 15 or 12 to 1 per teacher. Would the program be more effective with the application of more professional expertise?

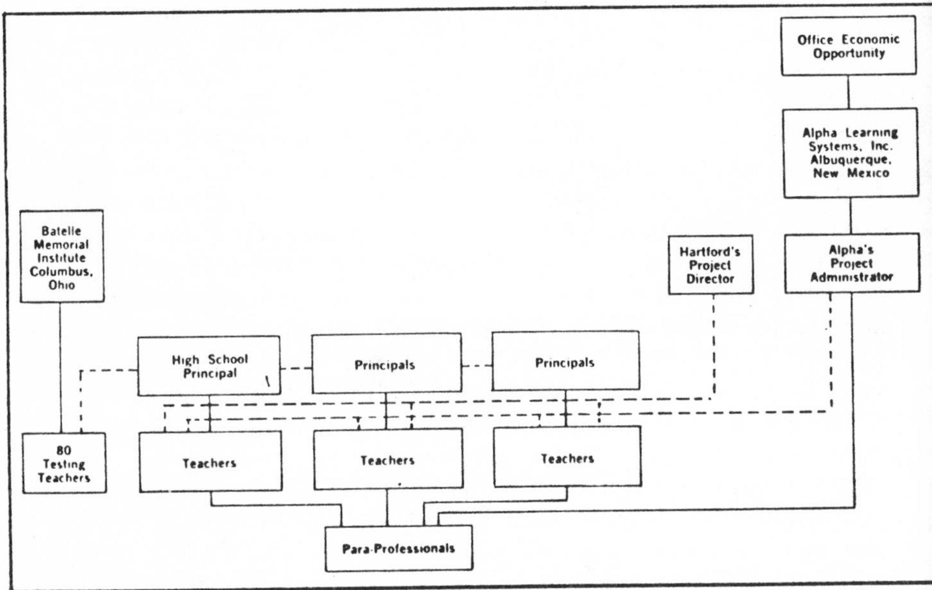

Nature of Incentives

The last group of questions are posed as a philosophical concept versus a psychological concept. Is behavior modification through the use of incentiveness ethically, morally, or philosophically desirable? Who is to getermine the "good" for a child? Should the same standard of performance be expected of all students? How far can incentive motivation or behavior modification go before it is too far, or before it insults the inherent right of freedom of choice of an individual?

Very little philosophical discussion is evey mentioned in the prevailing literature on Performance Contracts. Rather, in an attempt to be accountable, the System Managers who write most of the articles set qualifiable goals, use specific rewards, and then achieve specified results. All answerable questions, albeit, not always easily measured and analyzed as to their educational benefit. It is interesting to note that the design of the Hartford contract was predicated on the knowledge of what kinds of awards motivate students. Does a profit seeking company have the right to direct the manipulation of students? It was explained that at first students enjoyed receiving a reward of free time or leisure time for games and other play activities, but eventually some students got more involved and absorbed in what they were doing and gave up the aimlessness and purposelessness of leisure for the patterns to which they had been conditioned. Then more tangible rewards were substituted for good performances. These included such things as tokens, small toys and other redeemable notes. It is apparent and reassuring that good teachers are essential to learning. It is also obvious that many questions have to be asked as to the proprietary interests of the industries selling Performance Contracting.

Perhaps the teachers and administrators are capable of good performance without the intrusion of big business. At the recent National Association Elementary School Principals' Convention, James Craigmile, a professor at the University of Missouri, said the same achievements provided by performance contractors could be accomplished by teachers and principals if they were given the same opportunity to eliminate deadwood, to work extra hours and have available all the hard and software poured into the programs. □

This article is based in part on the writer's interpretation of conversations with Ernest Cermola, Project Director for the City of Hartford's Performance Contract with Alpha Learning Systems, Inc. Funding for the Hartford contract was provided by the Office of Economic Opportunity with some $320,573 allocated to the overall project. Involved were 600 students in grades 1, 2, 3, 7, 8, 9 in the Alpha program and another 600 students in a control group.

IV

INCENTIVES ONLY: MESA, ARIZONA

"One of my little boys (said a teacher) took a story home to read. His mother said she'd love to hear it. The little boy replied, 'OK, but what are you going to give me for it?' "

Doug Barnard, director of the "Incentives Only" program, explains the way it works, as follows.

"We began this project with the assumption that, for the average child, a report card and teacher praise is all that is needed for incentive. We believe that the economically deprived child must be rewarded more frequently and in different ways."

Designated experimental schools were presented with an overview of the project task. Each faculty voted to be a part of the project or to be excluded. No students were transferred, bussed, or homogeneously grouped for the study. In all schools, normal classroom teaching methods and materials are being utilized. Project classes remain basically as they were when the school year began—the addition of incentives is the only difference. Some classrooms of thirty students may contain only seven or eight designated as project students, but in such cases, all students receive incentives.

Don Blair, principal of Lehi Elementary, one of the participating schools, says:

"Our teachers establish with each student a set of goals to be achieved. When students reach the goals, they are rewarded. Our incentives program corresponds with the student's level of achievement. It consists of immediate rewards, such as candy and small toys, and delayed rewards, such as time to use educational games, watch movies, and go on field trips. Each teacher tailors a reward system to fit the personality of the child involved."

Lois Williams, who teaches a first-grade class at Lehi School, is happy to be involved in the project.

"It requires a very individualized approach which is very different from the traditional teaching methods you learn in college—it's challenging but gratifying when you see the results."

How does she feel about the reward system?

"I use the incentives in two ways: to reward scholastic achievement and to modify behavior. Because of the rewards I think the students are more motivated, and I've noticed fewer discipline problems. Let's face it, children will clean up their desks faster if they know they'll get a piece of candy when the job is done. Giving little but meaningful rewards seems to make the school day go along much more smoothly now."

How lasting are the effects of the incentives?

"This is a question parents ask—we began with small material rewards which we are slowly replacing with social incentives such as group activities. Of course, our ultimate objective is to make gaining knowledge the incentive for learning."

Mrs. Audrey Young, a second-grade teacher at Jefferson School, was opposed to the program at first.

"I didn't like the idea of giving tangible rewards—it seemed that praise and the satisfaction of understanding should provide enough incentive for achievement. Now I view the program more objectively—it works very well for some children. For others, I've had to find different ways of 'turning them on' to learning. The teacher must be very perceptive—he must sense what will motivate a child and how much pressure he can take. Rewards must be given for real mastery of a skill, real accomplishment of a goal—not just the appearance of having accomplished it.

Do students get used to being rewarded for what they do?

"One of my little boys took a story home to read. His mother said she'd love to hear it. The little boy replied 'OK, but what are you going to give me for it?'

"We try to explain to children that receiving rewards for achievement is a little arrangement we've made just to use in school—most children understand this."

How have parents reacted to the Mesa project?

"Favorably, for the most part," says Mr. Blair. "The Mesa School District has always made it a point to work closely with the community and this porject is no exception. We held briefings, wrote newsletters, and had extensive coverage in local newspapers and on television. No parents have requested that their child be removed from the project thus far. Many have been impressed with the results they see—kids actually say they like school and attendance has improved."

The program's teacher incentives are given in June if project students gain more than one grade level over their pretested achievement. Incentives are of four types: a cash salary supplement, cash for hiring aides, cash for purchasing additional materials, and released time for planning. At this writing, each school would decide what to do with the money it receives.

Teachers at Jefferson School are thinking about using the money to buy materials for the school but the Lehi School faculty favors giving each teacher a salary bonus for each project student who shows a grade-level gain.

What will happen next year when the funds are gone? Mrs. Williams feels no teacher could afford to personally sponsor a program of this nature, but she's convinced rewards work and she plans to purchase small items with her own money and make use of intangible incnetives such as free time for games and play.

Dr. Barnard says that the results in June will determine whether a similar program will continue.

"We're simply asking ourselves, 'Will a child who knows he'll receive candy or a toy for a successfully completed task work harder than a student rewarded only by praise and a good grade?' The incentives approach may not work for all students, but if it proves to be a way of reaching some, then educators should consider it." □

Major features: OEO-funded; involves one junior high and three elementary schools and an equal number of control schools; offers remedial work in math and reading for 100 students per grade in grades one through three and seven through nine; involves use of incentives to increase reading and math skills of selected disadvantaged students who show low achievement; no outside private contractor; carried out by regular teachers, using regular methods of instruction in their own classrooms; project participants selected on basis of low income and low achievement; students not aware of experimental grouping; began in November, ends in May; incentives for both students and teachers; all students in project classes receive incentives even though not all are part of testing group.
Contractor: Mesa School District and Mesa Education Association.
Contract objective: To determine if the use of student and teacher incentives can accelerate mastery of basic skills by disadvantaged students.
Evaluator: Battelle Memorial Institute.

V

PERFORMANCE CONTRACTING: THE DALLAS EXPERIMENT

by Dr. Donald R. Waldrip and Dr. Nolan Estes

"Accountability asks educators to place their careers on the line. Since our students had no choice of schools, but we had a choice of careers, this seems to me a fair trade."

For five years—ever since the passage of the Elementary and Secondary Education Act gave us the extra financial boost we needed to develop compensatory programs—we had been trying all the old tricks and most of the new to improve achievement among those children whom we call the "culturally disadvantaged." Along with other school districts all over the country, we bought shiny new hardware and clever new software; invested in workshops and seminars for our teachers; sent our kids to concerts and museums and factories and even—courtesy of Braniff Airlines—up over the city in planes. In sum, we waved the banner of innovation as energetically as anyone.

Naturally, even though we got a considerable boost from Title I and other forms of federal aid, our costs went up. They tripled in the last 10 years—mainly because of new construction, salary increases, and improvements such as air-conditioning; but partially because we asked the citizens of Dallas to stretch federal dollars with their own. And when we totalled the results of this financial exertion on the part of the taxpayers, and of the spiritual exertion on the part of our teachers, we found we didn't have much to be proud of.

Our target had been those schools in which students were averaging only a half-year's achievement gain for every full scholastic year. By the time we finished, we had not managed to

---

Reprinted with permission of the authors.

improve on this sad record; in fact, some of our Title I schools were worse off in 1970 than they had been in 1965.

Any sane school administrator is reluctant to hang out his dirty linen for public viewing. I cannot suppress a certain sense of embarrassment even now, as I speak. All that gives me courage to do so is the knowledge that virtually every other large city school system in the country has had the same experience as Dallas. Five years and five billion dollars after Title I was passed, we still have not learned how to break the cycle of under-achievement that sees children from poor homes do poorly in school; find poor jobs or none; marry—and then send their own poor children to school.

But though this failure remains constant, some things *have* changed in education—notably the public attitude toward those who run it. Ten years ago, we educators confidently asserted that we knew how to cure educational illness. All we needed was enough money to lower pupil-teacher ratios, put a library in every school, an overhead projector in every classroom, and so on and so forth. Our prescriptions for educational excellence were based on traditional notions that went unchallenged because a stingy public had never allowed us to try them.

During the 1960's, we got a chance to try them; not as much of a chance as we would have liked, perhaps—too many school systems spread Title I funds around so thinly that the extra money could not have any impact. Nevertheless, we were given a reasonable chance—and the results did not justify the investment. And today, it is clear, the public does not believe it is getting its money's worth from public education.

Thus there is a public frustration as well as a professional frustration behind the drive for accountability. Public school systems have developed extremely precise methods of accounting; most of them can tell you to the penny how much they spent for teachers' salaries, textbooks, red and blue litmus paper, and the wax on the gymnasium floor.

But they cannot tell you what this investment *produced.* Our focus in educational accounting has been on *input,* not *output.* Professor Dwight Allen of the University of Massachusetts has quite properly criticized the accounting methods of school systems as being irrelevant for purposes of devising new educational strategy. Per-pupil expenditures do not really tell us what it costs to *educate* a student; all they tell us is what it costs to keep a student *seated* for a year.

A much more relevant measure, Dr. Allen argues, would be a "learning-unit" cost—the total sum, including teacher's salary, portion of total building expense, cost of textbooks and other learning materials required to move a student from one skill-level in reading, writing, or math to the next highest level. These costs, moreover, would vary from one school to another; they would be higher in a school with a majority of children from low-income, black or Spanish-speaking families than they would be in a school with a majority of white children from upper-income homes.

Developing such a new accounting system would enable educators to show the public how much *learning* was produced by a certain amount of investment. It would, moreover, enable educators to shift resources back and forth within a budget—testing, for example, the value of teacher-aides in one classroom against the value of educational technology in another and of programmed texts in a third. In each case, *input* would be related to *output*—and educators who prescribed various teaching strategies would be held *accountable* for the results they produced.

Accountability is, in essence, a statement of policy. It states that educators will accept responsibility for their performance—or lack of it. It implies that there is a contract between school personnel and the public, and that that contract involves more than showing up for work on time. It accepts the fact that culturally different backgrounds make the task of educating more difficult, but it asserts that, as professionals, educators can overcome—or will *learn* to overcome—cultural difference.

Now statements of policy are fine things, if for no other reason than that they look nice framed on a wall. But if a statement of policy is to be a genuine *program* rather than just a fashionable enthusiasm, it must be translated into a strategy—a set of practical steps for turning an *idea* into a *reality*.

Performance contracting is one such technique. It is not the only one. Voucher plans are another—and so, indeed, is any systematic effort to relate educational effort to student achievement.

Our sense of frustration in Dallas led us to try performance contracting. Our interest in it led us to two distinct programs—one financed by the Office of Economic Opportunity, and the other by Title I. I wish today to describe the Title I program because we controlled it from the start: chose the student population, outlined the performance criteria, wrote the request-for-proposals, defined the conditions under which any successful contractor would have to work, and negotiated the final contracts.

The entire process has been carefully monitored by the most precise scientific methods. According to our most recent figures, for example, every administrator involved has lost an average of 13.1 pounds, given up 46.3 percent of his weekends, and antagonized 75 percent of his wives to the point where 100 percent of them threatened to go home to mother an average of 3.4 times. Nevertheless, innovation marches on in Dallas.

First, a note on the OEO program. It involved about 600 students in grades one through three and seven through nine in two schools; these students are matched with another 600 in a control group. The subject areas are reading and mathematics, both of which were subcontracted by OEO to Quality Education Development, Inc., of Washington, D.C. Contracts for two service components, audit and management support—I'll explain these terms a little later on—were awarded by OEO to Battelle Memorial Institute and Education Turnkey Systems, Inc.

The two programs resemble each other in principle, of course; the major distinction is that OEO designed one program, Dallas the other—hence I feel I can discuss the Dallas program with more authority.

First, the target group. Last May, we ran an analysis of underachieving high school students and selected a group whom, on the basis of our experience, we believed were highly susceptible to dropping out. By August 31, the first day of school, our predictions were proven unfortunately accurate: fully 50 percent did not show up. We divided the survivors into an experimental group of 960 and a control group of 700. The experimental group were all students in grades nine through twelve attending five Title I high schools.

We decided the program should concentrate on three kinds of instruction: first, basic skills—communication and mathematics; second, occupational skills; and third, achievement motivation—helping youngsters develop a determination to succeed.

The characteristics of both experimental and control groups were as follows: they were 4.8 standard scores below the national 50th percentile in reading, 6.2 scores below on vocabulary, and 4.9 scores below on mathematical skills. Their teachers and counselors indicated that each seemed to lack any desire to succeed in school, or any realistic goals in life.

When we set up this new shop, then, we chose to go after the toughest customers. Long before we picked them, however, we began thinking about the kind of program we would ask contractors to bid on. We started our planning in November 1969, with a Planning Advisory Group that comprised 30 people—and I think it important to describe this group.

The membership included only five employees of the school district: two central staff administrators, a principal, and two teachers. The other 25 included the president of the Classroom Teachers of Dallas, which is the local NEA affiliate; seven students and ex-students; one school board member; and the rest, residents of the target neighborhoods, representatives of local colleges, local businessmen, and officials in Dallas civic agencies.

The cynical way to view this is that we were trying to minimize opposition—and that, indeed, was one of the fringe benefits. Performance contracting seems by implication, at least, to impugn the competence of teachers, and one might expect their representatives to oppose it. But we are fortunate in Dallas to have NEA representatives who are equally alert to the interests of their members and to sound ideas for improving education. They agreed that performance contracting was a concept worth testing. Perhaps, they felt, it might be a step toward training teachers to aim for performance.

Yet minimizing opposition was not our principal objective in expanding the membership of the Planning Advisory Group. It is difficult for any educator to admit that laymen might know a thing or two about educating, but we decided to investigate the possibility.

Our humility paid off. Among many other benefits, it led us to include a somewhat offbeat course in the occupational training portion of our request-for-proposals: drafting for girls. That suggestion came from the businessmen on the advisory group—and every girl enrolled in the drafting program has already been spoken for by a local industry.

By February 1970, the Planning Advisory Group had helped us develop a "wish-list": what we hoped the contractors could do for us. By April, we had refined that list into the RFP. (The RFP is simply a request to eligible companies to submit proposals to direct the guaranteed performance programs. It includes all the constraints imposed by the district, such as limits of students and financial resources, and it outlines the objectives as perceived by the district. Dallas mailed EFP's to thirty-one companies.) We held a pre-bid conference in May, and chose the successful contractors in July.

Now–what had we asked for in the RFP?

The total list of performance criteria and conditions is much too exhaustive to repeat here. The most important requirements–those which, I believe, you will be interested in–are these:

First, in mathematics and communications, the students would have to gain 1.4 grade-levels in one scholastic year–in contrast to the 0.5 grade-levels this particular population had been gaining. Payment to the contractor would be based on individual student gains; unless every student achieved a 1.4-year gain, the contractor would not be able to recoup his costs.

Second, in achievement motivation, the contractor would have to reduce dropout rates below those of U.S.O.E.'s five most successful Title VIII dropout prevention projects throughout the United States. The retention rates, however, would not be based on attendance in the achievement motivation classes–since all a contractor would have to do to maintain high attendance would be to make these classes fun. Rather, measurement of the effectiveness of the achievement motivation classes would be based on attendance in the math and communications classes.

Third, with regard to occupational training, we could not define performance criteria as strictly as we could with the other two components. The essential test of occupational training is employability–but this is affected by economic conditions as well as by educational excellence. However, we did the best we could to specify performance standards for this component by enlisting 25 local companies to work with the contractor; they participated not only in the actual training, but also in judging the quality of the program.

The New Century Company, a subsidiary of the Meredith Corporation, won the contracts for communciations and math. Thiokol Corporation won the contracts for achievement motivation and occupational training. We also requested proposals for two other components: audit and management support.

Audit, essentially, is intended to keep everybody honest–to prevent a repetition of the unfortunate experience in Texarkana. We wanted an outside agency to approve the tests given to experimental and control group students throughout the program; to check our research design so that we could appraise the effectiveness of various treatments, singly and in combination; to ascertain the reliability of data; and, finally, to certify the results so that the contractors could be properly compensated.

In contrast to the instructional components, which were contracted for on a penalty-incentive basis, the audit contract was for a fixed fee. We chose Educational Testing Service to provide the audit.

Management support, as the name implies, is to help out management—in this case, the Dallas school system. Performance contracting was new to our staff; all of them have full-time duties, and we did not want to divert them to an unfamiliar job. Hence we contracted with the Council of Great City Schools—again for a fixed fee—to provide a supplemental staff that would act as liaison between the school system, the contractors, and the auditor.

In addition, the Council of Great City Schools felt that placing a few of its representatives on our staff temporarily would increase their expertise in performance contracting. In a sense, even though their people have significant experience in this area, they would be serving an internship—learning along with us so that they could later help other school systems.

The last aspect of performance contracting that I feel you should know about is the "turnkey" aspect. The three instructional components of our program—math, communications, occupational training—employed the contractors' methods and materials, but they employed Dallas personnel. We insisted on this in our RFP. Moreover, we insisted that the contractors' programs be so designed that they could be adopted throughout the school system if we elected to do so.

That is what "turnkey" means. Thus performance contracting can be viewed not only as a tool for improving student achievement, but as a tool for improving the effectiveness of teachers. Each contractor agreed to train our teachers in his methods if those methods work. Each also agreed to supply us with his real expense figures, so that we could appraise the cost-effectiveness of his program. We expected each of them to make a profit; we signed the contracts, and if they could deliver, we didn't care how much each of them made. But we did want to be able to compare *their* learning-unit costs against ours, so we could decide whether their methods could be extended to other students within our budget restrictions.

In connection with the "turnkey" aspect of the program, I venture the opinion that performance contracting poses no threat to any school district's teachers. But it does pose a threat to teacher-training institutions. If Thiokol or New Century or Jim-Dandy Educational Systems can teach teachers to teach potential dropouts to read, after all the tenured Ph.D.'s in our universities have so resoundingly failed—then I predict, we will see a lot of Ph.D.'s out of work during the next decade.

It is too early in our experiment to judge all the results. We *do* know that our target population had a much higher attendance record than their controls; these youngsters whom we identified as probable dropouts—*probable,* not *possible*—showed up much more often than they had in previous years.

The evaluation of the OEO project in elementary and junior high reading and mathematics has not been made available to the participating school districts at this date. Indications are, however —based on the results of interim performance objective tests—that students averaged more than one year's growth during one year of instruction. These results suggest that individualized systems of instruction below the high school level, when supported by sound, almost continuous monitoring and staff development, stand a good chance of succeeding with educationally disadvantaged students. It is difficult at this point to generalize about "individualized systems," but most observers agree that the teachers in the QED program generated much enthusiasm among their students, bringing about an obvious zest for learning among the participants. Some studies, though, have discovered negative correlations among disadvantaged students between scores on criterion referenced tests and scores on standardized tests—indicating that the cultural bias of standardized tests might be influencing results, that the criterion referenced test items are too easy, or that any number of additional factors could be blamed for the disparate results.

The high school reading and mathematics program under New Century did not bring about the expected results, although a cursory examination indicates that the New Century students did make greater gains than did the control group, even though the company did not approach its expected gains. An economist might consider the results the best of all worlds. The company did not receive its total fee because it did not reach its guarantees; at the same time, the evaluation did indicate a slight, if not statistically significant, supremacy for the treatment group.

The initial design for the high school reading and mathematics program called for all students from a 1400-student target population to be randomly assigned to experimental and control groups. As was mentioned earlier, many of these students did not show up for school during the first three or four weeks; consequently, random assignment was virtuously impossible. As the less interested students began arriving, they were put into a treatment group, leaving a great disparity in aptitude between the treatment and control groups, even though both groups were from the "target population." The bias resulting from this disparity was covaried out in all analyses—an almost totally unsatisfactory technique because of the difficulty of totally adjusting for mathematical differences in measured intelligence. The average intelligence of the treatment group for mathematics was 75.16, while the average for the control group was 86.31. The average intelligence of the treatment group for reading was 72.39, while the average for the control group was 82.16. These figures indicate that although the research design called for students with IQ's of less than 70 to be excluded from the program, principals let many of these special education students enter the treatment groups while excluding them from the control groups. Some of our principals needed desperately a place to put their problem students. Inasmuch as most of them are more interested in kids than they are in research (this is not all bad), they decided the New Century program with all its carrels, hardware, and contingency management systems could provide a new opportunity for these students.

Students in the mathematics program averaged .33 years mean gain based on the results of pre-and-post standardized tests. The control group, although averaging 11 points in IQ more than the treatment group, lost .09 years. Although the gain was greater for the treatment group, it is not great enough to be deemed significant at the .05 level of confidence; therefore, the conclusion was that performance among groups did not differ more than what would be expected by chance. But again the results were confounded by the lack of randomness within the two groups.

That the correlation between the scores on the criterion referenced tests and the post standardized tests was a mere .06, indicating no relationship between scores on the two types of tests, was an interesting discovery. Other major findings of the mathematics program are: (1) students with higher IQ's performed better; (2) eleventh and twelfth graders performed better than ninth and tenth graders; (3) the more a student was absent, the poorer he did in the program. These three conclusions are not very startling, but they do provide cooroboration for some of our biases.

Students in the reading program gained an average of .53 years, while their counterparts in the control group gained .48 years. As with the mathematics students, this conclusion persists in spite of the fact that the average IQ of the students in the treatment group was 10 points less than the average of the students in the control group. But again, the differences in achievement were not greater than would be expected by chance.

The finding of no significant difference is difficult to explain. 315 of the 334 participants in the reading program scored better than 75% on their criterion referenced tests. The correlation between scores on the criterion referenced tests and scores on the post standardized tests was -.15—not a very significant correlation, but one which indicates that students who tended to do better on the criterion referenced test tended to do poorer on the standardized test.

In addition to the questions concerning difficulty of criterion items and cultural biases of standardized items, perhaps the most relevant question we could ask would be "how do we get disadvantaged students to do their best on post tests?" One student whose scores indicated an eight year loss in reading ability—a preposterous conclusion—had actually answered more than 75% of his criterion test items correctly. Three more whose scores indicated a loss of six years also answered more than 75% of the criterion test items correctly. In fact. 79 students showing a loss of 1.0 years or more in reading fell into the same category of 75% or better on the interim performance objective tests. As in the mathematics program, the brighter students in reading performed better; the eleventh and twelfth graders performed better than the ninth and tenth graders; and the more the students were absent, the poorer they did in the program. One additional finding relates to the reading portion of the experiment only: females performed better than males.

Reading and mathematics scores were increased if the students were also assigned to achievement motivation classes. Attendance in these classes, a segment of the contracted program with Thiokol Chemical Corporation, definitely contributed to greater reading achievement. Students in achievement motivation classes attended school—their regular classes, not just the achievement motivation classes—86% of the time, a marked improvement over the 73% attendance of the target population the previous year. Results of deportment scale evaluations of regular teachers would indicate that the attitudes of these students toward school improved over the course of the year. 91% of the achievement motivation students—all probable dropouts—were still in attendance at the end of the year.

Vocational training under Thiokol was in three areas: auto mechanics, machine metals, and drafting. 26.7% of all students in the three courses reached the graduate level of training and were placed onto jobs. 13.3% reached the apprentice level. 21.3% achieved the level of assistant, and 23.3% reached the helper level. Since all of these achievement levels are varying levels of employment, 84.4% of the students enrolled into these specialized, individualized programs achieved an exit level of employment. This figure rises to 95% if one considers only those students who attended more than 84% of the time. (84% was a payoff goal in the Thiokol contract.)

Inasmuch as all reading and mathematics participants did not make positive gains, the computation of costs per learning unit was confounded. This computation, which was the responsibility of the management support group, was made by assuming that all students making a negative gain made zero gain. In reading, of those students for which both pre-and-post test scores were available, 213 made some kind of gain and 181 did not. Using 1.0 as the base performance unit, it would require $374.00 invested per student for each one year growth in the program.

In mathematics, 188 of 319 students made some gain, while 131 made no gain at all. The cost of this program was $442.38 per student/year growth. Of course both of these figures would decrease if more students could be moved from the negative gain column to the positive side.

All per unit costs include the cost of the teachers' salaries. These costs were a part of each contract, even though the Dallas

Independent School District paid the teachers and the contractors reimbursed the District for these costs. All contract teachers were on the Dallas Independent School District payroll and were considered Dallas employees.

We should be discouraged in Dallas inasmuch as our high school reading and mathematics programs did not approach our expectations, but we are not. This year is the first time we were able to tell our citizens, "Here is where X amount of your dollars went, and here is the amount of difference which that investment produced."

We know that a large inner city is a difficult place in which to carry out controlled experimentation, but we are not quitting. We are encouraged somewhat by the results of the interim performance tests. We are encouraged by the interest displayed by primary and junior high students in our OEO project. We are encouraged by the effect the achievement motivation classes had on attendance and achievement. We are very encouraged by the performance of our vocational students. 84% of them did in one year what it has taken two years in the past to accomplish.

Besides, we were not really evaluating performance contracting. Rather, we were evaluating certain instructional systems, and some of them will always work better than others. Our direction has changed somewhat for the coming year, and hopefully we will not repeat the same mistakes. We will be concentrating on reading in the early grades as over 11,000 primary students begin operating under some kind of performance contract during the 1971-72 school year.

We believe the results of our first year experience offer some hope. We have not found nearly enough answers to the learning problems of the disadvantaged child; but if one thing doesn't work, we will try something else. We feel we owe this to the citizens who are investing their taxes in the special knowledge which professional educators claim to possess. More important, we owe this to the parents who are investing their *children* in that special knowledge.

Most important of all, we owe it to the students, for they are investing *themselves.* Whether they know it or not, those children whom we term the "culturally disadvantaged" place most of their hopes for the future on the line when they enter our schools.

Accountability asks educators to place their careers on the

line. Since our students had no choice of schools, but we had a choice of careers, this seems to me a fair trade. □

Dr. Donald R. Waldrip is Assistant Superintendent: Accountability and Personnel Development for the Dallas, Texas, Public Schools. He received his B.A. and M.A. degrees from Midwestern University and his Doctorate from Northern Colorado University.

VI

PHILADELPHIA DISTRICT 4 RESULTS

by Ruth W. Hayre

"This was the first time in the history of Philadelphia Schools, during which millions of dollars had been spent on reading materials with various and sundry publishers (including uncounted years and dollars with 'Dick and Jane'), that any publisher indicated willingness to be accountable and to share partnership with the school staff for measurable results in reading."

"We are willing to guarantee that pupils will achieve a year's progress with our program." When the president of Behavioral Research Laboratories said these words in June 1970, and backed this up with a guaranteed performance contract for nearly 15,000 elementary school pupils in District 4, he initiated an innovative and controversial program. For this was the first time in the history of Philadelphia Schools, during which millions of dollars had been spent on reading materials with various and sundry publishers (including uncounted years and dollars with "Dick and Jane"), that any publisher indicated willingness to be accountable and to share partnership with the school staff for measurable results in reading. And the company was willing to include 506 retarded pupils along with the others.

The Philadelphia Board of Education voted in August 1971 to accept the proposal, though not unanimously.

The Institute for the Development of Educational Auditing, (IDEA), was selected by mutual agreement of the School Board and BRL to serve as the independent evaluating agency for Project Read G.

News release by Philadelphia District Four Superintendent Dr. Ruth W. Hayre on July 23, 1971 regarding the "Results of Nation's Largest Reading Performance Contract."

During the first week of October 1970 the firm administered pre-tests to approximately 14,500 pupils, grades 1-6, and to 600 seventh grade pupils. A form of the California Test was used. Scores on this test were not made available to any of the parties involved—teachers, principals, the District 4 Reading Team, or the central Office of Research. Eight months later, during the first week of June 1971, a post test was given to each pupil in the program to determine how much progress had been made. It seemed fair to assume that whatever difference emerged between the pre-test and the post-test could be attributable to Project Read G. On the basis of these tests, pupil achievement was measured, and the decision reached regarding which pupils would be paid for at the rate of $40 per pupil, $20 per pupil or nothing per pupil. A pupil was considered to have made one year's gain in reading if the differential between the pre-test and the post-test was 1.0 or ten months, despite the fact that actually there had been only 8 months of instruction. BRL accepted this. The attendance factor was the only limiting factor in the contract—namely 150 days (out of the total 180) of attendance in the program. The highest number of days actually attainable was 170 because of the delay in starting the program.

On July 23, IDEA made a preliminary report to representatives of BRL and of the School District, preparatory to a report to the Board of Education.

The report was a massive listing of pupils by schools in the program, with the pre-test, post-test scores on the California tests, the differential in scores, pupil attendance, and amount to be paid by BRL for each pupil.

Already it has been well publicized that:

4,929 pupils, or approximately 50%, gained at least one year's progress and were present 150 days or more during the school year. For these, the School District will pay $40 per pupil for a total of $197,160.

4,347 pupils attended less than 150 days and, regardless of progress made, will be paid for at the rate of $20 per pupil for a total of $86,940. No charge is made for the 4,985 pupils who attended the required number of days but who gained less than one year's progress.

It must be emphasized that all first, second and third grade pupils were in the program, which is basically a primary program, and the highest degree of achievement was shown in these grades.

In the grades above primary, namely 4th, 5th, 6th and 7th grades, pupils were selected for the program chiefly because they were underachievers, most of whom had never made a year's progress in reading, or anywhere near it. BRL was receptive to including 5000 or more of these youngsters in the guarantee, although they stood to lose, and did lose, as the majority of these youngsters still failed to achieve a year's progress. However, many of them (and this figure can be ascertained in more detailed study of the IDEA report), did make gains of as much as six to nine months, or more than they had ever achieved previously.

In summary, the following can be noted:

1. Approximately 50% of those students in Project Read for 150 days or more, gained one full academic year or more for the eight months between the pre and post test.

2. Approximately 60% of those students in Project Read for 150 days or more achieved month for month gains.

3. The average growth for the 14,261 students in Project Read was nine months during the eight month period.

4. Fifty percent of these children in grade 3 through 7 did as well or better in the post test as in the pre-test indicating a reversal in the downward trend of achievement.

The number of children gaining in the Iowa Test went from 32% upward. These were not in Project Read G but were using BRL Sullivan materials.

6. For year 2 children, a decided movement upward was noted as measured by the Stanford Achievement Tests. All these children used BRL Sullivan materials. □

VII

THE PERFORMANCE CONTRACTS IN GRAND RAPIDS

by James A. Mecklenburger and John A. Wilson

"You've got to be prepared for success, and it can cost like hell."

A good show of performance contracting has played Grand Rapids, Michigan, this year.

Three private corporations have spent the year displaying their techniques for remedial mathematics and reading instruction. Combined Motivation Education Systems (COMES), from Chicago, taught 500 junior high school students; Westinghouse Learning Corporation, from Albuquerque and New York City, taught 400 elementary students; and Alpha Learning Corporation, from Albuquerque, as part of the national OEO experiment taught 300 primary and 300 junior high students. "The competition has been one reason Grand Rapids is such a good show; all three are hustlers. Our kids have benefited," said Joan Webster, the contract learning research project director of the Grand Rapids school system. Her enthusiasm is infectious.

"We're dealing with kids who have been turned off, and many of them are now turned on," Elmer Vruggink, assistant superintendent for instruction, told us. "There are some good things going, excited kids and excited teachers." Our visits to the three projects confirmed his impression.

The Grand Rapids contracts, like the contract in Gary, Indiana, and others, did not begin with the formalized advance planning advocated by Charles Blaschke, Leon Lessinger, and others. Like Gary's contract and others, these are out on a psychometric limb; the contractors are to be paid based on test scores derived from standardized achievement pretests and posttests. Like

---

Gary's contract and others, the evaluation design is haphazard, the experiment anything but rigorous, and the legality of performance contracting questionable. Other issues, such as the growth of an educational-industrial complex, pressure-cooking kids, or threatening organized teachers, could be raised. But in Grand Rapids these issues have lain dormant.

The performance contract accoutrements—the document, the testing, the guarantee, the rhetoric of accountability—are acknowledged to be politically expedient and probably important; but the participants have become impatient with discussion of these topics, as they simply are not at issue. Elmer Vruggink dismisses them with a wave of the hand as "all that confusion." His acceptance of performance contracting has been "pragmatic." If standing on his head would improve student achievement, he'd try that too.

"When all is said and done, the performance contract can act as a vehicle for internal reform," Elmer Vruggink says. "Performance contracting is a management technique for getting people to look at something new," Joan Webster believes. Jack Goldberg, Westinghouse's center manager, intensely proud of the system his company has developed, says of the guaranteed performance contract, "It gets us on the market. That's all." Clay Coleman, COMES director, agreed, saying companies would be just as committed without the guarantee as with it.

Why the Performance Contracts?

Unlike the situation in other major cities (Grand Rapids is Michigan's largest after Detroit), racial tensions in Grand Rapids have not grown so potent that they dictate school policies; financial crisis has. Because fully one-third of Grand Rapids's children attend parochial schools, financial support of the public schools is rarely generous. Public interest peaks not over racial confrontations or substantive issues, but over school taxes.

Secondly, standardized test scores have revealed that Grand Rapids does not excel in teaching basic skills. Many inner-city students do not fare well in reading and math and, as elsewhere, parents complain. Grand Rapids has tried compensatory programs. Elmer Vruggink recently completed his doctorate studying compensatory education and "found many good things, but one thing I didn't find was improved achievement in terms of the cognitive skill areas."

The first statewide assessment in Michigan, a year ago, confirmed this problem that school people were already aware of, but the visibility caused by the assessment's coinciding with a school tax election intensified pressure from parents to innovate.

"We had to set priorities. One was to teach these kids to read and do mathematics. A second was to find new ways to do this, because the old ways obviously weren't succeeding," says Joan Webster.

Publicity over Texarkana sparked Grand Rapids's interest and planted the term and concept of "accountability" in the minds of school leaders, particularly Superintendent Norman Weinheimer. He sent a team to visit Texarkana, and they were intrigued. He sent another team to visit the Westinghouse remedial program at Albuquerque. Grand Rapids bid for an OEO performance-contract project. Then a former researcher in the Grand Rapids area, Walter Thomas, now with COMES, suggested to Grand Rapids that COMES contract a project.

The national political urge toward accountability was not lost on the Michigan State Department of Education either; in April, State Superintendent John Porter announced the availability of state and federal funds for experiments with performance contracts.

By mid-summer, Grand Rapids had confirmed the three projects, using mostly state and federal funds, and was scrambling to get them ready for September opening. As one school official wryly summarized, "There was this new thing. We're high risk takers in Grand Rapids. 'Let's try it.' We figured, what did we have to lose? First of all, we could do it on somebody else's money; secondly, it's a great tool—you can tell the public you're doing something. The population is liberal toward innovation, but they're very conservative every other way." (This is Congressman Gerald Ford's home district.)

Accountability

The three contracted projects are similar. Some of the similarity grows out of circumstances, for in each a private corporation has agreed to a one-year performance contract to teach reading and mathematics two hours per day to underachieving children; some of the similarity grows out of method, for each uses a mix of teachers and paraprofessionals, each relies heavily on programmed teaching materials, and each employs some kind of reward system for students.

But the fundamental similarity is ideological. These contractors anchor their practice in the belief that every child can learn. If children fall short, the companies regard themselves as ineffective. As one observer remarked, "These people obviously appear to be trying to do something for kids, while we don't."

While their techniques are new and imperfect, and there may be some failure, the atmosphere in these centers is charged with success. Kids are enthused and busy, as are teachers. Contractors and school people alike believe that most kids will reach the achievement levels that are contracted.

Educational technology, as practiced by these companies, means the organization, management, and use of school resources to accomplish a prescribed goal in a satisfactory manner—in this case, reading and mathematics achievement.

Elmer Vruggink calls this being "systematic." "Sometimes in education," he says, "we have scattered shots. . . . I think we have to zero in on what we're supposed to do. What is successful here may not be *the* system, but merely being systematic."

One potential danger that Grand Rapids school people see in the national interest in performance contracting is that some may see it merely as a money-saving means of "writing off kids." They may say, "Our kids aren't going to make it anyway; if we're going to write them off, let's not lose money on them." As Joan Webster cautions, "You've got to be prepared for success, and it can cost like hell."

Initially, this systematic instruction may cost more dollars, although it is actually cheaper in terms of cost per achievement gained. If last year it cost $135 to raise most children one-half grade in reading, and if with 200-dollar methods one can raise most children a full year in reading, "As a businessman," said former Superintendent Norman Weinheimer, "I'd say it's got to be done this way. This is good business. But it also means you may be spending more per child, until these kids get caught up, than you ever did before."

Accountability has three distinct meanings, as seen in Grand Rapids. First, the schools feel compelled to provide the community with better instruction; second, the fault if children don't learn is collectively shared by teachers, management, and community—

all the school resources; and third, dollars should be spent in the most efficient manner.

Choice and Preparation of Teachers

Teachers and paraprofessionals for the program were selected from volunteers, on four criteria: Preferably, they had taught in the building; they concurred that any child could learn despite his past record; they were willing to try new methods honestly; and they did not believe it unholy—as many do—to reward children materially for their successes.

Martha Golden, now teaching with Alpha, a 17-year veteran in Grand Rapids, two years ago the president of the Grand Rapids Education Association, was one choice; recently her voice has been raised throughout Michigan in praise of the promise inherent in these programs.

Each contractor held teacher training sessions during August and has followed with in-service training during the year. This training served several purposes: first, to familiarize teachers with the new methods to be used; second, to explain the rationale behind these methods; and third, to sensitize teachers to the changes in role they would experience.

It is probably significant that new titles have been applied to the staff in these projects, such as learning director, center manager, aide (not teaching aide), and specialist.

This change in teacher role is described by some as making teachers more professional, or as freeing teachers to use their training more effectively. Others feel teachers have been reduced to the role of technician. Experience in Grand Rapids reveals that the attitude teachers accept is critical to the success of these projects. Despite the teacher training, some teachers remain uncomfortable.

It has not been lost on many observers that such programs as these in Grand Rapids represent evidence that there are both shortcomings in teacher training institutions and alternative effective ways to train teachers. The Michigan Education Association is "looking at alternative ways of handling the training of teachers," according to one insider, and has explored this with the companies now contracting in Grand Rapids.

Role of Teacher, Materials, Students

Teaching materials are abundant in these projects, and

students spend much more time with them than students do in standard classrooms. The teacher becomes facilitator, manager, guide, and tutor to students, while the materials carry the bulk of minute-by-minute instruction.

In each project, a student's needs are diagnosed, a series of instructional activities is outlined for him, and he takes a pretest and later a posttest monitored by an adult. Unless he has difficulties, however, the student may not need to interact with a teacher at all during instruction.

None of these companies is a publisher; the materials they use can be purchased by anyone. At Alpha, all teaching materials are printed; at Westinghouse, most are printed but many are on audio-cassettes; at COMES, the bulk are delivered through teaching machines.

At Alpha, some diagnosis is done by test, some by the judgment of teachers. At COMES, diagnosis relies more heavily on testing. At Westinghouse, a computerized diagnosis-prescription system does most of this work.

The Westinghouse approach pleased teachers at two other elementary schools enough that, at mid-year, they asked and were granted permission for the Westinghouse system to be installed in their schools, also, although without performance contracting.

Clearly there is also a new role for the student. Many parents report that their children are getting personal attention. That is, each student feels in this system that he is important, worthy of concern. For some students at COMES, the existence of a room full of fancy machinery says, "You're important"; kids often refer to these machines in the same way they talk about teachers, even to one student's calling the Hoffman machines "Mr. Hoffman."

To the criticism sometimes heard that the Hawthorne or halo effect is responsible for success in performance contracts, one is reminded that the Hawthorne effect was recognized to occur when people perceived themselves as important. Elmer Vruggink remarks, "Sometimes that's what I think education ought to be about, the Hawthorne effect. We ought to capitalize on it."

One story people like to tell in Grand Rapids exemplifies these changes in role for teachers, materials, and students. As Joan Webster told it, "When one teacher said a book wasn't suiting her kids' needs, in two days the contractor had another book. In the local school system, she'd have to request it, she'd have to go through the principal, who'd have to go through the assistant director of elementary education, through the purchasing department, and they'd say, 'Order it in March for next year because we haven't got the money.' This guy went out and bought it and gave it to her."

The curriculum decisions were made before the projects began; the school system wanted reading and mathematics achievement. COMES, however, has added "achievement motivation" to its formal activities. As Mrs. Simms, center manager (teacher), describes this, "AMS – it's called achievement motivation sessions – is a reward in itself. This is where we sit and discuss any problems; if I have done something they don't like they get a chance to tell me. . . . I give them a chance to say what they wish and we discuss it realistically. Then we express our viewpoints, we share ideas, express things that happened to them, and also–the main thing–we discuss values, which is very important, because the idea of values is the basis for this program, really–what you think about yourself, accepting higher goals, having a high or nice self-concept, developing in other words a spirit of 'I can.' "

The COMES centers appear impressive, banks of wooden carrels filled with flashy machines, carpeting, and a lush atmosphere by classroom standards. Westinghouse centers are carpeted but small, resembling a library reading room filled with students. The Alpha centers are unadorned classrooms.

Positive Reinforcement

But the most unconventional feature, and the most debated feature, of these projects is the RE room or free room. In this reinforcing events room, children are rewarded for success in the classroom.

To create the free room, three class groups were regrouped into two, somewhat crowding the learning centers but thereby freeing a classroom for other use.

At the COMES center, a student sets a goal that after he successfully completes so much material he will be allowed time in the RE room. At Westinghouse, each unit of material completed is worth a "buzz," which is four minutes in the RE room. A student may take each buzz separately or accumulate them. Also, for exemplary behavior, students are awarded points; accumulated points may be swapped for desirable activities, such as a trip or a picnic. In both these centers, RE-room activities include pool, games, toys, music, comic books, and the like—things that kids enjoy.

Many performance contractors have adopted this approach to student rewards in which control is maintained by rewarding good behavior (rather than by punishing unacceptable behavior), which derives from Skinnerian principles of operant conditioning and goes under the rubric of "contingency management."

At Alpha's centers, contingency management is considered the dominant technique (whereas Westinghouse emphasizes its diagnostic-prescriptive approach, and COMES emphasizes achievement motivation). At Alpha, token economies operate. With tokens at the elementary level, and SKINs (Supplemental Knowledge Incentive Notes) at the junior high level, students may purchase free-room activities or items such as Coke, candy, potato chips, etc. This token economy frees the child to select his own kinds of reinforcement, SKINs and tokens may be converted to money. Elementary pupils "are just like people, strangely enough; they handle tokens like adults handle money," says Martha Golden. "We've got stingy ones and we've got kids who can't hold onto one for a minute. We had one youngster who had saved 900 tokens! He didn't want money, he just wanted lots of tokens." Some kids string them around their neck or collect them in jars; one youngster is saving for a bicycle, in a matching-funds arrangement with his father. According to Martha Golden, the results of this system are "fantastic!"

Alpha also uses contingency management with its teachers by presenting periodic cash awards to successful staff members. COMES also promises to reward teachers at the end of the program. This raises the merit-pay issue with teachers and teacher organizations. The GREA is talking about an unfair labor practices suit.

"Bribing children" and "buying learning" are charges leveled at this activity by many educators, including some staff members in Grand Rapids. "It was very hard to accept, at first, the extrinsic motivation," Melvin Leasure, MEA president, told us, but "when we were able to go to Grand Rapdis and see how it was used to motivate the kids, and we were also able to see that after w while the rewards became less and less important to the kids, well then apparently it was doing the job."

One benefit of this arrangement is that teachers gain a flexibility in classroom management, so that for special instruction they can send some students to the free room, while others stay to learn.

But the major benefit, advocates claim, is that children who have lost the motivation to learn can be rekindled; eventually intrinsic motivation will return. John Cline, the Alpha project manager, stated it most eloquently:

"When you put kids who are two or three years behind into that social studies class down the hall, and this kid is 15 years old and reading at a third-grade level, and you say to him, 'Read pages 14 to 21 and answer the 12 questions at the end,' what you're doing to that kid is saying, 'Hey, loser! We want to reassert that you are a dummy! A loser! You have no inherent value!'

"And we do this to him time after time, day after day, year after year. Sure the kid believes he's a loser! He doesn't like himself. He doesn't like school. He doesn't like anything. That's a sad, sad thing.

"And to expect that that kid is going to be intrinsically motivated to do anything in school is stupid! The way we justify extrinsic motivation is to say, 'We've got to get him motivated. And since it is stupid to assume that he has any inner motivation, let's give him outward motivation to get him started.'

"We hear from people that the kid should *want* to succeed. Well, goddamn it, yeah, he should. But he doesn't."

Contracting's Effect on Grand Rapids

Performance contracting has affected the Grand Rapids public schools in the same way that contingency management affects a student's self-concept. Here was a school system that had come to accept itself as being not too sharp, creditably serving some of its students but incapable of doing well with others. Along came this token, this SKIN, this buzz called a "performance contract" which seemed to promise to take the school just a little bit beyond its self-perceived capabilities (and for free). It was an extrinsic motivation, a little bauble, relative to the immensity of the school system, but enough to get the school system to select a few good teachers and try a small experiment. The steps were small, nothing the system couldn't handle, and soon people began to perceive success. The importance of the extrinsic motivation–oh, it was still there, the contract and the guarantee and all—began to fade, and in its place grew intrinsic motivation. "Maybe we should think of doing this again next year," some thought. As additional reinforcements—happy kids, teachers, supervisors, parents—occurred, some thought, "Maybe we should do it some more this year." So two more sites began in February. And they did well; more reinforcement.

So, by April, when we visited, this school system had come to think of itself as more powerful, more capable, saying "I can!," and was in fact taking the bit in its teeth and heading toward all kinds of things. Good test scores in June will be more reinforcement, but the "student" is already self-motivated.

Now the school people speak of themselves as becoming "sophisticated," of being beyond performance contracting. They say that now it is the school system's philosophy that every child will learn or the schools are to blame. While other school systems, they say, may need the protection from bureaucratic constraints that performance contracts allowed Grand Rapids this year, Grand Rapids now feels it can remold itself and move mountains.

The contractors, too, feel that a service has been performed far beyond the teaching of reading and mathematics to several hundred children.

The Michigan Context

One of the reasons that Grand Rapids has been able to skirt legal and philosophical issues that have bedeviled other cities that have tried performance contracting is that the State Department of Public Instruction, the Michigan School Boards Association, and the Michigan Education Association have been supportive.

The state department sees itself leading the quest for "accountability" and stimulating "local school districts to engage in guaranteed performance contracting." The state department has not only failed to raise issues, but has actively attempted to preclude their being raised by developing a technical assistance guide to performance contracting. This guide expresses the belief that "planning programming, and budgeting in curriculum areas should engage school officials as deeply as building a new high school or buying a fleet of buses." The guide details 50 pages of considerations for using performance contracting as a means for "curriculum renewal."

Superintendent of Public Instruction John O. Porter said in a winter speech to the Michigan Association for Curriculum Development, "It does seem that *now* is the time for someone to require that the schools guarantee student performance. . . . While performance contracting may not have all the answers. . . I am willing to give it a try if it reduced considerably the number of school disturbances and the number of complaints voiced by parents."

Norman Weinheimer, last year superintendent of schools in Grand Rapids, is now the executive secretary of the Michigan School Boards Association and an outspoken source of continued support and encouragement to performance contracting.

Melvin Leasure, only slightly less positive than the state department, told us that while the MEA has had some reservations from the beginning, "the first major attitude that we accepted was, 'You can't be against experimentation!' " The MEA's attitude of cautious openness is shared by the local Grand Rapids Education Association. "If the techniques being proposed by these corporations work," President David Thompson stated, "we had better take a second look toward adopting them ourselves."

The MEA does not seem to see as great a threat in performance contracting as do some other teacher groups. "What the performance contractor sells is not new ideas per se, but the way in which new ideas are put together to produce a result," says a recent MEA position paper. President Leasure has not found anything the contractors are doing, he says, that could not "be done ourselves," provided that proper training and support of "middle management" were forthcoming.

Ultimately, says the MEA position paper, the reason for the success of the "outsider" is that "he brings to the school a *well thought out system* and operates the system free and *unencumbered by the school administration of the district.*" (emphasis theirs) □

James A. Mecklenburger and John A. Wilson are EPDA Fellows in instructional systems technology at Indiana University. They authored "The Performance Contract in Gary" in the March *Kappan.*

VIII

WILL PERFORMANCE CONTRACTS REALLY PRODUCE?

by Mrs. Carolyn Rice
VEA Staff Assistant for Communications

"Give an average teacher a good system and you can get a 1.7 grade level increase in a year."

Performance contracting has tiptoed into 18 schools in seven Virginia localities with little fanfare or public attention in contrast to the commotion it has caused in some other states.

In a performance contract, private companies hinge their profits on student achievement. The companies guarantee specific educational achievements for a specific cost. This concept got off to a dubious start in Texarkana, Arkansas last year when it was found that the educational business firm, Dorsett Education Systems, Inc., had been "teaching to the test." They had primed students with answers to the tests on which the company's fee was to be based.

In spite of the Texarkana scandal, the Education Commission of the States estimates that schools signed 150 performance contracts this fall. Contracts differ from company to company in their emphasis on materials, machines, instructional methods or a combination of these things.

Most money for these contracts has come from the federal government: the Virginia localities are using Elementary and Secondary Education Act Title I funds.

Charles Blaschke from Educational Turnkey Systems, Inc., organized the Texarkana project and is now serving as a management consultant to the Virginia localities. This Washington, D. C. consultant believes that the climate in Washington is favorable

---

Reprinted with permission from the *Virginia Journal of Education,* January, 1971.

toward performance contracts. "Out of fiscal year 1970 funds," he said, "I estimate that close to $35 to $55 million will be spent on performance contract projects during the school year 1970-71. It is conceivable that as much as $75-$150 million will be spent under the fiscal year 1971 budget."

With funds like this up for grabs, performance contracting has risen to the limelight. Its appearnce has caused educators to criticize, question and specualte on how well it will work. Some wonder whether standardized achievement tests are an adequate measure on which to base payments; others have questioned whether teachers could not get comparable results in student achievement, given the same amount of money as the companies have for materials and instructional training. Finally comes the philosophical question: should a student's education be linked with a private company's profit?

Virginia grabs performance contracts

While educators busily aired such qeustions this fall, the Virginia localities plunged into the performance contract business at the State Department of Education's urging.

The State Department selected seven localities which according to Alfred Wingo, special assistant for federal programs at the State Department, have a high concentration of disadvantaged children. Three of the localities have had complications related to desegregation; all the localities have a high rate of lower socio-economic students who have failed to achieve satisfactorily in reading.

Last spring when the State Department announced plans for the contract, 117 private companies from across the United States responded. Fifty attended a meeting to hear the specifics and eight companies submitted proposals.

The administrators and some teachers from the seven localities studied these eight proposals. So did Educational Turnkey Systems, (ETS) Inc., the Washington firm hired by the State Department to act as a management support group for the Virginia localities.

Two proposals were selected and the final choice made at a meeting in Richmond late last summer. Besides superintendents and administrators from all the localities, the reading teachers from Prince Edward and Dickenson were present and according to

Mr. Wingo, "these gals really drilled the companies to the wall with their questions."

Most of the teachers and administrators favored Learning Research Associates' program, but this New York City concern promised only a one-grade level increase in student achievement.

"That's what we are doing ourselves," seemed to be the general reaction from the Virginia educators. After some quibbling, LRA upped their guarantee to 1.7 grade level increase per student. So the localities made the bargain, but the quibbling was just beginning. In December, although the instructional program had begun the first week of November, all the localities had not signed their contracts because of technical points concerning insurance for the children in the program.

This difficulty, along with the tremendous amount of work it took to implement the project, caused some project directors to complain about the program's administrative aspects. "We really should have had a year to evaluate proposals and put the program into action," Frank Barham, Prince Edward project director, said. Others complained that ETS was not doing the work it should.

In staffing the project, the seven school divisions employed their teachers and a project director while LRA employed two project supervisors. Each school provided several teachers who wanted to work in the program and LRA selected the ones they wanted. All personnel were Virginia educators.

"We looked for flexible teachers who were excited about trying the program and who were willing to try something new," Anne Mueser, a LRA consultant, said.

Students do not learn, if not taught

Several consultants provided by LRA prepared the teachers for the instructional program in an intensive, week-long, training session in Farmville during the last week of October.

LRA's main consultant is Dr. S. A. Cohen, a nationally known reading specialist from Yeshiva University in New York City. The appearance of Dr. Cohen—wearing levis and cowboy boots, with hippie length hair—and a mod female assistant—disconcerted some administrators at the workshop, but one project director said, "I kept telling them to listen to the ideas. I didn't care what they looked like because they had the ideas."

Dr. Cohen told the teachers that the reason the disadvantaged students do not learn is because they are not taught. "Teachers have not had the materials or methods because their college or school divisions have not given it to them," he said, adding that the good teachers who are successful have just "stumbled" onto systems which work.

"Give an average teacher a good system and you can get a 1.7 grade level increase in a year," Dr. Cohen claims.

His system is a High Intensity Learning Center which is a learning lab where students spend 85 to 90 per cent of their one-hour per day class individually working on prescribed reading activities. According to his research, students in a traditional teacher-directed classroom spend only 35 to 40 per cent of their time in actual learning-to-read activities.

With Dr. Cohen's system, the teachers diagnose the behaviors in which the students are weak such as alphabet knowledge, phonic spelling, and many other categories. Then they prescribe an assignment to remediate the deficiency. Each student gets an individual plan which assigns materials for a self-directing, self-correcting program, individually tailored in content, level, and rate. Students grade their own work right after completing it, learning immediately whether their response is adequate and are motivated by their progress, according to Dr. Cohen.

Classrooms are loaded with tradebooks—each room has 500 and for every five a student reads, he can choose one to keep. By the first week in December one Prince Edward student had read 50 books. Other teachers reported that students who had not been interested in reading were eagerly taking books home, reading them on the playground and in other classes.

"The payoff or student incentive in the program is allowing them to read," Dr. Cohen explained. "Basically what we are saying to them is, 'if you read this book, we'll let you go in the corner and read that book.' "

Other rewards which the students can have after completing their work include listening to and recording tapes and looking at filmstrips which illustrate stories. Each student has an opportunity to take the tape recorder home to play his recording for his family. This incentive system contrasts strikingly with the Texarkana one which relied on green stamps, transistor radios and a portable TV to generate student enthusiasm.

Teachers in the program have had much extra work in getting

it started, but so far those contracted are happy with what is happening in their classroom.

"To me this approach is what all students need," commented Mrs. Nancy Nance, a Prince Edward teacher. "It has taught me how to be a good manager."

"The materials do the teaching; the students spend all their time working–not listening to me. If they need me for more than two or three minutes, something is wrong with the assignment I have given them."

She also noted that the system helps combat short attention spans and restlessness, as the students must move to different areas of the room in carrying out their assignments."

The system would not work for the teacher who has to be the center of attention, she said, because the teacher's role becomes one of director from the sidelines.

What will happen?

"If this program works," Mr. Barham said, "we will have the majority of our students reading on grade level. We need something to help our students in a hurry. I don't think this program has all the answers, but it has some."

Harley T. Stallard, program director in Wise County, commented that "all along we have bought all kinds of material, but nobody has guaranteed they will work. This company is saying their materials and their methods will work."

In answer to educators who object to the profit motive in performance contracting, Mr. Stallard said, "to a certain extent the profit motive is in education anyway. Teachers teach for a profit. All suppliers make a profit. I don't object to people making money."

Miss Anne Mueser, the LRA consultant, explained her reaction to profit-making in simple terms. "When the money is on the line, you have to deliver the goods. Schools sometimes talk about it, but don't deliver. We have to deliver."

Both her salary and Dr. Cohen's salary will be based on the program results. "Besides the money, it is kind of an ego thing for us," Miss Mueser commented.

Miss Mueser, who is an advanced candidate for her doctorate degree at Yeshiva University, has been a TV demonstration teacher and has taught all grade levels. She hopes that performance contracting will spur some changes in teacher preparation, school curricula and instructional methods.

"We don't feel this program should be a threat to teachers," she said. "We are working with districts and teachers, and feel we are providing them with materials and methods which they have always wanted."

Both LRA consultants believe that performance contracting would be a way to make teachers accountable.

"But it is a lousy way unless the contract is between teachers and the school board," Dr. Cohen stated. "I don't want to see private industry teach kids; I want to see teachers teaching them."

When questioned why he was a consultant for a private company he said that it is an unusual company because its administrators are educators who are more interested in education than making money. "I wouldn't invest my money in their stock," he added.

This contract is LRA's first and according to Mr. Blaschke, "any firm will have difficulty making a profit the first year it enters into a performance contract."

Dr. Cohen also said that eventually he hopes to enter into performance contracts directly with the teachers. He plans to do all his future consulting work under contracts because he is tired of going into schools, offering suggestions, and seeing schools go right back to their old way of doing things the minute he leaves. With a contract the teachers must use the prescribed system for a certain length of time and it gets a fair chance, he believes.

"Teachers should become militant with performance contracts," Dr. Cohen said. "They should demand them from their school boards and then go after consultants who can give them the methods."

He predicts teachers may do this in reaction to communities which are becoming militant about accountability.

According to Daniel Avent, project director at Norfolk, "this is the era of accountability. The public wants to know what the schools are doing, how much it costs, and what it accomplished."

But he looks at performance contracting as "basically just another instructional approach in which we are using a company's expertise to teach us and supply materials."

Some teachers' groups have not so kindly viewed performance contracting and have even said that private industry will try to take over public schools by using it. Mr. Avent calls this accusation "really facetious."

Across the state the attitude towards performance contracting seems to be one of responsible neutrality. The Norfolk Education Association's instruction and curriculum committee and the executive board plan to look at the materials and classroom methods being used in the Norfolk contract.

"We don't want to make up our minds before we see it," Robert Richards, Norfolk executive director, said.

"If it's just another gimmick we'll denounce it as that," he said. "The one thing that concerns me is that people might look at performance contracting as a magic shortcut. If these companies bring in better materials and methods, it could be beneficial. But if performance contracting replaces teachers, then it has another connotation."

The Virginia localities will have results on this program by next fall, so educators will have some guide as to how it worked here. The localities have a turnkey option in their contracts which allows for program expansion. Teachers now in the program would teach other teachers the methods.

Whether the program becomes a terrific success or a thudding failure, educators will want to keep in mind that companies have established a wide variety of performance contracting—a fact which should cause educators to investigate closely before they obligate themselves. □

Virginia's performance contracts

Seven localities–Wise, Dickenson, Buchanan, Prince Edward, Lunenburg, Mecklenburg counties, and the city of Norfolk employed Learning Research Associates, a New York City company, to teach reading to 2,250 students in grades one through nine. Students had to be under their grade level in achievement and not below 70 IQ. LRA guaranteed these localities that they can raise each individual student's grade level by 1.7 grade in 150 one-hour classes, and they have staked their profits on the guarantee.

The total contract is $85 per child, with 75 per cent of the payment based on the 1.7 increase and the other 25 per cent based on instructional objectives which the teachers working with LRA specify for each student at the beginning of the year.

For each student who raises his grade level by 1.7, the localities pay $63.75. They pay $4 less for an increase of 1.6 and another $4 less for 1.5 and so on down. The localities pay nothing for the student who advances just one grade level during the year.

The localities must pay more than $85 for students who advance more than 1.7 grade level and who meet their instructional objectives, but the contract specifies that the localities will pay no more than an average of $85 per student. If the company earns the $85 on each student involved, it will receive $191,250.

The localities employed the University of Virginia education research department for pretesting, interim testing and post testing.

University evaluators are using three standardized achievement tests in each of the 18 classes and the contractors do not know which children had what tests.

Charles Blaschke, Washington consultant for the Texarkana project, said he did not feel that performance contracting got a fair test in Texarkana, but "it would very definitely get a fair test in Virginia."

According to Alfred Wingo, troubleshooter for the project from the State Department of Education, the test system in this project will eliminate all possibility of teaching to the test.

He said the State Department will be studying this experimental project to determine whether cost/effectiveness in education can be improved. "We need to get as much as possible for the money spent," he said, "and we do need to pay attention to output as well as input."

Besides the State and University of Virginia evaluation of the program, the Rand Corporation will be studying Norfolk's program. This Santa Monica, Calif., company received a $300,000 Health, Education and Welfare grant to study performance contracting in the United States and to develop guidelines for schools interested in it.

Mr. George Hall, Rand project leader in this study, said the message he had so far for educators is that "there is no typical performance contract." He explained that those he has seen vary greatly in technology, goals, and number of outside people involved.

Mr. Hall believes that in Virginia the contractor places more emphasis on classroom management and materials than in other contracts he had observed. He also said the Virginia project was unusual in that the State Department initiated it.

IX

EVALUATING VIRGINIA'S PERFORMANCE CONTRACT PROGRAM

by Mrs. Carolyn Rice
VEA Staff Assistant for Communications

"We are still quite baffled by the test results because in our judgment, they do not reflect the impact of the program. Every piece of evidence that we can accumulate shows that the kids were making much greater gains than were reflected in the standardized test results."

Testing variance vexes educators

Newspaper headlines have labeled Virginia's performance contract reading project a "flop," but many educators who worked in the program disagree with the assessment.

Last fall a New York City company promised that for $85 a child it could raise 2,430 low income students' reading level by 1.7 grades in a school year. The State Department of Education bought the promise and initiated the program in seven localities—Lunenberg, Mecklenburg, Norfolk, Prince Edward, Wise, Dickenson, and Buchanan.

This spring at the program's close, testing by the University of Virginia showed that, although a few children made impressive gains of 4.5 grade levels, most students made less than one-half year grade level gain in reading. Overall they did not better than control group students in regular reading programs.

Project directors and teachers were puzzled, as they had expected good results from the program. Also perplexing to some teachers was the fact that their students had done quite well on State standardized achievement tests in March, but did not do at all well on the University of Virginia tests at the end of the year.

Reprinted with permission from the *Virginia Journal of Education*, September, 1971.

The Bureau of Educational Research, University of Virginia, was paid $74,000 to administer pre- and post-standardized achievement tests and interim tests on instructional objectives, as specified in the contracts. The payoff of $121,173 to Learning Research Associates (LRA) the contracting company, was based on these tests; one-fourth on the instructional objectives and three-fourths on the standardized achievement tests.

Roy Stern, president of LRA, openly admits his company lost $39,000 on the program. "We are still quite baffled by the test results because in our judgment, they do not reflect the impact of the program," he claimed. "Every piece of evidence that we can accumulate shows that the kids were making much greater gains than were reflected in the standardized test results."

Several project teachers and directors have echoed Mr. Stern's sentiments. "I am still trying to get over the results of these tests," commented Sadra Farmer, a Dickenson county project teacher. "I had one student who was reading only 10 words out of the basic 220 when he began. At the end he was reading all but 10 of the 220. Yet on his test results, he regressed. There were too many incidents like that."

Miss Farmer's main concern was "that my students did so much better than the results showed they did."

Other project teachers were also upset when they got the test results. Mrs. Gwendolyn Daniels, a Norfolk teacher, described herself as "very disappointed. The results I could see daily in my classes just did not show up on the tests."

Many teachers stated that they had worked harder this year than ever before as a teacher. They liked the materials which came from 18 publishers and the instructional aids. Most teachers reported an upswing in student attitudes in their classes. Norfolk's Jacox Junior High principal, Romeo U. Lambert, said there was as much difference between his performance contract and regular reading students as between "chalk and cheese."

Frank Barham, Prince Edward County project director, said students in his performance contract classes had better attendance, fewer discipline problems, and better attitudes than students in his other classes.

Knowing these positive factors of the project, teachers and administrators have been trying to explain why on the standardized tests the students showed only .3552 grade level gain in the lowest division and .4376 in the highest division.

Dr. Charles Woodbury, Bureau of Educational Research director, University of Virginia, concluded that "the standardized tests did not adequately cover the reading objectives taught in the performance contract program." The Bureau of Research selected three standardized achievement tests as the contract specified.

At a later date after receiving the learning objectives of the program, Dr. Woodbury said "we discovered that the test items did not adequately measure the word attack skills, just fairly adequately measured the study skills, but adequately measured the comprehension skills."

Some teachers and principals complained about the testing program. In a Dickenson County school the testers showed up twenty minutes before school dismissal. They had given no advance notification of their coming but demanded that they have the students for testing. The principal refused, explaining that he could not hold the buses for several hours while a small portion of his students took tests.

Also, some southwestern teachers complained when a Scottish woman with a pronounced brogue was sent to test children who had trouble understanding her.

Although some educators in the program did have various objections, Dr. Woodbury stated that he was "absolutely satisfied with test conditions."

But teachers began to raise more questions when they compared the performance contract tests with State standardized achievement tests which had been given to fourth and seventh graders in March. They were finding that the students had scored much higher on the state tests.

Dr. Robert Turner, State Department of Education special assistant for federal programs, compared the tests and noted that very frequently children got 3.5 on the State test in March and 1.5 on a University of Virginia test in May.

Dr. Woodbury refused to discuss the discrepancy between the State's and University of Vriginia's tests, saying that State data was "scattered and would not be significant."

But Dr. Turner who administered the project for the State Department after Alfred Wingo's retirement this spring admitted this was quite a discrepancy. He felt that the test given by the State might have been easier and that children might get some carry over on the test as it has been used for a number of years.

Also, he noted that teachers give the State test and their attitudes might have encouraged the students to work harder on it.

He also thought that the students might have done better on the University of Virginia tests if they had taken them at an earlier date instead of during the last few days of school as the contract specified.

Late Testing Never Again

LRA President Stern said that "one thing we will never do again is specify that the testing be done as late as possible. We were naive in testing so late while other kids in the school were having parties and going on picnics."

He still believes that a 1.7 grade level increase was not too much to expect, but said that in the future contracts "the company might want to reduce the grade level increase guarantee a little bit out of business sense—but not from the conviction that we can not do it."

The interim testing on instructional objectives showed "that the students were indeed mastering the objectives of the program," Dr. Woodbury said. "We would concur with the teachers that these kids were really performing quite well," he concluded.

The students' success was so great on the interim testing that Dr. Turner, said that if one-half of LRA's payment had been based on the instructional objectives instead of one-fourth, they would not have lost money. "If all the payment would have been based on instructional objectives, LRA would have made a nice little profit," he noted.

In another evaluation which was unrelated to the payoff, the testers found that in a "statistically very significant way" the project students liked reading much better than their counterparts in the control groups.

Meanwhile, back at class

"We are getting a lot out of children that we have not been able to get much from before." . . . Carter C. Collins, Wise Primary principal.

"The thing that has amazed me is that interest has continued throughout the year. I thought interest would lag by the end of the year." . . . Mrs. Francis Riggs, teacher at Wise Primary.

"One boy whom I expelled from school for bad behavior asked me if he could come back just to attend the performance contract reading class. He did not get into trouble in there because he learned he could succeed–something he was not doing in his other subjects." . . . Romeo U. Lambert, Norfolk's Jacox Junior High principal.

This last incident points up what LRA's main consultant, Dr. Alan Cohen, tried to make an integral part of the program–success for every child.

Dr. Cohen calls his program diagnostic and prescriptive. First a teacher locates a child's weak points and then prescribes specific materials to remedy the weakness. Each child works at his own level and his own speed.

Many teachers commented that this program helped children learn how to follow directions and work on their own. The teachers made out prescription cards which the children followed to complete their assignments. They checked their assignments immediately upon completion. Even the first graders worked independently in the program.

The instructional program did not feature much hardware, but the children were responsible for operating the equipment it did use. They learned to operate tape recorders and film-strip machines.

Other teachers not involved in the program reported that they noticed a carry over into their classes. According to them, the children from project classes could follow directions better.

Also, the teachers and administrators felt the program probably had some carry over into the homes as the children were awarded one free paperback book for every five books they read. For many children, the paperback was the first one they had ever had of their own.

One teacher said that this program had completely changed his attitude toward educating slow learners. He had debated whether to place one slow learner in the performance contract class but finally decided to. The student made such significant progress that the teacher said he was forced to completely rethink his ideas concerning educating the slow learner.

The classes had low absentee rates, low dropout rates and discipline problems, for the most part, just did not exist.

On the negative side, some administrators complained that the State Department shoved this program at them so fast last fall that they did not have time to properly plan for it.

Some administrators just could not adjust to students having the freedom of walking around their classrooms, of working on their own daily, and of talking with other students during the class.

A few teachers had trouble adjusting to the prescription/ diagnosis form of teaching. They were used to being the center of attention in their former classes, and when they became a prescriber from the sidelines, their egos suffered.

Performance contracting's future in Virginia

All seven localities which participated in the performance contract program plan to use the program in some manner next year, according to Dr. Turner. Currently two localities are negotiating contracts; the others plan to work the program on their own or use consultants rather than a contract.

The program did not save the localities money, according to an analysis by Educational Turnkey Systems, Inc., the Washington, D. C. company employed by the State Department for $30,000 to be watchdog over the project. In most cases the cost per student in the performance contract was about equal or a few dollars higher than that of control students.

Dr. Turner said that State Department data on this program is inconclusive. "What we now have shows some positive and some negative evidence," he said, adding that he would need information on the program in future years before he could make recommendations concerning it to other localities.

Dr. Cohen spoke glowingly of performance contracting at the beginning of the program. Now he says he is a bit discouraged with the concept because it seems to involve educational politics rather than the performance of kids in the classroom. "People were often distrustful of me simply because I was in a performance contract. As a consultant I do not have to face this kind of distrust."

Dr. Cohen will be using his reading program in several other states this fall, but will be in a consultive rather than a contractor role.

LRA President Stern is not as discouraged. LRA is also going into several more states this autumn with performance contracts. "We are going to chalk our performance contract up in Virginia as a good experience. We've learned a great deal and we think we have helped the schools change. To me this is the most exciting aspect of what has happened. And we are convinced that the kids grew a lot more than was indicated by the standardized achievement tests." □

Chapter Three

BANNEKER

I

THE PERFORMANCE CONTRACT IN GARY

by James A. Mecklenburger and John A. Wilson

"Let's get the bugs and work them out by experience, rather than on paper," McAndrew said. "I wasn't interested in developing all kinds of fancy objectives; what I want to know is, can we teach the kids to read and add? And here's a school where 75% of them can't. That's the objective."

Never before, anywhere, has a private corporation contracted with a city school board to manage the entire program of one school—as Behavioral Research Laboratories, of Palo Alto, California, have done this year with the School City of Gary, Indiana. (Gary's public schools are called "School City.")

BRL, as consultant to School City, manages Banneker Elementary School, an inner-city school of 850 students. Gary has pledged its average cost per student to BRL; no federal money is involved. BRL guarantees to raise the achievement of Banneker's students; the guarantee states that BRL will return its fee for any child who fails.

In 1971 jargon, BRL is "accountable" for results. This "performance contract" involves more money (over $2,000,000), more responsibility (an entire school), and a longer period of time (four years) than any performance contract yet written in education.

Three Partisans

Gordon McAndrew, Gary's superintendent, once called this project a trial balloon at which everyone can shoot. "It has lost air, but not as much as I thought it would—and the best evidence is that the balloon is still up there," he told us early in January. He predicted that the project will work the kinks out of itself within this first year and operate smoothly thereafter.

"I think it's a badly administered and badly run school," Charles Smith, president of the Gary Teachers Union, states. "If I had to make a prediction right now," he told us in December, "I would predict BRL would not be here for the duration of their contract unless they change the system and they change the administration of the school."

"Banneker School is not being operated in accordance with the State Board of Education rules and regulations," State Superintendent Richard D. Wells stated at the conclusion of several months of investigation. At the January 19 meeting of the state board, a resolution called for Gary to comply with all rules and regulations by February 18, or the Banneker School would automatically be decommissioned.

A Brief History

BRL's *Project Read* – a sequence of programmed textbooks developed by M. W. Sullivan – has been used in Gary in recent years and has shown promise, first in summer remedial programs, then in six schools. Friendship developed over time between BRL and Gary.

"George and I got to talking once," McAndrew told us, referring to George Stern, BRL's president. "This must have been a year ago, and somehow we got to talking about what we thought about this whole 'accountability' notion. I said, kind of facetiously at the beginning. 'Tell you what. We'll contract with you to do this on a school-wide basis, not just reading but the whole shebang. Two conditions: One, it can't cost any more money than we're now spending, and two, you have to take a school as it now exists.' Out of that came a proposal." That was April. By August, in-service training of staff had begun.

Most performance contracts begin, unlike Gary's, with elaborate preparation. A school board prepares a "request for proposals" (RFP) which specifies the board's purposes, standards, funds available, constraints, and preferences for entering, then evaluating, then terminating a contract. Frequently a management consultant assists in the preparation; often teachers, parents, and community leaders assist also. Finally, the RFP is published, requesting potential bidders to submit proposals; bids are received and bidders chosen to receive contracts. (BRL was among 10 bidders on the Texarkana RFP, for example.) This procedure is commonplace in the defense industry, new to education.

None of these steps occurred in Gary. Despite national efforts to establish RFP's as preconditions for performance contracts,[1] only one school board member in Gary even questioned that no bids except BRL's had been sought.

"Why no RFP in Gary?" we asked McAndrew. "I don't know that there were any hard and fast reasons," he said. "I suppose one could argue we should have done that. I knew something about the BRL program, I had some indication of it; I think also in talking with Stern and some of his people, I felt they kind of grabbed the concept as well as I did. For those kinds of reasons, we went that route."

Charles Smith attributes the lack of bids to BRL's merchandising expertise. We surmise deeper reasons also. One can ask, What was the hurry to begin this project? Why not wait a year, plan the project thoroughly?

Impatience to innovate. Impatience, we sensed in Gary, permeates the city's large minority-group populations and its school board, which has only recently become minority-group dominated. Moreover, desperation characterizes many parents and schoolmen over the failure of many students, particularly nonwhite students, to acquire adequate basic skills. Banneker School, for example, ranked twenty-seventh among 29 elementary schools in achievement test scores by one reckoning; it had only one student in four reaching national norms for reading and mathematics. School City administrators tell us that the school board and the community are zealous believers in test scores, and such scores are hard to swallow.

Impatience and desperation prompted a declaration by the school board in 1970 of a "right to learn" philosophy, which calls for innovative attempts at teaching basic skills. Gary is studded with experiments to achieve better learning of basic skills, including experiments with BRL's *Project Read.* In this setting of impatience and experimentation, the nationwide emphasis on accountability made performance contracting seem irresistible.

Moreover, some insiders judged that if Gary had waited, union and Indiana state education policies would likely have scuttled such a project politically. BRL may be scuttled yet.

McAndrew himself embodies Gary's impatience. "Let's get the bugs and work them out by experience, rather than on paper," he said. "I wasn't interested in developing all kinds of fancy objectives; what I want to know is, can we teach the kids to read and add? And here's a school where 75% of them can't. That's the objective."

The Grand Design

McAndrew's "trial balloon" may not survive the slings and arrows the Gary Teachers Union, the state of Indiana, some parents, some teachers, and others are hurling. Or it may spring its own leaks and collapse. Survive or not, the grand design of the program – as revealed in BRL's proposal, the contract, press statements by BRL and School City, and in interviews – will remain tantalizing.

To orchestrate its systems approach to schooling, BRL provides a center manager, a "systems man," so to speak. Gary provides a learning director, responsible for supervising the academic portion of the system. Five curriculum managers bear responsibility for each of the five curriculum areas. These are language arts, mathematics, science, social studies and foreign language, and enrichment – "enrichment" being arts and crafts, music, drama, and physical education. Seventeen assistant curriculum managers perform the major instruction; 27 learning supervisors recruited from among the parents of Banneker students round out this differentiated staff.

In keeping with Gary's "right to learn" philosophy, the project began with heavy concentration on reading and mathematics, and as performance at Banneker improves, BRL will phase in the other areas.

BRL's *Project Read, Project Math,* and *Project Learn* serve as the cornerstone of teaching materials; BRL has chosen Allyn and Bacon's social studies materials and AAAS science. In-service training prepares the staff to teach each of these materials.

BRL liberally employs consultants from outside Gary to aid whenever necessary; in fact, several consultants serve full time. As many as 15 consultants at once were present during the two weeks of in-service staff training in August.

Day-to-day evaluation of student progress is built into the teaching materials; frequent evaluation will also be provided by the staff. A "profile" on each student's mastery of a host of skills in reading, mathematics, and other areas is to be updated by the staff monthly and supplied to the child and his parents.

Moreover, two independent firms provide long-range evaluation of each child's progress. One firm, Bernard Donovan's Center for Urban Redevelopment and Education (CURE) from New York, periodically administers the Metropolitan Achievement Test. CURE also monitors the program monthly to see that BRL and Gary both adhere to the terms of the contract. The second firm will audit CURE's findings.

Banneker is designed to be a truly nongraded school, for each child begins at a point where his own knowledge ends and proceeds at his own pace. "Classes" as such disappear in these circumstances, and classrooms become "learning centers." In each center, games and activities daily supplement and reinforce book learning. In practice, children of varied ages share one learning center based on their level of skills; over time children move from center to center as they learn.

An extensive community relations program and an advisory council of famed educators and local persons are promised by BRL.

Some Leaks in the Balloon

The letter of the Gary-BRL contract sometimes lacks the grandeur of the design.

For example, advocates say the program "costs no more," but analysis shows that – if successful – it will cost more, for two reasons.

First, roughly $34,000 per year accrues to BRL as "extra" income; this is so because Indiana schools determine cost per pupil based on "average daily *attendance*" while BRL is paid based on "active *enrollment.*" If enrollment is 850 students, and daily attendance averages 95% of enrollment, BRL receives 5% more than a Gary school would; 5% means 43 students BRL is paid for that a Gary school would not be.

Second, BRL is paid the average annual cost per pupil in grades one through 12, which is roughly $800. However, in Gary, the average elementary school cost per pupil is less. McAndrew estimated for us that K-6 expenditures average $700; the union says $696. This means Gary pays BRL approximately $85,000 per year more than it would spend in an average elementary school.

Based on these estimates, the program could cost Gary nearly 20% more than it spends for an average elementary school.

Three qualifications modify this analysis. First, if BRL were only 80% successful at raising achievement of every child, BRL would return to Gary roughly 20% of its fee. That is, at 80% success, it is true that the Banneker program would cost no more. In fact, if BRL were less successful than 80%, Gary would save on Banneker School. Second, because salaries differ among schools, based on the staff's experience, some elementary schools in Gary may cost \$800. Some also may cost less than \$700. (McAndrew did not know the cost per pupil at Banneker last year.) Third, this analysis does not criticize School City for deciding to commit more money to one school, which is its prerogative; it only questions the many public assertions that this program costs no more.

When one estimates BRL's costs at Banneker, he begins to doubt that BRL is motivated by profits to be made there, even at \$800 per pupil per year. Every observer we interviewed concurred with the conclusion of Otha Porter, Gary's assistant to the superintendent, that "I don't see BRL carrying dollars away from Gary." However, BRL does profit in Gary from the visibility BRL receives nationally (such as from this article), from whatever increased sales this visibility brings to BRL's publications, and – if the Banneker project succeeds – from the subsequent prestige for BRL.

In the January *American School Board Journal,* BRL's president, George Stern, reveals that BRL can afford not to make a profit. If one considers the large profit margein that business usually requires in a high-risk enterprise, and if one suspects that BRL may not even recoup costs in Gary, he begins to wonder what it would really cost to contract with a corporation that had to make its profit on site. It seems that Gary has gotten a bargain rate; one may look askance at the publicity that says this project can be endlessly duplicated at the Gary price. It might better be thought of as a "loss leader" aimed at the education market.

While BRL is nominally "accountable" for every student, the contract reveals a substantial minority of students for whom no guarantee applies. The annual turnover of students in Banneker School is reported at 5% to 7%. Because a student must be in the program a full year for either portion of the guarantee to apply, as many as 15% of the students at Banneker, over three years, will not qualify. Moreover, even at Banneker some students are already at grade level or above and should remain so without BRL. If these number 25%, as is said, then BRL has no effective accountability under the contract for this one-fourth of the school's students.

Most intriguing, there will be a number of students for whom an overwhelming effort would have to be mounted to raise them to grade level – special education students, for example, or simply children years below grade level who do not work well in programmed texts – much more than $800 worth of effort. Would a corporation make this effort, or instead concentrate on the vast majority most likely to succeed? That is, if one is motivated by profit, are there some students too expensive to teach?

School City's contract with BRL makes an intriguing contrast to School City's agreement with the Gary Teachers Union. The latter is precision honed to cover every contingency, while the BRL contract is often sketchy, even incomplete. It reads as if the two parties had agreed more to each other's good intentions than to a program. One wonders how CURE can monitor such a contract.

For example, the "differentiated" staff, from center manager to learning supervisors, consists mostly of the titles of positions; the contract says little about their functions or responsibilities. There shall be teaching in all curriculum areas; but there is no statement of how much instruction, its substance, or how anything but reading and math will be evaluated by School City. Who holds proprietary rights to materials developed at Banneker? What will the advisory council do? What might happen in the fourth year? When is payment refunded for any sixth graders who fall this year? For all these there are no provisions. Subject to School City's final authority, the contract provides BRL tremendous latitude with few guidelines.

The powerful 120-day withdrawal clause provides that either party may withdraw at will on written notice to the other. If either party withdraws, what happens to the guarantee? No answer. It appears to be a contract based more on good faith than on good business sense.

Slings and Arrows

One criticism during the first semester was that several provisions of the contract had not been implemented fully, some not at all. Despite the provision for monthly student evaluation on a profile of basic skills, the profile has yet to be issued. One "mini-report" was released in December. That report prompted some adverse community reaction, for some parents realized for the first time that their children had studied only reading and math; they feared their children might be getting shortchanged. Apparently, the promised extensive community relations program had not been extensive enough to reach many parents.

Even Superintendent McAndrew became critical of the slow pace with which the three other curriculum areas had been phased into the school; meetings over Christmas vacation resulted in a promise that by second semester these areas would all have begun. In mid-January, Mrs. Sandra Irons, vice-president of the Gary Teachers Union, repported that BRL was still teaching "only reading and math, *all day long!*"

The second evaluator, the so-called auditor, was to be selected by BRL, according to the contract, in September, 1970. It has not yet been named. There never has been an advisory council.

In addition, the Gary Teachers Union (GTU) which represents virtually every teacher in Gary, has some specific grievances. A strike vote, called in September, was rescinded in the face of a threatened court order, and at mid-winter, the issues remained in advisory arbitration.

GTU objected to what it saw as three violations of its agreement with School City. One related to class size – the pupil-teacher ration was said to be greater than 40-1 (850 students, 22 teachers). School City responded first that there are no "classes" as that word is used in the union agreement, and second, that the many paraprofessionals create a ratio of pupils to adults more nearly 20-1.

A second grievance related to a clause in the BRL guarantee; School City agrees to transfer any staff person within 15 days of written notice from BRL; otherwise the guarantee will not be valid. School City responded to the union that certainly the union has no grievance until such a transfer occurs.

The third grievance related to the summary transfer of 14 teachers from Banneker in August. In Gary, teachers are virtually secure within their buildings unless they request transfer, and several provisions of the agreement prescribe procedures for involuntary transfer; these were violated, according to GTU. School

City points out that none of the teachers involved filed a grievance, which indicates that the transfers were not involuntary, and that the experimental nature of the program necessitated the transfers.

Fundamental Issues

Performance contracting in schools, like a crystal dropped into a steam of light, acts as a prism, displaying a colorful spectrum of fundamental educational issues and requiring they be examined anew.

Advocates of the RFP procedure state that fundamental issues are best met in the planning stage – there conflicts can be anticipated and resolved before they disrupt a program. In Gary, where much planning was postponed until the program began, only now have major issues surfaced. And they may indeed disrupt the program.

Of what importance are teachers? for example. The emphasis on "performance," "guarantee," and "evaluation"; teachers "replaced" by paraprofessionals, reliance on "teacher-proof" materials; the denial to teachers of "professional" decisions traditionally made by teachers, such as pupil placement, or curriculum decisions – these have prompted many in Gary, not only teachers, to wonder what respect BRL and School City have for teachers. Charles Smith, of the union, echoes a frequently heard sentiment in Gary that BRL would rather have hired "technicians" than teachers.

By some reports, teacher morale throughout Gary has been affected. Rumblings were reported in the *Gary Post-Tribute* of December 20 that half the teachers in Banneker are considering or requesting transfer; Smith affirmed this for us in mid-January. Some observers charge that teachers are being made scapegoats for School City's financial inability to pay for needed new programs.

Who determines what schools shall be like? This question lurks behind a standing offer to the union by Gary's school board and superintendent. They propose for the union a project like the one with BRL, "under the same arrangements we've made with the contractor. We'll give them the same fees, the same help, the same control, if they'll agree to the same terms," in the words of Gary school board president Alphonso Holliday. The union is very much interested in implementing better schools, the union will tell you. But not being in the business of publishing and selling materials, the union cannot afford to compete on the same terms as BRL offers. Besides, says Smith, just sit and watch one or two classrooms at Banneker for a few hours, and you won't be so excited about trying to compete with BRL on BRL's terms. Smith deems the board offer not worthy of formal reply.

How shall we know who has learned what? Testing, an issue educators have slipped under the rug of collective guilt for two decades, emerges with a vengeance in a contract like BRL's. For Gary and BRL have agreed to raise test scores, and it is for test scores that BRL is accountable.

The suggestion, to student and community alike, is that standardized achievement tests provide, a precise yardstick against which an individual student's learning can be measured. Educators have sold this notion – or allowed school boards and politicians to sell it – for a long time.

But such tests are not that precise. As measuring devices for individual learning, they have more nearly the precision of a fist than a fine yardstick. While these tests yield "scores" that can be treated as if they are precise data, these numbers are very imprecise data. (See "Testing for Accountability," in the December, 1970, *Nation's Schools,* for a fuller treatment of testing problems.) Moreover, many factors besides learning – such as maturation, testing conditions, the timing of the tests, and student attitudes toward a test – can cause scores on standardized tests to improve sufficiently to fulfill a contractor's guarantee.

While a contractor could contract on the basis of specific skills taught, most, including BRL, have not yet done so. In this ill use of testing, contractors may undercut their own future.

Raise the testing question among people involved in performance contracts and they get defensive. For example, McAndrew responded, "In fact, for better or worse or right or wrong, that's the way we do it! We let kids into college based on the SAT, and we let them into graduate school based on the Miller Analogy, and we let them into industry based on all kinds of standardized tests."

Who wields authority in education? This issue has been especially virulent in Gary, because BRL, as an interloper, makes public school authorities tense. The contract itself does little to clarify the division of authority between BRL and Gary. Between Superintendent McAndrew and BRL's George Stern, this proved tolerable. But facing this issue at Banneker, the division of authority between learning director and center manager became crucial. The learning director, a former principal, and the center manager, not a professional educator, found themselves sharing the kingpin position that Banneker's principal had for years occupied alone. The contract's only guidelines was that the learning director manage academic affairs, the center manager manage nonacademic affairs. By January, sensitive feelings had grown into conflict and a host of BRL and Gary referees belatedly rushed in to straighten out the gnarled problem.

By this time, the Indiana School Board, a more powerful referee, decided that neither the contract split of authority nor the true split (according to some observers, the learning director had unwillingly become a figurehead) was legal. A man who performs the administrative duties listed in state regulations must be certified as an administrator. The question of who wields authority jumped, then, to the state level.

The state investigators identified other violations of state rules and regulations. After s series of summertime events as the contract was being written and signed, and subsequently as Gary and BRL forged ahead on their own, regardless of statutes, they communicated to the state superintendent "an attitude of . . . complete contempt" for the state office. State investigators identified six of Banneker's 22 teachers as improperly certified and found that BRL's materials had never been approved by the State Textbook Adoption Commission (and Gary never asked for a waiver of that regulation), that the teacher-pupil ratio at Banneker exceeded legal limits, and that BRL's heavy dose of reading and mathematics violated regulations about time allocation for a well-rounded curriculum.

So on January 19, the General Commission of the Indiana School Board resolved that Gary would comply with all rules and regulations within a month, or the state would decommission the school, thus withdrawing all state money from the Banneker budget.

In the face of the state's resolution, the arbitration with the Gary Teachers Union, some unrest in the community, and several fundamental issues still unresolved, we hesitate to predict (as we write this article January 20) the health of the BRL project as you read this in March. □

James A. Mecklenburger and John A. Wilson are EPDA Fellows in instructional systems technology at Indiana University.

II

QUALITY OF THE EDUCATIONAL PROGRAM OF BANNEKER ELEMENTARY SCHOOL, GARY, INDIANA February 12, 1971

by John S. Hand

"There is nothing uniquely innovative about the Banneker program except (a) the abdication of professional responsibility on the part of the School City of Gary and (b) the placement of the primary emphasis upon building and maintaining a systems model instead of upon the children and their needs and interests."

Appearing before the State Board of Education on January 19, 1971, I stated that I and other OSPI staff members have serious reservations about the quality of the educational program presently conducted at Banneker Elementary School, Gary, Indiana, under the control and direction of the Behavioral Research Laboratories, Inc., a private corporation based in Palo Alto, California, and New York City, New York. It is the purpose of this report to specify the basis for the statement.

The quality of the educational program could be evaluated from various perspectives, such as whether this year's program is more effective than last year's, whether the program violates basic educational principles, whether the program conforms to the expectations and promises built into the contract, etc. To some extent any report on such matters would reflect the philosophical bias of the reporter and would inevitably, in some respects, be subjective. The report will be more or less convincing to the reader to the extent that the reader shares or rejects the reporter's philosophical position and perception of what is important in education.

Since I had never visited Banneker School prior to my first

Contents of this memorandum were widely reported in the Indiana press in the early part of 1971.

visit in October 1970, I am not qualified to render an opinion as to the comparative effectiveness of this year's and last year's Banneker programs.

I *shall* attempt to assess the quality of the current program at Banneker School from two perspectives: (1) the promise and performance of the contractual relationship as it relates to educational quality and (2) additional specific observations not directly related to the contract.

1.0 Quality of the Contractual Services

1.1 Curriculum

1.1.1. Item 2. (A) (1) of the contract provides that BRL shall "develop a curriculum. . . ." and Item 2. (A) (5) states that "curriculum objectives" will be established. In response to my requests for information concerning this item, I received a voluminous packet of materials from Banneker School on January 19, 1971. The materials appeared to have been hastily assembled and consisted of lists of content items and lists of instructional materials. The document was not bound, contained no title page or introductory statement, and was not accompanied by any explanation; so its purpose must be guessed at. The science section of the packet consisted of Xeroxed copies of the copyrighted flow charts from AAAS, (Science-A Process Approach." The materials lists occupied many unnecessary pages (which contributed substantially to the bulk of the package) since in many instances only one instructional item was listed on a single page. (Although it is not germane at this point to the question of educational quality, the packet did clearly show that the Banneker program violates the intent of State textbook rules and laws.)

By no stretch of the imagination could the materials submitted to me be considered a curriculum design. There was no indication of desired behavioral outcomes, no scope and sequence description or charts, and no indication of instructional procedures that would be followed. In addition, there were serious grammatical and usage errors in the narrative portions of the document, fragmented sentences, and sentences that made no sense.

1.1.2 Item 4 of the contract defines six curricular areas to be provided in the program, as follows:

(i) *Science* – As noted in my January 19, 1971, report, science instruction had not yet been implemented as of January 7. Since I was informed on January 7 that January 11 had been set as a target date for beginning science instruction at Banneker, the science situation may have changed by this time.

(ii) *Social Science* – According to the contract, Social science at Banneker is to include black history, foreign languages, economics, government, and society. Although I am at a loss to define "society" as a social science discipline, I can attest that as of January 7, 1971, none of the five areas specified were included in the instructional program at Banneker. Map and globe skills were being taught at all levels; but it could be cogently argued that these are reading skills rather than social studies skills even though they are essential tools for social science comprehension. There is also an interesting statement in the contract in regard to social science that "respect for the change of institutions *by lawful means*" shall be taught. The flagrant disregard BRL and the School City of Gary have shown toward State rules and regulations during the first four months of the operation of this program raises an interesting question about the credibility of this contractual item.

(iii) *An Enrichment Program* – The enrichment program, according to the contract, shall include choral and instrumental music, arts and crafts, and physical education. To balance and add perspective to my own impressions, I sent our State fine arts consultants and the Assistant Director of the Division of Curriculum to Banneker on February 5, 1971. Unfortunately, school sessions were cancelled on February 5 because of serious weather conditions; but our consultants did confer with Banneker professional staff members. They have reported to me that (1) there is no organized instrumental music program and (2) the children at Banneker are receiving about ½ the amount of time in music and art that is considered average for the State as a whole. In other words, the fine arts program is limited by the inadequacy of the time allotted to it. The physical education program appears to be largely a games program supervised by a teacher who also is assigned to teaching science and mathematics. I seriously question that physical *education* is taking place even though I believe that the teacher is conscientious in his desire to offer such a program.

(iv) *Literature* – Our staff has been unable to locate any evidence that "literature" is being taught or that it is even being encouraged within the Banneker program. Use of the library has noticeably declined since last year as revealed by a spot check of the check-out files in the librarian's desk and a random sampling of the shelved books by two members of the State Board of Education and two OSPI staff members. (Nearly 200 books were examined at random in the school library). Teachers informed us that they were kept so busy teaching to the two "guaranteed" areas, reading skills and mathematics, that they had no time for literature or enriching activities which they would normally have provided.

(v) *Mathematics* – The mathematics program concentrates heavily on computational skills and considerably less on mathematical reasoning. The mathematics program appears somewhat unbalanced because of its nearly total reliance on programed instructional materials and seatwork review sheets of previously presented skills; but it seems to be adequate, though unimaginative and pedestrian in its insistence that all children must tread the same path. Only the pace is individualized, and a few of the teachers appeared to be trying their best to keep that from becoming too pronounced.

(vi) *Reading and language arts* – Reading is the area

of concentration; the other language arts, particularly handwriting, receive a token nod and occasionally some sporadic special efforts. Some work is being done in creative writing. But reading is the precious jewel of the whole program for which all other disciplines, including mathematics, must, upon occasion, step aside. At least this is how the teachers perceive the relative importance to BRL of the various curriculum areas. In the Banneker program, reading has become an end in itself to the extent that its usefulness as a functional tool for other learning seems, at times, to be ignored or forgotten. Even social science grouping is by reading level with the conceptual abilities of the students ignored, i.e. whenever the social science program actually is begun, the grouping will be by *reading levels.*

In summary the contract calls for the implementation of quality programs in six curricular areas. In mid-January there were adequate programs in two areas, an inadequate program in one area, and no programs in three areas. The total program is perceived by the teachers as a reading program rather than as a complete elementary curriculum.

1.2 Individualizing Instruction

The contract indicates various devices which are to be used to achieve an individualized instructional program at Banneker. Some of these are in operation; others exist in the contract, but not in the school. Item 2 (A) (4) mentions the terms "student centered" and "non-graded." Item 2 (A) (5) refers to "individual student profiles." Item 2 (B) (4) says that BRL will diagnose, prescribe, monitor, and help implement an individualized educational program for *each child"* (the italics are mine). Item 2 (B) (5) states that BRL will "present *detailed* plans for organizing instructional activities around a number of learning centers. . ." (Again I added the italics). Item 2 (B) (6) mentions "individualized instructional materials" and self-pacing. Item 2 (b) (7) refers to a "monthly evaluation of each child's progress."

All of these things sound very good *if* they are taking place. The next two sections of this report will examine the extent to which they are.

1.2.1. *Non-graded* – The Banneker program is non-graded in respect to the fact that the children were grouped in September according to their scores on BRL placement tests for mathematics and reading. There is also some degree of self-pacing permitted by some teachers within the three groups assigned to a particular teacher for a particular one-hour instructional module. There appear to be two serious flaws in the procedure: (1) the placement tests seem to be somewhat lacking in validity as placement instruments and (2) too little flexibility has been built into the placement procedure. Teachers are not permitted to correct placement errors by reassigning improperly placed children into more appropriate instructional groups; and, apparently, the Center Manager has been too deluged with other managerial problems to make the needed re-assignments himself. In addition to this, there seems to be no way by which a child may achieve his way out of his originally assigned group; or, if there is, few children are making that much progress because few transfers have been accomplished.

1.2.2. *Student Centered* – The central concern repeatedly expressed by the Center Manager is the development of a total systems managerial scheme for manipulating all of the components of the "mix" at Banneker. The Center Manager gives the distinct impression of perceiving the management of the educational process as primarily a matter of identifying and classifying components into groups of generally similar items to be arranged into systematic relationships. Little differentiation seems to be made within the system for coping with the great variability of the human components, i.e. children are grouped by achievement on placement tests but little attention is paid to variables of personality, interests, physical maturation, learning style, empathy for particular adults, etc. It seems obvious that the program is more systems-centered than student-centered.

Additional evidence of this systems-centering is provided by the neglect of certain key elements of the program. No "individual student profiles" were yet available in mid-January. Although the contract called for monthly reporting on the progress of each student, only one report had appeared by mid-January; and that report resulted in controversy rather than in understanding of student progress. There was still no evidence in mid-January that a diagnosis, prescription, or monitored individualized instructional or learning program had been developed for *any* individual child at Banneker, let alone for *each* child in the school.

A "detailed plan for organizing instructional activities around a number of learning centers" does exist but seems to be in a constant state of flux as the Center Manager tries to bring the components of his system into some semblance of balance and stability. In fact, one of the major reasons for the delay in fully implementing the program has been the Center Manager's inability to bring the system to sufficient equilibrium to risk adding new components to the mix. The detailed plan, however, only serves to confirm the impression the program is system-centered. This confirmation is further strengthened by the statement in Item 2 (B) (6) that the children are "moving in and out of learning centers according to a schedule" set up by BRL. The schedule does not rely, in any respect, upon the child's preference of learning activities or modalities, nor even upon any teacher's perceptions of the needs of particular children.

1.3 Instructional Materials

The contract says that BRL will provide "individualized instructional materials"; yet *all* of the children in the school are using BRL programed reading and mathematics materials. Although the children are placed at various locations within the BRL continuum for reading and mathematics, every child progresses through exactly the same sequence of programed frames. There is nothing individual about subjecting *all* 800 children to the *same* materials, even though the materials are assigned at different times and at different intervals of time.

Our staff members in three different visitations have yet to find situations in which there is a differentiation in seatwork. In most cases, at some time during a sixty-minute instructional period, every child in the room worked on the same seatwork sheets regardless of which of the three instructional groups he was assigned to.

"Individualized instructional materials" is probably a misnomer except in those few cases in which a teacher has prepared an instructional procedure specifically to meet the need of a particular child. To individualize materials, the teacher must diagnose the student's needs and, then, select and prescribe materials that will most adequately meet that need. This is not occurring with any noticeable frequency at Banneker; in fact, some teachers commented that they are so regimented in the procedures and materials they are required to use that they cannot do the individualizing that they were already competent to do prior to the beginning of the project.

1.4 Improving Staff Quality

Various items in the contract clearly indicate the importance of staff development to this project. Item 2 (A) (2) refers to workshops for teachers. Item 2 (A) (4) indicates the topics to be dealt with in the staff training and development program. Item 2 (A) (7) provides for "intensive preservice training" for the staff which, I presume, refers to training to have been given last summer. Items 2 (A) (9) mentions a "yearly calendar of activities. . .including staff development." Item 2 (B) (3) again refers to "intensive staff development and in-service training."

It is, unfortunately, impossible for me to offer any assessment of the quality or content of these staff development activities. I cannot even testify as to whether the promised sessions have been held. I have been informed that the "calendar of activities" still has *not* been prepared. Beyond this, BRL and the School City of Gary have demonstrated a strange reluctance to provide information about these activities. Four requests for this information have been ignored.

Whatever skills or insights the staff may have acquired, the BRL project does not appear to afford much opportunity to use professional skills. Instructional decision-making is restricted to the BRL staff members. The teachers are little more than technicians applying the instructional formulas mandated by the Center Manager and the BRL consultants. The project appears to operate from a profound distrust of the competencies of the Banneker staff.

1.5. Community Information Program

On paper the community information program promised by the contract looks impressive. The same problem attains here as in the previous item; BRL and the School City have been willing to talk in general, somewhat vague, terms about the community information activities; but no documentation has been provided our office.

2.0. Additional Observations

2.1. *Regimentation* – It would seem to me that one hallmark of a truly individualized instructional program is flexibility, so that the program may be readily adjusted to changes in needs and perceptions and to differentials in student progress. In contrast to this, regimentation of both students and teachers is one of the most noticeable features of the Banneker program. The sixty minute instructional periods are neatly divided into three segments, exactly twenty minutes in length. The teachers observe these precise limits with diligence, and the children move to their next assigned learning area each hour with almost machine-like precision. As observed earlier, teachers rarely make significant educational decisions in the Banneker program.

2.2. *Paucity of Options* – Individualizing instruction would seem to call for providing a vast array of options in instructional materials, strategies, and media. Our staff members all remarked surprise at the serious lack of such options in the Banneker program. Not only does this lack of options pertain to teacher behaviors, but also the children are similarly locked in by the program. Materials are limited. Learning and teaching behaviors are rigidly prescribed. And exploratory time seems lacking.

2.3. *Loss of the Human Touch* – The Banneker staff members should be commended for the persistence of their concern for the children as children. The system, however, works against this concern. The teachers and aides see too many children for too short a time each day to develop the kinds of warm, supportive relationships that elementary school children need with significant adults.

Also, the teachers profess that the demands of the system militate against their developing or making use of enriching activities which have generally brought elements of humanity to elementary classrooms.

2.4. *A Question about Pupil Personnel Services* – As noted in my January report, our investigations have not uncovered satisfactory evidence that effective pupil personnel services are being provided for the students of Banneker School. As of mid-January, no referral of a student had been fully processed. It seems strange that in four months there would be no need for such referrals for a student body of 800 in a disadvantaged area.

3.0 Conclusion

The information I have presented in this report clearly establishes that:

(1) The Banneker program is *not* a well-rounded instructional program.

(2) BRL has *not* succeeded in fulfilling a sizeable number of its contractual obligations.

(3) The Banneker program is *not* what the contract purports it to be.

(4) There is nothing uniquely innovative about the Banneker program except (a) the abdication of professional responsibility on the part of the School City of Gary and (b) the placement of the primary emphasis upon building and maintaining a systems model instead of upon the children and their needs and interests. □

John Hand, Indiana Asistant Superintendent of Instructional Services, had been instructed to investigate specifically those violations of state laws and regulations that might have occurred at Banneker. However, much of what he had seen in the school had disturbed him sufficiently that at the January meeting of the General Commission he remarked on the poor quality of the program. Subsequent to that remark, he addressed this report to the general commission to clarify his views. Hand continued to observe the Banneker program into the next year, and over time moderated most of his criticisms as the program changed and matured. As of February 1971, however, this was probably the most candid observation anyone had reported about Banneker.

III

PERFORMANCE CONTRACTING

by Richard D. Wells

"The current fad of 'whipping' the public school system has led many private-for-profit corporations to use slick public relations campaigns in an effort to give credibility to 'get-rich-quick schemes.' "

The Indiana State Board of Education desires innovative and experimental efforts in the public school system. Instructional methods and materials should be continually upgraded and revised.

The current fad of "whipping" the public school system has led many private-for-profit corporations to use slick public relations campaigns in an effort to give credibility to "get-rich-quick" schemes. A careful and thoughtful analysis of these schemes indicates parents, taxpayers, and students should remember the warning "let the buyer beware".

In Indiana, the Gary Public Schools have contracted with the Behavioral Research Laboratories of California for performance contracting. The State Board of Education welcomes new ideas; however, the "new ideas" must provide quality education and economy. Laws or rules or regulations which stifle advances should be amended. Under the same considerations, honesty, real performance, and full evaluation are necessities of consideration of both old and new ideas. The State Board has the responsibility to oversee all essential aspects of educational performance with no considerations to emotional public relations.

Gary school officials have failed to publicly release the many reports and items of information issued by the State Board. I am, therefore, issuing this brief summary of the criticisms relative to

---

Contents of this memorandum were widely reported in the Indiana press in the early part of 1971.

Banneker School. Additional information may be obtained upon written request.

Most performance contracts begin with elaborate preparation. A school board specifies the board's purposes, standards, funds available, constraints, and preferences for entering, evaluating, and terminating the contract. Specifications are published, competitive bids are sought and received, and the contract is awarded to the most qualified bidder. The Board of School Trustees for the Gary Schools has done none of these things. No competitive bids were sought or received. Only one contractor was considered.

Because of the irregularity of the procedure and specific provisions of the contract, the Indiana State Board of Education last summer advised the Superintendent of the Gary Schools to defer action until a thorough investigation and evaluation of the proposed contract could be made.

The Gary school board and superintendent rejected the advice and entered into a contract with the Behavioral Research Laboratories (BRL) which gave BRL control of Banneker Elementary School.

From September 1970 through February 1971, numerous visits to Banneker School were made by members of the State Board of Education and by staff members of the Office of the State Superintendent of Public Instruction (OSPI).

The OSPI staff reported to the State Board in December, January, and again in February. The State Board recommended the de-comissioning of Banneker School because satisfactory explanations had not been offered in the following areas:

Textbooks – The Commission on Textbook Adoption has a liberal policy on granting permission for using experimental materials that are not on the State-adopted list. No permission was sought for the use of experimental materials at Banneker School until February 17, 1971, five and one-half months after the beginning of the program.

Pupil/teacher ratio – The commission held by Banneker School requires a pupil-teacher ratio of no greater than 30 to 1 in grades one through three and no greater than 34 to 1 in grades four through six. Banneker School submitted figures which show an overall pupil-teacher ratio for the school of 38.2 to 1.

Administration – The laws established by the Commission on

Teacher Training and Licensing require that schools must be administered by a person licensed in the State of Indiana for this purpose. The Center Manager operating the program is not eligible for such license.

Budget – The budgets of the School City of Gary on file with State Board of Tax Commissioners for the calendar years of 1970 and 1971 do not show required appropriations for this project nor for paying any consultant or contractual fees to BRL.

Accounting Procedures –

(1) The State Board of Accounts had never been consulted concerning proper contractual procedure or accounting and bookkeeping operations in regard to this project.

(2) The agreement between BRL and the School City does not say when the refund for non-achievers will be made.

(3) The discrepancy between the available revenue of $673.86 per pupil, indicated in the 1971 budget of the School City, and $800.00 per pupil to be paid to BRL has not been satisfactorily explained. This results in money being taken from other Gary elementary schools to support BRL.

(4) The contract provides for BRL to pay for water, fuel, and insurance. As of January 1, 1971, in violation of the contract, no charges had been made for these items.

(5) There is no charge to BRL for rent or depreciation for the use of Banneker School and no such charges are stipulated in the contract. In effect, the Gary taxpayers are providing rent-free facilities to a private-for-profit corporation.

(6) BRL is being paid for the 800 students enrolled as of October 30, 1970. The enrollment has since declined by approximately 45 students, yet there is no provision in the contract to adjust payments in accord with enrollment fluctuations. Estimates of per pupil costs for Indiana schools are based on ADA, but BRL is being paid for enrolled students. This will result in BRL receiving approximately $36,000 for students no longer at Banneker School.

(7) Financial records for Banneker School indicate, through mid-February, an overdraft of $215,762.60 to BRL for Survey and Consultant Fees.

(8) The agreement was entered into on September 22, 1970, but was made retroactive to July 1, 1970.

Curriculum – From the beginning of the school year to mid-January, adequate instructional time was provided only in the areas of reading and mathematics. Social studies and science were not taught. Examination of the library showed that use of the library had measurably decreased during the BRL project. Because of the pressure of repeated warnings from the OSPI, all required subjects are now being taught, but only after a lag of four months.

Profits for BRL are based solely on achievement in reading and mathematics. No other achievement is measured or considered. All public schools could show enormous increases in just two areas of teaching if all other areas are excluded. If science, social studies, music, and art have any cultural values as courses of study, consideration must be given to these areas.

Special Education – From September through mid-January, special education services were not available to Banneker children. This lack was repeatedly called to the attention of Gary school authorities. Since mid-January, once again because of pressure from the State Board of Education, this deficiency has been corrected.

Unqualified Teachers – In January, six teachers were identified as lacking proper teaching licenses. One of the six could not qualify for a license and has been transferred out of the program. The other five now hold limited certificates. □

Superintendent Wells spearheaded the attack on Banneker. He left office March 15, 1971 after he lost his bid for re-election during the Banneker controversy. Under his administration, the school had been "decommissioned"– that is, dropped from the rolls of officially recognized and state financed institutions. A week after this memo, at his final state board meeting, the school was recommissioned. Despite the crusading tone of much of this memo, it remains an excellent summary of Banneker's troubles with the state of Indiana.

IV

PLANNING FOR DEVELOPMENT, May-September, 1971

by Brian Fitch

"WE ALL NEED TO SHARE OUR IDEAS AND TO WORK TOGETHER! Our goal must be to provide an increasingly better program for each learner."

Attached is a description of the kinds of steps which should be taken to improve the program at Banneker. What I have written reflects your statements about the program, what I have observed, and where I think we can go from where we are now.

Please feel free to criticize constructively and to make suggestions. The attached paper is very general. We will get much more specific in committee meetings as we work together to plan our development program. WE ALL NEED TO SHARE OUR IDEAS AND TO WORK TOGETHER! Our goal must be to provide an increasingly better program for each learner and to make it easier for teachers to manage that program.

Sections "I" and "II" are especially important. I'm looking forward to your comments and reactions.

Introduction

The performance contract at Banneker is nearing the completion of its first year of operation. A number of accomplishments of considerable educational value have been achieved; foremost among these are the nongraded curriculum, a differentiated staffing pattern, and the first crucial steps toward individualized instruction.

However, no program of the scope intended for Banneker can be complete after one year of operation. Rather, a substantial amount of developmental activity must be initiated now to

---

Reprinted with permission of Behavioral Research Laboratories, Palo Alto, California.

capitalize on the good start already made. Without such a development effort, much of the knowledge gained from the past year will be lost because it will not be organized in a manner useful to instructional and managerial personnel.

The activities proposed in this document will consolidate what has been learned during the 1970-71 school year. In addition, crucial steps will be taken to ensure smooth operation during 1971-72 and to make it both possible and desirable to replicate the Banneker program in other schools in Gary.

Plans for Development: May-September, 1971

The activities discussed below will lead to needed development in four main areas:

I. Improved scheduling and class assignments for instructional personnel and learners.

   Goal. To facilitate pupil movement through the learning continuum and to capitalize on the expertise of classroom managers.

II. Organization of materials and learning activities into Curriculum Management Guides (for Language Arts, Mathematics, Social Studies, Science, Enrichment).

   Goal. To enable classroom managers to prescribe the appropriate activities for every learner, on a continuous basis.

III. Staff development programs for curriculum managers, learning supervisors, and administrators.

   Goal. To present improved techniques of classroom management and to become familiar with these techniques before using them in the classroom.

IV. A management information system.

   Goal. To optimize the allocation of resources (time, effort, dollars) to the individual learner.

Work in each of these areas will result in written documents that can be used by instructional and managerial personnel.

I. Scheduling and Class Assignments

Creating a schedule which is flexible enough both to accommodate a program of individualized instruction *and* to honor teacher preferences for class assignments is a difficult task. Progress is being made, however, and soon it will be possible to make assignments for next year.

In a program of individualized instruction, it is very important that pupils be able to progress at their own speed. Naturally, some will move ahead faster than others. Our job is to make sure that pupils can move from level to level when they are ready. At the same time, we have to be sure that the range in a given classroom (for example, the number of books) does not get too large for the manager to handle. Therefore, what we need to do is establish levels. As a pupil completes a level (for example, four books in Sullivan Reading and related activities) he should move on to the next level and a new manager. There must be enough sections at each level so that classes don't get overcrowded as pupils transfer into the level.

Most of the staff indicated that they would like to have just one or two subject assignments for next year. It would also be nice if managers taught two sections at the same level. That is, a manager who teaches a section of Language Arts in the morning at a given level could teach that same level to another section in the afternoon. Such an arrangement would facilitate preparation activities and help the manager to become a real expert at the level to which he or she was assigned.

II. Curriculum Management Guides

Once managers have been assigned to levels, it will be possible to talk to each manager in detail about the kind of development work to be done this summer. Basically, this work will involve putting together Curriculum Management Guides for each level of each of the five subject areas. Whenever possible, managers will be assigned to develop the Guide for the level they will be teaching next year.

What exactly is a Curriculum Management Guide? We've all seen guides before but the kind we need is different because our program is individualized. Let's consider an example of what we need to do in an individualized program.

Let's take any pupil and call him "Bobby". Bobby has been

tested and placed at a level that we know he can handle. He is assigned to a manager who teaches that level. What do we do with him then? Given Bobby's placement in the program and knowledge of how far he has gone in the level, the manager should be able to open the Curriculum Management Guide and say, ". . .hmmm. . . This is how far Bobby has gone, and here are the materials and activities that he should do next." In other words, the manager uses the Curriculum Management Guide to locate the appropriate materials and pages and then to prescribe or assign Bobby's next learning activity.

How do we get to having Curriculum Management Guides from the point where we are now? A lot has been done this year to provide materials and activities to supplement the basic curriculum in each of the five subject areas. What we need to do next is to pull all that has been done together into a logical sequence and write it down in the Guides in a form that managers will be able to use next year.

To do this, consultants should be called in between now and July 1. They will write and organize objectives to provide a continuum in each subject area. For example, in Language Arts the consultants will show us the sequence in which to present the programmed texts, spelling, handwriting, etc., to the learner. By July 1, the continuums in each subject will be completed. Then we go to work!

Given a continuum in each subject, managers will begin to specify and develop the learning activities at each level. These activities will be written down in the Curriculum Management Guides so that they can be used next year. By the time we are done, we will have guides that tell us what to do and when for each level of each subject.

One more word about using the Curriculum Management Guides to prescribe for individual learners. What's so good about prescribing? The point is that no two learners are at exactly the same place at the same time, even when classes are grouped according to learning levels like ours are. Therefore, in order to meet the needs of the individual learner, we must enable him to move ahead at his own speed. That is why we need to prescribe for each individual. If there are thirty children in one classroom, it is difficult for the teacher to prescribe for all thirty unless the materials are organized so that she can. But if the materials are organized, as they will be in the Curriculum Management Guides, the manager will know exactly what to prescribe because it is spelled out in the Guides.

III. Staff Development Programs

The total individualization of instruction calls for new tasks to be performed by the school staff. Managers and administrators work together to perform the tasks required to provide each learner with the opportunity to maximize his learning potential.

The staff training program, initiated before school starts and continued throughout the year, provides staff with an opportunity to "get it all together". Managers must have an opportunity to become familiar with the Curriculum Management Guides and to write their first prescriptions. A training program will be written to show managers how to use the Guides to manage the activities of their learners.

In addition to managing the curriculum, staff must control the behavior of the learners assigned to them. Much of the learners' behavior is controlled by adhering to the classroom management cycle. That is, the learner is placed initially at a point in the learning continuum where he can function. His needs are diagnosed and the manager prescribes the appropriate learning activities. Because records are kept of his performance, the manager knows when to provide special assistance and therefore much of the frustration often experienced in school is avoided.

However, some learners need extra help to become acclimated to school and the behavior expected of them. A system of positive reinforcement should be devised which gives managers the option to provide a positive consequence (reward) when the learner performs as desired. In these situations, the learner typically is given an assignment and performed as the manager expects him to, his behavior is reinforced by letting him do something that he wants to do. This reinforcing activity can and probably should be directly related to school life. The learner can spend time with books, records, animals, plants and other activities which he finds enjoyable and which supplement his learning activity. As the learner is acclimated to school and what is expected of him, the duration of his assignments increases and reinforcement may be administered more intermittently. In this way, his school behavior is improved by positively reinforcing him for doing what he is expected to do.

Consultants will be used to help devise a reinforcement system which can be integrated with the classroom management cycle at Banneker. In addition, staff will be trained in the use of positive social reinforcement. By learning how to verbally reinforce individuals and groups for desired behavior, managers and supervisors acquire a powerful tool for maintaining the kind of behavior desired in the classroom.

IV. Management Information System

A management information system will be developed to provide a means for coordinating the vast amount of information needed to operate a program of individualized instruction. Central files will be kept on pupil performance and progress. These files are referred to by administrators to acquire the information they need to support the classroom management operation and to facilitate pupil placement and transfer. In addition, a materials inventory is maintained so that the vast amount of material needed in a program of individualized instruction will be available at the right time. A program budget will be prepared so that resources can be allocated according to program objectives and learners' needs. □

After the first and problem-ridden year at Banneker, BRL chose to change its project director. BRL hired Brian Fitch, a young instructional systems developer. Fitch changed the tone of the rhetoric about the program and, following the guidelines set forward in this memo to the staff, created in the second year of the project a more complex and sophisticated instructional system at Banneker. By the middle of the second year, spokesmen for the district, the company and the State Department of Public Instruction expressed greater hope for the ability of BRL to achieve its initial promises.

V

SCHOOL CITY OF GARY REPORTS SUCCESS AT BANNEKER ELEMENTARY SCHOOL

by Gordon L. McAndrew

"During the first year at Banneker, 72.5%, or 396 of 546 children in the program in grades 2 through 6, made average or better than average gains in reading, mathematics or both. . .As encouraging as the first year's results are, no definitive conclusions will be drawn at this time. Up to now, much effort has gone into organizing this new program and making improvements."

The School City of Gary, Indiana, today reported success in its first annual review of the Banneker Elementary School, which last year became the first public school in the nation to be operated by an educational service company under a contract whereby the cost to the taxpayers depends on the children's progress.

During the first year at Banneker, 72.5%, or 396 of 546 children in the program in grades 2 through 6, made average or better than average gains in reading, mathematics or both. Thirty-two per cent, or 176 students made one and one-half year's gain or more. In addition, 90%, or 72 of 80 kindergarten children in the program scored at or above national academic "readiness" norms, indicating the likelihood of their future success in school.

The review was based on studies by the school system, parents, faculty and administrators; an independent evaluation by the Center for Urban Redevelopment in Education (CURE); an outside audit by Price Waterhouse and Company and appraisals by educators and observers such as the Rand Corporation and the Office of Economic Opportunity.

Under the four-year contract, the company, Behavioral

Press release in the fall of 1971.

Research Laboratories (BRL) of Palo Alto, California, and New York, is attempting to bring the achievement levels of Banneker students up to or above national norms in all basic curriculum areas, with early emphasis on the fundamental skills of reading and mathematics.

Today's announcement indicated that, based on at least one measure, standardized achievement tests, marked progress had been made toward this goal.

"Banneker was the next to lowest achieving elementary school in Gary prior to this new program in September, 1970," said Dr. Gordon L. McAndrew, Superintendent of Schools, at a briefing in Gary's School Service Center.

"Seventy-five percent of the school's graduates were below grade level in reading and mathematics. Given the present rate of gain in the new program at Banneker, that statistic will be reversed and children now in the primary grades will graduate from Banneker performing at or above grade level.

Last school year, student performance was measured in terms of gains between October 1 and June 1 administrations of the Metropolitan Achievement Tests. The 546 students measured in Grades 2-6 in the Banneker program averaged nine and one-half months growth in reading and mathematics combined during the eight months between the two tests.

Kindergarten students were tested at the end of the year on the Metropolitan Readiness Test, an indicator of the child's kindergarten preparation and his likelihood to succeed in first grade work. Seventy-two of eighty students, or 90% of those in the program scored "A", "B", or "C" (superior, high normal, or average). National norms for this test indicate that only 69% of all children in the nation do this well. The average achievement level of 91 first grade students in the project was 1.7, reflecting time that was devoted to teaching readiness skills during the first two months of the school year.

Eighteen students who entered Banneker last fall averaging 6.9 in both reading and math ended the year averaging 8.4 in both.

"As encouraging as the first year's results are, no definitive conclusions will be drawn at this time," Dr. McAndrew said. "Up to now much effort has gone into organizing this new program and making improvements. The second year at Banneker began this month, and we are optimistic that future results will be even better than those obtained so far. Final evaluation of the program will be made at the conclusion of the project in 1974."

Following an audit by the accounting firm of Price Waterhouse and Company, which also certified the accuracy of the CURE report, the amount payable to BRL for the first year of the program was determined to be $662,982.08, out of a potential maximum of $737,671.20.

Price Waterhouse reported that the average cost per student to the Gary schools was $830 for Banneker, almost $100 per child, or 10% less than the $924 spent on each student city-wide last year. Gary's school costs have been rising by 10% per year despite a fixed income.

Dr. George H. Stern, President of BRL, said today, "The program's first year's results demonstrate enormous effort by teachers, parents, students, administrators and all others in Gary concerned with the welfare of the public schools. We have never worked with a more dedicated and responsible group of educators. We all still have a lot more work to do. But considering the kind of energy everyone is putting into the Banneker program, nothing but success is possible." Dr. Stern also said that BRL would earn a profit in the project.

As part of the C.U.R.E. evaluation, parents' reactions to the program were surveyed. Eighty-seven per cent of the parents felt that the Banneker program should be continued. Seventy-nine per cent thought their children had made greater improvement this year than last year in reading; eighty-four per cent, in mathematics. In addition, 76 to 81% of the parents said that their children had made good progress this year in social studies, science, art and music.

Seventy-one per cent of the parents noted that their children read more at home and seventy-nine per cent indicated that their children talked more about school. Seventy-eight per cent said that their children liked school more.

C.U.R.E. interviewed each staff member at the school and reported that both "curriculum managers" and "learning supervisors"—teachers and paraprofessionals—at Banneker expressed a unanimous desire to continue the program into the next school year and wanted to return to Banneker.

The Banneker program was initiated last year by the Superintendent and Board of School Trustees. Then Board President,

Dr. Alfonso D. Holliday, II, stated that "the basic educational reason for this contract is the gross underachievement of our children. We are at rock bottom and must try new approaches. We must be willing to be pioneers and no longer say our children can't learn."

Dr. Holliday said that the Board decided to sign the unique $2.6 million contract with BRL because it couldn't continue to present an increase in educational costs to the public in view of the fact that three out of every four sixth graders were achieving below grade level.

"With education costs rising every year, our projected budget this year (1970-71) is for $61 million. Under our arrangement with Behavioral Research Laboratories, Banneker will not cost us any more than we are presently spending," Dr. Holliday had explained. □

VI

THE BANNEKER CONTRACTED CURRICULUM CENTER

by The American Federation of Teachers

"The figure of 72.5%, when it reached the press wires, was, of course, striking. It was also a calculated deception. . .Only about one-third of the sixth grades at Banneker achieved satisfactory gains."

What Was the Real Comparative Cost to Gary?

Behavioral Research Laboratories, a private Palo Alto-based firm, was awarded a four-year performance contract in 1970 to take over the operation of Banneker Elementary School, Gary, Indiana. In the original proposal submitted to the Board of Trustees and Dr. McAndrew, BRL stated, "The basic premise of the Contracted Curriculum Center is that striking improvement can be made at no increase in cost. Therefore, the total annual charge per pupil under this contract will be $800, the average amount now spent per inner-city pupil in Gary, including special funding." (June 1, 1970). Under the guarantee clause, if *all* sixth-graders made satisfactory gains, the company would be paid $640,000 for 800 students.

By September 1971 these estimates had changed radically. In late September, the Gary school board announced a payment of $662,982.08 to BRL for its first-year operations. This was the total payment despite the fact that *only about one-third* of the sixth graders at Banneker achieved satisfactory gains.

How as this payment determined? The payment was computed on the basis of $924.40 (the board's figure for average per-pupil expenditures in Gary, 1970-71, grades 1-12), multiplied by the 798 enrollment at Banneker, and minus a penalty of $74,689.12. (See table.)

Press release by the American Federation of Teachers on November 5, 1971.

The penalty was charged against BRL because 88 of 131 sixth-grade students *did not* achieve at least month-for-month advancement in reading and mathematics guaranteed by BRL. First, however, "non-instructional" costs for clerical and custodial expenses were deducted from the $924.40, leaving an "instructional-costs" figure of $848.74. This was multiplied by 88 to determine the penalty.

After these computations, the balance due BRL was $662,982.08. When divided by 798 students, the per-pupil cost to Gary was only $830.80, compared to the $924.40 citywide average. Gary Supt. Gordon McAndrew boasted, "This was almost $100 per child less."

Most school authorities can document that the average per-pupil costs in elementary schools are from 10-22 percent less than the grade 1-12 average costs. Gary school officials have not released to the public a breakdown on the difference between elementary and citywide costs claiming such details are not maintained by their finance officers. *But the American Federation of Teachers has obtained a copy of a letter from a school official to George Stern, President of BRL (the private contractor) that reveals the real elementary per-pupil costs are at least 20 percent less than the average for grades 1-12.* In short, the Board of Trustees and Superintendent McAndrew knowingly wrote the contract with BRL to maximize the company's profits and/or minimize potential loss.

Thus, *even granting that per-pupil costs increased by 16 percent at Banneker,* the increase reported by the school board for citywide per-pupil costs over the previous year, (from $796[1] to $924) computation of the elementary-school/citywide costs differential of 20 percent shows a significant over-payment to BRL. Such a computation indicates that the real per-pupil cost at Banneker in 1970-72 would have been approximately $765.00. If we use the same formula for determining the penalty against the company, we find that the payment would have been $689.87 per student, not $830.80, or a difference of $141. *Had the board of education and Superintendent McAndrew demanded that BRL be paid on the basis of elementary per-pupil costs, the citizens of Gary would have saved $112,462.14.* (See Table.)

Thus, the McAndrew-BRL claim that "improved performance has been achieved *at no additional cost* to the Gary schools" is not valid. The validity of the first part of the claim—"improved performance", must be judged after the reader examines the following analysis prepared by Dr. Bhaerman and Sandra Irons.

Gross Inconsistencies in Testing Data

In addition to the very questionable circumstances which surround the financial matter, the data encompassing the testing issue is equally troubling. Gross inconsistencies are evident at practically every turn of the page of the report prepared by the Center for Urban Redevelopment in Education (CURE), Inc.

Utilizing the same data on pages 46 through 74 of the report and utilizing the same criteria of "satisfactory gain" (indicated by "a more than month-to-month gain"), major inconsistencies appear on the summary charts for reading achievement (p. 12) and for mathematics achievement (p. 13). In the case of reading achievement, *20 fewer total cases* of satisfactory gain in reading result from the analysis made by the AFT (173 rather than 193) and *44 fewer total cases* of satisfactory gain in mathematics result from the AFT analysis (317 rather than 361 shown in the CURE report.)

The comparative figures are as follows:

		Satisfactory Gain CURE Analysis	Satisfactory Gain AFT Analysis
Reading—	Grade 2	23	22
	Grade 3	15	11
	Grade 4	62	58
	Grade 5	46	39
	Grade 6	47	43
	Total	193	173
Mathematics—	Grade 2	50	43
	Grade 3	59	48
	Grade 4	87	86
	Grade 5	73	66
	Grade 6	92	74
	Total	361	317

Time and again our analyses disclosed total figures of pupils at various grade levels and total figures of pupils at various achievement levels which were not consistent with the data presented in the CURE report. The Gary School City must make certain that these inconsistencies are clarified. Both the school administrators and the CURE researchers must be made "accountable" for the clarification of their data and how their various "totals" were arrived at. How they "used" this data is a separate matter!

Even more troubling – and significant – inconsistencies are evident in the testing data of the Price Waterhouse audit. Using two data bases for the analysis of "at least month-for-month advancement in reading and mathematics for the fiscal school year 1970-1971" (1.0 and 0.9 months of growth, with the latter figure giving the school system the "benefit of the doubt") there is simply no clear resulting way in which the figure of "88" sixth-grade students was arrived at: 98 perhaps or 94 maybe, but the figure "88" again raises the question of "accountability" for those involved. They must be held accountable for their statistical manipulations.

Finally, the figure of 72.5% "average or better gain in reading, mathematics, or both" (as presented in the press release of 9/24/71 is an outright deception. It is a case of administrative statistic juggling and a neat public relations job on top of it. While perhaps 6 out of 10 students appear to make this gain in mathematics, only 4 out of 10 appear to make it in reading. The figure of 72.5%, when it reached the press wires, was, of course, striking. It was also a calculated deception. □

American Federation of Teachers,
AFL-CIO
1012 14th St. N.W.
Washington, D.C. 20005

Robert D. Bhaerman
Director
Educational Research

John H. Oliver
Director
Collective Bargaining Services

---

[1]The current per-pupil expenditures, grades 1-12, reported by Gary for 1969-70, Dept. of Public Instruction, *Report of Statistical Information,* Part I, Section E-1, p. 5.

Chapter Four

INTERNAL PERFORMANCE CONTRACTS

I. Performance Contracting–Yes
Myron R. Blee
(An argument for internal contracting rather than contracting with private corporations.)

II. Performance Contracting . . . Proceed with Caution
Jerry D. Reynolds
(Internal Performance Contracting in Keokuk, Iowa)

III. Performance Contracting in *Cherry Creek!?*
James A. Mecklenburger, John A. Wilson
(External and internal contracts in the same school district.)

I

PERFORMANCE CONTRACTING–YES

by Myron R. Blee

"Performance contracting, first by forcing school boards to clarify their expectations of the school, and then, by freeing teachers to seek to attain those objectives through procedures deemed by them to be most promising, offers promise for improving the relationship between a school board and its teachers; and the students should be the beneficiaries."

The concept of 'performance contracting' when applied to the relationship between the teachers of a school system and their school board, offers a basis for the improvement of that relationship and of professional practice as well.

While the use of performance contracts for the purchase by public school boards of teaching services from private enterprise appears to be prompted by dissatisfaction with the results being obtained by the public schools, the concept itself has great promise for use *within the school system.*

The concept involves:

(1) Defining the objectives to be achieved through the teaching/learning process.

(2) Fixing responsibility for attaining those objectives and

(3) Assessing the results of teaching in order to determine the extent to which the desired results have been achieved.

This statement argues the pro's of casting those functions in the context of performance contracting for use in differentiating the respective roles of school boards and their professional staffs.

Teachers ought not to determine the basic objectives to be

Reprinted with permission by the author and the *Florida Schools* magazine, January-February, 1971, an official publication of the State of Florida Department of Education.

sought through the public schools. The need to make such determination consistent with the value systems of the people in a free society is the very reason which prompted the "invention" of school boards. The use of performance contracts requires that a school board face that responsibility, make the necessary decisions and then be accountable to its constituency for defining the basic goals of the school.

Professionals Needed

Similarly, school boards ought not to determine the professional procedures to be employed in order to achieve the goals for which the schools are operated. Such determinations relative to the teaching/learning process require the teacher's professional expertise; and the reliance upon demonstrable results that is required in performance contracting permits the teacher great freedom in structuring the learning environment so long as the agreed-upon objectives are being obtained.

Under conditions required for the effective use of the performance contract, both the school board and the teacher can know what the expectations for the schools are. Knowing that, the school board can wait for evidence to indicate the extent to which the schools are meeting those expectations. Likewise, when the teacher knows what objectives he is expected to meet, he is free to structure the teaching/learning process in such ways as, in his professional judgment, are most likely to yield the results for which he is to be held accountable.

The teacher should expect and the school board should require that the assessment of results of the learning process be subject to an independent audit in order to safeguard the interests of both parties.

Responsibilities Are Clear

For teachers, the use of the concept of performance contracting defines more precisely what is expected of him. It places squarely upon his shoulders the responsibility for obtaining measurable results, and it gives the teacher the opportunity to display evidence of the outcomes of the teaching process. Moreover, the conditions required for the use of the performance contract should be expected to afford the teacher freedom for determining what teaching methods and what teaching styles he will employ.

For the school board, the use of the concept of performance contracting means that it must make determinations in operational terms that define the results expected of the schools. While a lay school board must look to its professional staff for recommendations concerning the outcomes to be expected of the schools, the school board itself must shoulder the responsibility for making those determinations.

Likewise, it means that the school board must be prepared to make its judgments concerning the effectiveness of the teaching/learning procedures employed by their professional staffs on the basis of evidence that demonstrates the extent to which the objectives have been achieved—rather than upon conjecture relative to goals that are not clearly and mutually agreed to by both parties.

Were the ambiguities in the responsibilities which appear to exist between a school board and its professional staff to be found in a contractual relationship between a board and a private firm, it is doubtful that the interests of either party could be protected. With such ambiguities removed under an effective performance contract both the teacher and the board are protected.

Moreover, performance contracting concepts, utilized within the school system, should help eliminate the very dissatisfactions that appear to have prompted the development of the concept for use in purchasing services from outside contractors.

Performance contracting, first by forcing school boards to clarify their expectations of the school, and then, by freeing teachers to seek to attain those objectives through procedures deemed by them to be most promising, offers promise for improving the relationship between a school board and its teachers; and the students should be the beneficiaries. □

Dr. Blee is Executive Director of Associated Consultants in Education, Inc. in Tallahassee.

II

PERFORMANCE CONTRACTING . . . PROCEED WITH CAUTION

by Jerry D. Reynolds

"The factor of performance for all concerned provided the needed motivation to make the project succeed."

Performance contracting is another promise for education to guarantee more return (output) for the time and dollars (input) invested in instruction . . . a yet unproven innovation in which private corporations and teachers will be paid according to their ability, as assessed by pre- and post-standardized tests, to improve specified skills of a given group of students. Thus far, the several programs in operation have been geared to improving reading and mathematical skills of students who are performing substantially below grade level.

Because of the qualified success of the program operated this past year at Texarkana, Arkansas, under a Title VIII grant from the Office of Education, the Office of Economic Opportunity (OEO) has decided to expand the program to eighteen school districts, with six firms working with over 15,000 children in a five-million-dollar, one-year experiment. Government officials and the six firms involved are optimistic about the revolutionary changes that could evolve from these experiments. Many educators, and reading specialists are more cautious: educational contractors, incentives, and learning machines do not assure the realization of the goal, as articulated by formore U. S. Commissioner of Education James E. Allen, Jr., "that by the end of the 1970s . . . no one shall be leaving our schools without the skill and the desire necessary to read to the full limits of his capability."

The purpose of this writer is neither to support nor to find fault with the performance contracting-accountability concept. He would rather share his experience in which one Iowa school district has tried to help some of its students improve their reading performance by selecting those aspects of this program which were considered desirable and could be adapted effectively to the local school system.

In an effort to determine early last spring whether the Keokuk Community School District should seriously consider such a venture, we applied for and received Title I funding to evaluate the performance contracting concept such as that found in the Texarkana, Arkansas, schools and to launch a pilot summer reading project that incorporated some of the desirable features found in our evaluation of the Texarkana program.

Five of us flew to Texarkana in May, where we spent several days observing the project in operation, visiting with supervisory and teaching personnel, and studying the materials and machines used in the reading instruction. Our group was representative of different perspectives—Janet Hayes, a seventh-grade reading teacher; Mary Olson, a fourth-grade teacher; Velma Anderson, an active PTA worker who recently launched a Paperback Read-In program in several of our elementary schools; Bruck Meeks, a junior high principal; and I. Although we had some serious reservations about certain parts of their experiment, we decided that many aspects of the program could be adapted to our pilot summer reading project in Keokuk. Based upon the results of our project, we could then decide whether to incorporate particular approaches to reading within our regular school program in the future.

The Texarkana project is a Dropout Prevention Program: help the child to succeed and, thus, to stay in school by improving his math and reading skills. The gains made by the students from October to May were impressive, particularly in light of several factors. The program did not begin until well after the opening of school in the fall. The target group of about 360 students had poor attendance records, were achieving at least two years or more below grade level as measured by the Iowa Tests of Basic Skills, and were diagnosed as potential dropouts. In its first year the Project Staff was understaffed—six teachers (instructional managers) and six paraprofessionals; the project director for Dorsett, the company selected from a group of ten companies to operate, staff, and equip the Rapid Learning Centers on a guaranteed performance basis; the project director for the school system, Martin Filogamo, a former elementary school principal; one qualified reading teacher; and twenty local teachers who served as consultants to help in making the transition when the program is fully implemented within the entire system. Students were admitted to the program if their I.Q. was 75 or higher (the average I.Q. score was approximately 84 for the entire group).

In spite of these factors that would tend to limit performance, after sixty hours of instruction in reading, the students had grown, on the average, 2.2 grade levels; and after a comparable number of hours of study in math skills, the group had progressed 1.4 grade levels. Eighty hours is about one semester of the school year. Typically in the past the dropout rate for these students was about 12 per cent, but under this program the rate dropped to 1 per cent. Although two-thirds of the students were counselled into this program and the other one-third were volunteers, there was a waiting list in March of several hundred students who wanted to enter the program when space was available.

The "contingency management concept," commonly known as incentives, is another feature of the Texarkana program. Extrinsic motivation is not new by any means, but giving students Green Stamps, transistor radios, "free" time to listen to records and to read paperbacks and magazines for their achievement based on periodic tests is another factor that produces motivation. What happens when the motivation of the candy is removed was best answered by Project Director Filogamo: "When all of it is said and done, the kid is still basically motivated by a desire to improve . . . personal achievement is the true incentive." This explains why the tangible incentives fall off in their appeal soon after the student begins to experience the success of his own efforts.

With more funds being poured into the one-year experiment in eighteen school districts, OEO will have to refine its assessment procedures to separate the actual or permanent factors accounting for the achievement from those Hawthorne effects that often produce immediate gains but which for various reasons are not sustained over a period of time. In the original letter of intent, the Dorsett Company and the school agreed to the clause specifying that the target students would be retested at a time six months following completion of the program. However, later this important clause was dropped because of the many problems in administering it. The effect of this clause would have determined the degree of retention of skills supposedly acquired through the program. Final payment of the contract would have been predicated, in part, upon this clause. What is achieved immediately upon completion of an intensive program like this one may be far different from what is actually *retained* six months or longer beyond the completion date.

How some of these techniques could be adapted to our summer project was our first concern when we returned to Keokuk. We decided to employ one of our own reading teachers to handle the instruction because we believe that diagnosis should be an on-going part of such a program, with a qualified reading diagnostician to handle these duties. At Texarkana, however, none of the six project teachers had any formal training in reading other than several weeks of inservice study at the beginning of the project. Qualified diagnosis with follow-through remedial or corrective work was practically nonexistent in their program. By selecting one of our experienced and qualified reading teachers who has a master's degree in reading, we would have a qualified reading instructor who could provide competent and on-going diagnosis for the students. Janet Hayes, a reading teacher in our junior high school and also a member of the group that visited Texarkana, was selected as the key teacher for the project.

It was decided that the target group would be comprised of sixty students who had just completed the sixth or seventh grade, who have an I.Q. of 90 or higher,, and who were reading one or more years below their grade level as determined by the Iowa Tests of Basic Skills, the Stanford Reading Test, or the Diagnostic Reading Test. Having no pattern to follow for writing a performance contract, we had to develop an agreement that would fit our purposes.

Since our summer school program lasts for six weeks, the contract specified that the teacher would instruct each of the sixty students a maximum of thirty days (comparable to six weeks of instruction during the regular school year) and a minimum of twenty-two class hours in a reading improvement program, and that the total number of instruction hours of the entire project not exceed 180 hours. These specifications were to help us later in assessing the correlation between achievement and hours of instruction.

Most of our students had taken the Iowa Tests of Basic Skills each year and it had been used as one of the basic instruments for the selection of students for this program. Therefore, another instrument was selected as the pre- and posttest to determine the degree of growth for each student during the instructional period. The Nelson Reading Test was chosen because of its reliability and its broad norming sample by percentiles and grade level scores.

The following table was developed to determine the amount of pay based upon each student's total gain in reading, with the stipulation that no payment be made for any student making less than two months of growth. Since this was an experimental program, it was agreed that the teacher be guaranteed a salary of $600. She could earn, however, a maximum of $1,500 if the test scores reflected a high degree of growth. Normally a teacher working a comparable number of hours in our summer program would earn from $750 to $900. Thus, the project teacher could earn $150 less and up to $600 more than she would normally earn under the traditional program. As it turned out, she earned several hundred dollars more under this contract than she would have under our regular summer school contract.

Total Gain Per Student	*Amount Paid Per Student*
0-1 month	no pay
2 months	$12.00
3 months	$15.00
4 months	$17.00
5 months	$19.00
6 months	$21.00
7 months	$23.00
8 months	$25.00
9 months	$27.00
10 months	$28.00
11 months	$29.00
12 months	$30.00

For gains of more than twelve months, one dollar was added to the $30 for each additional month of growth.

The teacher was also permitted to hire aides to assist in the non-teaching duties of the project; the aides were paid by the school district, the total cost not exceeding $300. The instructor also developed a modified performance contract for the aide, a recent high school graduate. She received a basic hourly rate plus 10 per cent of what the teacher earned above $600.

A relatively small amount of money—$75—was allocated to the student incentive concept that was built into the project. These incentives included paperbacks and candy given to students as rewards for their achievement on such items as comprehension checks, attendance, weekly progress, and vocabulary growth. At the end of the course, ten students were paid $1–$10 for the best gains in reading.

A large amount of the Title funds was also allocated for the purchase of instructional materials which would then be available for use by the school district upon the completion of the project.

One can see that no attempt was made to incorporate all aspects of the Texarkana program to insure performance or accountability. We did, however, include performance contracting with both teacher and aide, and we provided tangible incentives for students to work up to their full potential. The major thrust of the program was individualizing the instruction which permitted students to learn at their own rate. For example, upon arriving at the lab each day, the student picked up his own file folder which contained his progress sheets and outlined his assignment for that fifty-minute period. This assignment was based upon a periodic diagnosis of his progress and deficiencies. Although we had no contract with an outside corporation and we used no teaching machines, we did have a wide diversity of materials and activities: shadowscopes, programmed materials, skill builders, controlled readers and pacers, SRA Labs, Springboards, Phonics Rummy and other reading games, current magazines, and hundreds of paperbacks. Students who missed class because of vacations or illness were able to make up those days since the program was tailored to each child rather than to the entire group. Conducting this type of project in the summer proved to be tough competition with the host of camps, swimming and music lessons, and general summer vacation plans. That the attendance held up well could be attributed to the individualized approach, the variety of materials, the incentive concept, and the enthusiastic attitude of the teacher and the aide. The factor of performance for all concerned provided the needed motivation to make the project succeed.

Some of the results of the program:

*During the six-week period, gains in total reading scores as determined by the Nelson Reading Test ranged from 0 to 30 months. The average gains for the sixty students were seven months in vocabulary, seven months in comprehension, and seven months for the total score. Whether these gains are sustained will be determined by resting the students during the school year.

*At the beginning of the program, Test A showed that thirteen students were at or above grade level on total score and forty-seven were below grade level. On Test B, thirty-four students scored at or above grade level and twenty-six scored below grade level.

*Through the open lab which allowed students to make up absences or to extend their study by working beyond the end of their class, about forty students took advantage of the opportunity to work more than an hour on some days.

*The results of a questionnaire administered to the students at the end of the course revealed that twenty-seven students felt they had made much progress in reading, twenty-seven indicated some progress, and one saw no progress.

*Students also indicated they liked the incentive concept: forty-four favored it, seven said it made no difference, and three did not like the idea of incentives ("bribes" as one student labelled them).

*The results of the questionnaire also showed that many students changed their attitude toward reading during the course. Ten who had a negative attitude at the beginning of the course developed a positive attitude. Twenty-two who had been neutral in their feelings became positive. Two who had been negative now had no particular feeling toward reading. Three who were neutral at the first developed a negative attitude by the end.

Overall, the program was considered fairly successful and the average class gains were good. Since it ran for only six weeks and there was no control group to ascertain the effects of the incentive concept, the results of this program cannot be reliably compared with those of other programs. What the staff has learned, however, through this experiment should provide a more reliable basis for determining whether our schools should consider implementing aspects of this concept within the regular school program or limiting its application to our summer school remedial reading program. In either case, such a program could be improved in several ways—reducing class size, screening students more carefully for selection, tightening the controls on attendance, diversifying the techniques and materials in the teaching of reading, allowing more time for thorough diagnosis, and altering the performance contract to provide greater incentives for the instructor and aide.

Some of these same factors are recommended by authorities in the teaching of reading as means to improve any reading program. Regardless of the variety of methods, materials, and approaches employed in the teaching of reading, much of the research has generally shown that the single most important factor contributing to the success of a reading program is the *teacher*—the trained and experienced teacher who is open to new designs in reading instruction and one who is willing to implement these approaches in his reading lab.

Does a school need a private industry, with its managers, machines, and software, to come in and handle the program defined by the specifications of the contract between them and the local school? Or should the school use its own professional teaching personnel in more effective ways by giving them not only more opportunities to experiment with new methods and materials but greater pay incentives with built-in accountability features that protect the taxpayer, the teacher, and the child? After all, even though education is becoming computerized and occasionally imitates the jargon of corporate management, educators and taxpayers must remember that schools are working with human resources—students—and that the standards of performance for them should not be patterned after those of DuPont or General Motors. It is for this reason that although the concept of performance contracting—accountability may have promise in revolutionizing American education, the entire venture must be approached with caution. One of the challenges that have faced American education for years—helping every child "to read to the full limits of his capability"—can be met if we are careful to temper our high degree of commitment with a commensurate degree of caution and deliberation. □

Jerry D. Reynolds is Coordinator, English Language Arts of the Keokuk Secondary Schools in Keokuk, Iowa.

III

PERFORMANCE CONTRACTING IN *CHERRY CREEK*!?

by James A. Mecklenburger and John A. Wilson

The Cherry Creek School District has justified the premise that performance contracting does have a place—the place is within the school district, using the district standards and objectives and by the district personnel.

STEREOTYPE: Performance contracts occur in inner-city and depressed areas; they bring knowledge-industry businesses, with the profit motive at their heels, to salvage disadvantaged children; advocates of contracting believe schools and teachers are mossbacked, hamstrung, ineffective, and in need of salvation by contract; critics condemn contracts as the Devil's own instrument.

It is all too easy to believe the stereotype, to think that a few programs highly publicized during 1970-71 represent the whole of performance contracting in education. Cherry Creek's involvement puts the lie to the stereotype.

Cherry Creek is attractive metropolitan Denver suburbia. Clean. White. Solvent. Its schools are mentioned in the same breath with Newton, Berkeley, Nova, and Winnetka. It prides itself on devoted, energetic, innovative teachers. To many, Cherry Creek's name is synonymous with differentiated staffing. A recent study[1] praised its five-year planning design that brought and kept dozens of school innovations. Last year 10,000 visitors tramped through Cherry Creek's schools. "Cherry Creek is unique. I look to Cherry Creek for guidance, for what they're doing," Don Richardson of the Colorado Education Association told us. "The staff they've put together are really educational leaders. Cherry Creek is a unique bunch of teachers doing their thing, given the latitude, the freedom, and the atmosphere to do so."

Cherry Creek had two performance contracts in 1970-1971; there will be three this year; more are likely.

One contract last year approached the stereotype. It did not originate with Cherry Creek but with the state of Colorado, which hastily determined, late in August, that Colorado should experiment immediately with performance contracting. Having started so late that competitive bidding was impossible, the state chose the contractor, Dorsett Educational Systems of Norman, Oklahoma. Dorsett, recovering from wounds suffered in Texarkana,[2] was anxious to recoup its reputation. In whirlwind fashion, atypical for Cherry Creek but necessitated by circumstances, an experimental program was designed which included three Denver-area districts. Contracts were negotiated, staff hired and trained, an outside evaluator secured; Rapid Learning Centers were constructed, carpeted, and furnished; children entered early in November.

"A traditional performance contract set-up," one school board member called it. That is, a goal was set to improve student reading performance; students were pre-tested, taught, and post-tested; the contractor was paid for gains in student performance. Dorsett promised one year's gain for a child in reading after no more than 80 hours of instruction, and was paid $60 per student for success, nothing for failure. Each student worked one hour daily in the learning center, interacting with teaching machines and other programmed materials. A teacher and aide, as well as managing the center, helped any student having difficulty or requiring assistance.

Despite its similarity to other performance contracts, this one rapidly acquired a Cherry Creek personality. Since Colorado wished to experiment with performance contracting for disadvantaged students, the first draft of the contract called, in each community, for 100 students two or more years below grade level; few could be found in Cherry Creek. Only a few more could be found 1.5 years below. The final contract stipulated that students must be only one year behind national norms; that is, most of the Cherry Creek youngsters began near national norms. And most were capable students. Joseph Akiyama, the Cherry Creek teacher managing the project, remarked that in Dorsett's Texarkana program students generally completed one or two teaching-machine programs daily, whereas in Cherry Creek students completed three or four. (Of course one can argue that these students were still "disadvantaged," relatively, because in Cherry Creek the national norm is below the district average.)

No Green Stamps, no transistor radios, no trinkets were used as rewards to students, as Dorsett used them in Texarkana. According to Akiyama, that kind of motivation would not be effective with his population of junior high students. One area of the learning center was furnished with lounge chairs where students who completed a chunk of work could choose to relax or read or chat. "It's like our coffee break," Akiyama explained.

To guard against "teaching the test," which gave Dorsett a black eye in Texarkana, the three school districts each selected the test to be used; then the outside evaluator supervised the administration of the tests and both inside and outside evaluators kept a watchful eye.

Students we met in the learning center liked the program. However, some 15% either left of their own accord or were asked to leave, during the year, for reasons such as misbehavior, boredom, or "dissonance" with programmed instruction.

When Colorado determined to experiment with performance contracting, several communities, including the city of Denver, refused to participate. According to Cherry Creek Superintendent Edward Pino, Cherry Creek was intrigued for three reasons:

"Notwithstanding the quality of our program, we do have unmet needs. They may not be as severe or they may be of a different type from those in depressed areas, but they're there. That's the first reason. Second, performance contracting provides new ways of looking at unmet needs for children—which may be one of the lasting benefits, nationwide, of the whole movement. Third, I think it's going to be a vehicle for bringing about faster innovative practice."

Conversation with Mary East, a school board member, uncovered a fourth reason. Such programs appeal to many parents, which in turn appeals to the school board. Particularly the well-organized, conservative element that comprises perhaps 20% of the district can "feel in this program a specific thing they can get their hands on and know after a period of time that something concrete will take place." Cherry Creek school leaders are sensitive to the community. Such programs as Dorsett's, Mary East stressed, "do not lend themselves to many areas that Cherry Creek puts stress on, fine arts and these things." But in areas that can be so handled, she feels the board would "very much" favor expanding this program and entering into others.

In actual fact, accepting the Dorsett program required some compromise with both the spirit and the management scheme of the Cherry Creek schools. Normally, decision making is highly decentralized. Each school is required to have a five-year plan for itself, which it updates annually. Each school has considerable autonomy in matters of curriculum, instructional strategies, staff development, and more.

"The identification of the need to do something in reading, and the proposal to do something of the type we are now doing with Dorsett, was part of their plan," said Pino of the two schools now housing Dorsett learning centers. "But the decision was reached because I glommed onto some state funds that help support the first year of the program." Even at Cherry Creek, purity of intention can be compromised for budget reasons. Pino readily dismisses the popular belief that Cherry Creek is a wealthy district. "Every school district in America is bankrupt. Every state department. It's just the degree of bankruptcy." Cherry Creek does spend more per student annually than other districts in Colorado, but many ordinary districts elsewhere spend more.

The independence of individual schools in Cherry Creek makes for a district of incredible diversity. Also, it encourages each school to draw upon the resources of its own community. More and more, schools actively solicit the participation of parents and community leaders, encouraging them to sit on advisory committees, planning committees, and evaluation committees, along with the staff, administration, and students. The decision-making procedure in Cherry Creek is complex, time-consuming, and frustrating.

As suggested earlier, Cherry Creek attracts teachers who value their freedom. Such criticism as we hard about the Dorsett program from teachers centered around their dissatisfaction at a decision delivered from on high. Many who respect the superintendent nevertheless fear a streak of impatience in him, of which the Dorsett decision became an example. However, most reachers in Cherry Creek seem quite unperturbed by performance contracting in their midst.

When we visited in May, the faculty of one of the schools had just voted to discontinue the Dorsett program in favor of their own reading program. And that decision will be honored. The Dorsett contract called for the machines to remain with the district, however. This year Joseph Akiyama has contracted to run a similar program in one school. His contract calls for a 10% bonus if at the end of the year students reach the target achievement levels.

This shift from an outside to an internal contract is the more promising direction for performance contracting in Cherry Creek, according to Pino, although he isn't opposed to other outside contractors and can rattle off a list of outsiders with whom the district is "having dialogue." Also, some of his internal contracts may have outside subcontractors.

The only operating internal performance contract last year was an "I-Team," an interdisciplinary team effort to retain potential high school dropouts. That program continues this year and has been expanded.

This year's third contract involves an unusual approach to emotionally handicapped students. Isolated until recently from other students, these youngsters will return to regular classes accompanied by a team of adults who will give them special aid and supervision. This team has negotiated a contract with the board.

Another program, well through the planning stage and nearing approval, involves staffing an elementary school in a way that makes a team of teachers collectively responsible for specified goals. The second year of that program would include performance contracts with staff. Another proposal nearing approval will place the principal of one school on a performance contract. There are other notions "still pretty much in the idea stage" in vocational and physical education.

Last year the I-Team project served 50 high school students identified as probable dropouts. (This year 80 such students are involved.) There were three team teachers, an instructional aide, a secretary, two interns from a local college, and the director, who serves as team leader.

Rewards to the contractor (in this case the I-Team faculty), as in all performance contracts, are based on results. Unlike the Dorsett program and most other performance contracts, however, the performance criteria for the I-Team are complex. For example, whereas Dorsett was paid for success in meeting one criterion – reading gains on a standardized test – I-Team members received an end-of-year bonus if the group of students reach 80% or better on several distinct criteria. These criteria include not only several kinds of student test gains but also measures of attitude change, attendance, and work experience. Outside evaluators determine whether the criteria are met.

Students placed with the I-Team are "educationally handicapped"; they have difficulty coping with the traditional school setting. They have been "discipline problems" in high school, absent more than present, and hostile to both school and teachers. Lyle Johnson, the project director, believes that least half of the I-Team students would have dropped out of school had it not been for the project. But only two girls and one boy dropped out. This year's graduates are either working, are in vocational training, or are entering college.

I-Team faculty received their bonus last June. Their accomplishment was the product of a year of extensive counseling, of relating the curriculum to the community, of a strongly individualized approach to instruction, and of a very personalized approach to kids. A "learning laboratory" was used for reading and math, since most students, in the words of the final evaluation, were "exceptionally deficient in the basic skills." (Average improvement was 2.0 years in reading, 3.3 years in math.) The regular high school schedule of classes was adapted to the program, but heavy emphasis was placed on the community as classroom. I-Team not only had a bus assigned to it, but also could subcontract with community businesses and individuals for mini-courses. field experiences, service activities, and individual tutoring. Also, most of the students gained work experience.

Johnson finds significance in the I-Team's location in a cottage five miles from the high school. The separate location, away from the school where these students had had difficulties, helped the I-Team to be a new start, a new chance for kids.

Not only were all criteria met last year, but there were other benefits. Don Brown of the University of Northern Colorado, one of the evaluators, wrote in his interim report, "[I believe] that a good indication of behavioral change is to be found in the absence of behavior which marked the first days of the I-Team project. Thievery, violence, and disrespect which were common during the first month or so have virtually disappeared. The students take pride in protecting the property and facility."

The I-Team is partially supported by a Title III grant. One of its purposes, therefore, was to take maladjusted students, adjust them, and feed them back into the high school. But as Johnson said, "We're discovering over here that once the students have found out the alternative route, and it's a success to them and a joy, they don't want to go back where failure was before." Last year only two students elected to go back.

It is too early to assess the impact of the I-Team on the rest of Cherry Creek. Some high school faculty envy the advantages enjoyed by the I-Team – its student-teacher ratio, consultants, the bus to which it has access. Curiously, after two years of the I-Team, the high school faculty is "looking at" similar groupings into interdisciplinary teams within the high school. Johnson won't claim credit for the coincidence, but it is easy to suspect that the I-Team's exemplary success with the most difficult students must have had some effect on the rest of the faculty's thinking.

The outside evaluators judged the program "a notable example for other special programs to emulate," "overwhelmingly successful," and "richly deserving" of regional and national attention. Concerning performance contracting, they offer these comments:

> A fifth recommendation is the extension of the bonus pay feature of the project for at least another year. The Cherry Creek School District has justified the premise that "performance contracting" does have a place – the place is within the school district, by the district standards and objectives and by the district personnel. The district personnel from the top (Board of Education) on down has been enthusiastic about helping students learn and adjust and [become] dedicated enough . . . to fulfill this task, and thus made the I-Team Project a successful "performance contracting" part of their total educational program. This feature which provides incentive pay to *teachers within the district* (not to commercial educational entrepreneurs) would seem to have merit. Each of the involved staff members noted some concern relative to his effectiveness in achieving his bonus. No ill effects have been noted so far. This recommendation is for increasing the number of staff members who might receive such a bonus; specifically, the two interns, the secretary, and the director.

Those who ride herd on this decentralized school district –

the board, the superintendent, and his small administrative staff – speak the language of management. The question always bubbling beneath the surface of their decisions and their conversation is, How can the district's resources be best employed for students? Leon Lessinger's term, "educational engineering," would provoke no fear or hostility here. "Middle-level management" is as likely to trip off a tongue as "principal." "Management by objectives" is the keynote. Pino speaks of the district as "doing business for kids."

In thinking about how best to spend district funds, Pino, Mary East, and other district leaders chafe at some of the restraints upon them. They find performance contracts appealing for their ability to challenge some of these restraints.

For example, we asked Mary East the significance of paying bonuses to teachers in the I-Team. "I think it probably is a test area where we can find different variables, different methods of compensating those who work, rather than find ourselves trapped in the traditional pay pattern. . . . We're trying to find other alternatives that would reward people for doing excellent jobs." She is talking, of course, about that perennial bugaboo of teachers, merit pay.

"Performance contracts are a form of merit pay," admits Pino, "but the two probably shouldn't be identified with each other because of the connotations of 'merit,' plus the fact that a person would draw a misconception of how it works. It is saying, on the basis of performance criteria, now objectified (lack of criteria has always been the reason for objecting to merit pay): 'Here is a new way to provide bonus arrangements on a fairly objective basis.' "

Pino disparages as "Mickey Mouse" the legal problems in "finding the proper vehicle for internal performance contracting." According to one legal interpretation, the district's master contract precludes individual contracts. Pino suggests putting teachers on leave, then contracting with them privately. This was considered for the educationally handicapped program this fall, and perhaps for the reorganized elementary school. But Pino notes that this "is no longer internal performance contracting; it is just like Dorsett competing for a job." We asked, "If the second year of the Dorsett program were opened to bidding, could staff members bid?" Pino said, "Of course. Anyone should be able to bid; but you're back to the contractual problem and, very frankly, I don't know where the solution to that is." His position here is characteristic: "We're going to go ahead and we'll just find a way!" At present, all contracts are like the I-Team's – a salary bonus if the final evaluation is satisfactory.

Ron McIntire, whose proposal it is to performance contract the elementary school, chafes at tenure. "If I've got a person here who isn't worth a damn, I can't fire that person because he's got tenure." His solution – if it is legal, and he fears it isn't – is to staff the school with teachers willing to sign a contract renouncing tenure, then to create within the school a staff review committee.

Pino speaks of his district as a leader in satisfying the "goal of accountability." And by accountability he seems to mean two things simultaneously – financial responsibility and customer satisfaction. He writes that the goal of accountability will necessitate three major changes in education: a shift in focus from teaching to learning, a developing technology of instruction based on learning objectives, and a rational relationship between costs and benefits in the system.

One might summarize performance contracting in Cherry Creek as taking small steps in these directions.

Whether the Cherry Creek contracts are good or poor arrangements is not the point of this article. The point is simply that exploration of the range of alternatives opened by the performance contracting concept has barely begun; that definitive statements, beliefs, and stereotypes about the device of performance contracting in education are premature; that if creative people have the opportunity, you ain't seen nothin' yet. □

James A. Mecklenburger is a School of Education fellow at Indiana University and research assistant at Phi Delta Kappa International, Bloomington, Ind. John A. Wilson is an administrative assistant for instruction of services, State Department of Public Instruction, Indianapolis.

---

[1]Michael Kalk and Bob L. Taylor, *Evaluation of the Operation of a Model for Planned Change in the Cherry Creek Schools, Metropolitan Denver, Colorado.* Boulder, Colo.: University of Colorado, August, 1970. Summarized in "Effective Innovation: Cherry Creek, Colorado, Shows the Way," *Nation's Schools,* April, 1971.

[2]During 1969-70, Dorsett operated a similar program in Texarkana on the Texas-Arkansas border. Gains reported were impressive, but subsequent events and evaluation revealed that students had been taught items used in the standardized test which was to determine payments to Dorsett.

Chapter Five

THE CONTRACTORS

I. My Visit to BRL
   James A. Mecklenburger
   (A visitor asks, 'what motivates this company?')

II. Private Firms in the Public Schools
   Reed Martin, Peter Briggs
   (An analysis of what motivates companies by two skeptical insiders.)

I

MY VISIT TO BRL*

by James A. Mecklenburger

"Materials teach."

While preparing a book about performance contracting, I wrote to several corporations seeking information. Dr. Allen Calvin, chairman of the board of Behavioral Research Laboratories (BRL), responded to my letter by inviting me to California. So, I went.

Aware of the "Hucksters in the Schools!" assertions that the American Federation of Teachers is making, and suspecting as I do that 'hucksterism' is a state of mind, I hoped to assess the state of mind of BRL, to grasp what makes it tick, and to learn how it sees its own role in the contemporary education turmoil.

BRL is an elder statesman among learning companies, dating back to the early sixties. Along with Linguist M. W. Sullivan (now principal stockholder in BRL), Calvin has been developing and marketing programmed instruction for a decade. The cornerstone of every product and service offered by BRL is Sullivan-developed programmed books and materials. Strong convictions about the bankruptcy of current educational practice, reinforced by years of struggling to introduce programmed instruction into the nation's classrooms, lead Calvin to believe that he and his company represent a challenge to "the system." In recent years, BRL has grown until Calvin boasts that this year 8,000,000 kids will be learning to read with Sullivan materials.

A heady feeling of having won the first round permeates the company. "In a time when other educational publishers are having a very hard time, we're busting out all over!" Calvin beamed. "Look at these!" he urged, handing me test results from BRL's

---

*James A. Mecklenburger visited BRL in October, 1971.

Philadelphia performance contract. "These are the best results anybody's ever gotten with inner-city kids. Anywhere. And the Gary results will be better!" "You know," he claims with an ear-to-ear grin, "We killed Dick and Jane."

Materials teach. This is an article of faith at BRL. *Project Read* is BRL's frontrunning product, a series of programmed texts designed on linguistic principles, coupled with teacher training and management support. Project Read has an admirable track record of improving the reading (or, at least, the achievement test scores) of thousands of inner-city kids. BRL people are proud of Project Read and disdain the use of other materials. This helps explain BRL's resistance in Gary to pressures to add other publishers' materials to Banneker School (however, this second year, other texts have been 'coordinated' with Sullivan texts). "Why should we use other people's reading materials in our projects?" Calvin asked. "Ninety percent of the other companies in performance contracting are using our materials!"

Wind Calvin or his associates up—all the BRL people I met had been public school teachers—and they tear into American education like Charles Silberman, in high gear, lambasting schools for their heartless, mindless, inefficient, hideously mismanaged character. BRL people depict public schools as prisons, designed to deny the principle that every child can learn; they are hellbent for change. When parents have a choice, says Calvin, they don't choose the typical public school for their children. As Calvin sees it, BRL is in the business of creating alternatives. "What I like about working for BRL," said one executive, "is that when BRL goes into a school, you see changes happen; kids start to learn."

Though, in Gary, many are still shaken from the headaches suffered last year, Calvin shrugs them off and regards last year as positive. The Gary contract resulted in significant gains in learning, he claims. Also, it increased the company's visibility, provided hard-won experience in operating a school, and most important, signified two new directions for BRL: BRL has moved toward warranteeing its product, and BRL has begun operating schools.

BRL is willing to sign new performance contracts, and will have several this year. These contracts have an historic character. As Philadelphia's District #4 superintendent Dr. Ruth W. Hayre expressed it, BRL's performance contract for 15,000 elementary school pupils "was the first time in the history of Philadelphia

Schools, during which millions of dollars had been spent on reading materials with various and sundry publishers (including uncounted years and dollars with 'Dick and Jane'), that any publisher indicated willingness to be accountable and to share partnership with the school staff for measurable results in reading."

More than contracting its materials, BRL has reorganized the corporation this year to begin operating schools itself. "Our school system," as Calvin calls it, includes Sullivan Reading Centers, where a parent can bring his child for reading and math instruction, Sullivan Language Schools (who espouse the goal of putting Berlitz out of business), and Sullivan Pre-Schools. Perhaps most intriguing, BRL has its own Sullivan Elementary Schools. Calvin claims BRL can operate elementary schools at a profit for less money than typical public schools. BRL's schools are staffed with highly qualified teachers, maintain a 15-1 teacher-pupil ratio, have non-graded open space classrooms, handsome facilities and the entire range of Sullivan readiness, reading, math, science and social studies materials. In these schools, teacher salaries are geared to student enrollment; that is, teachers are rewarded for parent satisfaction. No teachers are tenured. The schools will operate all 12 months; for an extra fee, they offer day care services. My visits were brief, but first impressions were favorable. Teachers I met expressed pleasure in having more professional responsibility than when they had worked in public schools. Though the schools had been open only a few weeks, most were nearly filled to capacity.

An undercurrent throughout the BRL operation is money. The people I met, whether in classrooms, reading centers or the corporate offices all speak matter-of-factly about making a profit. These are venturesome people, willing—even anxious—to prove themselves accountable in a public marketplace. For BRL, parents are the rightful arbiters of educational quality; if parents don't like the school, they don't pay, they don't send their children. "If the voucher plan is funded, we'll be in it!" Calvin asserts; he favors those European school systems in which parents can choose to send their children to public or private schools at the state's expense.

It would be unfair, from my experience, to stereotype BRL as slaves to the almighty profit-margin. However, to public educators accustomed to thinking of themselves as tireless self- sacrificing individuals, BRL's interest in profitable ventures is a point of deep suspicion. The very notion that profit-making enterprises would attempt to compete with public education jangles one's complacency.

For good or ill (and I think that is open to serious question) BRL represents the arrival of the entrepreneur in education. He has proprietary interests, he disdains the status quo and desires to compete with it, and he measures his achievement not only by standards customary to schoolmen but also in marketplace terms—in dollars, in satisfied customers, in growth. He dares to claim he will do a better job, cheaper. In his own mind, he is not a huckster—BRL, for example, has things to offer it believes are worthwhile—but almost a knight in shining armor.

Still, as interloper, he represents a new breed in the cautious realm of public education, and to the homefolk he sometimes appears brash, crass, and slick; humility is not his style, nor patience his virtue; he delights in rocking boats. Because other educators are his competition, he is quick to capitalize on their weaknesses—for example, getting better standardized test scores than the public schools can, since schools insist on using the tests.

In this age of Ralph Nader, companies such as BRL will face skeptical consumers, anxious to stereotype them as evil wolves stalking children for profit. No doubt there are temptations—as the 'teaching the test' brouhaha over Texarkana made clear.

Because, as the recent Gallup Poll of citizen attitudes toward public schools reveals, most people still regard the public schools highly, the stereotypical contest of the virtuous school versus the evil capitalist will face every learning company—hence the cry of "Hucksters in the Schools!" The burden of proof of virtue will be on BRL and its ilk. Certainly in Gary, the evidence is not yet in, and remains inconclusive (Should one place faith in a company called Behavioral Research Laboratories that does no research and has no laboratories?).

Still, in BRL's offices, one cannot miss the earnest David facing Goliath atmosphere. BRL's stones are in the sling, and one day soon, it thinks, the public school giant will tumble. □

II

PRIVATE FIRMS IN THE PUBLIC SCHOOLS

by Reed Martin and Peter Briggs

"Last year, costs were relatively low and guarantees were high. These factors represented the firms' desire to 'buy into' a project to establish their reputation, and their naivete about the persistence and magnitude of remedial education problems."

Why Performance Contracting?

You probably heard something about performance contracting in education for the first time about one year ago. The idea that private educational firms were going to attempt the instruction of public school children – particularly potential dropouts–and promised to do better than the public schools or not get paid, had gotten a little attention in the fall of 1969. Many people who had heard about the experiment considered it either a gimmick or of limited significance. But, when initial test results were released this time last year and showed potential dropouts to be achieving a growth of 2.2 grade levels in reading and 1.4 grade levels in math after only half a year of instruction, Texarkana became the Mecca of the education world, and the pilgrimages began.

Also, in the news at that time were continuing reports that our public school system was a colossal failure and nearing financial collapse. Teachers were demanding higher salaries and in some schools were going on strike. Taxpayers were voting down bond issues, and funding agencies were demanding to know what they were getting for their money. Some administrators suggested long-term funding of education, differentiated staffing, and merit pay. Students demanded relief from stifling boredom of the curriculum, while principals wanted less controversy and more order in the

---

Reprinted with permission by *Education Turnkey News,* February-March, 1971.

classroom. Whole communities of blacks and Chicanos felt the education system had so totally betrayed them that they must take things into their own hands in the form of community control of public schools or alternative community schools.

Texarkana Seemed To Make Sense

No wonder the simple little experiment in Texarkana seemed to make so much sense. The community could join teachers and administrators in setting the goals they wanted from their educational system. It avoided the battle over what inputs to make into the public schools – salary raises, stronger student discipline, classroom instruction, paraprofessional clerks, smaller class size, a new reading or math approach – and simply stated the output the community wanted from the instructional system. Their most critical problems concerned black students recently integrated from a du dual-track system who were several grades behind their white peers in reading and math. The output Texarkana desired was accelerated achievement in reading and math for deficient students.

They asked private firms to propose an approach to reach this goal and to state the costs necessary. Schools often purchased technical assistance or components of instructional systems, *but now the school would purchase an entire instructional system and a private company would run it inside the school house for a year.* A payment-only-for-performance contract gave taxpayers confidence that money would be well spent. "Turnkey" provisions assured that the firm would leave as quickly as possible, training local teachers and administrators, then turning the system over to them.

The winning bidder "guaranteed" his system would raise deficient students one grade level in reading or math for each 80 hours of instruction for $80. The age of guaranteed ecuation for $1 an hour had began. And proponents predicted that during the 1970-71 school year as much as $150 million would be spent in 75-100 projects.

What Actually Happened This Year?

The Texarkana project sought to bring a student up to grade level as quickly as possible and return him to the regular operating classroom. To do any less, particularly because many of the students in the program were black, would appear that this was merely a segregationist dodge – integrate your schools, but keep the black kids in special centers. Thus, the students who seemed to be achieving the best were the first to be tested. The results were understandably dramatic but did not really furnish a sample of what was going on in the overall project.

Before final testing occurred in Texarkana, it was discovered that on the third round of tests some students had been taught test items in the curriculum. (This was not specifically prevented by the contract; safeguards against "teaching to the test" had been considered too vague by the Office of Education and had been struck from the contract. The contractor knew what test was going to be given, and it would be a simple matter to include test items.) The result was the claim that the whole project had been contaminated and that no real evaluation would be possible.

Faced with the possibility of widespread adoption of an unproved technique, federal agencies reacted in different ways. The Office of Education decided to continue funding the Texarkana project until they had learned what there was to be learned from it. The Department of Health, Education and Welfare awarded a $300,000 sole-source contract to the Rand Corporation to study the approach and to report its value in November of 1971, unfortunately after schools would have had to decide whether to commit funds to projects for the '72-'72 school year. The Office of Economic Opportunity decided that what was needed was a national experiment that would demonstrate the costs and effectiveness that schools might expect from performance contracting.

The OEO Experiment

To evaluate the impact of performance contracting upon as many learning situations as possible, OEO included in its experiment grades 1, 2, 3, 7, 8 and 9, with white, black, Mexican-American, Puerto Rican, and Indian children. A total of 18 large and small school districts in rural as well as urban settings were selected, with 600 students per site. Six companies from 32 responding to an OEO bid were chosen to display a variety of approaches, from heavy reliance on machines to improved teacher training. Each of the six companies was matched with three school districts and contracted to raise students a minimum of one grade level in reading and math.

Other projects pushed the concept even further. Dallas, Texas contracted with two firms to meet performance specifications in vocational education and achievement motivation, as well as reading and math. The State of Virginia grouped seven predominantly rural counties together to provide enough students for an efficient experiment and also became the first project to use E.S.E.A. Title I (compensatory education) funds. In Mesa, Arizona and Stockton, California, the Classroom Teachers Association became the "contractor" rather than a profit-making company, and agreed to raise students in reading and math under the OEO nationwide experiment. Duval County, Florida (Jacksonville) contracted with a firm to teach all subjects at the first grade level. Gary, Indiana turned an entire elementary school over to a private firm, which may have extended the concept too far – State funds were cut off over the question whether school personnel had delegated policy making authority.

Funding sources were significantly increased from the original Dropout Prevention grants in Texarkana. Providence, Rhode Island; Grand Rapids, Michigan; and Texarkana used Model Cities dollars. Seven projects used Title I, and Savannah, Georgia used its initial grant under Emergency Assistance (desegregation) funds for a performance contract to accelerate remediation of deficient students.

A "knowledge" explosion also occurred. Three books were published, ranging in price from $3 to $95, and this newsletter was begun. Performance contracting was treated in at least a workshop and possibly as the major theme in virtually every education conference over the past six months. A recent bibliography listed several dozen articles that had appeared in education journals over the past year.

Compared to all this activity and the confident predictions of $150 million in projects, the actuality seems almost meager. Fifteen firms are performing under 46 contracts dealing with 42,000 students at a total cost of $9½ million. If guarantees are not met, the actual amount expended could be cut in half.

However, there will undoubtedly be more "activity" next year. Studies are underway at the Bureau of Indian Affairs considering performance contracting as a way to improve federal education of Indians and also as a vehicle to transfer responsibilities to local tribes; and at the Department of Labor, where performance contracting may serve as a stimulus to manpower development efforts under the Family Assistance Plan. Locally directed efforts are underway to use performance contracting techniques: for accelerated remedial work with deficient college students enrolled under Open Admissions plans, in junior colleges, and with veterans preparing for college level work. Firms involved in performance contracting have approached the Justice Department, which provides skill and attitudinal retraining in its prisons; and state rehabilitative institutions concerned with modifying behavior of inmates through educational strategies. There is no longer any way to make a responsible prediction of how many educationally related projects next year will use performance contracting techniques.

Consumers Have Lost the Initiative

As yet no final academic achievement measures have been reported from any performance contract project so the answer to our question, "What actually did happen this year?" cannot be given in terms of statistics on student performance. It is in terms of a trend which has unfortunate implications for public policy. The trend is that, in the absence of school personnel caring about it, business has gained the initiative in this new approach. Performance contracting offered great hope for the school/consumer of educational services to have an impact on what was offered in the education marketplace. But most of the contracts developed over the past few months have shown that hope was misplaced.

In these recent contracts, there has been no public goal-settin setting that would involve a community in a new enthusiasm for what the school system might have to offer. Even in the few contracts sought through open bids, the Request for Proposals does not stimulate the supplier of educational services to create an approach that is new and worthy of demonstration. It is safe to say that since Texarkana, no significantly new approaches have been offered by the firms. Each project now has the same old wine in new bottles. There is typically no short demonstration period in which teachers and administrators are taught how to use the approach. The trend is toward sole-source contracts initiated by companies who offer the same approaches they have offered for many years at costs determined by the companies and not in a competitive bid situation. Contracts are sometimes for three or four years and may have no obligation to turnkey the approach.

Location	Contractor	Subjects	No. Students
Anchorage, Alaska	Quality Education Development	Reading, Math	600
Dallas, Texas	Quality Education Development	Reading, Math	600
Rockland, Maine	Quality Education Development	Reading, Math	600
Athens, Georgia	Plan Education Centers	Reading, Math	600
Selmer, Tennessee	Plan Education Centers	Reading, Math	600
Wichita, Kansas	Plan Education Centers	Reading, Math	600
Bronx, New York	Learning Foundations	Reading, Math	600
Hammond, Indiana	Learning Foundations	Reading, Math	600
Jacksonville, Fla.	Learning Foundations	Reading, Math	600
Fresno, California	Westinghouse Learning Corp.	Reading, Math	600
Las Vegas, Nevada	Westinghouse Learning Corp.	Reading, Math	600
Philadelphia, Pa.	Westinghouse Learning Corp.	Reading, Math	600
Grand Rapids, Mich.	Alpha Learning Systems	Reading, Math	600
Hartford, Conn.	Alpha Learning Systems	Reading, Math	600
Taft, Texas	Alpha Learning Systems	Reading, Math	600
McComb, Mississippi	Singer/Graflex	Reading, Math	600
Portland, Maine	Singer/Graflex	Reading, Math	600
Seattle, Washington	Singer/Graflex	Reading, Math	600
Stockton, California	Classroom Teachers Assoc.	Reading, Math	600
Mesa, Arizona	Classroom Teachers Assoc.	Reading, Math	600
Buchanan Co., Va.	Learning Research Assoc.	Reading	500
Dickinson Co., Va.	Learning Research Assoc.	Reading	250
Lunenberg Co., Va.	Learning Research Assoc.	Reading	250
Mecklenburg Co., Va.	Learning Research Assoc.	Reading	250
Norfolk, Va.	Learning Research Assoc.	Reading	500
Prince Edward Co., Va.	Learning Research Assoc.	Reading	250
Wise Co., Va.	Learning Research Assoc.	Reading	500
Texarkana, Arkansas	Educational Development Labs.	Reading, Math	300
Texarkana, Arkansas	Dorsett (Turnkey Phase)	Reading, Math	250
Gilroy, California	Westinghouse Learning Corp.	Reading, Math	100
Compton, California	Reading Foundations of Amer.	Reading	3,000
Cherry Creek, Colorado	Dorsett Educational Systems	Reading	100
Denver, Colorado	Dorsett Educational Systems	Reading	100
Englewood, Colorado	Dorsett Educational Systems	Reading	100
Oakland, California	Education Solutions	Reading	400
Jacksonville, Fla.	Learning Research Assoc.	1st Grade Sub.	300
Savannah, Georgia	Learning Foundations	Reading	1,000
Gary, Indiana	Behavioral Research Labs	All Subjects	800
Boston, Mass.	Educational Solutions	Reading	400
Grand Rapids, Mich.	Westinghouse Learning Corp.	Reading, Math	400
Grand Rapids, Mich.	Comb. Motiv. Educ. Systems	Reading, Math	600
Flint, Michigan	Educational Development Labs	Reading	2,160
Philadelphia, Pa.	Behavioral Research Labs	Reading	15,000
Providence, R.I.	New Century	Reading	1,500
Greenville, S.C.	Comb. Motiv. Educ. Systems	Reading	480
Dallas, Texas	Thiokol	Voc. Ed. Motiv.	960
Dallas, Texas	New Century	Reading, Math	960

Grades	Begin	Total $	Source $	Guarantee
1-3, 7-9	September, 1970	$444,632	O.E.O.	1.0 Grade Level Gain
1-3, 7-9	September, 1970	$299,417	O.E.O.	1.0 Grade Level Gain
1-3, 7-9	September, 1970	$299,211	O.E.O.	1.0 Grade Level Gain
1-3, 7-9	September, 1970	$301,770	O.E.O.	1.0 Grade Level Gain
1-3, 7-9	September, 1970	$286,991	O.E.O.	1.0 Grade Level Gain
1-3, 7-9	September, 1970	$294,700	O.E.O.	1.0 Grade Level Gain
1-3, 7-9	September, 1970	$341,796	O.E.O.	1.0 Grade Level Gain
1-3, 7-9	September, 1970	$342,528	O.E.O.	1.0 Grade Level Gain
1-3, 7-9	September, 1970	$342,300	O.E.O.	1.0 Grade Level Gain
1-3, 7-9	September, 1970	$299,015	O.E.O.	1.0 Grade Level Gain
1-3, 7-9	September, 1970	$298,744	O.E.O.	1.0 Grade Level Gain
1-3, 7-9	September, 1970	$296,291	O.E.O.	1.0 Grade Level Gain
1-3, 7-9	September, 1970	$322,464	O.E.O.	1.0 Grade Level Gain
1-3, 7-9	September, 1970	$320,573	O.E.O.	1.0 Grade Level Gain
1-3, 7-9	September, 1970	$243,751	O.E.O.	1.0 Grade Level Gain
1-3, 7-9	September, 1970	$263,085	O.E.O.	1.0 Grade Level Gain
1-3, 7-9	September, 1970	$308,184	O.E.O.	1.0 Grade Level Gain
1-3, 7-9	September, 1970	$343,800	O.E.O.	1.0 Grade Level Gain
1-3, 7-9	November, 1970	$ 55,154	O.E.O.	1.0 Grade Level Gain
1-3, 7-9	November, 1970	$ 33,976	O.E.O.	1.0 Grade Level Gain
1-7	November, 1970	$212,500	Title I	1.7 Grade Level Gain
1-7	November, 1970	For	Title I	1.7 Grade Level Gain
1-7	November, 1970	All	Title I	1.7 Grade Level Gain
4-7	November, 1970	Seven	Title I	1.7 Grade Level Gain
4-9	November, 1970	Virginia	Title I	1.7 Grade Level Gain
4-6	November, 1970	Project	Title I	1.7 Grade Level Gain
4-9	November, 1970	Sites	Title I	1.7 Grade Level Gain
7-12	October, 1970	$ 65,788	Title VIII	1.0 Grade Level Gain
8-12	September, 1970	$	Model Cities	
2-4	September, 1970	$ 60,000	Title I	1.3 Grade Level Gain
7	1970	$120,000	Title I	Reading Speed Quintupled
6-8	1970	$ 50,000	Title I	Reading Speed Quintupled
6-8	1970	For All	Title I	Reading Speed Quintupled
6-8	1970	Three	Title I	Reading Speed Quintupled
6-8	1970	$ 80,000	Title I	Reading Speed Quintupled
1	1971	$ 70,000	Title I	Reading Speed Quintupled
	1971	$ 97,000	Emer. Assis.	
K-6	September, 1970	$640,000	Dist Funds	Above National Norm
K-6	September, 1970	$120,000	Title I	1.6 Gain
1-6	September, 1970	$143,700	Title I	1.0 Gain
6-9	September, 1970	$164,000	Title I	1.0 Gain
9	September, 1970	$210,000		
1-2, 7-8	September, 1970	$600,000		1.0 Gain
2-8	December, 1970	$145,000	Model Cities	1.2 Gain
6-9		$100,000		
9-12	September, 1970	$209,000	Title I	
9-12	September, 1970	$256,000	Title I	1.4 Gain

This is not to say that there are not private firms who have anything unique to offer to the public schools or that performance contracting is not a very good way to harness the innovative energies of the private sector for public use. It is to say, however, that the general trend is not so much toward educational reform under the initiative of the public sector as it is toward marketing and sales with the private sector setting the terms. The public may find that in the majority of cases it is simply paying a higher price for a company to put last year's product in this year's favorite package. Several firms have announced their prices will be higher under a performance contract, and one states it will sell its materials either under a regular agreement, or under a performance contract at exactly twice the price. Last year, costs were relatively low and guarantees were high. These factors represented the firms' desire to "buy into" a project to establish their reputation, and their naivete about the persistence and magnitude of remedial education problems.

Recently, one West Coast firm sought out schools to participate in a project contrasting two firms and a teacher organization. When it was suggested that it had little chance of receiving funding, the marketing representative replied that they did not care if it were funded; all they wanted was the publicity that they were willing to engage in a "horse race" and therefore they must be the best. Thus, rather than schools seeking out firms to see if they have anything to offer, firms now seek out schools for marketing stunts. Performance contracting has come a long way in only one year, and the public – the real consumer of educational services – must work hard if it is to get the initiative back.

PERFORMANCE CONTRACTING AND ACCOUNTABILITY

Most of our public institutions and professionals are under attack for their failure to render adequate services to all their clients. And the employees of these institutions are often criticized for an arrogant attitude when approached by a client. In the case of public schools, there seems to be little responsiveness to the increasing demands of the poor that schools do a better job, or to the middle class taxpayers' demand that the job not cost more each year. Accountability for both cost and results has thus become this year's central demand.

The public school system has grown into a vast bureaucracy

which tangles friend and foe in red tape. Consequently, those inside the system direct most of their attention inward and have little time to respond to outside demands. Their response to this new interest in "accountability" was a series of questions; accountable to whom, for what, and judged by what standards? To the public the answer was simple: Teachers (which comprise the majority of individuals the public contact about education) are accountable for a child's education and can be judged by how well (or how badly) a child performs.

How Can A Teacher Be Judged?

The education profession was aghast. The criteria it used to judge a teacher's worth was never student performance; it was educational background plus years of teaching experience. Similarly, criteria for the school system as a whole did not focus on educational accomplishment, but rather on the various ingredients of the system: teacher salaries; employment security; size of classes, square footage of foot space available for instruction; number of volumes in the library, etc. This fundamental difference in perception between the public and the professionals had erupted into ugly confrontations in northeastern cities in the past few years and it appeared that the desire for accountability would be another casualty. "Accountability" in 1970 was destined to become stalemated, with the public demanding public evaluation while the education profession insisted on the right to judge itself.

But private industry, through performance contracting, picked up the gauntlet. The initial performance contracts undertaken were highly "accountable": a single goal was specified; a single criteria for judging performance was agreed upon; an independent and public evaluation was undertaken; and the contractor was paid for success but received nothing for failure. Measurement presented a problem but in most cases standardized tests were used because the public felt competent to judge the results themselves – if a student begins the year at the fourth grade level of reading and ends the year at the fifth grade level, then he has had one year of growth. Professionals might insist that this may be the least important thing to know about the student, but the public feels it would know all it needed to know.

It is understandable that many educators viewed with alarm the introduction of private industry into the public schools. The initial reaction was ironic: groups that had besieged Capitol Hill demanding more federal funds, particularly in the area of research, now demanded that Congress cancel the $10.5 million being spent by OEO in performance contracting research. The long-term reaction was a demand that funds not be diverted to private companies and away from the traditional participants in the public school system.

The Turnkey Concept

This implicit competitive threat almost disappeared with the development of the "turnkey" approach. The turnkey concept is that private business is involved only if they have some unique capability to demonstrate, not just as competitors; and that the services of private business are dispensed with when the demonstration is complete, and they "turn the key" over to the public school teachers. Thus, teacher opposition to performance contracting was qualified: performance contracts planned by teachers and including the turnkey phase in which the status quo absorbed the experiment were all right. Any institutionalized competition, such as the "voucher" plan under study by OEO, would, of course, be intolerable.

After the year or so of discussion, accountability has boiled down to whether those outside the system can change the workings inside the system by contrasting performance against public standards. The various performance contract projects, in theory, seemed the best chance of testing this out. They contain agreed upon standards for measurement; they focus responsibility for performance in one place; they make the evaluation public; and there is a point – the payment or non-payment of money; the continuation or non-continuation of a contract – beyond which one advances only after successful performance. They stand in vivid contrast to a regular school system which continues from year to year with hardly a pause for evaluation.

Unfortunately, the type of performance contract projects which have been developed over the past few months do not contain this high degree of accountability. Responsibilities of contractors and regular school system personnel are blurred; contracts are for periods of years; the company is usually guaranteed to be reimbursed for its costs and possibly receive a profit even if student achievement is not increased; and there is little guarantee that evaluation will be made more public than in the regular school system.

As suggested earlier, public schools have been rendered almost non-accountable because of an internalizing focus on "professional" concerns. The one year of evolution of performance contracts indicates that business, which also has internal concerns such as profits, will follow a similar path. Unless, schools, as consumers of education suppliers, insist on accountability from business, there is apparently no magic that would guarantee greater responsiveness under a performance contract.

IS IT LEGAL?

The Texarkana experiment was never challenged on legal grounds. During this year, most performance contract projects are either federal experiments or state experiments, as in Virginia. During a year of experimentation, laws can be waived where they are found to contradict an experiment, but in most cases they simply are not raised. For example, in New York State, state and local funds could not be used for performance contracting. However, since federal funds are being used in the OEO experiment in the Bronx, the legal obstacles are not confronted. If the Bronx were to attempt to continue the experiment next year, it might be susceptible to legal attack. Thus, the general public has gotten the impression because of all of the activity during this year that there are no legal problems with performance contracting. The opposite is the case.

The most difficult problem with performance contracting is whether a public school can contract with a private agency for instruction of public school children. The first problem is the authority to contract for such a purpose, and it is not clear from an examination of state statutes and case law whether such authority exists in all cases. There is some evidence to suggest that the current state of the law in some states would prohibit a school district from contracting with a private education firm for instructional services.

Schools Cannot Delegate Policy Role

The second and more far-reaching dimension of this problem is that of delegation of policy-making functions. The local school district is delegated very specific policy duties from the state which cannot be shared with a private agency. If a private firm approaches a school district and convinces it that it should undertake an experiment using a particular approach offered by that firm, then the school district may have defaulted on its policy-making function. This appears to be the case in many performance contracts now being negotiated for next year.

For the fullest exercise of the policy-making role, a school should have a public setting of goals, an open bid before awarding a contract, and the constant ability to exercise discretion (both financial and programmatic) over the contract without simply terminating it. In other words, it must always retain control over policy matters.

The competence of the staff is a factor into which a court might inquire. Even where a contract specified that the school board was to retain total control over the operation of the program, if the competence of the school's staff was not sufficient to really be in control, then effective delegation of policy matters would occur, and the private company would be in control.

To help solve these problems, some school districts have hired an independent party called a management support group. But the same constraints apply in that situation. A school district cannot delegate to the management support group the authority to plan the program—for example, to decide the subject matter areas, the grade levels, the types of children in the experiment, the method of evaluation, etc. The management support group can work as a consultant to the school district and continually advise on all these matters, but if a court found that effective control had passed to the management support group, then a school district would be as unable to contract with that entity as it would be with a private educational firm.

Turnkey Has Legal Ramifications

The turnkey concept seems to provide an answer to the delegation problem because it assures that even if a private firm is able to wrest policy control away it must eventually surrender it. Further, turnkey affects the problem of authority to contract for it presumes an overriding interest on the part of the school in learning how to do its job better. A one or two year contract with a private firm may be an aberration and thus illegal, but with turnkey built in it appears clearer that the purpose is directly related to the constitutionally mandated provision of public instruction.

But the turnkey concept also muddies the legal waters. By its nature, it may commit a school to following the results of an experiment before results are even known. It could also produce conflicts of interest which might be impossible to reconcile. For example, a management support group monitoring the demonstration phase and also expecting to plan or monitor the turnkey phase would be unlikely to expose a contract violation which would terminate the experiment and thus jeopardize its own business for the next year. As schools contract with management support, instructional and auditing firms, they must be aware of natural and legal conflicts of interest.

It is impossible to say what would make a performance contract project legal next year. Even if the contract were "internal" (i.e. between the school board and a group of teachers) many legal constraints still apply. Depending upon the funding source, various guidelines must be followed, in some cases requiring community representatives in the planning phase. Contracts already negotiated, such as with a teacher association, may contain requirements for joint planning, and use of personnel. Federal, state, and local court decisions, laws, statutes and ordinances must all be observed. (Two projects this year ran afoul of health and fire ordinances.)

The first year of performance contracting was spared legal problems because of federal and state interests. During the second year, schools and contractors, whether companies or teacher groups, would be well advised to treat the legal problems seriously.

WHAT DOES BUSINESS BRING TO SCHOOLS?

When the year of performance contracting began, many teachers and administrators asked, "What does a private company know that it can guarantee our deficient students will learn or the company will not get paid?" A few assumed it was a trick, such as teaching students test material or selecting outstanding students for participation. Others who visited experimental sites and saw carpeted, air-conditioned rooms filled with machinery and new curricular materials concluded, "If I had those resources, I could produce the same results."

The most typical comment was, "If teachers did the same thing the companies are doing, they could produce the same results." This, of course, was the stated object of performance contracting—for an outside party to demonstrate a successful approach and then for teachers to adopt it. But the most perceptive comments were the understandably bitter analysis, "All they're doing is what we teachers have wanted to do for ten years." In order for business to demonstrate what it had to offer, school boards allowed them great flexibility. Where companies then extended that flexibility to their classroom teachers, the creativity that was tapped had been there all along, stifled by the public school system. (To be fair, one must note that some companies impose an even more inflexible program on the teachers than do the public schools).

Diagnosis and Prescription

What, then, do companies have to offer? Basically, it is a more systematic (that does not mean less humane) use of what schools already attempt to do. When one pierces the thin veneer of corporate uniqueness in these projects, one finds certain common ingredients.

First, each student is diagnosed in the subject area to be treated. The diagnosis often uses the same standardized tests used by public schools but with an analysis of what problems the student has rather than simply where he stands.

More important, the contractor has the flexibility and resources to act upon the diagnosis. This comprises the second step. prescription. The idea is for each student to have an individual course, for example in math. In a regular class, with automatic promotion policies, a student may find himself in an eighth grade math class but really still at the sixth grade level. Equally as important, he may read at the sixth grade level and be totally lost with his eighth grade math materials. As the group-paced instruction continues, the student will fall farther behind. Where there is individual diagnosis and prescription, the student will begin at his own level of competence, using materials adjusted to his reading level.

A typical performance contract project will therefore have a wider range of materials available than the regular classroom with its standard textbook. Materials are often arranged in clusters like a reference library and each student, working at his own pace, will go wherever he needs to complete his day's assignment. If the diagnosis of the student showed he learned more quickly through hearing than through seeing, the materials he uses might be on audio-visual equipment in addition to written formats. This ideal, unfortunately, is seldom attained in this year's projects. Most students end up using programmed workbooks.

Contingency Contracting

The third basic component involves motivation. Any student, placed on his own, needs a strategy to motivate him to proceed through the materials. This is doubly true of the student with a history of failure who is the subject of virtually all performance contract projects this year. The motivation strategy is simple: If the student completes an assigned task satisfactorily, he may then do something he wants to do.

This approach, developed nearly twenty years ago by educators and called contingency contracting (a student *contracts* to get a reward *contingent* upon successfully completing a task), is nothing new to public schools. A student begins with extrinsic educationally-related rewards for performing short tasks and soon moves to intrinsic motivation for lengthy tasks as he tastes his first success in school. Extensive research has validated the approach but its largest publicity occurred under performance contracting when the Texarkana contractor offered green stamps and color television sets as rewards. Obviously, the approach can be used poorly, but in several cases it is being used very well, with rewards that are educational in themselves and student attitudes toward school have been dramatically changed.

It is significant that so many performance contract companies, given the flexibility to use anything that they feel is educationally effective, choose contingency contracting.

The fourth basic component is a continual evaluation of student progress. For a student to receive a reward, he must "check out" on his assigned task. If he is unsuccessful on these interim tests, then the teacher knows not only that he is having trouble but precisely what the problem is. Armed with this system, the teacher can then approach each student individually to work on specific problems. This evaluation is, of course, in itself a diagnosis which leads to further prescription, and so forth.

Contingency contracting has been described as the glue which holds the system together so the last component is pre-service and in-service training of teachers in this approach (See *How to Use Contingency Contracting in the Classroom* by Dr. Lloyd Homme, Research Press, PO Box 3327, Country Fair Station, Champaign, Illinois for a full but simple explanation of the process.)

In answer to the question, "What does business bring to the public schools," each company will understandably argue that something unique which only it offers makes all the difference. One company has a computerized diagnostic service, another uses a special teaching machine, and yet another uses its own programmed learning materials. But what seems to be most significant is a classroom/instructional management system rather than a particular proprietary approach, with training of teachers, and, as mentioned earlier, the flexibility to follow that system. That bitter comment—all that business is doing is what we teachers have wanted to do—is very persuasive.

DOES IT WORK?

Current performance contract projects hope to report results in terms of both cost and effectiveness, as contrasted with control groups. Effectiveness will be the easiest thing to determine, despite complaints about use of standardized tests and conditions under which pre-tests were administered in some projects. Unfortunately, no achievement results are available as yet, and it may be late Fall 1971 before any are reported.

Cost figures pose a much greater problem. Many experiments do not require much in the way of cost reporting from the firm: thus the firm will tell the public its cost. In the OEO and Virginia projects, rigorous reporting has been attempted. Some of the problems encountered are getting actual figures, as opposed to what the firm wants its costs to appear to be. There may be hidden research and development costs, and a firm might be willing to take a loss on its first project but want to obscure those operational costs it considers non-recurring.

Even when accurate costs are obtained, it is difficult to compare them with school costs to see which is less, since school costs are kept and reported differently. The comparisons may reveal nothing more than different figures, especially since the firm may depreciate certain items much more rapidly than schools.

Cost and Effectiveness

It is even more difficult to try to contrast effectiveness with cost. If effectiveness is reported in tenths of a year's achievement, which some statisticians feel is cutting it too closely, and that figure is divided into cost data which is part hidden and part hypothetical, what does the public get? Will a school board really base a major decision on curricular changes on such a "cost per unit of student achievement" figure? It is likely that school boards will proclaim the virtues of cost-effectiveness during these years of taxpayer revolts but in the absence of adequate data will have to resort to other bases for their decisions.

Assuming that accurate cost and effectiveness data is developed and contrasted with comparable data for schools, and it is thus determined that the firm did a better job, what was the reason? The typical project uses: volunteer teachers (some of the school's best and most creative personnel); new materials and perhaps machinery; a new classroom environment with carpeting, air conditioning, drapes, and perhaps individual study carrels; students work at their own pace; there are incentives for students, and perhaps for teachers, to achieve; the student: adult ratio is lowered by the use of instructional aides; and the total system is operated under a managerial flexibility quite different from the regular school. So if there is a difference, what caused it? A thorough analysis will be needed to decide what components are worth turnkeying.

WHERE WILL PERFORMANCE CONTRACTING LEAD?

Businesses involved in performance contracting this year recognized that one cannot successfully separate authority and responsibility. Personnel cannot be accountable for results strongly influenced by factors over which they have no control. Therefore companies decentralized decision-making to the classroom level, or coordinated it among several classrooms. Rather than using traditional procurement procedures which take months to get new materials, or district-wide standardized curriculum, private firms placed resources and the decision to use them in the hands of the teachers and principal/project director.

In Mesa and Stockton, this model is already being attempted by teachers without the involvement of private firms. There will be legal problems as changes in curricular flexibility, student scheduling, budgeting, and others are attempted, but this managerial approach may well be the legacy of performance contracting.

Next year in Michigan, which has four performance contracts this year, selected elementary schools will receive the total budget allocated to the building for instructional materials and staff. A school-community advisory committee (including principal, staff *and parents*) will select educational goals, stated in terms of behavioral objectives. The building personnel will then decide how to meet those objectives (staffing patterns, instructional strategy, materials). Locally developed tests will supplement nationally normed instruments and ensure school effectiveness in areas thought important by the community. Measures of effectiveness will be made public.

It is likely that this coming year school personnel and communities will press for this type of institutional flexibility. Schools and teachers would then be able to be much more effective consumers of what private industry and others might have to offer through performance contracting. □

Reed Martin, editor of *Education Turnkey News,* is an attorney and former legislative aide to Senator Ralph Yarborough. He has drafted performance contracts currently in use in 27 sites and written on the public policy problems involved.

Peter Briggs is a doctoral candidate at Stanford Graduate School of Education and was a special assistant to the Associate Commissioner of Education, U.S.O.E. He planned the landmark Dallas performance contract and has managed the twenty-city OEO experiment and the statewide Virginia project now underway.

Chapter Six

TESTING AND EVALUATION

I

ACCOUNTABILITY AND PERFORMANCE CONTRACTING

by Roger T. Lennon

"Having in mind the Dorsett experience in Texarkana, I am tempted to put it that, with respect to several performance contract situations, we were the successful bidder–we did not get the contract."

PART I

The perspective that I bring to this discussion of accountability and performance contracting is one growing out of my association with an organization which proffers instructional materials and services, measuring instruments, and evaluative services. The opinions that I shall voice are not necessarily those of my colleagues, nor do they in any sense constitute a declaration of official policy of the house. They are an outgrowth of protracted discussions in which my associates and I have attempted to define how we might, as responsible publishers, act in relation to requests for "guarantees" of the performance of our materials and services, and equally protracted discussions of the measurement and evaluation problems in performance contract arrangements.

We are, in fact, providing some instructional materials and support services on a contract basis, and we are furnishing measurement instruments for use in evaluating many performance contract programs; but our experience, like everyone else's at this stage, is limited.

Having in mind the Dorsett experience in Texarkana, I am tempted to put it that, with respect to several performance contract situations, we were the successful bidder–we did not get the contract.

Reproduced with copyright permission of the *Journal of Research and Development in Education,* College of Education, University of Georgia, Volume 5, no. 1, Fall 1971, pages 1-14.

Accountability

Few terms that have come into the language of education have evoked the ready acceptance and nearly universal approbation that has attended the term "accountability." The reasons are not hard to find. Most observers credit Dr. Leon Lessinger with the earliest and most vigorous advocacy of both the concept and the term, during the time when he was serving as Deputy Commissioner in the Office of Education. In that role he witnessed the frustration felt by many members of Congress as they sought to assess the efficacy of the federal monies being expended on education, and as they sought to develop policy for educational expenditures. Legislators were distressed to learn how little could be asserted with confidence, for example, about the impact of funds expended under Title I of ESEA. Schooled in the "more bang for the buck" approach espoused in Department of Defense budgeting, they raised questions about the cost-effectiveness of various educational programs which the Office of Education and school people found very difficult to answer.

Increasingly, their concern was echoed by school boards across the country confronted with never-ending requests for additional funds, and by taxpayers beginning to wonder whether the ever-increasing expenditures were really buying more or better education for their children.

Dissatisfaction with the lack of success that attended most efforts to improve the level of achievement of inner-city and disadvantaged pupils, and the growing concern that schools be rendered more responsive to the communities which they served, particularly in the large metropolitan centers, combined to create a readiness for the proposition that school officials at every level should in some fashion be made accountable, that is, responsible for bringing about learning that could be shown to be commensurate with, or satisfactory in relation to, the resources being committed to the effort.

Educators, so the accountability message ran, habitually sought to justify requests for funds in terms of needs such as buildings, books in the libraries, books in the pupils' hands, teachers' salaries, learning equipment—in short, process variables—rather than in terms of manifest product—pupil learning of demonstrable magnitude.

Some accountability spokesmen, to be sure, grossly overstated the case that school men had not been concerned with pupil achievement. We all know better. To pretend that only under the goad of accountability would we recognize that the effectiveness of education must be sought in evidences of pupil learning is to impugn needlessly the good sense and good will of countless generations of educators.

After all, the notion that compensation of an instructor should depend on student attainment goes back at least to the time of the medieval universities. We are told that at the University of Bologna in the 15th century, student-enacted statutes required that the "professor start his lectures at the beginning of the book, cover each section sequentially, and complete the book by the end of the term;" if the professor failed to achieve the schedule, he forfeited part of funds that he himself had had to deposit at the beginning of the term!

The concern of governmental bodies that they were getting their educational dollar's worth was manifest in 1911 when the Board of Estimate of the City of New York, critical of the demands made by the Board of Education on the city's treasury, launched a comprehensive survey of the city's schools, one aspect of which was an analysis of the tested arithmetic achievement of its pupils.

The first wave of textbooks in educational measurement—those published say between 1912 and 1922 or 1923—abound with references to the utility of standardized achievement test results as indicators of the effectivenesss of schools and even of teaching efficiency. So, the notion of pupil learning as the proper criterion in the establishment of accountability is in no sense new. Accountability, we might say, is an idea whose time has come—again, or perhaps an idea whose time is always.

I do not allude to the historical concern with student outcomes in any way to minimize or disparage the importance of the current concern with accountability—quite the contrary. I think that the perennial concern with student outcomes as indices of effectiveness attests both to the validity of the notion of accountability and to the extreme difficulties that have been experienced over the years in implementing the concept. What is new about accountability as currently advocated is the realization of the necessity for relating output in some sense to input, defining input as all professional staff effort, financial resources, materials, etc., and the search for appropriate methods and systems of accomplishing this.

In any case, it is not the novelty of the concept that gives it importance; it is, as Lieberman has pointed out, its utility as a unifying theme around which may be organized a number of the most prominent concerns on the current educational scene: systems analysis, operations research, performance contracting, even the voucher system and other freedom-of-choice plans.

This umbrella aspect of the concept, by the way, accounts for the difficulty of providing any neat definition of the term accountability. It means many things to many people (a reason, perhaps, for its easy acceptance?). Yet, for establishment of accountability in any formal, systematic sense, certain common elements are discernible:

1. What are the schools to be accountable for? For student accomplishment and development—cognitive, affective, motor. This is taken to imply explicit, detailed statements of desired outcomes or goals, set forth in behavioral terms susceptible to observation or, preferably, measurement, in the absence of which statements there can be no evaluation of the enterprise.

2. Who shall be accountable? Our senses of logic and justice tell us that each person, whose task it is to influence learning—teacher, supervisor, principal, curriculum coordinator, counsellor, whoever—should be held accountable for precisely that part of the educational outcomes which he can affect directly, through his own efforts. This highly specific imputation of responsibility is, as we shall see, a requirement which, if slavishly followed, nearly gives the whole game away.

3. How shall accountability be established? Clearly there is need for an accountability information system, providing systematic information on output and input. Further, there is need for a method for relating input factors, including staff efforts, instructional materials, support systems, etc., to the outcomes in a manner—and here is the critically important point—that will permit the attribution of the outcomes in proper measure to the various input elements.

4. By whom shall accountability be determined? There is substantial feeling that, whatever a school or system may do in its own self-evaluative endeavors, independent auditors or "accounting" agencies are desirable.

By far the most comprehensive and sophisticated discussions of these elements of a formal accountability system that I have seen are contained in articles by Barro and Dyer in the December 1970 issue of the Phi Delta Kappan. Both papers manifest a very healthy awareness of the complexity of the data-gathering task and of the analytical methods that must be employed if it is to be possible to assign responsibility properly to the various contributing agents. Barro and Dyer have seen that it is extraordinarily difficult, perhaps impossible, to disentangle the several contributions of the variety of professionals to the learning of pupils. Dyer proposes that accountability always be thought of as joint accountability, by-passing, in a sense, any attempt to divide up the responsibility of various staff members and concentrating on responsibility at the school level through the creation of what he calls School Effectiveness Indexes.

Both, interestingly enough, arrive at a multiple-regression approach as the appropriate analytical scheme, seeking thereby to partition the variance in student performance according to its various sources. Both approaches, it is interesting to observe, address themselves to the simpler case of a uniform set of outcomes for all learners.

The alternative, and probably more nearly realistic case, in which desired outcomes are permitted to vary across learners, across classes, schools, and systems, is so very much more complicated as quite possibly to have seemed impossible to cope with at the present state of the art.

In fact, if I read correctly between the lines of these two presentations, I sense a small suspicion that even the models proposed may be seen by their authors as unattainable in the real world; yet, I take it that they are advocating that we must make the effort, whatever the likelihood of success—and if this is a proper interpretation of their sentiments, it accords with my own view of the matter.

Another attempt to establish accountability, somewhat in the Barro-Dyer model though less elegant and sophisticated, which has at least been pilot tested, is Project Yardstick, under the direction of Fred Pinkham in Cleveland. Yardstick provides a schema for relating test performance to several input measures. All three of these approaches, incidentall, are reminiscent of the New York State Quality Measurement Project of a decade ago, certainly the most sustained and ambitious effort of this kind. It would be instructive to know why it has not flourished.

The Performance Contract

The Barro and Dyer models, in my opinion, point the way in which serious efforts at the assessment and location of accountability must proceed in the long run. In the meantime, in a more immediate ad hoc effort to establish accountability for certain aspects of the educational program, we have the phenomenon of the performance contract.

In concept, the performance contract is simple: a school system specifies desired outcomes, defines the target group of pupils, establishes certain parameters within which education of the pupils is to take place, and enters into a contract with an agency for the provision of an educational experience that will bring the target group of pupils to the desired outcomes.

The agency typically to date, though by no means necessarily, has been a private, commercial purveyor, leading to such witless treatment in the press as headlines which cry, "Can Big Business Succeed Where Schools Have Failed?" Let us hope we may be spared this red herring in considering the merits of performance contracting; the contracting agency may perfectly well be a university, a teachers' organization, a professional society, or the like. Methods and materials are left to the discretion of the contracting agency, and it is hoped that they will bring innovative and extraordinary modes of instruction to bear. The contracting agency undertakes to bring about stipulated amounts of progress or improvement, generally but not always in a basic skill area, often agreeing to a penalty should pupils not reach the desired level, and, about equally often, stipulating that it shall have a bonus or premium for bringing the learners to a level in excess of the goal.

The contractor, in other words, undertakes to insure gains or growth in accomplishment of a stipulated amount subject to penalties in the event of failure. The outcomes of the services provided under the contract are to be audited by an independent agency whose assessment of the amounts of gain that have taken place shall form the basis, in part at least, for the payment to be made to the contractor.

In the pure-culture performance contract—the Lessinger-Blaschke model—two additional features are regarded as central. These are the functioning of a so-called Management Support Group, which offers advisory assistance to the school with respect to the development of the specifications for the contract, the location of appropriate bidders, the award of the contract, and subsequent services; and the so-called "turnkey" provision, by which is meant the explicit inclusion in the contract of arrangements that will permit the methods, materials, practices, etc., of the contractor's intervention to be incorporated in the regular operation of the school or school system and carried forward by regular personnel.

In much of the early discussion of performance contracts, there was reference to them as "guaranteed performance" arrangements, the implication being that the contractor warranted that every pupil would attain the stipulated goals. The guarantee notion seems to be less prominent lately, perhaps in grudging recognition of a still-existing law of individual differences. The talk now is of performance contracts with premium and penalty clauses. (Speaking of guarantees, do you remember how last Sunday we all anguished with our astronauts as they struggled with the recalcitrant docking device? It is reported that Mission Control called the manufacturer of the device seeking his assistance and counsel, only to be told, "We're sorry; that unit has gone more than 50,000 miles and it's not under warranty any more." One wonders for how long some of the contract learnings may be guaranteed.)

A considerable number of school administrators, habituated to the purchase of a wide variety of services, such as maintenance, transportation, food services, etc., on a performance contract basis, responded enthusiastically to the notion that instructional services might be handled on a similar basis, particularly with respect to instructional problems that had resisted previous efforts.

As Blaschke has repeatedly pointed out, the performance contract has appeal as a low-risk approach—low financial risk because of the guarantee or penalty clauses, and low political risk because failure could be imputed to the contracting agency rather than to the school system. The early favorable reports from the Texarkana project undoubtedly contributed to the eagerness of school men to explore and even to enter into such seemingly attractive arrangements.

But from the beginning there were also voices of caution, and not a few of outright opposition. Critics of the approach saw in it an abdication of professional responsibility, committing a part of the responsibility for the primary mission of the schools to non-professionals. Teacher organizations voiced particular concern on this score, in spite of assiduous efforts on the part of some of the contracting agencies to woo the support and collaboration of these groups. Some of the early advocacy of performance contracting was not without a note of hucksterism.

Albert Shanker, President of the United Federation of Teachers, denouncing performance contracting as a kind of ecucational "cure for cancer," declared that to guarantee performance in certain complex fields of human endeavor is to engage in deception. To "guarantee" to bring every child, regardless of ability, prior achievement, etc., up to the national norm seems to bespeak either a lack of awareness that the "norm" is by definition a level below which half of pupils in general achieve, or an extraordinarily, perhaps recklessly, high level of expectation. One should not begrudge a publisher or other contractor boundless confidence in his materials; but in the nature of things, not every pupil can wind up "above average."

Some publishers and other purveyors of instructional materials and support services regarded it as inappropriate for schools to seek guarantee of performance for the materials, since the purveyors had little control over the way in which materials and services were used.

The notion that textbooks or other instructional materials could be "guaranteed" to produce specified amounts of learning struck many as reflecting a serious misapprehension of the nature of the learning process and the role of the textbook—as if a textbook had a definite, uniform, predictable impact on a pupil's learning, as a drug might on his body chemistry or physiological processes.

Moreover, such research as is available on the contribution of the text or instructional materials to variance in pupil performance (as in the First-Grade Reading Study) suggests that this contribution is small—very much less than that of teacher competence, for example.

Thus, many suppliers refrained from bidding on contracts where they could not exercise major control over the total instructional system, but were merely to provide materials. Those of us with long memories in textbook publishing remember when the harsheet cirticism of the textbook was its supposed strait-jacketing or control of instruction and curriculum. Now it almost seems as if the instructional materials are to be required to display —guarantee—this monolithic impact on learning.

Other critics voiced uneasiness that the performance contracts would divert disproportionate amounts of resources to the pursuit of narrow and short-time goals, to the detriment of other objectives; some administrators felt that if the funds available for performance contracting could be channeled into their regular operations, they could accomplish as much or more as the performance contract arrangement. And some critics, lay and professional, took a dim view of the use of extrinsic motivators, such as trading stamps, radios, etc., employed, for example, in the Texarkana project.

The performance contract, as you all know, received its initial fame through the Texarkana project, and you are all aware of the melancholy fate that befell it at the end of its first year. The Office of Equal Opportunity has mounted a massive investigation of performance contracting, sponsoring performance contract programs in some 18 school districts and arranging for a comprehensive evaluation of them. Meanwhile, it is reported that some 150 school districts have entered into one or another type of performance contract, covering a variety of programs over most of the elementary and secondary grades, with a wide range of conditions and through a sizable number of purveyors.

PART II

Measurement Problems In Performance Contracting

The philosophical, political, and economic aspects of performance contracting are not my major concern tonight. They have been amply discussed in other forums, and I shall not dwell on them here, much less pass judgment on any of the issues in these areas. My mission is, rather, to invite your attention to certain of the measurement problems that inevitably arise in the conduct and, more particularly, the evaluation of a performance contract. These problems may be subsumed under familiar rubrics – validity, reliability, and unit and scalar properties of the measuring instruments.

Validity. The performance contract begins with a specification of the educational outcomes to be achieved through the contracted intervention; there is strong emphasis on the necessity for detailed enumeration of the behavioral objectives to be achieved. Under these circumstances, one would suppose that identification of appropriate instruments that would validly measure the attainment of these particular objectives would be greatly facilitated. So, indeed, it might – except for the overriding insistence that the results be expressible in units that are thought to be meaningful and comprehensible. This has eventuated, in the case of most performance contracts written to date, in a stipulation that the gains be measurable in terms comparable to "normal progress," generally defined as progress in terms of grade equivalents or, less often, age equivalents. This requirement has driven the contractors – reluctantly in some instances – to adopt one or another of the more widely used achievement series as the instrument for measuring gain, since these are the only series having dependably established normative systems yielding grade- or age-related measures. But these series are, almost in the nature of things, concerned with a much wider range of content and outcomes than the narrowly defined, more specific ones of the contract interventions, so that the fit between the goals of the intervention and the content or functions measured by the test often leaves much to be desired. A considerable part of the variance in the scores on these general achievement tests may be unrelated to the specific goals of the contract program.

There is a widespread belief among laymen (including legislators, in this context) and, for that matter, among a great many school people, that measurement of growth in reading ability can be satisfactorily accomplished through the repeated use of any of half a dozen of the better series of reading tests now available – and in a sense this is true. But everyone who is familiar with reading tests knows that the several reading tests do not correlate perfectly with one another, even within the limits of their reliabilities. The tests vary with respect to subtest composition, relative emphases on component skills, and so on; they may be equally defensible on rational grounds as samples of the reading domain, but it does not follow that each of them is equally valid or, indeed, that any one of them is valid as a measure of the particular reading objectives of a given performance contract. And as with reading, so with arithmetic and, to an even greater extent, so with the content areas of science and social studies. In a word, the nationally standardized tests on which performance contractors (or the evaluating or auditing agencies) have relied because of their credibility and their normative systems may, from a validity standpoint, be considerably less than ideal for the evaluative task.

Under the general heading of validity, I would like to dwell for a moment on the touchy issue of *teaching for the tests.* It is repeatedly suggested that the performance-contract type of arrangement, with its concentration on relatively narrow and specific goals, conduces toward instruction undesirably and narrowly focused on those behaviors that are the immediate target behaviors and which will presumbably form the basis of assessment. Since most contract situations involve a pre- and a post-test situation, almost necessarily calling for use of alternate forms of a given instrument at the beginning and the end of the program, all concerned clearly are likely to know what the character of the final assessment device will be, if not, indeed, to know precisely what its content will be. We need not be altogether cynical about human behavior to anticipate that this knowledge will condition and shape the pattern of some instruction. Such patterning may take the form of familiarization of the subjects with the actual exercises they will encounter in the final test, and we would say, ordinarily, with resulting contamination of the final test resutts and a subversion of any attempt at evaluation of gains. But the question is not quite so simple. At the early grade levels particularly, a performance-contract instructional sequence may be directed to the attainment of goals in realms where the universe of outcomes is limited. We may think, for example, of knowledge of letter names, a very early prerequisite for learning to read. The universe of outcomes consists of ability to recognize 26 lower-case letters and 26 capital letters. Here, clearly, the appropriate instruction program must consist of having the child perform precisely those behaviors that will be included on any test of his competence. The same is true of, let us say, mastery of the basic addition and subtraction facts, or of mastery of the spelling of the fifty most common words in primary reading materials. So we cannot say that any instructional practice in which a learner is exposed to precisely the tasks that he will encounter on a final assessment instrument is necessarily bad or wrong; but it is important to point out that the more specifically the desired goals are defined, and the more narrowly focused the instruction on these particular goals, and the more closely the post-test reflects and measures attainment of these goals, the more acute becomes the question of deciding what is and what is not legitimate approximation of test content and instructional content.

Reliability. On the matter of reliability, evaluation of performance contracts is particularly vulnerable to all the perennially vexing problems of the reliability of a *gain score* for an individual pupil. Even with tests having satisfactory reliability as measures of status of an individual pupil – say .90, about as high a level as is reached by most subtests in the commonly used batteries – the reliability of gain measures over relatively brief periods, say four to six or seven months (the common duration of most of the early performance contracts), is distressingly low, influenced as it is by the measurement error in both pre- and post-test scores. The error of measurement of a gain score may very easily equal or exceed the amount of gain normally to be achieved in a short-term intervention. Yet it is on the basis of these gain scores that it is proposed that contractors be rewarded or penalized. It is ironic that whereas measurement textbooks caution against taking individual decisions or actions on the basis of measures having reliabilities of .4, .5, even .6, no one thus far seems to be very excited about amking or withholding payments to a contractor on the basis of a piece of information of this degree of reliability. One recently announced contract, for a horrible example, "guarantees" individual gains of half a grade level in four months, for first-grade pupils, in social studies and science. To essay to discern, much less measure reliably, such differences in individual pupil attainment in these areas in grade 1, is really to wander in cloud-cuckoo land. (This same contract, by the way, calls for a bonus to the contractor for every child showing a significant increase in IQ. Well, why not?)

It is almost instinctive to react to this state of affairs by saying, "Well, let compensation be based on *average* gain for a group, and avoid the messy question of unreliability of individual gain scores." Such a proposal, acceptable though it might be to the contractor, is likely to be seen by the school as a cop-out – and, I feel, not without some justice. It is clearly an intent of a performance contract to foster the academic growth of *every* participating learner, and no evaluation plan will be acceptable that allows failure by a significant fraction of the group to make good gains to be offset, in calculating payment, by better-than-average gains by others. The situation can be improved but not corrected by striving for greater reliability of both initial and final measures; for example, these measures might be based on administration of two forms rather than a single form. But not only is this time-consuming and costly; it is not often the case that there are four equivalent forms of a measuring instrument available. Moreover, the increase in reliability of either initial or final status measures to be achieved by doubling the length of the test is modest, as is the reduction in the error of measurement of the gain scores from the lengthened measures. The more promising way of coping with this problem is to design projects of longer duration and not attempt to assess short-term changes, at least as a basis for compensation.

Alternate-form comparability. We have spoken of the use of alternate or equivalent forms as pre- and post-measures, and it is proper in this connection to observe that, even under the most conscientious test-building procedures, alternate forms may yield results, whether in terms of raw scores or converted scores, that are not precisely comparable. Determinations of equivalence of forms are necessarily specific to the equating sample and do not necessarily apply with equal precision to any other groups. Moreover, they involve necessarily apply with equal precision to any other groups. Moreover, they involve necessarily their own sampling and estimation errors. The degree of imprecision is, in most uses of the tests, slight enough to be tolerable, but it can become important in a context where variations in compensation may turn on such minimally perceptible differences as a month or two of grade equivalent.

Level comparability. A similar situation prevails with respect to the equivalence of converted scores across successive levels of the more commonly used achievement series. For most of these series, the test development enterprise includes the articulation of successive levels, to permit translation of raw scores on the successive levels to some common set of units. Again, even when this is done with all conscientiousness, the precision of the translations can never be fully guaranteed. Contracts of the kinds entered into thus far may appropriately involve administration of different levels of a test at the beginning and end of the program; and the imprecision of the conversions may introduce additional distortions into individual pupil gain scores.

Inter-test differences. Everyone knows, of course, that scores on standardized tests are likely to vary systematically from one test to another, as consequences of differences in their standardization groups, times at which they were standardized, varying content even in like-named tests, etc. Less well recognized is the fact that the various tests yield distributions of grade equivalents for given subjects at given grade levels that also differ systematically from one another. Test A, for example, will yield distributions of reading grade equivalents at grade 4 having larger standard deviations than Test B. The standard deviation of scores, whether raw or derived, is a function in part of the distribution of item difficulties and their intercorrelations, and is thus partly at the test-maker's discretion. Use of one or another of the available tests, accordingly, may produce different financial results for school and contractor, entirely as a consequence of this artifact and for no reason related to the effectiveness of the program provided.

The grade equivalent system. Faced with the financial consequences, to either school or contractor, of gains measured in grade equivalent terms, it is surely prudent to inquire whether the grade equivalent system is not too slender a reed to support such weighty baggage. One might have supposed that in 1970 practitioners of educational research would need no reminders of the limitations and deficiencies of grade equivalents, yet some of the practices built into performance contracts make one wonder. Grade equivalent scales are notoriously unequal-unit scales, having no zero points. They are most certainly not ratio scales. Thus, talk of "125% of normal gain," such as occurs in some performance contract language, is altogether meaningless; thus, gains of given numbers of months of grade quivalent represent accomplishments of quite different difficulty for a contractor to bring about according to the level and subject; thus, efforts to assess cost-effectiveness in any realistic sense are foredoomed, if output is measured in grade-equivalent terms.

The deficiencies of grade equivalents are particularly egregious in connection with the measurement of achievement at the secondary level. The Texarkana project, for example, sought, among other things, to raise the reading level of 9th-grade pupils by "one grade level." One has to wonder whether it was realized that a gain of one grade level, as measured by most reading tests for the secondary level, would correspond to a raw-score gain of not more than two or three points – in almost all cases well within the error of measurement of an individual score. The within-grade variance of scores on secondary achievement tests is so great in relation to the between-grades variance as to render grade equivalents altogether inappropriate. The logic underlying the development of the grade equivalent for secondary achievement tests is so irreconcilably at variance with the realities of curricular and instructional practices in secondary schools, and with the facts of student growth in academic achievement, that it is surely time for us to lay to rest this mode of interpreting – or should I say misinterpreting? – scores on secondary achievement tests.

Scarcely less unfortunate are efforts to interpret elementary achievement test performance exceeding the median performance of end-of-ninth-grade pupils by way of so-called "extrapolated grade equivalents" that purport to express performance of superior pupils in sixth, or seventh, or eighth grade as like the performance of typical 10th, or 11th, or 12th graders. Such extrapolated values are commonly identified by test publishers as artificial. Maybe it is now time to declare that their artificiality exceeds any potential utility and that they, too, should be quietly dispensed with.

And maybe the cumulative impact of all the problems enumerated above is sufficient to lead us finally to speak the unspeakable: to declare that the grade equivalent, at whatever level is an inappropriate unit for the measurement of gain of an individual pupil over relatively brief periods – say as much as a year of ordinary growth. Those of you who are familiar with the instruments that we publish, and their espousal of (though not exclusive reliance on) grade quivalent systems of interpretation, may be listening to me in wonderment and tempted to say, "Well, when did you kick the habit?" My answer to you, a little wistful perhaps, must be, "Not yet"; and please notice that my renunciation of grade equivalents is far from total. For all their limitations, they can, in my opinion, serve useful functions, particularly with respect to the assessment of progress of groups over longer periods of time. And if one asks, "Well, what better way is there, what better set of units for measuring academic gains?" we are hard put for an answer. We can point to efforts that have been made to develop continuous scales having units more nearly defensible as equal units, or to the utilization of within-grade status measures, such as percentile ranks or stanines, as bases for estimating magnitude of growth. For a variety of reasons we do not have time to go into here, these alternatives are considerably less than ideal.

The foregoing enumeration of technicalities will have seemed to many of you, I know, tedious, not to say boring; indeed, to those of you familiar with measurement, the cataloging must have seemed rudimentary. My justification for this discussion is that, in all the literature on performance contracting, I find few references to these measurement issues, and it has seemed to me worthwhile to get them into the record in a meeting such as this. The evaluation of performance contracts and the implementation of the accountability concept can ultimately be no more secure than the measurement data on which they rest; if these data are flawed by psychometric difficulties of the kinds I have suggested, we will never be in a position to assess properly the usefulness of this approach.

Criterion-referenced Tests. I must not leave you with the impression that resort to grade-equivalent interpretation in performance contracts entered into thus far means that the contracting parties have been unaware of these difficulties. Confronted with the annoying metric characteristics of norm-referenced tests, they, and others, have sometimes sought to exorcise these demons by invoking the magic phrase *criterion-referenced tests.* There is much that might be said about the adequacy of this alternative, and much of that favorable. Certainly, strong arguments can be advanced to support the proposition that criterion-referenced tests might be more valid measures of certain performance-contracted outcomes. But it is not yet altogether clear how results of a series of criterion-referenced tests can be translated into units that will yield measures of gain or growth. This is not an impossible task conceptually; perhaps Rasch-model operations can point the way. Neither is it easily accomplished, nor can it escape many of the problems that we have enumerated above with respect to norm-referenced tests. Secondly, there seems to be an easy assumption that criterion-referenced tests of respectable quality and adequate scope can be called into being reasonably easily and quickly. The truth is quite otherwise. The methodology for development of criterion-referenced tests is less well explicated than that for the development of norm-referenced tests, but it is clear, to me at least, that the production of batteries of criterion-referenced tests equal in quality and scope to the better norm-referenced tests will be no mean accomplishment – and, in the long run, I suspect, not less costly than the development of norm-referenced tests covering essentially the same domain of knowledge and skills.

As an aside, the difficulties in arriving at any satisfactory estimate of "growth" of individual pupils, especially over short periods of time, have prompted some of us to have second thoughts about the entire concept of "growth" in academic attainment. The notion of "growth" in reading or arithmetic or language skills comes easily to us by ready analogy with growth in height or weight; but we may well wonder whether the process by which a learner acquires more information in a given discipline or attains greater skill in, let us say, reading or arithmetic computation accords well with the model of growth in height or weight. We may further wonder whether tests built according to the methods used in constructing norm-referenced tests, having as their goal the maximization of individual differences, are efficient instruments for measuring this supposed growth – and we may ask ourselves how to define "normal" growth: normal for whom, under what conditions, etc. But these are speculations for another time.

Am I saying, then, that it is not possible to evaluate satisfactorily the outcomes of short-term interventions such as are called for in most performance contracts (having in mind, for the moment, only the psychometric considerations, and not other obviously relevant issues such as performance of gains, Hawthorne effects, regression phenomena, comparison with control groups, transferability of the instructional programs and skills from the contractor group to the regular staff, etc.)? That is a rather harsher judgment that I am ready to make. I believe reasonably dependable estimates of average gains, at least in reading and arithmetic, can be obtained in most of the contract situations going forward at the present time, but I do not see a satisfactory answer to the question of sufficiently reliable measurement of individual pupil gains. Neither do I discern the logic that will permit a school system to ascribe even average gains unerringly to the contractor's performance or his special type of intervention. It would be my hope that performance contracts negotiated hereafter would contemplate intervention programs of greater duration than a few months, that greater attention be paid to reliability of initial and final measures, that the selection of evaluative instruments receive far more searching attention prior to writing the contract than I think has been true heretofore, and that far more comprehensive testing for formative evaluation purposes be built into the programs – systems of continuous performance monitoring.

What of the future of performance contracting? My crystal ball is as clouded as any man's, but that does not deter me from a little forecasting. Of course, we would all be well advised, would-be contractors and interested bystanders, to await the evaluation of the OEO-sponsored performance-contract programs now in progress before venturing to look too far ahead or to risk too much. My own opinion is that, within a couple of years, performance contracting as we now know it will be seen as a rather primitive, simplistic approach to the establishment of accountability. Blaschke has reminded us that the performance contract should not be viewed as an end in itself – that it is just one way in which a local school system may experiment effectively. Perhaps, given incentives such as those made available by performance contracts, local school systems may be motivated to seek change by other arrangements.

But whatever the fate of performance contracting, it is my feeling that the notion of accountability will continue large in our thinking, and a powerful influence on the educational scene. How can it be otherwise, when as a poeple we are committing such vast sums to education? I hope that our view of accountability will be a large one, that we will not permit ourselves to worry overmuch about paralleling precisely the accountability methods available to industry. For all our insistence on bringing every child "up to standard" in reading, arithmetic, etc., we still know that this is far from the whole of schooling. We know that education, unlike a manufacturing operation, must concern itself with raw material infinitely varied, and that it seeks a product, not of unvarying sameness as does the manufacturing operation, but with its initial richness and variety enhanced and multiplied. Who of us wants it otherwise? How to translate that richness and variety into behavioral objectives, how to assess their attainment in all their richness, and how to capture it all in cost-effectiveness equations, I do not know. But I believe strongly that even modest and limited successes are greatly to be preferred to faint-hearted failure. □

Mr. Lennon is senior vice president, Harcourt Brace and Jovanovich, Inc., and president, The Psychological Corporation.

II

TESTING HAZARDS IN PERFORMANCE CONTRACTING

by Robert E. Stake

"Would that our problems withered before stern resolve. But neither wishing nor blustering rids educational testing of its errors."

In the first federally sponsored example of performance contracting for the public schools, Dorsett Educational Systems of Norman, Oklahoma, contracted to teach reading, mathematics, and study skills to over 200 poor-performance junior and senior high school students in Texarkana. Commercially available, standardized, general-achievement tests were used to measure performance gains.

Are such tests suitable for measuring specific learnings? To the person little acquainted with educational testing, it appears that performance testing is what educational tests are for. The testing specialist knows better. General achievement tests have been developed to measure correlates of learning, not learning itself.

Such tests are indirect measures of educational gains. They provide correlates of achievement rather than direct evidence of achievement. Correlation of these test scores with general learning is often high, but such scores correlate only moderately with performance on many specific educational tasks. Tests can be built to measure specific competence, but there is relatively little demand for them. Many of those tests (often called criterion-referenced tests) do a poor job of predicting later performance of either a specific or a general nature. General achievement tests predict better. The test developer's basis for improving tests has been to work toward better prediction of later performance rather than better measurement of present performance. Assessment of what

---

a student is now capable of doing is not the purpose of most standardized tests. Errors and hazards abound, especially when these general achievement tests are used for performance contracting. Many of the hazards remain even with the use of criterion-referenced tests or any other performance observation procedures.

One of the hazards in performance contracting is that many high-priority educational objectives – for various reasons and in various ways – will be cast aside while massive attention is given to other high-priority objectives. This hazard is not unrelated to testing but will not be discussed here. This article will identify the major obstacles to gathering direct evidence of performance gain on targeted objectives.

Errors of Testing

Answering a *National School Board Journal* (November, 1970) questionnaire on performance contracting, a New Jersey board member said:

> Objectives must be stated in simple, understandable terms. No jargon will do and no subjective goals can be tolerated. Neither can the nonsense about there being some mystique that prohibits objective measurement of the educational endeavor.

Would that our problems withered before stern resolve. But neither wishing nor blustering rids educational testing of its errors.

Just as the population census and the bathroom scales have their errors, educational tests have theirs. The technology and theory of testing are highly sophisticated; the sources of error are well known.[1] Looking into the psychometrist's meaning of a theory of testing, one finds a consideration of ways to analyze and label the inaccuracies in test scores. There is a mystique, but there is also simple fact: No one can eliminate test errors. Unfortunately, some errors are large enough to cause wrong decisions about individual children or school district policy.

Some educators and social critics consider the whole idea of educational testing to be a mistake.[2] Unfortunate social consequences of testing, such as the perpetuation of racial discrimination[3] and pressures to cheat,[4] continue to be discussed. But, as expected, most test specialists believe that the promise in testing outweighs these perils. They refuse responsibility for gross misuse of their instruments and findings and concentrate on reducing the errors in tests and test programs.

Some technical errors in test scores are small and tolerable. But some testing errors are intolerably large. Today's tests can, for example, measure vocabulary word-recognition skills with sufficient accuracy. They cannot, however, adequately measure listening comprehension or the ability to analyze the opposing sides of an argument.

Contemporary test technology is not refined enough to meet all the demands. In performance contracting the first demand is for assessment of performance. Tests do their job well when the performance is highly specific – when, for example, the student is to add two numbers, recognize a misspelled word, or identify the parts of a hydraulic lift. When a teacher wants to measure performances that require more demanding mental processes, such as conceptualizing a writing principle or synthesizing a political argument, performance tests give us less dependable scores.[5]

Unreached potentials. Many educators believe that the most human of human gifts – the emotions, the higher thought processes, interpersonal sensitivity, moral sense – are beyond the reach of psychometric testing. Most test specialists disagree. While recognizing an ever-present error component, they believe that anything can be measured. The credo was framed by E. L. Thorndike in 1918: "Whatever exists at all exists in some amount." Testing men believe it still. They are not so naive as to think that any human gift will manifest itself in a 45-minute paper-and-pencil test. They do believe that, given ample opportunity to activate and observe the examinee, any trait, talent, or learning that manifests itself in behavior can be measured with reasonable accuracy. The total cost of measuring may be 100 times that of administering the usual tests, but they believe it can be done. The final observations may rely on professional judgment, but this could be reliable and validated judgment. A question for most test specialists, then, is not "Can complex educational outcomes be measured?" but "Can complex educational outcomes be measured with the time and personnel and facilities available?"

When it is most important to know whether or not a child is reading at age-level, we call in a reading specialist, who observes his reading habits. She might test him with word recognition, syntactic decoding, and paragraph-comprehension exercises. She would retest where evidence was inconclusive. She would talk to his teachers and his parents. She would arrive at a clinical description – which might be reducible to a statement such as "Yes, Johnny is reading at or above age-level."

The scores we get from group reading tests can be considered estimates of such an expert judgment. These objective test scores correlate positively with the more valid expert judgments. Such estimates are not direct measurements of what teachers or laymen mean by "ability to read," nor are they suitably accurate for diagnostic purposes. Achievement gains for a sizable number of students will be poorly estimated. It is possible that the errors in group testing are so extensive that – when fully known – businessmen and educators will refuse to accept them as bases for contract reimbursement.

Professional awareness. Classroom teachers and school principals have tolerated standardized test errors because they have not been obligated to make crucial decisions on the basis of test scores. Actually, in day-to-day practice they seldom use test scores.[6] When they do, they combine them with other knowledge to estimate a child's progress in school and to guide him into an appropriate learning experience. They do not use tests as a basis for assessing the quality of their own teaching.

In performance contracting, the situation is drastically changed; tests are honored as the sole basis for contract reimbursement. The district will pay the contractor for performance improvement. An error in testing means money misspent. Course completion and reimbursement decisions are to be made without reliance on the knowledge and judgment of a professional observer, without asking persons who are closest to the learning (the teacher, the contractor, and the student) whether or not they *see* evidence of learning. Decisions are to be made entirely by objective and independent testing. Numerous human errors and technical misrepresentations will occur.

Which Test Items?

It is often unrealistic to expect a project director to either find or create paper-and-pencil test items, administrable in an hour to large numbers of students by persons untrained in psychometric observation and standardized diagnostics, objectively scorable, valid for purposes of the performance contract, and readily interpretable. The more complex the training, the more unrealistic the expectation. One compromise is to substitute criterion test items measuring simple behaviors for those measuring the complex behaviors targeted by the training. For example, the director may substitute vocabulary-recognition test items for reading-comprehension items or knowledge of components for the actual dismantling of an engine. The substitution may be reasonable, but the criterion test should be validated against performances directly indicated by the objectives. It almost never has been. Without the validation the educator should be skeptical about what the test measures.

It always is unrealistic to expect that the payoff from instruction will be apparent in the performances of learners at test-taking time.[7] Most tests evoke relatively simple behavior. Ebel wrote:

> . . . most achievement tests . . . consist primarily of items testing specific elements of knowledge, facts, ideas, explanations, meanings, processes, procedures, relations, and so on.[8]

He went on to point out that more than simple recall is involved in answering even the simplest vocabulary item.

Much more complex behavior is needed for answering a reading-comprehension item. These items clearly call for more than the literal meanings of the words read. The student must paraphrase and interpret – what we expect readers to be able to do.

These items and ones for problem solving and the higher mental processes do measure high-priority school goals – but growth in such areas is relatively slow. Most contractors will not risk basing reimbursement on the small chance that evidence of growth will be revealed by *these* criterion tests. Some of the complex objectives of instruction will be underemphasized in the typical performance-contract testing plan.

The success of Texarkana's first performance-contract year is still being debated. Late winter (1969-70) test results looked good, but spring test results were disappointing.[9] Relatively simple performance items had been used. But the "debate" did not get into that. It started when the project's "outside evaluator" ruled that there had been direct coaching on most, if not all, of the criterion test items, which were known by the contractor during the school year. Critics claimed unethical "teaching for the test." The contractor claimed that both teaching and testing had been directed toward the same specific goals, as should be the case in a good performance contract. The issue is not only test choice and ethics; it includes the ultimate purpose of teaching.

Teaching for the test. Educators recognize an important difference between preparation for testing and direct coaching for a test. To prepare an examinee, the teacher teaches within the designated knowledge-skill domain and had the examinee practice good test-taking behavior (for example, don't spend too much time on overly difficult items; guess when you have an inkling though not full knowledge; organize your answer before writing an essay) so that relevant knowledge-skill is not obscured. Direct coaching teaches the examinees how to make correct responses to specific items on the criterion test.

This is an important difference when test items cover only a small sample of the universe of what has been taught or when test scores are correlates, rather than direct measurements, of criterion behavior. It ceases to be important when the test is set up to measure directly and thoroughly that which has been taught. In this case, teaching for the test is exactly what is wanted.

Joselyn pointed out that the performance contractor and the school should agree in advance on the criterion procedure, though not necessarily on the specific items.[10] To be fair to the contractor, the testing needs to be reasonably close to the teaching. To be fair to parents, the testing needs to be representative of the domain of abilities *they* are concerned about. A contract to develop reading skills would not be satisfied adequately by gains on a vocabulary test, according to the expectations of most teachers. All parties need to know how similar the testing will be to the actual teaching.

A dissimilarity scale. Unfortunately, as Anderson observed,[11] the test specialist has not developed scales for describing the similarity between teaching and testing. This is a grievous failing. Educators have no good way to indicate how closely the tests match the instruction.

There are many ways for criterion questions to be dissimilar. They can depart from the information taught by: 1) syntactic transformation; 2) semantic transformation; 3) change in content or medium; 4) application, considering the particular instance; 5) inference, generalizing from learned instances; and 6) implication, adding last-taught information to generally known information.

For any student the appropriateness of these items depends on prior and subsequent learning as well as on the thoroughness of teaching. Which items are appropriate will have to be decided at the scene. The least and most dissimilar items might be quite different in their appropriateness. The reading-comprehension items of any standardized achievement battery are likely to be more dissimilar to the teaching of reading than any of the "dissimilarities." Immediate instruction is not properly evaluated by highly dissimilar items, nor is scholarship properly evaluated by highly similar items. Even within the confines of performance contracting, both evaluations are needed.

For the evaluation of instruction, a large number of test items are needed for each objective that – in the opinion of the teachers – directly measure increase in skill or understanding. Items from standardized tests, if used, would be included item by item. For each objective, the item pool would cover all aspects of the objective. A spearate sample of items would be drawn for the pretest and posttest for each student, and instructional success would be based on the collective gain of all students.

Creating such a pool of relevant, psychometrically sound test items is a major – but necessary – undertaking.[12] It is a partial safeguard against teaching for the test and against the use of inappropriate criteria to evaluate the success of instruction.

What the Scores Mean

At first, performance contracting seemed almost a haven for the misinterpretation of scores. Contracts have ignored 1) the practice effect of pretesting,[13] 2) the origins of grade equivalents, 3) the "learning calendar," 4) the unreliability of gain scores, and 5) regression effects. Achievement may be spurious. Ignoring any one of these five is an invitation to misjudge the worth of the instruction.

Grade-equivalent scores. Standardized achievement tests have the appealing feature of yielding grade-equivalent scores. Each raw score, usually the number of items right, has been translated into a score indicating (for a student population forming a national reference group) the average grade placement of all students who got this raw score. These new scores are called "grade equivalents." Raw scores are not very meaningful to people unacquainted with the particular test; the grade equivalents are widely accepted by teachers and parents. Grade equivalents are common terminology in performance contracts.

Unfortunately, grade equivalents are available from most publishers only for tests, not for test items. Thus the whole test needs to be used, in the way prescribed in its manual, if the grade equivalents are to mean what they are supposed to mean. One problem of using whole tests was discussed in the previous section. Another problem is that the average annual "growth" on most standardized tests is only a few raw-score points.

Most teachers do not like to have their year's work summarized by so little change in performance. Schools writing performance contracts perhaps should be reluctant to sign contracts for which the distinction between success and failure is so small. But to do so requires the abandonment of grade equivalents.

The learning calendar. For most special instructional programs, criterion tests will be administered at the beginning of and immediately following instruction, often in the first and last weeks of school. A great deal of distraction occurs during those weeks, but other times for pretesting and posttesting have their hazards, too. Recording progress every few weeks during the year is psychometrically preferred, but most teachers are opposed to "all that testing."

Children learn year-round, but the evidence of learning that gets inked on pupil records comes in irregular increments from season to season. Winter is the time of most rapid advancement, summer the least. Summer, in fact, is a period of setback for many youngsters. Beggs and Hieronymus found punctuation scores to spurt more than a year between October and April but to drop almost half a year between May and September.[14] Discussing their reading test, Gates and MacGinitie wrote:

> . . . in most cases, scores will be higher at the end of one grade than at the beginning of the next. That is, there is typically some loss of reading skill during the summer, especially in the lower grades.[15]

The first month or two after students return to school in the fall is the time for getting things organized and restoring scholastic abilities lost during the summer. According to some records, spring instruction competes poorly with other attractions. Thus, the learning year is a lopsided year, a basis sometimes for miscalculation.

Another possible overpayment on the contract can result by holding final testing early and extrapolating the previous per-week growth to the weeks or months that follow. In Texarkana, as in most schools, spring progress was not as good as winter. If an accurate evaluation of contract instructional services is to be made, repeated testing, perhaps a month-by-month record of learning performances, needs to be considered.[16]

Unreliable gain scores. Most performance contracts pay off on an individual student basis. The contractor may be paid for each student who gains more than an otherwise expected amount. This practice is commendable in that it emphasizes the importance of each individual learner and makes the contract easier to understand, but it bases payment on a precarious mark: the gain score.

Just how unreliable is the performance-test gain score? For a typical standardized achievement test with two parallel forms, A and B, we might find the following characteristics reported in the test's technical manual:

Reliability of Test A = +.84.
Reliability of Test B = +.84.
Correlation of Test A with Test B = +.81.

Almost all standardized tests have reliability coefficients at this level. Using the standard formula.[17] one finds a disappointing level of reliability for the measurement of improvement:

Reliability of gain scores (A-B or B-A) = +.16.

The test manual indicates the raw score and grade-equivalent standard deviations. For one widely used test, they are 9.5 items and 2.7 years, respectively. Using these values we can calculate the errors to be expected. *On the average,* a student's raw score would be in error by 2.5 items, grade equivalent would be in error by 0.72 years, and grade-equivalent *gain score* would be in error by 1.01 years. The error is indeed large.

Consider what this means for the not unusual contract whereby the student is graduated from the program, and the contractor is paid for his instruction, on any occasion that his performance score rises above a set value. Suppose – with the figures above – the student exits when his improvement is one grade equivalent or more. Suppose also, to make this situation simpler, that there is *no* intervening training and that the student is not influenced by previous testing. Here are three ways of looking at the same situation:

Suppose that a contract student takes a different parallel form of the

> criterion test on three successive days immediately following the pretest. The chances are better than 50-50 that on *one* of these tests the student will gain a year or more in performance and appear to be ready to graduate from the program.
>
> Suppose that three students are tested with a parallel form immediately after the pretest. The chances are better than 50-50 that one of the three students – entirely due to errors of measurement – will gain a year or more and appear ready to graduate.
>
> Suppose that 100 students are admitted to contract instruction and pretested. After a period of time involving no training, they are tested again, and the students gaining a year are graduated. After another period of time, another test and another graduation. After the fourth terminal testing, even though no instruction has occurred, the chances are better than 50-50 that two-thirds of the students will be graduated.

In other words, owing to unreliability, gain scores can appear to reflect learning that actually does not occur.

The unreliability will give an equal number of false impressions of deteriorating performance. These errors (false gains and false losses) will balance out for a large group of students. If penalties for losses are paid by the contractor at the rate bonuses are paid for gains, the contractor will not be overpaid. But according to the way contracts are being written, typified in the examples above, the error in the gain scores does not balance out; it works in favor of the contractor. Measurement errors could be capitalized upon by unscrupulous promoters. Appropriate checks against these errors are built into the better contracts.

Errors in individual gain scores can be reduced by using longer tests. A better way to indicate true gain is to calculate the discrepancy between actual and expected final performances.[18] Expectations can be based on the group as a whole or on an outside control group. Another way is to write the contract on the basis of mean scores for the group of students.[19] Corrections for the unreliability of gain scores are possible, but they are not likely to be considered if the educators and contractors are statistically naive.

Regression effects. Probably the source of the greatest misinterpretation of the effects of remedial instruction is regression effects. Regression effects are easily overlooked but need not be;

they are correctable. For any pretest score, the expected regression effect can be calculated. Regression effects make the poorest scorers look better the next time tested. Whether measurements are error-laden or error-free, meaningful or meaningless, when ther there is differential change between one measurement occasion and another (when there is less-than-perfect correlation), the lowest original scorers will make the greatest gains and the highest original scorers will make the least. On the average, posttest scores will, relative to their corresponding pretest scores, lie in the direction of the mean. This is the regression effect. Lord discussed this universal pehnomenon and various ways to correct for it.[20]

The demand for performance contracts has occurred where conventional instructional programs fail to develop – for a sizable number of students – minimum competence in basic skills. Given a distribution of skill test scores, the lowest-scoring students – the ones most needing assistance – are identified. It is reasonable to suppose that under unchanged instructional programs they would drop even farther behind the high-scoring students. If a retest is given, however, after any period of instruction (conventional or special) or of no instruction, these students will no longer be the poorest performers. Some of them will be replaced by others who appear to be most in need of special instruction. Instruction is not the obvious influence here – regression is. The regression effect is not due to test unreliability, but it causes some of the same misinterpretations. The contract should read that instruction will be reimbursed when gain exceeds that attributable to regression effects. The preferred evaluation design would call for control group(s) of similar students to provide a good estimate of the progress the contract students would have made in the absence of the special instruction.

The Social Process

The hazards of specific performance testing and performance contracting are more than curricular and psychometric. Social and humanistic challenges should be raised, too. The teacher has a special opportunity and obligation to observe the influence of testing on social behavior.

Performance contracting has the unique ability to put the student in a position of administrative influence. He can make the instruction appear better or worse than it actually is by his performance on tests. Even if he is quite young, the student will know that his good work will benefit the contractor. Sooner or later he is going to know that, if he tests poorly at the beginning, he can benefit himself and the contractor through his later achievement. Bad performances are in his repertoire, and he may be more anxious to make the contractor look bad than to make himself look good. Or he may be under undue pressure to do well on the posttests. These are pupil-teacher interactions that should be watched carefully. More responsibility for school control possibly should accrue to students, but performance contracts seem a devious way to give it.

To motivate the student to learn and to make him want more contract instruction, many contractors use material or opportunity-to-play rewards. (Dorsett used such merchandise as transistor radios.) Other behavior modification strategies are common. The proponents of such strategies argue that, once behavior has been oriented to appropriate tasks, the students can gradually be shifted from extrinsic rewards to intrinsic. That they *can* be shifted is probably true; that it will happen without careful, deliberate work by the instructional staff is unlikely. It is not difficult to imagine a performance-contract situation in which the students become even less responsive to the rewards of conventional instruction.

In mid-1971, performance contracting appears to be popular with the current administration in Washington because it encourages private businesses to participate in a traditionally public responsibility. It is popular among some school administrators because it affords new access to federal funds, because it is a way to get new talent working on old problems, and because the administrator can easily blame the outside agency and the government if the contract instruction is unsuccessful. It is unpopular with the American Federation of Teachers because it reduces the control the union has over school operations, and it reduces the teacher's role as a chooser of what learning students need most. Performance contracting is popular among most instructional technologists because it is based on well-researched principles of teaching and because it enhances their role in school operations.

The accountability movement as a whole is likely to be a success or failure on such sociopolitical items. The measurement of the performance of performance contracting is an even more hazardous procedure than the measurement of student performances.

Summary

Without yielding to the temptation to undercut new efforts to provide instruction, educators should continue to be apprehensive about evaluating teaching on the basis of performance testing alone. They should know how difficult it is to represent educational goals with statements of objectives and how costly it is to provide suitable criterion testing. They should know that the common-sense interpretation of these results is frequently wrong. Still, many members of the profession think that evaluation controls are extravagant and mystical.

Performance contracting has emerged because people inside and outside the schools are dissatisfied with the instruction some children are getting. Implicit in the contracts is the expectation that available tests can measure the newly promised learning. The standardized test alone cannot measure the specific outcomes of an individual student with sufficient precision. □

Robert E. Stake (2084, University of Illinois Chapter) is associate director of the Center for Instructional Research and Curriculum Evaluation, College of Education, University of Illinois.

---

[1] Frederick M. Lord and Melvin R. Novick, *Statistical Theories of Mental Test Scores.* Reading, Mass.: Addison-Wesley, 1968.

[2] Banesh Hoffman, *The Tyranny of Testing.* New York: Collier Books, 1962; and Theodore R. Sizer, "Social Change and the Uses of Educational Testing: An Historical View," paper presented at the Invitational Conference on Testing Problems, New York, October, 1970.

[3] David A. Goslin, "Ethical and Legal Aspects of the Collection and Use of Educational Information," paper presented at the Invitational Conference on Testing Problems, New York, October, 1970.

[4] Barry R. McGhan, "Accountability as a Negative Reinforcer," *American Teacher,* November, 1970, p. 13.

[5] Benjamin S. Bloom *et al., A Taxonomy of Educational Objectives: Handbook I, the Cognitive Domain.* New York: McKay, 1956.

[6] J. Thomas HastingsPhilip J. Runkel, and Dora E. Damrin, *Effects on Use of Tests by Teachers Trained in a Summer Institute,* Cooperative Research Project No. 702. Urbana, Ill.: Bureau of Educational Research, College of Education, University of Illinois, 1961.

[7] Harry S. Broudy, "Can Research Escape the Dogma of Behavioral Objectives?," *School Review,* November, 1970, pp. 43-56.

[8] Robert L. Ebel, "When Information Becomes Knowledge," *Science,* January, 1971, pp. 130-31.

[9] Dean C. Andrew and Lawrence H. Roberts, "Final Evaluation Report on the Texarkana Dropout Prevention Program, Magnolia, Arkansas: Region VIII." Education Service Center, July 20, 1970 (mimeo). Commentaries on this report include Henry S. Dyer,

"Performance Contracting: Too Simple a Solution for Difficult Problems," *The United Teacher,* November 29, 1970, pp. 19-22; and Roger T. Lennon, "Accountability and Performance Contracting," paper presented at the annual meeting of the American Educational Research Association, New York, February, 1971.

[10]E. Gary Joselyn, "Performance Contracting: What It's All About," paper presented at the Truth and Soul in Teaching Conference of the American Federation of Teachers, Chicago, January, 1971.

[11]Richard C. Anderson, "Comments on Professor Gagne's Paper," in *The Evaluation of Instruction,* ed. M. C. Wittrock and David E. Wiley. New York: Holt, Rinehart and Winston, 1970, pp. 126-33.

[12]Dorsett indicated the desirability of such an item pool in the original Texarkana proposal.

[13]Not discussed here because of space limitations.

[14]Donald L. Beggs and Albert N. Hieronymus, "Uniformity of Growth in the Basic Skills Throughout the School Year and During the Summer," *Journal of Educational Measurement,* Summer, 1968, pp. 91-97.

[15]Arthur I. Gates and Walter H. MacGinitie, *Technical Manual for the Gates-MacGinitie Reading Tests.* New York: Teachers College Press, Columbia University, 1965, p. 5.

[16]L. Wrightman and W. P. Gorth, "CAM: The New Look in Classroom Testing," *Trend,* Spring, 1969, pp. 56-57. Project CAM is described as a model for a continuous (perhaps biweekly) monitoring and recording of classroom performance.

[17]Robert L. Thorndike and Elizabeth Hagen, *Measurement and Evaluation in Psychology and Education,* 3rd ed. New York: Wiley, 1969, p. 197.

[18]Ledyard R. Tucker, Fred Damarin, and Samuel Messick. *A Base-Free Measure of Change,* Research Bulletin RB-65-16. Princeton, N.J.: Educational Testing Service, 1965. This is a discussion of change scores that are independent of and dependent on the initial standing of the learning. A learning curve fitted to test scores could be used to counter the unreliability of individual scores.

[19]This would have the increased advantage of discouraging the contractor from giving preferential treatment within the project to students who are in a position to make high payoff gains.

[20]Frederick M. Lord, "Elementary Models for Measuring Change," in *Problems in Measuring Change,* ed. Chester W. Harris. Madison, Wis.: University of Wisconsin Press, 1963, pp. 21-38.

III

EVALUATION OF TWENTY-THREE NON OEO PERFORMANCE CONTRACTS

RAND News Release

Two Federally funded reports on performance contracting were released in the winter of 1971-1972.

OEO, which had funded 18 contracts similar to the first one in Texarkana, (see Chapter I) concluded "We have found no panacea," in the words of OEO's director Philip Sanchez.

RAND Corporation, which studied 23 non-OEO performance contracts including those in Gary and Texarkana, however, concluded that performance contracts can be effective catalysts for change in schools.

Here is RAND's own brief summary of its report:

Santa Monica, Calif., Dec. 14 – Performance contracting, a new process in which business firms are brought into the classroom and paid for results achieved, shows promise of being able to introduce change into the schoolhouse.

But based on the results of a 16-month evaluation that The Rand Corporation conducted for the Department of Health, Education and Welfare, no consistent level of improvement in reading and mathematics has emerged that would be likely to lead educators to believe performance contracting is ready to replace traditional remedial programs for disadvantaged children.

Those are among the findings today in a six-volume report from Rand to HEW's Office of Planning and Evaluation. Rand is an independent, nonprofit research center.

While some contractors' program results outstripped those of more conventional programs, scores on standardized tests given at

RAND news release, January, 1972.

the beginning and the end of the performance contract programs evaluated by Rand were generally below the expectations of both private contractors and school districts, according to Dr. George R. Hall, who directed the Rand team.

Five of the six volumes of the Rand study deal with programs in Gary, Ind.; Gilroy, Calif.; Grand Rapids, Mich.; Norfolk, Va., and Texarkana, Ark. The sixth volume is a summary and also draws on information gathered from 15 other program sites.

In reviewing the results, Dr. Hall pointed out that in conventional schooling average students achieve one grade level of advancement each year, while students from disadvantaged environments are more likely to gain a half grade level or slightly more than that in remedial programs.

Student achievement in the five performance contracting programs on which Rand concentrated ranged from a low of one-tenth of a grade level in a Norfolk fifth grade reading program to a 1.7 grade level advancement for first graders in both reading and math at Gary.

The contractor in Gary achieved a reading gain of seven-tenths of a grade level and a math gain of 1.2 for the second through sixth grades. Other Norfolk results were a half grade level for reading in both a seventh and a ninth grade.

There were three contractors in Grand Rapids. One, serving first through sixth grades, showed a seven-tenths gain in reading and six-tenths in math. Another contractor, serving sixth through ninth grades, posted a gain of 1.2 in reading and one grade level in math. The third contractor's results have not been released.

In Gilroy, where the contractor worked with second, third and fourth graders, reading advances were six-tenths of a grade level and math advances were eight-tenths.

In Texarkana, the birthplace of performance contracting experiments, the test results observed by Rand were so low – a half grade level in reading and only three-tenths of a grade level in math in sixth through 12th grades – that the school district decided to discontinue contracting with private firms and operate the program itself.

In those programs were achievement was markedly above others, further studies could be productive to determine how those successes could be repeated in other schools, Dr. Hall said.

Performance contracting scored better as a catalyst for

change in school systems, primarily in getting more individualized instruction into the schools.

"People who are not a permanent part of the school system seem to be freer to implement radical changes in the classroom than are regular school personnel," the Rand report says.

Rand also noted that initially educators had expressed concern that performance contracting would be "dehumanizing," that it would force a student into a mechanized environment in which he would produce to satisfy the profit motive of the contractor.

The Rand team found, instead, that the individualized approach of most systems tended to foster more self-reliance in students by requiring them to accept greater personal responsibility.

"Teachers and pupils tended to interact more informally," the Rand study said. "Contractors fostered the informal approach and strove to stimulate enthusiasm because they were convinced that unhappy students do not learn."

How do per-capita costs of performance contracting stack up against those for other programs?

Rand found that they are about the same—or slightly less expensive—than the costs for more conventional remedial education programs. Both are more expensive, of course, than for regular education programs.

Conventional remedial education costs usually are higher because classes are generally limited to fewer students than in regular programs. Performance contracting programs, in contrast, tend to keep normal, or larger, class sizes, then employ more materials and new teaching techniques.

Performance contracting has dramatized the need for more accurate measures of teaching effectiveness than standardized tests, which have presented many problems for school districts attempting to use them for educational accountability purposes, Dr. Hall said.

Because of the experimental status of performance contracting, legal and labor problems which have arose have generally been swept aside, according to the Rand report, "but those unresolved questions will eventually have to be answered," Dr. Hall said.

The study team represented many different professional skills in order to permit Rand to examine a wide range of questions about performance contracting.

Participating with Hall were Polly Carpenter, Mathematician

and teacher; Arnold W. Chalfant, educational psychologist; Sue Haggart, cost analyst; Marjorie L. Rapp, educational psychologist, and Gerald C. Sumner, statistician. □

Chapter Seven

INCENTIVES

I. School 'Percentomania'
New York Times
(An editorial slam at rewarding students and teachers for learning results.)

II. Incentives for Performance
Education Turnkey News
(How performance contractors use incentives.)

III. Every Kid a Hustler
Gary Saretsky
(Some ways students can achieve power over performance contractors.)

I

SCHOOL 'PERCENTOMANIA'

(The editorial appeared in the July 25, 1970 issue of *The New York Times.*)

"Even worse (than incentives to teachers) is the use of 'incentives' for children in the form of trading stamps, tokens, candy or money."

It is a measure of the American public school establishment's lack of imagination and initiative that industrial concerns and other private agencies have been entering the critical business of trying to upgrade the schooling of disadvantaged children. The extent to which private enterprise can help solve these problems remains to be demonstrated by far more sustained efforts than have been made to date; but it would be folly to reject expert aid through innovated experimentation from any source simply because such aid did not originate within traditional pedagogic channels.

A disconcerting element in the new approach is, however, the introduction of direct fiscal awards and penalties for the managers and teachers of these projects, narrowly based on pupils' test scores. Even worse is the use of "incentives" for children in the form of trading stamps, tokens, candy or money.

Those participants in one of the projects who were said to have raised achievement records by feeding their pupils the proper test answers may actually have done American education a service. They underscored the danger in putting schooling on a basis of direct payments for the right answers. When Soviet school authorities tried the same procedure in holding teachers too narrowly accountable, they were soon faced with a professional disease known as "percentomania"–jargon for cheating by teachers.

Accountability of professionals is essential and it has too

often been lacking in a self-satisfied and defensive educators establishment. But the piecegoods mentality is not the answer to making educators responsive to the true goals of schooling.

As for the children, the reward for solid accomplishment in reading ought to be in the pleasure of new and more exciting books—interesting to the children, not merely prescribed by dull pedagogic tradition. Whatever is wrong with education now, it would be a devastating commentary on American values if crass materialism of profit or loss were to be the only hope for a brighter future of learning in the United States. □

II

INCENTIVES FOR PERFORMANCE

Education Turnkey News

"The teacher's role is being changed to one of instructional manager, and like most managers. . .incentives are offered based upon productivity."

One of the most critical and significant elements in performance contracting is the incentive structure which it creates at the student and the school system levels. The incentive structure thus created is a philosophically new approach to innovation which differs greatly from policies and procedures at the Federal and State levels – a bottom up approach rather than a top down approach to school system innovation.

Well over 70% of all performance contract configurations allow for contingency contracting or incentive structures for the students. Not only does this structure create the management contingencies for conditioning environment, recognized as an essential ingredient in skill development, but it also provides a psychological break from what exists in the classroom. The instruction is learner centered and, to a large extent, learner controlled, in that the student becomes the focus for determining who gets paid how much, and for doing what. Some have attributed a large portion of the success of the Texarkana project to the fact that students are working for their "partners", the paraprofessionals whom they know and like. In other cases, the students have hinted about potential sitdown strikes if certain teachers, who have been improperly trained, would not leave them to learn at their own rates without interruption.

The teacher's role is being changed to one of instructional

Reprinted with permission of *Education Turnkey News,* July, 1970.

manager, and like most managers in a decentralized environment, incentives are offered based upon productivity increases. Most performance contract configurations allow for incentives to the "teachers" as well as the paraprofessionals and other staff involved. One specific company would pay its staff 70% of total salaries with additional bonus based on student performance. Another configuration would pay teachers, employed by the school system but on sabbatical to work on the project, cash bonuses or stock bonuses based on individual student gains beyond a certain amount. In other instances, where the economic man is frowned upon in education, the firm would still reward teachers on the basis of productivity, but teachers would spend the money collectively on new equipment or other materials which they could utilize in their programs in future years.

Incentives for School Performance

Incentives have to be provided for the school system as well to insure that the program is implemented on time and is executed in the most effective manner, thus realizing the full potential of the contractor's learning system. In specific instances, firms have proposed to award cash gifts directly to particular school sites which have proven to be most effective in ensuring student attendance, cooperating with the contractor, and providing other functions which create a better learning environment for the contractor.

In other instances, Requests for Proposals have been developed and contracts written in such a way that no equipment is purchased by the school system until the successful achievement of the goal is made at the end of the first year. If the goal is achieved, then the school system reserves the right to purchase the equipment at its fair market salvage value. Since most of the teachers in the school system, if properly exposed and sensitized to the program, will want the teacher aids equipment and materials for their use, there exists incentives, both among the teachers as well as the administrators to cooperate to the greatest extent possible with the contractor, ensuring the potential success is achieved. In several other instances where programs have been planned, the particular firm has indicated an interest in allowing the school system a small fee for all material validated in a successful performance contract.

There are indications in several of the State-wide performance contracts being planned that new grants management systems will be developed to provide incentives to local education agencies to "search the market" for the most effective teaching methods available. Initial emphasis will probably be on performance contracts to assist in removing math and reading deficiencies in Title I schools. It is quite feasible that in the near future certain States will allocate dollars to local education agencies based on the number of grade level deficiencies being removed at a fixed unit price. Hence, it will allow for local initiative to contract out, adopt new learning systems and upon proper staff development, operate performance budgeting projects within the school system. What is evolving in certain States, at least in the thinking of policy planners planners, is that there eventually will evolve a performance budgeting system whereby dollars are allocated according to needs and institutions are held accountable for ensuring that students actually do achieve.

Performance contracting seems to be necessary to demonstrate the power of this new incentive structure. If a school system would reward students upon successful achievement, or reward teachers based on productivity, or allocate dollars within school sites within the system on the basis of principals' performance, then performance contracting would probably not be necessary. However, the world of reality indicates that attitudes can be changed only as viable, credible alternatives are demonstrated, and performance contracting seems to be the best current tool for demonstration. □

III

EVERY KID A HUSTLER

by Gary Saretsky

"We understand that if we do well on the test tomorrow, you're going to get a lot more bread than if we don't do well. Me and the brothers wonder what you intend to do for us if we do well tomorrow."

For performance contracting to make "every kid a winner,"[1] must it allow some opportunity for every kid to become a hustler? Teachers and firms who have performance contracted may have placed new power into the hands of students, unwittingly making themselves accountable to the students.

Under most performance contracts, the measure of success – for the teacher or contractor – is the performance of students on tests. Contractors are rewarded for good student performance and sometimes penalized for poor student performance.

Students have the option of performing at a lower level on the tests than they are capable; that is, students have the potential to influence the financial rewards or penalties of the contractors. Therefore, students could have power over the contractor and force him to meet and satisfy the needs and desires of students.

The majority of students involved in performance contracting are the poor, blacks, Puerto Ricans, Chicanos, Appalachian whites, and American Indians. The schools have evidenced their inability to provide many of these students with even basic academic skills, which provide access to the usual rewards of schooling. Perhaps in reaction, many of these students have substituted hassling and hustling as sources of rewards.

Hassling, or making life difficult for teachers and schools –

---

assaults upon and intimidation of teachers, school demonstrations, and school boycotts – has become a rewarding activity in which students can demonstrate their alienation from and discontent with the schools.

Performance contracts could serve as new ways to hassle the teacher, new methods for retribution.

Hustling, on the other hand, is the inner-city version of cost-effective private enterprise. Hustling is simply maximizing perceived payoffs from energy expended within the enterprise. That is, playing the numbers; dealing in drugs; theft; extortion; betting on handball games, basketball games, pool – these are means by which the hustler receives the greatest dollar-per-man-hour return. Where else can an inner-city resident get $25 for five minutes' work? (Four kids can completely strip a car in less than four minutes for that payoff.)

Aside from material rewards, hustling provides the intrinsic reward of beating the system. This is a powerful reward for those who otherwise feel helpless in the face of the system. In fact, it may be far more powerful than a monetary reward. By making a teacher's salary or payment to a contracting firm contingent upon student performance, performance contracting has made those responsible for instruction vulnerable to being hustled.

The most obvious way that students can hustle the contractor is through extortion, threatening to perform poorly on the posttest unless the teacher meets certain demands. A more sophisticated and more profitable approach would be an offer, by a group of students, to perform poorly on the pretest. The students could then perform better on the posttest, regardless of the quality or effect of the teacher's instruction. Payment to the contractor (and his student coconspiritors) usually increases proportionately to student progress. If students realize that better performance will yield more financial rewards, hustling may actually serve to motivate students to learn how to perform well on the posttest.

Is it likely that, someday soon, a group of students may approach a teacher and say, "We understand that if we do well on the test tomorrow you're going to get a lot more bread than if we don't do well. Me and the brothers wonder what you intend to do for us if we do well tomorrow"? Is it just as likely that members of the Black Panthers, the Young Lords, or the SDS will soon approach a major commercial performance contractor and use similar leverage to get contributions for their free breakfast program or their free health clinic? Would a performance contractor who also has contracts with the Department of Defense be forced to choose among his clients because of student influence on the company's income? Certainly far more elaborate scenarios, concerning personnel selection, retention, and curriculum determination, could emerge from the possible dilemmas caused by the simplistic performance measures used in most current performance contracts.

Among the questions raised by the proposition that students can hustle performance contractors are: Why hasn't it happened yet? (or has it?) What changes in the student's self-image and his academic performance might result from his new power? Should the schools and the contractor attempt to close or utilize this loophole existing in many performance contracts?

Most students presently involved in performance contracting experiments are in elementary and intermediate schools and are not into hustling. Many of them aren't aware that others (teachers and commercial firms) are receiving money on the basis of their (the students') performance on a test.

Texarkana established the precedent for performance contractors to "pay off" students in the form of merchandise, green stamps, etc. Even those students "determined" the nature of some of the rewards, which the Dorsett company had not anticipated. The practice of providing rewards in the form of merchandise and money has been continued in most performance contracts. In essence, then, some of the potential hustlers have already been paid off. The more activist, underground-newspaper genre of public school student who might become a hustler has not been involved in performance contracting ventures; nor have the outside organizations which have organized and radicalized the high schools latched onto the potential inherent in performance contracts.

Hustling the contractor may increase the student's tendency to perceive his school experiences as dependent upon his own actions. Studies indicate that a person who has a strong belief that he can control his own destiny is likely to "be more alert to those aspects of the environment which provide useful information for his future behavior" and "place greater value on skill or achievement reinforcements and be generally more concerned with his ability. . . ."[2]

Industrial studies indicate that workers who participate in management, decisions evidence greater productivity and satisfaction with their work.[3]

Wouldn't it be interesting to find that the inner-city student, when given this hustling leverage, increased his reading achievement?

If contracting teachers and firms have a responsibility that goes beyond facilitating student performance on some measure of cognitive achievement, they must be accountable for enriching the child's learning experiences and making them intrinsically more rewarding than hustling or hassling.

Until a better way is found, the loophole to which I referred may be the only means by which society, the immediate community, and the ultimate client, the child, can hold the performance contractor accountable for more than test scores. □

Gary Saretsky (3998, Indiana University Chapter) is a doctoral candidate at Indiana University.

---

[1]Lessinger, *Every Kid a Winner: Accountability in Education.* New York: Simon and Schuster, 1970.

[2]J. B. Rotter, "Generalized Expectancies for Internal versus External Control of Reinforcement." *Psychological Monographs,* 80 (1, Whole No. 609), 1966.

[3]F. Herzberg, *The Motivation to Work.* New York: Wiley, 1959; and *Work and the Nature of Man.* Cleveland: World Publishers, 1966.

Chapter Eight

REACTIONS TO PERFORMANCE CONTRACTING

I. NEA's Policy Statement on Performance Contracting
Virginia Journal of Education
("If performance contracting is to succeed the key will be teacher involvement from the beginning.")

II. Accountability: The Great Day of Judgement
Robert D. Bhaerman
(The AFT officially condemns performance contracting.)

III. AFT Resolution
Education Turnkey News
(An advocate of performance contracting addresses the AFT critique.)

IV. Performance Contracting is a *Hoax!*
Girard D. Hottleman
(The most hostile teacher reaction in print.)

V. Performance Contracting: Is it the New Tool for the New Boardmanship?
Harold V. Webb
(A positive response from the National School Board Association.)

VI. Two out of Three Boardmen Buy Performance Contracting
American School Board Journal
(A survey suggests performance contracts have wide appeal.)

I

NEA'S POLICY STATEMENT ON PERFORMANCE CONTRACTING

Virginia Journal of Education

NEA warns of pitfalls in performance contracting – outlines nine conditions to guide teachers.

–The National Education Association has adopted a policy statement cautioning its 1.1 million members against the pitfalls of performance contracting in schools, Mrs. Helen Bain, NEA president, has announced.

The controversial concept, which typically brings business firms into the schools and rewards them according to how well students perform, is being boosted by the Nixon Administration through the Office of Economic Opportunity.

Mrs. Bain likened performance contracting to earlier educational fads, designed "to provide simple, cheap solutions to problems that are both complex and costly."

The president of the nation's largest teacher organization said that probably none of the so-called performance contracts now in effect is acceptable. The NEA is asking teachers to be wary of contracts that do not meet basic requirements outlined by its executive committee. These include realistic teacher and community involvement in the development of learning objectives and a strong role for local education associations from the initial planning through final evaluation of the program.

"As things stand now," Mrs. Bain stressed, "we don't know whether the contracts are written to serve the needs of children or of special interest groups. We don't know the extent, if any, to which contracts are written to meet their learning objectives–or,

---

Reprinted with permission from the *Virginia Journal of Education*, January, 1971.

indeed, whether the objectives are consistent with sound educational policy."

The NEA supports a systematic approach to education, Mrs. Bain stressed, noting that the policy statement asserts that an orderly, thoughtful approach to education can help provide the changes that will make schools more humane. But the contracts now in operation, she said, are subject to potentially serious abuses that are not in the best interest of students, teachers and society.

The Nashville, Tenn., teacher of speech and English said no program can replace a good teacher, working with small classes and with adequate time and materials in which to help individual students having difficulty grasping new concepts. "Providing a child with these advantages," she said, "is, and always will be, costly. It requires far more financial help—particularly from the federal government—than we're getting today."

Performance contracting is generally described as a formal agreement between a local board of education and a private business organization or a group of teachers already employed by the board to achieve certain specified gains in student performance. These gains frequently are measured solely by standardized achievement tests—a practice challenged by the NEA in one of nine conditions for involvement in performance contracting it outlined to its members. The condition: other measurements in addition to the so-called standardized achievement tests should be used to evaluate student learning.

If performance contracting is to succeed the key will be teacher involvement from the beginning. Therefore NEA lists as its first requirement that teachers be involved through their local association as a basic condition of the contract. The involvement must extend from the planning of the contract objectives through the evaluation of the performance of the contract.

Other requirements set by the NEA are that:

—learning objectives be developed with community and professional involvement and be the basis for the requests for bids on the contract;

—contracts make maximum use of school personnel, adequately prepared to meet contract goals;

—contracts adopt the so-called "turnkey" approach, whereby innovative aspects of the contract revert to the regular staff and program of the school;

—pupils be under the close supervision of professionally trained and certificated personnel;

—contracts be limited to genuinely innovative approaches that are neither likely nor possible within the school's program;

—contracts not be in conflict with negotiated agreements between school boards and local education associations and not violate the established rights of teachers;

—contracts assure that no performance contractor profits by virtue of any privileges given to nonprofit educational institutions or agencies under copyright law.

Mrs. Bain said the association developed the conditions after a series of studies on performance contract practices, including on-site visits and work with affiliate organizations throughout the country. □

II

ACCOUNTABILITY: THE GREAT DAY OF JUDGMENT

by Robert D. Bhaerman

"The pushers, for that is what they are, of such things as performance contracts. . .certainly have injected some 'innovative' verbiage into the rump of the educational system."

(In its August, 1970, convention, the American Federation of Teachers passed a strongly worded resolution criticizing performance contracts. Bhaerman summarizes this resolution.)

"The important criterion will be results–student learning," Leon Lessinger and other blind advocates of accountability tell us. Yet they ignore the most important questions: What is the major *function* of the school? In the light of the major function, what should the *results* be? What are the *kinds* of student learnings which should be stressed? In short, what *should* students learn? The answers depend on how one views social progress and the status quo. On the whole, I think, most educators have their lives pretty well adjusted to the status quo. Most probably resist any *major* disturbance which would require the redistribution of social energies of so broad a nature as to require a radically new frame of reference. Such extensive revisions–of school and society–usually are too precarious for many who call themselves educators.

The individualities of others, however, are so marked that they cannot be made congruent with things as they are. What of the teacher–and his "resulting" students–who cannot abide the status quo? What of the teachers in a school who are the incubators of social unrest and revision? How does one set up the criterion to evaluate the results, that is, of student learning, in order to

---

Reprinted with copyright permission of *Educational Technology,* January, 1971.

fit *this* view of education? In short, what does "accountability" mean in terms of *this* function of the schools? Is the function of schools merely to be a conservative one, the "trailing edge," as Van Cleve Morris has called it? Or, to use his term, should schools be at "the growing edge"? What of the teacher whose "results" are in terms of students undertaking acts of social reconstruction? What about those students who are undergoing a drastic reorganization of their outlook toward American society? What of those teachers who hold, with George Counts, that the school *shall* build a new social order? Who would the advocates hold accountable *if these teachers succeed?*

Leon Lessinger's position on accountability seems to be within a very limited view of the function of the school. In order to qualify his conception of education, Lessinger has said that there are and should be larger objectives in education that are difficult to define and impossible to measure as the consequence of any given program; the "training" components of education, illustrated in the basic skills of reading, arithmetic, vocational training and the like are amenable to performance contracts—or, I take it, amenable to his conception of accountability. Is he saying that teachers should be made accountable for the "training" component of education, but not the more important "education" component of education? Teachers want to know what this means. How do we answer parents who say, "If you don't teach my child, I'm going to have you fired"? Teachers want to know the answer to this, too. Do you tell the teachers of reading, or arithmetic, or vocational training, that their chances of being fired are 100 percent greater than the social studies teacher? The "training" component theory of education leaves much to be desired. It leaves a lot out: teachers of history and science and literature demand the equal right of being axed along with the teachers of reading and arithmetic and vocational training. You see, teachers demand "due process"!

I, for one, wish that Lessinger and his followers would be *more specific* in answering the question to be asked on that Great Day of Judgment when teachers' names shall be written in the Great Book of Accountability: *Who shall live and who shall die?*

I am afraid that their conception of accountability is nothing more than the old "pie in the sky" or perhaps "pie in the eye" of teachers.

The difference between the paradigm for accountability of Lessinger *et al.* and the AFT paradigm for accountability is that theirs is based on the black-or-white, simplistic dichotomy of "success or failure," whereas ours is based on the more complex notion of identifying "strengths and weaknesses" *of* teachers and then establishing continuous progress programs *for* teachers. Their paradigm is based upon the jehovah-like decree of life or death, whereas ours is based upon the belief of compassion, humaneness and human potential.

Their paradigm can be called the "Cult of Adoration," for they seem to worship at the feet of the almighty Efficiency of Industry, but seem to ignore the all too-frequent corruption of the high priests of the military-industrial and now the educational-industrial complex, so aptly illustrated by the highest priests of them all, those of Texarkana fame. How many of these high priests of industry have set foot in a classroom after their own youthful experiences? Can we honestly say that the educational engineers of IBM and Borg-Warner and the like know more about the teaching-learning process and "kids" than the educational workers of Gary and Pittsburgh and the District of Columbia? I will take the educational workers over the educational engineers any day.

It is said that the heart of the educational engineering process is the performance contract. This must raise some additional questions. These, in fact, come from over 200,000 teachers of the AFT, whose representatives passed a resolution at the August, 1970 convention with seven points which I shall relay in the form of questions:

1. *Can "the advocates" guarantee that performance contracting will not take the determination of education policy out of the hands of the public?* Already, the incipient performance-contracting lobby is telling school boards that independent contractors should not be tied down by school board policies. "The schools have to be very careful not to put constraints on contractors," the president of QED, Inc., one of the recipients of OEO funds, said recently.)

2. *Can they say, with a straight face, that performance contracting does not threaten to establish a new monopoly of education?* (While there are currently scores of small private educational corporations interested in performance contracting, the big hardware manufacturers like Westinghouse, Borg-Warner, IBM and

Xerox have set up "educational divisions." With their almost unlimited supply of capital, it is only a matter of time before the performance-contracting industry is in the control of a small group of big businesses which can use it (a) to sell their hardware and (b) to promote their ideology.)

3. *Can they stand up before groups of teachers and convince them that performance contracting does not dehumanize the learning process?* (Almost all performance contractors depend on programmed instruction tied to material incentives to motivate students to learn. The attempt to "individualize" learning actually creates a fierce competitiveness among students to see who will get the most money, green stamps or transistor radios.)

4. *Do they honestly believe that performance contracting will not sow distrust among teachers? (It has already.* Most performance contractors use a teacher-incentive program. Teachers whose pupils do the "best" on tests get a bonus—often stock in the performance contractor's company. No longer are teachers willing to share their good ideas with one another; to do so might cut back on their earnings.)

5. *Can they rationalize that performance contracting does not promote teaching to the "standardized" test? (It has already.* The Texarkana performance contract project already is mired in accusations that questions on achievement tests were identical to those specifically taught by the private contractor's staff. As long as tests and scores are the criteria for determining how much the private contractor is to be paid, the dangers of subterfuge, collusion and teaching to the test are present.)

6. *How can they state that performance contracting would not subvert the collective bargaining process and reduce teacher input?* (Contracts between teachers and school boards will be replaced by arrangements between private corporations and "their" staffs of teachers and paraprofessionals. The input of educational expertise from teachers to school board authorities will be lost. In its place will be substituted any kind of cheap, short-cut method of "teaching" that will make the most money for the contractor.)

7. *Is not performance contracting educationally unsound? Is performance contracting not predicated on the false assumption that educational achievement can be improved in the vacuum of a machine-oriented classroom, without changing the wider environment of the poverty-stricken child?*

The pushers, for that is what they are, of such things as performance contracts, developmental capital, and so on, *ad nauseam* certainly have injected some "innovative" verbiage into the rump of the educational system. They are correct in some ways though. The education system needs a good shot in . . . Trouble is, more often than not, the pushers miss their mark! □

Robert D. Bhaerman is director of research, American Federation of Teachers, Washington, D.C.

III

AFT RESOLUTION

Education Turnkey News

"Performance contracting in theory can serve the public interest; in practice, it could be as bad as the AFT resolution warns."

At their recent national meeting in Pittsburgh, the American Federation of Teachers adopted the following resolution opposing performance contracting:

"WHEREAS: the concept of performance contracting (under which a local school board turns over the management of the learning process to a private industrial corporation), threatens to become a common practice in U.S. education, and

WHEREAS: performance contracting incorporates such dubious educational practices such as merit pay incentives to teachers, over-reliance upon standardized testing and the utilization of teaching machines and such doubtful incentives as "green stamps" and transistor radios to children, be it therefore,

RESOLVED: that the AFT go on record as opposing any plan, such as performance contracting, which;

(1) will take the determination of education policy out of the hands of the public and place it in the hands of private industrial entrepreneurs,

(2) threatens to establish a monopoly of education by big business,

(3) threatens to de-humanize the learning process,

(4) would sow distrust among teachers through a structured incentive program,

(5) promotes "teaching to the (standardized) test",

Reprinted with permission of *Education Turnkey News,* September, 1970.

(6) subverts the collective bargaining process and reduces teacher input, and

(7) is predicated on the assumption that education achievement can be improved in the vacuum of a machine-oriented classroom, without changing the wider environment of the poverty-stricken child and be it further,

RESOLVED: that all AFT locals be urged to educate their members, boards of education, as well as parent and community groups to the educationally negative aspects of performance contracting, and that the AFT sponsor a major nationwide campaign to oppose performance contracting".

Probability or Possibility?

The AFT resolution is helpful to suggest many of the abuses that could occur under the name of performance contracting if the public interest is not carefully protected. Performance contracting is a tool. Its use can be enjoyed by anyone; and it is subject to exploitation by anyone. Performance contracting in theory can serve the public interest; in practice, it could be as bad as the AFT resolution warns.

Some comments on each of the resolution's points can clarify what is needed to enable performance contracting to provide the greatest amount of service possible.

First, the AFT feels that performance contracting might take education policy formulation out of the hands of the public and place it in private hands. Two important points need to be made. What the AFT claims to be worried about—placing education policy formulation in the hands of a private agency – is clearly illegal. (see August *Education Turnkey News).* It would be an abdication of responsibility delegated to local schools by the state. Two State Attorneys General have already examined performance contracts involving half a dozen companies on that specific point.

Private agencies – whether they be "industrial entrepreneurs" or a teacher's union – may participate in policy formulation, make inputs into the curriculum, advise on decision making, but they cannot take over the role as policy maker. Most corporations realize this limitation and they are being extremely careful not to assume education policy functions in their performance contracts, for they know they run the risk of having such contracts declared null and void.

Let the People Decide

The second, and more important, point is that education policy formulation today is not in the hands of the public. It is clearly in the hands of interest groups which work for their own goals, with the average student or taxpaying parent unable to make a difference. For example, in the District of Columbia, the popularly elected school board decided, with only one dissenting vote, to try a Reading Mobilization Year. But the teachers union has decided not to cooperate. At an emergency meeting, attended by 250 of the system's six thousand teachers, the union voted to block implementation. Policy formulation is definitely not in the hands of the public.

Performance contracting as advocated in *Education Turnkey News,* as developed in the Texarkana project, and as explained in the book, *Performance Contracting in Education* is devoted to the proposition that the public, not narrow interest groups, should control education policy formulation.

The problem has been that the public has not had adequate information on which to make decisions, nor adequate tools with which to translate their decisions into action. Without information or power, the public must yield to these competing interest groups which each claim to be acting in the public's best interests. School boards, the public's formal channel for representation, are often reduced to making decisions no more important than how many reams of paper and what grade pencil to buy.

Performance contracting can offer an opportunity for all citizens in the community to participate in setting educational goals. Once goals have been set, the performance basis of a well-planned contract means realistic information can be constantly reported back to the community on how the program is meeting those goals. And the performance guarantees, if properly required, give the school board the power to make programs conform to objectives. Thus, performance contracting can respond to the AFT fear. It can give an opportunity for a community-wide participation in education policy formulation as well as implementation, so that education can be taken out of the hands of narrow interest groups and self-styled experts and returned to the public.

Who Is The Monopoly?

The next major point of the AFT resolution is a fear that

performance contracting will establish a monopoly of education by big business. This implies two things: first, that there is no education monopoly today; and that performance contracting will establish a big business monopoly. The first is wrong; and the second need not be the case. Education today is a near monopoly over which the consumers of education services can exercise little influence. As Dean Theodore Sizer of the Harvard Graduate School of Education once characterized the problem: "The public schools are a monopoly and monopolies offer neither variety nor high quality. As America needs both varied and excellent schools, competitive pressure is clearly required. A marketplace must be created for education, with children and their parents as the choice making consumers." Performance contracting can create competitive pressure within the current public school system by letting consumers set goals and giving schools incentives to "search the marketplace" for the newest and best ways of teaching children.

The second part of this AFT argument is that a monopoly will be created of big business interests. The supporting document on which the AFT Resolution was based hints of a Nixon Administration – big business "conspiracy" to take over the public schools. The AFT may have reason to fear such a thing but so long as there is competitive bidding, the public can be protected.

Admittedly, there are some large companies which would like to effect a monopolistic takeover. Some companies make a practice of seeking sole source contracts. In a sole source contract there is by definition no public goal setting, no community participation, no accountability for the decision making process, and possibly a bad contract. *Education Turnkey News* has always opposed sole source contracting as being inconsistent with the idea of performance contracting. (see Volume 1, Number 1, April 1970). Their costs are usually much higher, the performance guarantees much lower and the public interest less likely to be served. If schools are so ill-advised that they negotiate sole source contracts, and Federal, state and local funding agencies allow funds to flow to these back-room procurements, then the AFT prediction might come true.

Competition Serves the Public Interest

Where contracting is on an open competitive bid, we find small businesses more likely to succeed than a big business monopoly. There is one key element in a successful bidder's proposal: his price per guaranteed student grade level increase. Many larger, more well established companies, have intricate marketing systems with layers of middlemen, high research and development costs, expensive consultant fees for members of textbook adoption committees, and large inventories of already produced materials. All of these factors lead to high market costs. A smaller company which searches the marketplace for the latest and most effective materials and approaches will most likely be a successful bidder. Thus, new companies are being formed daily to participate in performance contracts, diluting even further the possiblity that a monopoly will arise.

A further reason against monopoly is that business should not "take over" a school in perpetuity. Business should be used to demonstrate an effective approach in the shortest possible period of time, probably one school year. Then schools should make whatever changes are needed to adopt successful aspects of the program. If schools perceive performance contracting as a means to stimulate internal reform, rather than as a way to contract out their problems, then business contact with any one school system will be too short to monopolize the educational process.

The last reason that a monopoly of big business should not arise is the fact that business may in the long run not be the main practitioner of performance contracting. Charles Blaschke, a leading spokesman for performance contracting, as well as Christopher Jencks and James Coleman, two education authorities who have written on the subject, have always proposed that teachers, administrators, groups of parents, and universities are potential "contractors". Jencks, writing in "The Public Interest", Winter 1966, states, "A university might be given a contract to run a model school system in the slums . . . a group of teachers might incorporate itself to manage a school on contract to the city wide board . . . a group of parents, working through an elected board, might also take over a school." The AFT can guarantee that a business monopoly will not occur by working to get more teachers involved as contractors.

In the O.E.O. nationwide performance contract experiment, three of the twenty-one participating schools will have projects in which teachers will have the performance contract. In eighteen of the sites, six instructional technology firms employing a wide range of hardware and software will teach children under incentive contracts. In the additional three sites, teachers are being asked to guarantee one grade level increase for their students and then are to be left free to adopt their own approach. Their cost and effectiveness in terms of student performance at the end of the year will be contrasted with that of the six instructional technology firms. There is every reason to believe that some of the teachers will be so successful that many school systems seeking to adopt the performance contract approach will do so internally with their own teachers. Thus, performance contracting need not lead to a big business monopoly, for it will enable school decision makers to search the market place for the most effective blend of education in the public and private sector.

A Dehumanizing Experience

The third main point of the AFT resolution is that performance contracting threatens to "dehumanize" the learning process. Often the point is made that performance contracting will bring machines into the classroom and students will never again see a human face. Performance contracting, if developed properly, will indeed bring into the classroom whatever the most effective education strategy is for a particular child. The recent report of the President's Commission on Instructional Technology and initial analyses of the National Assessment of Education Progress, indicate that some students learn best from machines, particularly television. Thus, machine instruction should be used where it can be successful. But there is nothing in performance contracting that requires machines. Performance contracting is a way to apply management skills, not necessarily to increase the use of technology.

If the AFT fears a dehumanizing of education then they must welcome performance based programs. The most "inhumane" aspect of today's education system is that it gives up on some children. How dehumanizing must it be for a child to fall farther and farther behind, waiting only to reach the legal age to drop out. A system that allows a flexible instructional approach, judged on each student's performance is a much more humane approach.

But the AFT point apparently is that performance contracting dehumanizes the learning process by motivating students to learn for material rewards such as green stamps. One wonders if motivation is more dehumanizing than failure? Educators and sociologists who have analyzed failures of minority group children in the current educational system have consistently agreed that these children are not motivated to learn. Sometimes it is because of the expectations of failure held by teachers of minority children. But often it is because lower socio-economic class children see no relation between education and anything of value. Some sociological studies suggest that upper-middle class children can relate education and eventual rewards such as a high paying job, and receive more immediate gratification by material rewards for good report cards.

Let's Motivate Students

To break the cycle of frustration and defeatism and convince students that in fact they can learn and that there are rewards for learning, some psychologists involved in education have developed achievement motivation strategies which begin with externalized material rewards. Material rewards provide the best motivation because they receive the most approval among fellow students. However, the process practiced by most of those in psychological education quickly internalizes the reward system making a student's performance his own reward. An excellent, simple work that explains this process is *How to Use Contingency Contracting in the Classroom,* by Dr. Lloyd Homme (Research Press, Champaign, Illinois).

The AFT position is that a "dehumanizing" competition will be created among students. But everything in public school today, whether curricular or extracurricular, places students in competition. What is needed is an approach that meets such student's needs, giving him the tools he needs to be an effective competitor. This was the case in Texarkana, where potential dropouts were motivated to stay and compete, while fellow students, whose teachers did not have motivation strategies available to use, dropped out at an alarming rate.

The fourth general area of the AFT resolution argues that performance contracting will sow distrust among teachers through a structured incentive program. This need not be the case. There is nothing implicit in performance contracting that requires an incentive bonus. A performance contract could be developed internally with teachers, using incentives that did not amount to bonus pay; or if there were bonus pay it could be shared by groups of teachers or shared with students. Under the OEO nationwide performance contract experiment the three schools who will participate in teacher incentive programs have been asked to propose what would be the best incentive for teachers – bonuses, time off, more money for staff training, money for teaching aides, prizes for students, more materials – and it will be interesting to see what these teacher groups feel will be the best incentive for teacher performance.

Should Better Teachers Be Rewarded?

One can understand the AFT apprehension if incentive bonuses – which seem like merit pay – begin to be used. With no objective basis for comparing one teacher to another, bonuses might be used to reward complacency and penalize teachers whose attempts at innovation create administrative inconvenience. But performance contracting, by relating all inputs to get the most effective education output in terms of student performance, can determine if teacher incentives are inputs that make educational sense; and if they do, performance bases can then be used to assess teacher contributions and award bonuses.

The AFT is also afraid that teachers would begin to distrust each other and would fight for bonuses, keeping secret any successful approach. That might be the case where merit pay existed. But a well-planned performance contract will provide sufficient information about successful instructional strategies for the very purpose of formally implementing them among all instructional personnel. Success will not be kept secret.

The simple facts of the Texarkana program proved completely the opposite. There was so much excitement and sharing of information about the curriculum and new instructional strategies that in fact there was a "spill-over" effect and some students elsewhere in the Texarkana schools performed above expectations. Teachers who participated in the project, as well as those who did not, have overwhelmingly endorsed the program and asked that it be spread throughout the entire system in the current year. That has consistently been the philosophy of the turnkey approach: program successes demonstrated by industry are adopted by the school system at the end of the year.

The fifth concern of the AFT is that performance contracting promotes teaching to the test. The AFT has eagerly judged the contractor in Texarkana guilty before all the facts are in and ignored the existence of other "uncontaminated" achievement gains. But they are right in warning that, uncontrolled, contractors will teach test items just as regular teachers often do. But, once again, teaching test items is not inherent in the concept of performance contracting. The O.E.O. performance contract experiment has developed a series of safeguards to prevent teaching to the test: the contractors will not know what tests are given their curriculum will be audited in the beginning and during the program and any test items in the curriculum will be removed; and part of the payment will be on criterion referenced rather than on standardized tests.

Get Away from Standardized Tests

The AFT point also seems critical of using standardized tests as the measure for performance and as a basis for payment, although tests which use national grade level norms seem widely accepted by the lay public, in whose hands the AFT says it wants education policy to be formulated. One wonders what the AFT would suggest using–the professional judgement of teachers?–which would not be susceptible to abuse. In fact, everyone involved in performance contracting is painfully aware of the inadequacies of current testing and measurement and a great deal of research and developmental effort is underway to provide better measures for student achievement. *Education Turnkey News* has advocated using criterion referenced tests to measure the attainment of interim performance objectives. Let students be tested on what is actually taught in the classroom, and let the teacher help devise the test that accurately reflects his curriculum. The teacher can suggest interim performance measures as curricular goals and by testing can find how each student is performing. Such tests can serve as diagnostic tools as well by indicating precisely what part of the curriculum is causing trouble for a particular student. Such tests are being used in the OEO nationwide experiment, in the State of Virginia, and in Dallas performance contracts. They provide part of the basis for payments to contractors and could be made the basis for full payment.

Teachers' Inputs Will Be Used

The sixth point in the resolution is that performance

contracting would subvert the collective bargaining process and reduce teacher inputs into education. The AFT suggests that contracts between teachers and school boards will be replaced by arrangements between private corporations and their staffs. This need not be the case, and in fact might not be possible under current state and local legal requirements. Once again, there is nothing inherent in performance contracting that requires that private industry be involved unless in fact private industry can do the job better than anyone else. If teachers under the present system can do the job of teaching better than anyone else, then they should continue to be the prime supplier of educational services, and contracts between teachers and school boards will continue. Collective bargaining sessions will not be subverted unless information is subversive; these sessions will for the first time have reliable information on how well students are being taught, and how much various instructional approaches cost.

The second part of this argument is that "the input of educational expertise from teachers to school-board authorities will be lost. In its place will be substituted any kind of cheap, short-cut method of 'teaching' that will make the most money for the contractor." The AFT does a service in making such a warning for it suggests what might happen if the school board and teachers totally abdicate their responsibilities. But the school board can also use performance contracting to open up to it the full marketplace of educational expertise and receive inputs from new as well as old sources.

Teacher inputs into school board authorities will be lost only if teachers have nothing to offer, for inputs will be judged on educational relevance, not the power of the interest group making the suggestion. So long as goals are set and programs are adequately monitored, then "any kind of cheap, short-cut method" will not be established but, in fact, an informed community can choose among the most successfully demonstrated and credibly audited instructional approaches.

The last argument of the AFT resolution is that performance contracting is educationally unsound. One is not quite sure what the basis for this argument is. The tone of the argument—"The vacuum of a machine-oriented classroom"—suggests a traditional AFT reaction to the use of teaching machines. Of course the AFT does not speak for all teachers, and in fact teachers who have experienced the only performance contract in the nation, those in Texarkana, have asked that the system with its teaching machines be spread systemwide. Again, the argument assumes performance contracting means a total reliance on machine-oriented instruction and, of course, that does not have to be the case in a performance contract. A performance contract could specify that no machines be used.

Let's Stop Excusing Failure

Part of the argument is also a call for "changing the wider environment of the poverty stricken child." One assumes some reliance on the *Coleman Report,* a brilliant research piece which has been often abused by those who draw their own conclusions from it, and an often stated "conclusion" is that the education of a child is determined by his socio-economic condition. So long as one concentrates only on inputs into the educational process such as teacher salaries and socio-economic background of children, then it does appear that the most important variable that can be traced through to a change in the educational achievement is student socio-economic background. Would the AFT extend the argument to its logical conclusion and say that it makes no sense to raise teacher salaries, or lower teacher:pupil ratios, or that in fact teachers make no difference?

The AFT argument, apparently, is that only by removing poverty will we end poor education. *Education Turnkey News* has often suggested that we should shift our focus from input oriented analyses to output oriented analyses; we should stop talking about equality of educational opportunity which often proves so hollow to children while giving educators excuses for their failures, and begin striving for programs that guarantee equality in educational results. We know that we have instructional technology and approaches which can teach virtually any child the basic skills which today's teacher in today's schools are failing to teach.

We do not need to make excuses for poor children, or wait until we have a totally integrated society, or quit until poverty is wiped out and we no longer have children with low socio-economic backgrounds. We can take the tools available now and guarantee that each individual child will meet community adopted minimum standards of educational achievement.

Teaching Profession Has New Opportunity

The current business of education has failed so badly that taxpayers are beginning to turn their backs on the public schools and community sentiment for non-professional inputs into education is growing. The teaching profession has the opportunity to use performance contracting as a new management tool to develop more flexible approaches to instruction, to better meet the individual needs of students, to be responsive to their clients and to work with the community to return a sense of public confidence in the public school system.

The AFT has *told* us in their resolution how bad performance contracting can be if they, and everyone else, stand back and watch it abused by our failing education system. They can also *show* us how good performance contracting can be if teachers take the leadership in seeking to increase educational performance.

In summary, the AFT fears can be averted: if school boards take this opportunity to involve the public fully in educational policy formulation; if school boards protect the public interest by selecting contractors through open competitive bids; if funding sources refuse support to sole source contracts; if teachers and community groups as well as business become contractors; if programs are adequately monitored with safeguards against teaching test items; and if successful approaches are adopted by school systems as soon as they have been demonstrated and validated.

The AFT says it wants more money for education. Nixon has said if we get more education for our dollar we will get more dollars for education. Performance contracting may be the best way to get what the AFT wants—more money for education.

UFT Seeks Injunction

Al Shanker, President of the United Federation of Teachers in New York City, has announced strong opposition to the OEO experiment in performance contracting beginning there. Speaking in a recent radio address, he stated, "I think that what has been done in the Bronx is illegal and we are preparing a court action which will prevent the program from continuing.

Shanker referred to many of the arguments made by the NEA and the AFT: that teachers will teach tests and students will cheat in order to win television sets; that profits do not belong in education; and that some teachers might be replaced by machines.

A New Nixon Plot?

But Shanker has an even greater criticism: an insidious plot on behalf of the Nixon administration. Many Washington analysts have been trying to guess White House education strategy. The AFT thinks it has caught a glimpse of a conspiracy between big business and Nixon but the UFT sees a Nixon-Office of Education-OEO design to shift the blame for educational failures to the people.

The reason the present educational system is failing, according to this analysis, is lack of money. Nixon has vetoed education appropriations and now, in Shanker's view, must "figure out a way of satisfying parents without spending more money." Shanker attacks voucher plans and performance contracts interchangeably so it is hard to follow the argument, but it goes like this: if you have an opportunity to contract for whatever you want in education, then you obviously have to accept the blame for its failure. The blame for failure is thus "decentralized," moving from Nixon and other politicians down to the complaining parent. In Shanker's words, "It is a terrific device for taking the heat off of where the heat ought to be."

Who Wants Off the Hook?

Shanker concludes that performance contracting is "part of a government strategy to get off the hook." But observers concluded that the UFT is trying to get off the hook at a time when community demands for accountability threaten the way teachers have been doing things. The last two turbulent years in New York City have shown where the community places the blame for the public school system's failure to improve itself. And nationwide, the massive defeats of public revenue issues indicate many communities do not feel teachers have been doing such a good job that they should get salary increases.

Performance contracting can offer a way for the public to interact with schools in a postive way, not just in a game of assessing blame. Taking the White House at its word that it will fund programs after a demonstration that they work, performance contracts can demonstrate the newest techniques of diagnosis, instruction, and student motivation. With a turnkey approach, these can then be made available to teachers and students. That seems more promising than continuing the game of pin-the-tail-on-the-scapegoat. □

In response to the AFT's convention resolution, *Education Turnkey News* devoted its entire issue the next month to an analysis of the AFT's arguments.

IV

PERFORMANCE CONTRACTING IS A *HOAX!*

by Girard D. Hottleman
MTA Director of Educational Services

"It becomes obvious that it is not performance contracting at all, but profit contracting–and the kids are the waste products."

"I'm a ramblin wreck from Georgia Tech,
And a helluva engineer" . . . old drinking song from Georgia

"I'm a messenger
From Leon Lessinger
Proclaiming the accountability news
I'm just a meanderin', panderin' mandarin
And you'll pay, pay, pay for my views." . . . new song from Georgia, guaranteed to drive you to drink.

Leon M. Lessinger, former associate commissioner of education, United States Office of Education, and now Callaway Professor of Education at Georgia State University, has been variously described as the founder, father, or midwife of the concept of educational accountability. He is also a leading advocate of performance contracting as one means of gaining accountability in education.[1]

Dr. Lessinger contends that taxpayers are greatly concerned, even more so than usual, about whether or not they are getting the maximum value for their dollars. He quotes President Nixon to buttress his point:

> ". . . From these considerations we derive another new concept: accountability. School administrators and school

---

Reprinted with permission of the *Massachusetts Teacher,* April, 1971.

teachers alike are responsible for their performance, and it is in their interest as well as in the interests of their pupils that they be held accountable."[2]

Incidentally, the President in his message on education also called for an end to increasing education expenditures until we can be assured that we are getting maximum value for those expenditures.

Dr. Lessinger and President Nixon share several things in common besides their years of government service, but their major common belief seems to be that the best method of improving the value of the educational dollar is to reduce the amount actually spent on educating children. For example, the President this year has appropriated $6.5 million to private profit-making industries from his budget in the Office of Economic Opportunity (administered directly from the White House Budget) for the purpose of performance contracting. (A performance contract is an agreement between a school governing body and a contractor in which the contractor agrees to produce specified rates of learning for specified rates of pay. Any residue of payment above cost is profit.)

Lessinger's plan for greater economy is as follows: He says the LEA should hire an MSG to produce a RFP with a performance contract, and this should be evaluated by an IEAA.

Baffled? Don't be. Remember, Dr. L. worked at O.E. at H.E.W. in Wash., D.C. One hesitates to conjecture, but apparently, that, combined with the rarefied atmosphere of Academia in Georgia, tends to produce this kind of Scrabblese. Let me walk you through again:

Dr. Lessinger says that the Local Education Agency (LEA) should hire a Management Support Group (MSG) who would produce a request for a proposal (RFP) with a Performance Contractor (PC?), and that the whole operation should be evaluated by an Independent Education Accomplishment Audit (IEAA).[3] That's how we save money in education and produce results.

Let me review:

1. We pay a new group (MSG) to produce a proposal.

2. We pay a new group, a profit-making corporation to carry out the proposal.

3. We pay a new group (IEAA) to evaluate the proposal.

Shazam! Reduced costs.

Even with five years of Jesuit logic behind me, I still don't understand it, but there it is. We add a group of university or private business consultants to our payroll to help us hire a group of university or private business implementers, and we hire a group of university or private business consultants to evaluate what the previous consultants have done, and we reduce our costs.

A word of fiction

Compared to Dr. Lessinger, Isaac Asimov and Rod Serling are rank amateurs in the world of imaginative fiction.

Since both the NEA and the AFT have taken strong positions against performance contracting as it is currently being implemented,[4] we can assume that teachers everywhere will be faced with the usual accusation of "logjamming" that we encounter every time we oppose the most recent pontification that issues from the latest version of Mt. Olympus.[5] The arguments this time, however, will be much stronger than before and they will be framed by more sophisticated propagandists than ever before, because a lot of people stand to make a lot of money if this particular pontification is sold.[6] Also, the credentials of the new pontificators will be, in many cases, "impeccable". Consider for example the significant increase in income that will become immediately available to university consultants if Lessinger's concept of a M.S.G. and an I.E.A.A. were to be adopted on a wholesale basis. For example, Dr. Lessinger himself is currently being sought by several school boards who desire his services as a consultant to help them prepare performance contracts.[7] Also, he is a consultant to a firm established to audit the production quality of public schools, the Education Audit Institute, Washington, D.C.[8] I am by no means attempting to impugn the personal motives of Dr. Lessinger, but it is true that he is the major spokesman for the "accountability movement" and it is also true that if the movement moves according to his design, he will probably benefit significantly. Based on this knowledge, I merely allude to an old principle in Rhetoric I – "Consider the source".

The accountability and performance contracting movements are literally littered with mutual backslapping by those within the business. For example: "He (Leon Lessinger) wishes to acknowledge Charles Blaschke of Educational Turnkey Systems . . . for (his) valuable insights and assistance."[9]

"Blaschke gives much of the credit to Dr. Leon Lessinger,

former associate commissioner of education, for beginning the Texarkana project . . ."[10]

"Texarkana is the most successful dropout prevention program in history."[11] said Lessinger. (The Texarkana project was designed by Blaschke)

Blaschke (who now holds a $600,000 contract from OEO as the overall consultant to the OEO performance contracting experiments) and Lessinger are both alumni from the federal agencies which are now funding performance contracts. Blaschke's route was Pentagon to OEO to founder of Education Turnkey Systems, which now holds the $600,000 contract with OEO. Lessinger's route was superintendent of schools to HEW (OE) to Georgia State and consultant to Education Audit Institute. When Lessinger took over as Associate Commissioner for Elementary and Secondary Education, "he vowed to bring accountability to federal aid programs administered by his bureau."[12] Like Blaschke, he spent his term of office promoting his philosophy and imbuing his government agency with his own personal stamp. And like Blaschke, he left after a short stay only to become immersed in the contracting business recently adopted at his insistence.

Thiokol and Sullivan

Another Damon and Pythias team has turned up in Massachusetts Commissioner of Education Dr. Neil V. Sullivan and the Thiokol Chemical Corporation. Speaking to a joint meeting of the Massachusetts Association of School Committees and the Massachusetts Association of School Superintendents on Oct. 14, 1970, Sullivan said,

> "Industry has finally gotten its feet wet in the billion dollar enterprise called education. I not only applaud this involvement, but I urge each and every one of you here this evening to do all you can to sustain this partnership."[13]

Thiokol holds a $208,000 contract in the Dallas schools. On Tuesday, Dec. 8, 1970, Dr. Sullivan spent the morning visiting the Thiokol program at James Madison High School in Dallas. On Tuesday afternoon at a press conference, Dr. Sullivan said, "It is an exciting innovation and I'm very enthused by the student reaction. I like it very much."[14] Dr. Sullivan omitted revealing that he was a paid consultant of Thiokol until after the admission was brought about by questions from the Dallas Times Herald. "I'm a

Thiokol consultant and have been for many years," he conceded.[15] Superintendent Nolan Estes withdrew tapes of the news interview when the discovery was made that Sullivan was on Thiokol's payroll. Dr. Estes had "become suspicious" of Dr. Sullivan "when he (Sullivan) saw everything good and nothing bad."[16] "It just puts a shadow over everything,"[17] Estes said.[18]

Another shadow loomed large in the precedent-setting Texarkana performance contract. Designed by Blaschke, praised by Lessinger, and run by Dorsett Educational Systems of Norman, Okla., the Texarkana project made national headlines when it was disclosed by evaluator Dean C. Andrew that there had been direct teaching of test items to such an extent that the test results could not be used as a valid measure of achievement.[19] Further investigation revealed that the programmer, Rosella Scott, who resigned in April, 1970, to found her own company, was the sister of President Lloyd G. Dorsett.[20] "I did everything I could to see that company made money on the project,"[21] she said. She readily admitted that "teaching to the test" occurred. But, she said, this was largely to compensate for some low I.Q. students enrolled despite prior agreement that Dorsett would be working with normal I.Q. youngsters.[22]

A growing practice

Despite the resistance by experienced teachers and despite the widespread knowledge of the highly questionable practices of the advocates, performance contracting threatens to grow in leaps and bounds. One sure indicator is the recent announcement by OE official Albert Mayrhofer that, "Expenditures for management support, outside evaluation, outside audits and performance contracts are legitimate under Titles I and III of ESEA."[23]

Another significant omen can be seen through analysis of the background of the 16 newly-appointed top aides to Commissioner of Education Sidney P. Marland Jr. Not one is a teacher and four of the top aides are not educators at all, but systems analysts hired out of such places as the Rand Corporation. Interestingly enough, with the accountability panderers calling for outside audits, OEO chose the Rand Corporation (at a cost of $300,000) to evaluate the 18 projects currently let out to other corporations, despite the widescale availability of qualified educational research units from the non-industrial sector. Rand is a well-known systems management firm whose executives are already publishing articles publicizing performance contracting.[24]

In case you've forgotten, all this money that is going to Rand and Westinghouse and Thiokol and Singer-Graflex is out of the "poverty" budget at OEO. Now that Mayrhofer has opened up the Title I money, the corporations will also have access to the billion-dollar appropriation for disadvantaged students. Oh, the burden that the poor place on our society!

The real issues

The real issues in the "accountability movement" are far more significant than the wholesale emergence of the new educational profiteers, and far more important than any question of the respectability of the methods by which the advocates of the "movement" attempt to make it popular. As teachers, we ask only one question – will the accountability-performance contracting movement improve the education of children?

It is this author's contention that it will not. As a matter of fact it is most obviously apparent from an examination of the literature that the performance contracting industry will prove to be harmful to children.

One of the major reasons for this conclusion is the obvious lack of understanding of the education establishment by the practitioners of this new black art. For example, Lessinger asserts, "Professionalism . . . goes hand in hand with accountability; with clear-cut proof of performance. And in education we have time and again refused to produce that proof."[25]

Another advocate, J. D. Comas, dean, College of Education, University of Tennessee, Knoxville,[26] pronounces: "Public institutions always have had a moral obligation to be accountable. However, an examination of practices in public education often reveals that educators have hidden schools from the public by a selective system of communication and public relations."[27]

This kind of criticism, often stated by the performance contract advocates, that the teaching profession has refused to be accountable, is nothing more than pious, pompous pap. It is inaccurate. It is the pandering of the new self-appointed, would-be educational mandarins. Since teachers have been systematically and deliberately denied any meaningful role in the decision-making apparatus of public education, they are obviously not accountable for the mess we're in.

At this writing, the New York City School Board has just announced its intention to lay off 6500 city school teachers. Who's accountable for that move? And who will be accountable for the subsequent drop in educational quality?

School boards deal with money. Superintendents deal with money. The Federal Government deals with money. Thiokol Chemical Corporation deals with money. But teachers deal with children. It may warm the hackles of an assembled group of tax guardians to hear Commissioner Sullivan refer to education as "a billion dollar enterprise." It may be very reassuring to the hundreds of panting corporations to hear Lessinger calling for "educational engineering." But all the new jargon in the new lexicon will not resolve the basic issue that the new mandarins are tryint to avoid – education is woefully underfunded. More money is needed, much more money, and so is a substantially more powerful place for teachers in the school hierarchy. What is not needed are new ways to excuse the refusal of a society with inverted values to avoid its responsibility to school children.

The polluted child

Another reason to fear the performance contracting menace is because of the ultimately harmful effects of the usual process of education that is employed by most of the projects. It becomes obvious that it is not performance contracting at all, but profit contracting – and the kids are the waste products.

We have finally reached the age where we are about to sanction the wholesale production of the polluted child. The approach is almost universally mechanistic, automated, programmed, and built on extrinsic rewards. The Bronx project is typical. If a student learns at a predetermined accelerated rate (and by the way, what is being "taught" there are narrowly defined skills) he may earn enough green stamps to get a toy gun. "Why do you learn, Johnny?" "To get a gun, of course." When measurement becomes king and profit the motive, reading, for example, does not become "reading for pleasure" or "reading for appreciation" or "reading for leisure" or "understanding," but straight de-coding or "reading for profit."

Consider the obvious conditioning of a child caught up in the grip of a profit contractor. "If I can learn this thing called 'Hamlet' well enough and fast enough, I might double my green stamp reward." Many well-qualified educators have expressed themselves on this in an effort to prevent too many children from being crushed by the new runaway juggernaut.

Herbert M. Kliebard, professor at the University of Wisconsin, describes how the schools have taken on the principles of scientific management and have become "dominated by the criterion of social utility"[28] which results in channeling students into predetermined slots in the social order:

"Modern curriculum theory, currently being influenced by systems analysis, tends to regard the child simply as input inserted into one end of a great machine, from which he eventually emerges at the other end as output replete with all the behaviors, the 'competencies,' and the skills for which he hasbeen programmed." Says Kliebard, "Even when the output is differentiated, such a mechanistic conception of education contributes only to man's regimentation and dehumanization, rather thant o his autonomy."

The problem lies not so much in ferreting out the details of this new movement toward wholesale charlatanism, since many competent educators will be doing that, but in finding effective weapons to combat it.

Teachers are always at a disadvantage in the war of propaganda vs. truth because schools represent, generally, more than half of the tax rate of any local municipality. The politically ambitious and the special interest representatives who frequently populate school boards recognize this, and pander to the taxpayers' fiscal pains at every opportunity. Personal short-term gains are made at the considerable sacrifice of the quality of the future lives of succeeding generations. Only teachers can thwart this continuous long-standing lack of accountability displayed by those who have so long reserved power over schools for their own ends. It is time to hold them accountable.

Lessinger, for example, points with horror at the school's record: "Today, about one of every four American children drops out of school . . . hundreds of thousands of parents . . . have decided that their children are *not* stupid – that either some educators are incompetent, or that methods they are using are inadequate."[29]

This kind of statement is typical of the leaders of the new industrial-education complex. Tell the parents that teachers have cheated their children. Get the community angry enough and they'll beg for industry to solve their problems.

The myth of industrial sanctity

Before parents dial the hot line to industrial headquarters, perhaps we had better remind ourselves again about the humanitarian track record that profit-making corporations have compiled in their race to make America more productive: Lake Erie is dead; food companies are now selling their cyclamate reserves to overseas markets; the major car companies recall thousands of defective cars each year; no one eats fish any more without feeling anxious. Despite all this, a wholesale indictment of industry in America would not only be unfair, it would be inaccurate. Yet the fact remains that industry makes mistakes and industry has done extensive damage to our public good. Industry is no panacea. Furthermore the industrial mind-set (profit first/humanity second) has led to some appalling behavior that is totally unacceptable to experiended educators:

> Item: In Hartford, Conn., where Alpha Systems, Inc. holds the contract, a serious proposal (rejected by the teachers) was made that pinball machines and slot machine pool tables be installed in the schools. Children would be permitted access to these recreational outlets as a reward for learning, with a portion of the money in the till to go to the school system and a portion to the performance contractor.
>
> Item: In the Bronx, where Learning Foundations (one of Fran Tankerton's major economic interests) holds the contract, children were pre-tested in one large group in an assembly hall at 95 degrees temperature for five hours in one day. Learning Foundations' rate of payment depends upon the difference between the initial pre-test score and later scores computed from tests conducted under much more favorable circumstances. Also, the Bronx project incorporates a reward system of green stamps for learning (a common practice among performance contractors). Children are given a cheaply-printed company catalog displaying toy guns and other merchandise which is used to motivate achievement.

In addition to these bizarre practices, in almost all performance contracting experiments, the pupil-teacher ratio has been drastically increased by adding low paid para-professionals and reducing the number of professional teachers. (Now do you understand the school board's interest?) The money saved goes to the high-priced consultants that Lessinger advocates (10 to 15 percent of the total cost of a contract) and to the hoped-for profit margin. The major ingredients of most contracted experiments are machine-oriented programmed materials, and extrinsic reward systems (tokens, recreation time, green stamps, color TV sets, The American Way.)

Where teachers stand

Despite the pious pandering of the educational critics, these facts remain: Schools have been controlled not by teachers, but by school boards. Curriculum decisions, pupil-teacher ratios, availability of special services, availability of adequate textbooks, materials, equipment, etc., have always been touted as "management prerogatives." The shallow thinking that historically created the image of the teacher as a public servant, directed by the whim of elected laymen, has led to the wholesale abuse of talent that has created the horrendous statistics of failure which any cavalier critic of education can easily cite. These statistics are the product of irresponsible school boards who have always had the power to enact change and who, in fact, have not. There can be no accountability without power. School boards have had the power; they are accountable when teachers gain power over professional practices they will be accountable. But that time has not arrived – yet.

The time has arrived to end the unfair exposure that teachers have been subject to because they have been forced to teach under intolerable conditions.

The time has also arrived to end the drastically inferior conditions of education that have frustrated and cheated so many children. We must tell our school boards forcefully and, if need be, dramatically that we will not permit them to hide their irresponsibility behind the comfortable and deceiving illusion which the new catchwords, "accountability," and "performance contracting," really are.

We have for years been our own most active critics. We have been very deeply aware of the shortcomings of public education. We have repeatedly suggested what is needed to improve education, and our suggestions have been rejected. What is needed is not Lessinger's managerial triple play or Rumsfeld's double talk or Thiokol Chemical Corporation or green stamps, but the implementation of the suggestions of experienced teachers.

Since school boards won't listen, let us, as the critics have done, go to the community. We must fully inform the local communities, in paid advertisements if necessary, of the needs of children. We must also inform them that it is their elected representatives who are responsible for the failure of children, not us. When we request additional specialists, reduced class size, time for curriculum revision, opportunity for individualizing instruction, improved diagnostic and placement services, and money in the budget for curriculum experimentation or instructional improvement, and we are refused, we must notify the community at large that we have offered to be accountable and our offer has been refused.

When the day finally arrives when school boards become accountable to their public trust by permitting the conditions necessary for any real degree of teacher accountability to exist, the problems so glibly catalogued by the critics will begin to be solved. But in the meantime, let the pandering mandarins go peddle their green stamps elsewhere. □

---

[1] Lessinger, Leon, "Engineering Accountability for Results in Public Education." *Phi Delta Kappan,* December, 1970, pp. 217-225.

[2] President Richard M. Nixon, Education Message of 1970. As cited by Lessinger, Leon, "Robbing Peter to Pay Paul": Accounting for Our Stewardship of Public Education. *Educational Technology,* January, 1971.

[3] Op. Cit.

[4] See *Policy Statement by the NEA Executive Committee on Performance Contracting,* Dec. 5, 1970, and the *American Teacher,* Jan. 1971, pp. 20, 21.

[5] For example, Donald Rumsfeld, formerly with OEO and now a White House assistant in responding to NEA and AFT's attacks on Lessinger's new pet theory, said, "A major effort has been mounted by a handful of self-appointed education spokesmen to halt any inquiry into the possibility of educational reform. I doubt that these people speak for most teachers."

In a recent speech in San Francisco (See Boston Globe, Feb. 28, 1971) speaking further of professional organizations of teachers, he said, "They reject the idea of accountability and want to ensure that their paychecks . . . are maintained regardless of what is achieved in the classroom." Although Mr. Rumsfeld is not an enthusiastic teacher advocate, he does have some accurate insights. For example, in that same San Francisco speech, speaking of his disappointment with results of five years of federal funding, he said, "The poor have grown cynical. They are fed up with promises not kept . . ." Rumsfeld's answer to the cynicism of the poor is, of course, to transfer O.E.O. and O.E. money to Westinghouse and Thiokol Chemical. This magic plan will no doubt produce the same level of reduced cynicism that occurred when former U.S. Commissioner Allen announced the "Right to Read" campaign only to find that Nixon insiders refused to appropriate any money to fund it. The "Right to Read" campaign was to be the keystone of the Nixon thrust at H.E.W. When is the last time you heard that slogan?

[6] For example, a spokesman for the Wall Street firm of Dominick & Dominick told a recent conference called to promote private investment in pre-school day care centers that ' the education area is the last remaining capital investment industry" with "significant long term thrust." (See the *American Teacher,* Wept. 1970.)

[7]Report of NEA Resource Committee on Performance Contracts, an unpublished paper, p. 7.

[8]Sigel, E. and Sobel, Myra, *Accountability and the Controversial Role of the Performance Contractor,* Knowledge Industry Publications, Tiffany Towers, White Plains, N.Y. 10602 p. 39.

[9]Editor's note prefacing Lessinger, Leon, *"Engineering Accountability for Results in Public Education,"* Phi Delta Kappan, Dec. 1970, p. 217.

[10]*The Sunday Star,* Washington, D.C., July 19, 1970, Mathews, John "Contracting to Teach Opens Education Era".

[11]Sigel, Op. Cit., p. 11.

[12]Sigel, Op. Cit. p. 1.

[13]Sullivan, Neil V., *MASC Journal,* "Survive – or Thrive?", December 1970, p. 5.

[14]*Dallas Times Herald,* Wednesday, Dec. 9, 1970.

[15]Ibid.

[16]Ibid.

[17]Ibid.

[18]A telephone call by MTA to the *Dallas Times-Herald* revealed that Sullivan's appearance in Dallas had been preceded by a telephone call, a letter, and a telegram from the New York-based public relations firm of Zobel & Jacobs. None of the three releases mentioned Sullivan's relation with Thiokol. Zobel & Jacobs later revealed that they were acting as the public relations firm for Thiokol. Similarly, the Dallas paper discovered that School Superintendent Estes (also a former associate commissioner of education at HEW and a strong advocate of performance contracting, by the way) had no knowledge of Sullivan's relationship with Thiokol.

[19]*The Washington Post,* Sept. 20, 1970, Wentworth, Eric, "Teaching Experiment is Dropped."

[20]*Washington Post,* Op. Cit.

[21]Ibid.

[22]Ibid.

[23]Sigel, Op. Cit., p. 48.

[24]See Barrio, Stephen (an economist with the Rand Corporation), "An Approach to Developing Accountability Measures for the Public Schools," *Phi Delta Kappan,* Dec. 1970, p. 196-205.

[25]*Educational Technology,* Op. Cit., p. 13.

[26]Readers who are as interested in moral obligations and public relations as Dr. Comas purports to be also might be interested in the September issue of *Esquire* magazine. (Wills, G., *How Nixon Used the Media, Billy Graham, and the Good Lord to Rap with Students at Tennessee University,* p. 119-122.) This carefully documents the cooperation of the University of Tennessee in engineering the Nixon-Billy Graham public relations charade to convince America that college youth still loves the Nixon administration despite the then recent Kent State shootings.

[27]Op. Cit. p. 31.

[28]See Haubrich, Vernon F., Ed., "Freedom, Bureaucracy and Schooling," *A.S.C.D., Yearbook,* 1971, NEA, Washington, D.C.

[29]*Educational Technology,* Op. Cit., p. 13.

V

PERFORMANCE CONTRACTING: IS IT THE NEW TOOL FOR THE NEW BOARDMANSHIP?

by Harold V. Webb

"Performance contracting may suggest a new kind of relationship between school boards and industry."

It is a tidy idea and easy to express; the board decides what should be done and the administration carries out the order. That, essentially, is how the action is – in theory. And that is pretty much how it is *not* in reality. The line of management division in school district operation – as boardmen across the nation know all too well – is hardly holding, if in fact it ever did.

An increasingly vocal public keeps getting in the way. It is a public less inclined by the day to respect or care about fine differentiations in administrative theory. It is a public that wants solutions to the enormous problems of the schools. Citizens, especially in the cities, are bypassing even the superintendent's office; they are taking their grievances directly into the boardroom, and they are dramatizing the jarring truth that underlines the role of school boards in the 1970s:

An aroused and incredibly diverse public is making complex vocal demands on its schools and is insisting on a measurable accounting from the people it selected to be immediately answerable for what the schools accomplish or fail to accomplish.

The result already is visible: the emergence of a totally committed, totally involved school board member, determined – sometimes forced – to assert a vigorous presence not witnessed for a long while in American education.

I am not suggesting that this is likely to mean open conflict between school board members and the school staff, but I am stating that staff is going to have to get used to the idea that board members increasingly are awakening as functional managers of the educational process, with a sense of responsibility for the *productiveness* of what we call the teaching-learning process. That is reall really a principal reason that various methods of educational accountability to the public are being adopted by school boards and very likely will grow in application and number during this decade.

"Performance contracting" could very well turn out to be one such workable method. It is being tried out, under federal auspices, by a number of school boards in several parts of the country this year.

In addition to its obvious, albeit not fully tested, implication as a means for boards to demonstrate pupil achievement to their communities, performance contracting may suggest a new kind of relationship between school boards and industry and, as portentous, between boards and teachers.

So far as either is concerned, no factor in public education is more crucial to the success or failure of performance contracting – indeed to its very idea – than is the school board. Industry is already cognizant of this, realizing that, if the school board – the functional manager of education which determines the amount and purpose of education expenditures – is not committed to performance contracting, the idea can never amount to anything more than another of the passing fancies that have plagued public education on and off for decades. For this truth is more evident than ever: education's policy makers – its elected and appointed school board members – are chiefly among the people who can and will decide whether the concept of performance contracting is to become widespread educational policy.

Whether they will, and to what degree, is still unclear, but the nationwide scientific sampling of school board members on the subject, conducted by the *Journal* and summarized on page 35, [sic], provides important clues. A full two-thirds of the nation's school board members, the survey found, look with at least some favor on the concept of performance contracting.

Why? As the article on page 35[sic] points out, board members offer numerous explanations, but generally these can be refined to two major points:

☐ *A sensitivity to the public's demand for a humane education with opportunities for each child regardless of his personal, racial or economic circumstances.* This is compelling evidence of the emergence of school board members determined to take more seriously than ever before their responsibilities for all aspects of the school system for which they are responsible – to demand of their staff demonstrable *results* of the teaching-learning process, and to account to the public for those results.

☐ *An apparently widespread belief on the part of boardmen that teachers have turned, at least to some degree, from commitment to children as their primary responsibility to a commitment to their own occupational interests.* Board members participating in the national survey cited the overwhelming increases in the number of teacher strikes in recent years – along with intensified collective bargaining activities on the part of militant teacher groups – as indications of a new teacher preoccupation, not so much with whether children learn, but, as it was put by a board member from a school district on the East Coast, "with winning the highest possible pay for the least possible effort." Whether that conviction is entirely accurate or even completely fair is not the immediate question. What is significant is that this belief appears widespread among school board members and may indicate that school boards are willing to give aggressive consideration to new arrangements to achieve demonstrable results in getting children to learn – new arrangements with their own teacher employes, or indeed, beyond the teachers, perhaps to private contracting agencies.

Both points expressed in the survey by school board members deserve examination.

About the first – it is easy to state, as I did at the beginning of this article and as did so many school board members who participated in the *Journal* study, that the demands of an increasingly vocal public to share in the educational decision-making process mean that school boards will have to become more sensitive to their constituents and more thoughtfully demanding of their staffs. But is is a little more complicated than that.

Board members are not likely to ignore the demands from their new electorate for a voice in making decisions that affect the lives of the community's children. At the same time, neither can they abandon their legal responsibilities for making final policy.

Even though there is room for a new democracy in education – indeed, room must be *made* for it – we cannot embrace the extreme of regarding educational policy making as a populist free-for-all. While the new educational electorate is entirely within its rights in complaining about school deficiencies, it remains the task of the school board and its appointed superintendent to translate complaints about educational deficiencies into *programs.* So the school board cannot abdicate – to private contractors, to teachers or to anyone else – its legal obligation to make the final decisions about prudent public policy and effective plans for education.

That seems to be the real challenge facing school boards in their relationships with the new educational electorate. How are they to convince an apathetic, sometimes hostile, financially threatened middle class *majority* that only truly major changes can bring the schools into line with the needs of the Seventies?

General agreement has it, probably rightly, that this will be achieved by offering some measurable, believable proof of performance – performance *contracting* being one of several possible methods for achieving that, and, to be sure, the method currently receiving the greatest degree of national attention and experimentation in school districts.

The need for offering proof of performance is clearly recognized by many of the board members who expressed favor to the concept of performance contracting. But, as these participating boardmen also pointed out, there is reason to conclude that teachers, as a group, do not yet seem to share the belief that some measurable proof of performance is needed in education. Or, if they do, that they are unwilling or feel unable to accept responsibility for it – indeed, if recent statements by spokesmen for national teacher groups are to be taken seriously, to the specific idea of performance contracting.

Yet the facts tell an almost incredible story.

Our public schools enroll more than 44 million students, employ nearly two million teachers, and account for the expenditure of at least $35 billion in tax dollars each year. We have all kinds of measurements of where this money goes: We can pin down per-capita expenditures nearly to the penny, state how much any school district in the country spent for construction and debt service, and enumerate pupil-teacher ratios.

But we have virtually no measurement of the *results* that such an enterprise yields. We do not know, for example, what it costs on the average to increase a youngster's reading ability by one year; all we know is what it costs to keep him seated for that year.

Fortunately, the evidence, born of long and close association with school boards in all parts of the nation, is encouraging. It indicates strongly that in the Seventies we will see school boards moving beyond showing the public where its education dollars went (teacher salaries, textbooks, new buildings) to showing the public what it *received* for those expenditures – how youngsters moved from one level of learning achievement to a higher one.

It is reasonable to conclude, in view of the *Journal's* survey findings, that performance contracting seems to have a better than even chance of becoming one important means that school boards will employ to accomplish that.

It also seems reasonable to predict that school boards will enter into performance contracts not only with private corporations but, just as likely, with their own local teachers. The reason for that likelihood is this: boardmen, as they hold *themselves* accountable to the public for learning results, will in turn hold their administrators and teachers accountable to the board for the same results. The evidence of this change may manifest itself fairly early in this decade – in collective bargaining. If it does, it may indeed involve school boards with performance contracting of a very real sort, although not always with private corporations.

Collective bargaining between boards and teachers thus far has been largely one sided. In general, teachers have taken the offensive, boards the defensive. That teachers intend to retain and enhance their initiative seems clear enough from the plans teachers are announcing nationally with the intent of strengthening still further their bargaining position with boards. In the face of that, nevertheless, school board members are now being heard arguing forcefully that teachers have an inescapable *performance obligation,* an obligation that must be translated into measurable performance levels and written clearly into contracts.

Many board members are recognizing that it is futile and unfair to perpetuate the notion that some "mystique" about education precludes the spelling out and measuring of learning outcomes. The public no longer will accept that. A new conviction, in fact, is that learning outcomes can and must be spelled out and introduced as legitimate and essential items in bargaining between school boards and teacher groups.

The public has a right to expect a defined standard of performance by its teachers and it is holding the board itself accountable for that performance – to a greater degree each year. The buck is stopping with uncomfortable frequency at the boardroom door. It is this hard fact of life that is likely to spawn school board performance contracts both with private corporations *and* with teachers.

The degree to which the public is beginning to hold school boards accountable isn't entirely fair, of course. Perhaps as much as 75 percent of what school boards do is predetermined by (a) state law, (b) federal guidelines, (c) negotiated agreements, and (d) budget limitations. But to quibble about what is fair is useless. Some one agency must accept prime responsibility for education, and since accountability is thrust upon the school board, it is accepting that responsibility – and proceeding to act accordingly – with the knowledge that the options exercised in that 25 percent gap can spell a significant difference in the quality of education children are afforded. □

Harold V. Webb is executive director of the National School Boards Association and publisher of The American School Board *Journal.*

VI

TWO OUT OF THREE BOARDMEN BUY PERFORMANCE CONTRACTING

American School Board Journal

"If performance contracting can provide us with the means of demonstrating the results the public wants – and is entitled to – then I'm for it," said one board member. "I shudder at the thought of the pressures to which our children could be subjected," said another.

Simply providing an educational program for children is not enough anymore. The Sixties made it clear that school boards are going to have to *prove* to an increasingly concerned – and sometimes skeptical – public that *learning,* not just teaching, is going on in the schools.

And, if two out of every three school board members have their way, performance contracting is likely to be an important tool that boards will use to offer proof – teacher resistance notwithstanding.

That conclusion is drawn from a national sampling of school board members in 47 states, just conducted by the *Journal.* Results break down into neat categories: exactly 33 1/3 percent of boardmen emphatically favors performance contracting; another 33 1/3 percent also supports the concept but with reservations; and a final 33 1/3 percent opposes the idea.

First, a summary of how the responding school board members think. The majority generally gave these two reasons for supporting performance contracting as a means of helping youngsters learn – and of offering proof of their learning:

☐ A lessening of school board confidence in the dedication

Reprinted with permission, from *The American School Board Journal,* December, 1970.

of teachers to youngsters – teachers, school board members argued repeatedly, are demonstrating more interest in winning occupational gains from boards than in accepting serious responsibility for learning results.

☐ A growing awareness on the part of boardmen that *they,* perhaps more than any other group in public education, are being held increasingly accountable for what happens in the schools – "it's a responsibility that has been thrust on us," said a Michigan school board member, "but one we're accepting and can handle."

The minority generally offered these two reasons for opposing performance contracting:

☐ It threatens to "dehumanize" schools at a time when a humane approach to education is more crucial than it has ever been – "education," said a California boardman, "is not a profit and loss sheet or a mass production measurement." What it *is,* offered a Vermont board member, "– or had better be – is a determination on the part of every school board in this country to get to every child with what that child needs, not with some 'norm of achievement.' "

☐ Performance contracting is a näive idea – nobody, minority respondents insisted can "guarantee" learning as though it were a new automobile.

There is irony in the fact that most of the nation's school board members welcome performance contracting even in the face of growing resistance from teacher groups. It is plainly *because* of teachers that many respondents are willing to give performance contracting a try. Sample statements from boardmen: "Right now my fellow board members and I are ready to try almost anything that focuses on what's good for the pupils, and what's good for the teachers," said a plainly exasperated New Jersey boardman. "We're fed up, as I'm sure other school boards are, with the nonsense that the big teacher unions like the NEA and AFT are trying to sell the public – that paying teachers more money means better education for children. Who are they trying to kid?"

"Naturally teachers are going to fight performance contracting," said a member of an Illinois school board. "Performance contracting does what they won't do – it rises or falls on *results,* not on schedules and seniority and protected mediocrity."

"Just send the salesman in to see us," chorused board members from seven states in three regions (Pacific Coast, New England,

Mountain). "We'll give performance contracting more than an even chance." Added a Midwesterner: "As a member of a school board that is trying to make some reasonable demands of our own in collective bargaining with our teachers, I can tell you emphatically that we're ready for some kind of contract with somebody – we'll pay for results, gladly; but we're not paying for double-talk."

"It's as simple as this," explained a Missouri school board member: "let teachers come to the bargaining table and tell us how many kids they're going to have reading at grade level this year, and how much they think *that* ought to be worth to us. Let them use that approach instead of the old business of wanting more money for less effort, and they'll find school boards a lot less reluctant to stick out their necks to find money for teacher pay raises."

If those statements reflect the general attitude of boardmen who give a no-holds-barred approval to performance contracting because of disillusionment with teachers, this one (from Pennsylvania) clearly summarizes another view also held by board members in favor of performance contracting: "For decades we bought the tired old argument that policy making meant signing our names and casting our votes and letting the administration and teachers make the important educational decisions. But now,

---

WHAT BOARDMAN BELIEVE

Question to school board members:
Does the concept of performance contracting have validity for education?

How board members replied:
33 1/3% – Yes, definitely.
33 1/3% – Yes, with reservations.
33 1/3% – No, not at all.
From a scientifically representative sampling of school board members in 47 states.

---

thank God, the public has literally knocked some truth into the heads of those of us who sit on school boards. They [the public] don't give a damn about those administrative niceties. They want results and it's *our* boardroom they storm when they don't get them. If performance contracting can provide us with a means of demonstrating the results the public wants – and is entitled to – then I'm for it."

Performance contracting, suggested a board member from Oklahoma, "could be the moment of truth for school board members. If we're serious about accepting the real responsibilities for public education, as we're becoming fond of asserting, then we should be willing to try out some arrangement like this one – something that enables us to establish measurable goals, move toward them, and make them public, the consequences be damned."

It is, however, the Oklahoman's "consequences be damned" summation that is at least part of the reservation held by a third of the responding board members who attached strings to their approval of performance contracting. Their concern is summarized in this comment from a Californian, a board member from a rural district, who cautioned: "Performance contracting – whether the contract is with a private firm or, as certainly could be, with the local teacher union – can never be allowed to become one more of those terrible infusions that are making education less humane and less child-centered, at the very time that education needs to address itself more singularly than ever to the human needs of the individual child."

And this from an Illinois boardman who also cast an affirmative but qualified vote for performance contracting: "Evaluation must be made by a disinterested outside party, not under any circumstances by the contractor himself. There must be no possibility whatever of the contractor acting as litigant, judge and jury." To which a New Jersey school board member added this warning: "Objectives must be stated in simple, understandable terms. No jargon will do and no subjective goals can be tolerated. Neither can the nonsense about there being some mystique that prohibits objective measurement of the educational endeavor."

But for the one-third minority of board members opposed to performance contracting, there are no safeguards sufficient to avert what these respondents see as ill effects of performance contracting. From Texas: "We are dealing with human minds. I said *human.* No amount of force-feeding, no amount of mechanization, no amount of slick promises and guarantees is ever going to make up for lack of *interest* – a sincere, compassionate caring for the child as a human being."

Finally, amid numerous quotable responses from those one-in-three board members who want nothing to do with performance contracting is this one from a Chicago suburbanite, comprehensively representative of the group opposed to performance contracting: "Do I believe the concept of performance contracting has validity? I do not. We count kids with a computer, grade them via IBM, schedule them through the data processor, and now it's proposed that we employ someone to 'guarantee' their performance at so many dollars a head. No wonder we have student unrest. In the name of heaven, let's stop this dehumanizing of our educational institutions!

"How on earth can anyone 'guarantee' that all children will be able to perform at a stipulated level within a specified time period? These are human minds we're dealing with, not machines that can be revved up or slowed down to meet someone's idea of 'performance.' How can performance contracting possibly allow for the individual differences in children's capabilities? What provision can it make for the slow learner – or the late bloomer?

"I shudder at the thought of the pressures to which our children could be subjected under this concept.

"Is it really necessary that all our children read and comprehend at the same level, or even close to it? Is it really necessary that all of them are able to add a column of figures as fast as the fellow at the next desk? I think not.

"What is necessary is that our schools produce graduates who have learned all that they are capable of learning – young men and women who have been given the educational tools they'll need for the future no matter what their chosen work.

"So Johnny can't read – at least not 200 words a minute with 90 percent comprehension. But perhaps he can read at 150 with an 80 percent, or even at 120 with a 99 percent. So what? If that's the best he's capable of doing, and it's enough to enable him to become a happy, productive citizen, shouldn't that be 'proof' enough to the community of the success of our teaching/learning endeavor?" □

Chapter Nine

ANALYSES AND PERSPECTIVES

I. Better Education for the Children of Tomorrow
Richard W. Hostrop
(In 1967 an educator wrote about performance contracting before it happened.)

II. Performance Contracting for Public Schools
James C. Gillis, Jr.
(The first attempt to explain performance contracting as a new practice in education.)

III. Promises, Promises
Kenneth S. Goodman
(A researcher has fun with industry's guarantees.)

I

BETTER EDUCATION FOR THE CHILDREN OF TOMORROW

by Richard W. Hostrop

This fictionalized account, with its eerie resemblance to the events chronicled in this book, was written in the winter of 1967. Rejected at that time as "too controversial" by several leading educational journals it finds its first publication here.

The city is Tomorrow. It is the year 1975. Tomorrow withdrew from the city of Yesterday in 1970 because no noticeable school improvements had been observed for many years, in spite of assurances by Yesterday's Board of Education that good education already existed and would get better. But it didn't. If anything. the quality of schooling in Yesterday had seriously deteriorated over the past several years, despite VISTA, the National Teacher Corps, and the work of other governmental and quasi-governmental agencies.

Tomorrow is a community of the poor, the disadvantaged, the alienated. Its people have been degraded by years of abuse by the dominant group in the society. There is despair and there is hate. But in spite of these factors, there are occasional bright flashes of vision. It was one of these flashes of vision that enabled Tomorrow to have a school system vastly different than any that had existed heretofore. In fact, Tomorrow's vision has caused such an educational upheaval throughout the country as to astonish even the most avant garde.

It was February 24, 1967. A meeting was being held in a community center ostensibly to discuss ways in which the youth of the community could be constructively occupied during the forthcoming summer months. But Howard Jackson, with sudden insight, changed the direction of the discussion. "What we really need in our community," he said, "is a complete overhauling of our school system. Talking about summer programs for youth is fine, but that is just plugging another hole in a crumbling dike. We need a whole new dike. But we can't do this as long as we're under the control of Yesterday. We must establish our own city!"

After much argument, some of it heated, these community leaders finally agreed that establishing their own city was what was really needed. Through this nucleus of leadership and after three years of hard work, Tomorrow finally was able to establish itself as an autonomous city government. Recognizing that education is the central concern of the good society, the people of Tomorrow and their leaders readily adopted as their slogan and rallying cry, "Better Education for the Children of Tomorrow."

During the last year that cityhood was being achieved, Howard Jackson and others frequently met to discuss the shape education was to take in Tomorrow. Already, many of the teachers who had been teaching in the area had requested transfers to the city of Yesterday. They had tenure, and they were uncertain as to their future in the schools of the new city. Most of them were suspicious that the slogan, "Better Education for the Children of Tomorrow," implied a dangerous threat to their long-accustomed teaching modes. As it turned out, they were right. Most of them would have been misfits in the new school system which soon evolved in Tomorrow.

It was nearly two years to the day since that first meeting on cityhood that Howard Jackson, as chairman of the "Better Education for the Children of Tomorrow" group, synthesized the feelings of the group in what historians now say was one of the most significant meetings on education ever held in this country.

Howard Jackson opened the historic meeting by stating, "We have invited learned educators from school systems and from colleges and universities up and down this state. We have listened to government, workers representing VISTA, the Teachers Corps, and many other projects for the improvement of education. But, gentlemen, we have never heard from industry. Today, I have invited Dr. Jordan to talk to us about the company he represents as it relates to the Job Corps. Perhaps we can soon come to a decision as to what direction our school system should take when we achieve cityhood next year."

Dr. Jordan was introduced to the group and was asked to describe what results were being obtained in Job Corps centers.

"Gentlemen," he said, "it is a pleasure to be here today to tell you about our company's involvement with the Job Corps.

"As you may know, we are not the only corporation engaged in the Job Corps. RCA, Xerox, IBM, Packard Bell, ITT, and others are running Job Corps centers under contract to the federal government. These corporations have acquired educational companies of various kinds such as textbook publishing houses and test bureaus. Xerox, for example, has purchased five different educational companies. Our company has purchased three. Candidly speaking, we agree with Jack T. Conway, former executive director of the Industrial Union Department of the AFL-CIO, in an address sponsored by the U.S. Department of Labor. Conway said, 'The education industry is the most rapidly expanding industry in this country.' Harold B. Gores, president of the Educational Facilities Laboratories, essentially has said the same things as a spokesman from industry: 'It is apparent that education will be the new dynamic of our national economy. Learning is the new growth industry.'

"I mention this, gentlemen, to indicate to you why it is that my company and others are getting directly involved in the business of education. We use Job Corps centers as living laboratories. We combine our technology with experimental teaching patterns in an attempt to achieve a major breakthrough in educating those who have the least promise of being educated. As you perhaps know, in the Job Corps we are dealing with unemployed and rootless young people 16 to 22 years of age. For most of them, school has been little but one continuous sequence of failure. I must confess that we have had many failures too, but there also is no question that some highly significant advances are being achieved.

"We hope that what we are learning in our Job Corps centers will prove useful to educators in the public school system. In turn, we would hope to sell the schools software and hardware that we have found useful, and we would also like to promote the sale of systems programs, which we have developed and found successful."

After Dr. Jordan left, the group discussed what they had heard for a good many hours. Once more, Howard Jackson was the first to verbalize an insight that was emerging in the group.

"I remember reading a newspaper article several years ago in which Dr. Jean Noble of New York University stated that if industry were employed to run a school system, specifications could be set as to the amount of learning that was to take place within a given school year, and industry might be successful in meeting these specifications. Tonight we heard Dr. Jordan. As knowledgeable as he is, he has failed to grasp the next logical step for industry to take. He has failed to see that industry might play a bigger role than merely assisting education with technology and know-how. Industry could actually *run* the schools of Tomorrow.

Animated discussion followed. But there was little disagreement. Public education had failed the children of Tomorrow. VISTA was peripheral. The National Teacher Corps was too transitory. Yes, this might very well be the answer. The group agreed to meet the following day to begin to establish educational learning specifications and to plan their campaign for community support.

The educational specifications that were finally drawn up were perhaps not put in the best grammatical form, but it was clear what they meant. Essentially, they called for an outside testing agency to measure academic pupil placement in September in the areas of reading, spelling, language, mathematical computation, and mathematical reasoning. The outside testing agency was to test again in the first week in June. Bids were to be called on a contract which would include the provision that one percent of the bid would be withheld for every month below the specified year's academic progress that each age group failed to achieve within the academic school year. The contract would also provide an incentive bonus of one percent of the bid for every month beyond a year's progress achieved by each age group. A lawyer in the group volunteered his services to make out the contract and bid specifications in a proper, legal form.

After the contract and bid specifications had been properly drawn, the legal counsel of the State Department of Education was contacted concerning the legality of a school board using public tax money to contract with a corporation to run a school system. Although there was some apprehension in the group regarding this question, it was found that nothing in the Education Code prohibited such use of public funds as long as the professional staff met certification requirements of the state.

A number of "Town Hall" meetings were held in Tomorrow in which lively debates took place concerning this radical proposal. The eventual outcome, though, was overwhelming community approval.

Incorporation of Tomorrow was at last achieved. Howard Jackson was elected first mayor. In his victory he knew that his mandate was the incorporation slogan, "Better Schools for the Children of Tomorrow."

Under Mayor Jackson's prodding, the newly elected Tomorrow School Board contacted all major corporations in the country who were involved in educational enterprises, requesting the submission of bids to run Tomorrow's schools under a three-year contract. To their dismay, they found that the giants of industry were not as eager to get in the education business as had been anticipated.

The national publicity which had taken place when it became apparent that a city was to contract with a corporation to operate its schools has hardly ever been equaled or sustained over such a long period of time. The continuing national debate that ensued produced sharply divided opinions even within the ranks of educators. This was especially so at the university level.

The furor and national debate caused even more smoke in the smoke-filled board rooms of industry as equally heated debates took place there.

"If we bid on operating Tomorrow's school system we will lose the business of the traditionally operated public schools," one corporate tycoon said.

"It just isn't worth the risk," another remarked.

"But this could be the wave of the future, with profit potential far in excess of any we had dreamed of before in the education industry," said another. "Being first could give us an edge over our competitors. It would assure our dominance in the education field. I say, let's go all out to get the contract. I'm in favor of making a bid of just one dollar in order to get the contract. The temporary financial loss will be far more than offset by the profit potential of operating other school districts in the future."

Conservatism finally prevailed, however. None of the large corporations submitted a bid. They concluded that the risk simply was not worth the taking. Tomorrow's plan was just a flash in the pan—a novelty which would probably not be emulated elsewhere. The public school market for educational materials and machines was just too big to take a chance of losing. Moreover, hadn't industry made continuing reassurances to education that technology was only to aid the teacher; that industry was not to be feared; that technology would not displace the teacher? No, industry had a moral commitment to education. Business should remain as a service agent for the teacher and not take over the teacher's job.

However, there were smaller companies who had little to risk and no "moral commitments."

Innovations, Inc. finally obtained the contract for $9.76 million. The company had not even been sent specifications, but upon receiving their request the Tomorrow School Board had quickly responded.

The Tomorrow School Board had been disappointed that major corporations had failed to submit bids, but they were pleased with the apparent knowledgeability of this aggressive small firm. The contract was signed.

Innovations, Inc. has been operating Tomorrow's schools now for nearly five years. Their risk-taking venture has showed a handsome financial return. Their success with Tomorrow's schools has snowballed into eight other school districts with far greater community financial strength. Each of these districts is operated according to the specifications of the district and each is somewhat different than the others. In one of the districts, great emphasis is placed upon the arts, in another physical fitness, in another college preparation for the rest it is basic skills. Innovations, Inc. was approached by two districts after operating Tomorrow's schools for a year, three more the following year, and three more last year.

During the first year of operating Tomorrow's schools, Innovations, Inc. was successful in advancing the children of the district an average of one year in achievement. The company therefore neither suffered a penalty nor received a bonus. It was considered a moral victory by the company, however, since past performance indicated an average loss of two months per school year. Each year under the former system Tomorrow's children had fallen further and further behind the national average.

Each succeeding year of this exciting experiment has shown even better results. In the second year of operation, the average achievement level increased by a year and two months, the third year, another year and two months, and the fourth year a year and one month. In the last year that the schools were part of the public school system, the average national standing of Tomorrow's students in achievement stood at the 44th percentile. Now the students are achieving at a respectable 56th percentile.

Among the first things Innovations, Inc. did upon receiving Tomorrow's contract was to introduce its own testing devices. Among others, the Individual Performance Analysis, a test developed and used by the company, was utilized. IPA is essentially a combination intelligence test and achievement test within the same test booklet, results being recorded in percentiles according to chronological age. IPA thus shows how well a student is achieving according to his ability. This test permits underachievers to be readily identified. Innovations, Inc. gave special attention to the underachievers, since it was the children in this group who most needed help. Summing up, the testing program was designed to identify individual shortcomings so as to individualize instruction more efficiently.

Innovations, Inc. based its operation on certain concepts learned from two Job Corps centers which the company had operated as educational laboratories. Extensive research and experimentation at both centers produced valuable findings which have been adopted for Tomorrow's school system.

The structure and titles of the school staff have even been changed. For example, the schools do not have "principals" but "facilitators." The schools are organized along team teaching patterns with a master teacher and a support team consisting of a content research specialist, a media specialist, a systems specialist, a learning and guidance specialist, and a teacher aide. The teams are nongraded and multi-aged. Each school has an educational engineer. Nursery schools have been established and a new tuition-free community college has just opened its doors. Montessori methods are extensively used in the three-through-eight-year-old group.

The school week is also different from traditional schools. On Monday, Tuesday, Thursday, and Friday the students are required to attend school half an hour longer than schools in neighboring districts. This schedule was adopted in order to free the students for other activities on Wednesday afternoon and to provide time for staff planning. Students were free to go home or to engage in a variety of co-curricular activities. Individual counseling and tutorial sessions are held by both the counseling staff and the teaching staff. Teacher aides, with the help of cross-age teachers, provide academic assistance in both individual and group sessions. Teacher aides have all completed a specialized two-year community college program. Cross-age teachers are older students in the district who assist the younger students. They gain both satisfaction and spending money for their efforts. Clubs, school orchestras, Boy Scouts, and other groups also meet early on Wednesday afternoons in the schools while the children are still relatively fresh. Students are thus not removed from the instructional setting for these activities during the regular school day. Furthermore, parents are expected to arrange for music lessons, doctor and dentist appointments, and other items of personal business on Wednesday afternoons.

All the schools are tied in to a central computer, and the staff makes use of computer consoles. Primary grades have "talking" typewriters. Each classroom has a television receiver. In sum, all of the technological devices that have proven successful are in use, and some new ones have been developed by the staff itself. Programmed written materials, of course, are extensively used, including programmed reading texts.

Organizational patterns, hardware and software, teaching methods and materials are all under a continuous and rigorous evaluative systems approach which specifies under what conditions and to what extent certain kinds of student performance are expected to take place. Indeed, the entire school district is under a systems approach, with the prime objective of increasing academic performance.

Innovations, Inc. had found in its two Job Corps centers that they could not expect increased academic performance without first improving the self-image of the trainee. Therefore extensive and intensive counseling, including basic encounter groups (BE's), are an important part of the "Self-Image Program." Beside BE's, other group counseling techniques are used. A minimum of individual counseling is used. Innovations, Inc. has found it inefficient and less productive than group approaches in most situations. Experiments comparing these two counseling approaches have confirmed recent research in this area. Simulation techniques are used in both counseling and instruction.

Innovations, Inc. did not have a difficult time recruiting staff. Some were brought in from the Job Corps centers, but most of them came from outside. Outstanding teachers and others throughout the country were eager to participate in the most radical educational experiment on a large scale ever conducted. Innovations,

Inc. pays considerably higher salaries than most school systems, but is not apologetic to have a *certificated* staff/pupil ratio of 1 to 45. Thus a great deal more money has been expended for educational hardware and software, but a great deal less for instructional salaries than in typical public school systems. The use of teacher aides, cross-age teachers, programming, grouping patterns, and teaching technology have caused the staff to challenge the traditional concept of the ideal teacher/pupil ratio of 1 to 25. The teachers of the nation wagged their fingers at Tomorrow over this issue above all others. They could not see how the personal needs of a student could be met or how his learning could be individualized with a ratio of 1 to 45. Furthermore, they frankly felt this to be a threat to their livelihood. Even some of the corporations cringed, remembering that they had been telling the educational establishment that technology would not displace teachers. Notwithstanding these arguments, achievement test scores for Tomorrow's children have shown marked academic improvement, and personality inventories have shown better adjustment than when the schools were operated traditionally. Critics at first claimed that these "apparent" improvements were due to a "Hawthorne Effect." After nearly five years, this charge is no longer heard.

Innovations, Inc. used many "aspiration figures" among its staff. The professional staff was deliberately integrated. In fact, more than 50 percent of the professional staff were from minority group backgrounds. This was done in order to create a "success image" for students, most of whom themselves are from minority backgrounds. By the same token and with the same intent, not a single member of a minority group was hired as a janitor, custodian, groundsman, or bus driver. Even among cafeteria employees there were fewer employees from minority backgrounds than from the majority group. True integration could not be achieved at the child level, they felt, while maintaining a "lily-white" staff. For the first time, students were viewing a society in which their ethnic backgrounds were represented at an equal, if not higher, professional level than American society's majority group. This "innovation" in itself did more good than providing any number of individual counseling sessions or lowering the teacher/pupil ratio.

We can now see that Tomorrow has stirred up a revolution in school systems across the country. Other corporations, even the major ones, are now contracting with local districts to operate their schools. The debate still rages, but by bringing fundamental assumptions into open question, the debate has had a healthy effect on the public school system. Many districts and schools of education on university campuses are forging ahead as never before. The time lag between theory and practice has been shortened. It is apparent that the country is entering into a new educational era—an exciting era of frank competition between four major areas of educational power: industry, public education, private education, and the federal government.

It seems certain that these four patterns will dominate in the years ahead. It is expected that these competing systems will assure a healthy cross-fertilization of ideas to the ultimate benefit of the children and the nation. □

Richard W. Hostrop is Professor of Management in the Department of Media Sciences at Federal City College, Washington, D.C.

II

PERFORMANCE CONTRACTING FOR PUBLIC SCHOOLS

by James C. Gillis, Jr.

This article first appeared in May, 1969, in a special issue of Educational Technology edited by an unknown young scholar named Charles Blaschke. Even before Texarkana, the implications for education were clear, and the three models offered here range considerably beyond the narrow limits of most performance contracts to date. Indeed, Model III makes clear that performance contracting as a concept is closely related to the voucher proposals also advocated by the Office of Economic Opportunity which gave performance contracting a boost with its national experiment.

It is generally accepted that American public education is less successful than it could be. Its future directions also are uncertain, due to pressures and influences such as:

- ☐ great increases in knowledge, especially in scientific and technical areas, in the last few decades;
- ☐ continuing population increases, placing more children in schools – and for longer periods of time;
- ☐ increasing pressure from minority groups to have a voice in the administration of the schools;
- ☐ student demands for greater relevancy of courses and study material;
- ☐ dissatisfied teachers using collective bargaining techniques to make their demands known.

Local school boards and school administrators are searching for solutions to this rash of problems. Unfortunately, only a few

---

Reprinted with copyright permission of *Educational Technology*, May, 1969.

school boards and superintendents have seriously explored alternatives to the existing organizational structure. The public school system is over a hundred years old, and it is unrealistic to expect it to operate well in today's new environment.

Enormous strides have been made in management techniques and educational technology within the past two decades. I estimate that 75 percent of the knowledge required to build and operate a modern learning system exists today. However, very few schools employ any of the components of such a system, and virtually no one has synthesized a fully functioning system that takes advantage of all the components.

One is compelled to ask why. Usually the answer is a complicated one that places blame obliquely on everyone and squarely on no one. Furthermore, despite the fact that quality educational opportunities are not available to large segments of our population, there has not been an appropriate response from the citizenry – a demand to fully utilize the existing technological resources to provide the best learning opportunities for each student.

Few alternatives to current patterns of schooling have been presented for the student or his parents to consider. In a country that has risen to world leadership based largely upon open competition and technological advances, it seems strange that one of the most profound institutions, the school, should remain a direct **operational** responsibility of the government – whether local, county, state or federal. With the exception of a few private schools, some form of government exercises a monopoly over formal schooling below the college or university.

Most educators believe that learning is a linear process that takes place in a specified sequence over a predetermined period of time – at least the present system behaves this way.

Most of today's teachers and administrators were not trained in educational technology (it is not an option at most colleges), and are simply not aware of its potential. It is difficult if not impossible for them to envision a computer mediated instructional system with learning modules creating a mosaic pattern based upon student performance and interest option, rather than as an instructional system based upon a linear pattern and elapsed time.

Alternate models

Let us consider a few alternate approaches to the operation

of a school system. Though the public agencies should continue to have the best interest of the individual and community as their primary concern, better procedures than are now in widespread use may be available for discharging this responsibility. Let us briefly examine three models.

Model I – limited sub-contracting

The school system remains under local jurisdiction; it receives state and federal financial assistance and is operated by superintendents and their personnel, like most school systems today. The innovation of Model I, however, is the provision of certain courses or functional areas by another organization, either profit or non-profit, on a contractual basis.

For example, a request for proposals (RFP) might be sent out by the school system to corporations qualified and interested in providing learning experiences to students in, say, welding. The RFP would include the school system's criteria defining the kind and quality of student performance to be demonstrated at the end of the instructional block. The corporations would then submit a technical proposal and dollar bid, and the school system would select the one best able to meet the school's defined needs, at the best price. Depending upon the proposal, the corporation might send staff and equipment into the school, or transport students to a more appropriate facility in order to learn about welding.

The procedure of limited sub-contracting may be equally well applied to history, English, chemistry and other academic subjects and at any level. It would be possible to have a number of concurrent contracts with different organizations, depending upon the needs of the system.

In Model I, it is probable that vocational education would be one of the early candidates for contractual arrangements. This, along with music and certain of the arts, has long been done on a private basis. Aside from cultural values and the development of special talents, one of the reasons for such private contracting is that relatively clear-cut behavioral outcomes can be defined. Thus, the student's progress can be easily measured by observing his performance, and the contractor's performance can be inferred accordingly.

Although it is more difficult to measure abstract or verbal learning than skill acquisition, performance criteria in these areas can also be defined, and programs developed to meet them. Performance criteria can also be linked with payment, such that payment to a contractor for his services becomes contingent upon successfully meeting agreed-upon criteria related to student learning.

Proceeding still further, performance criteria may be linked to profit-sharing between the contractor, the teacher and the student, with profit-sharing becoming a reward system for attaining specific behavioral objectives. Obviously, the system could have many options. Money is not the only "profit" that can be "shared," nor is it necessarily the best. One could think of the contractor sub-contracting with the teacher, and the teacher sub-sub-contracting with the student. In each agreement, the criteria and the reward can be clearly defined.

Model II – total prime contracting

Model II, an extension of Model I, is to contract for the operation of the **entire school system** through one or more contractual arrangements. This model places the school board in the position of having to hire a very limited number of specialized staff to monitor the contracts and evaluate the contractors' performance. The responsibility for actual operation would be the contractor's, and pay would be on the basis of services received (learning by students), not on the basis of elapsed time. Each contract would be reviewed at the end of a two- or three-year period of operation, and put up for bid again.

In this model, the learning system might be characterized by the following:

- ☐ a large number of learning packages, each dealing with a few closely related concepts;
- ☐ modular learning packages that can either stand alone or relate to other learning packages within a given discipline or course;
- ☐ materials that are designed to provide constant feedback to the student regarding his progress;
- ☐ an instructional management system that constantly keeps track of each student, and presents alternatives for each on the basis of individual performance;
- ☐ a data bank that will allow researcher, curriculum developers and teachers to analyze individual performance, group performance, specific instructional items and tests;

☐ opportunities for teachers to earn additional money contingent upon levels of student behavior change (learning).

In short, the goal of Total Prime Contracting would be the production of a learning system using modern management techniques which are self-corrective and cost/effective. The system would require: (1) a well-defined instructional management system (IMS) utilizing the latest in hardware and software; (2) properly trained personnel capable of using the IMS and acting as guides and counselors to individual students; (3) physical facilities that enhance the program, and aid its proper functioning, and (4) learning materials that are self-paced, with many options to select variations in content and media format.

Model III – individual contracting

Maintaining the integrity of the concept of performance contracting, but drastically changing the organizational format, one could conceive of at least one more model: a severe modification of the "GI Bill," where each person shops for his own education. The government would provide free education to all citizens of all ages. Let each individual decide when he wishes to learn, what he is interested in learning, and where.

Sufficient educational technology exists today to offer learning opportunities in the home, at work, or at "play." Television, radio, telephone, portable cartridge tapes and visuals, plus the usual array of printed material are all available for instructional purposes. In addition, learning centers, run on a private or public basis, could compete for customers.

Learning centers might work according to the following plan. First, an organization (either profit or non-profit, private or public) would submit its operation to a public agency for examination and general accreditation. The learning center could be a single entity or part of a nationwide chain; it could offer comprehensive courses in all areas at all age (or competency) levels, or it could specialize in one subject area. Each learning module or course it offered would be approved for reliability of content and would meet minimum pedagogical standards.

Students of any age could then shop and choose what they wanted to study, where, and with whom. If they were not learning well enough with one school, they could go to another. The learning centers would receive money from the government, depending on two criteria: (a) "X" dollars for each student who is physically present, or taking the module or course, and (b) "Y" dollars based upon the performance level at the completion of the study.

Certain variations would have to occur in patterns of course offerings, dependent upon the general ability levels of students, the difficulty of materials, areas of national concern, etc. A supply and demand relationship would evolve between the government and the learning centers, with an incentive system to provide certain courses.

Implementation

Any one, all three, or some combination of the above models could be implemented within two to five years by communities and corporations. It is probable that many communities and several corporations would work together to achieve performance contracting.

Educational technology and a low labor-intensive posture must be the key to contractor-operated learning centers, or to involvement in schools as they are presently conceived. Materials must be self-paced and capable of direct student interaction. Individualized instruction – provided through the full use of hardware and individualized software, and managed by an instructional management system – must be the mode of instruction, if performance contracting is to succeed.

Individualized instruction on a large scale demands both the instructional management system which keeps track of learning experiences for each student **and** sufficient quantities of curricular materials for all abilities and styles of student learning. The curricular materials should be developed through an empirical process of test and revision until they produce in students the specified behaviors they are designed to produce – and do so with a predetermined degree of consistency. They should be presented in multi-media formats for necessary redundancy as alternate ways to achieve certain ends; more important, media format should be selected to best convey the particular information that is being presented to the student.

Many groups have independently devised and are currently following an empirical curriculum development process with these goals. The process borrows heavily from behavioral psychology, defining criterion tests in behavioral terms, and individualizing the instruction through pacing and through branching techniques. The student often has options, and can begin to feel that he is a responsible agent in his own education.

The recent development of educational technology – both techniques and hardware – has made such individualization possible. Unfortunately, educational technology is only beginning to be used effectively; given the state of the **possible** in education, the **actual** does not come very close. Only the rare school or college uses educational technology to any reasonable degree. Many organizations with greater technological capability are in a position of "outsider," and are only allowed to perform on a limited basis within the school setting, although they could be very helpful to the schools, used properly.

It costs money to upgrade any system. The research and development effort is expensive, and the actual installation of new procedures and materials, including training of staff, is considerably more expensive than maintaining the status quo. Once a new system is installed and operational, however, it is probably more cost/effective than the one it replaces; in other words, more student learning will be in evidence per dollar spent. Few school systems, least of all urban ones, can afford to install and maintain new technology without considerable help from other sources. A large portion of the work accomplished to date has been done as a result of funds provided under Title III and Title IV of the Elementary-Secondary Education Act of 1965 (P.L. 89-10). However, it might be possible to take advantage of existing technology by proceeding differently, and reallocating a system's available funds to contract out for specific services, paying according to student performance.

In this way, performance contracting would provide more relevant learning to more students at less overall cost to the taxpayer. Because there is a profit incentive for the contractor, he will constantly update his procedures and materials, thereby placing the latest research findings into practice within a year or two, rather than having the 30- to 50-year gap that has been traditional in education. American business has usually found ways to reduce cost and to provide the consumer with the quantity, quality and diversity for which he is willing to pay. There is no reason to believe that business cannot do the same in education.

In the past, textbook publishers and furniture manufacturers were the major businesses in the education sector. In the past five years, more companies, especially electronic firms, have begun to move seriously into the education market – and not just to sell hardware. They have begun to know the "market," and soon they will realize that they must provide the leadership and direction for the wise use of the new educational technology.

It can be expected that the various levels of government will continue to provide funds, guidelines and monitoring function for efforts to advance the state of the art. At the same time, it is equally predictable that industry's entry into the educational market will become an extended stay.

Performance contracting holds considerable promise for optimizing the relationship between these groups. It is a means by which the requirements of the school and the needs of the student can shape the application of sophisticated technological talent, so that all people, of any age or background, may have full educational opportunity.

James C. Gillis, Jr., is president of Quality Educational Development, Inc., Washington, D. C.

III

PROMISES, PROMISES

by Kenneth S. Goodman

"A pep rally might be better than in-service training, since the main thing is that teachers have faith in and enthusiasm for the program." A director of reading research, Kenneth Goodman digs his satirical spike deeply into performance contracts.

"It's not so much the input that counts as the output"; so said the San Diego Schools' leading authority on performance contracts in a conversation with this writer recently.

This is a rather remarkable but succinct distillation of the arguments in favor of performance contracts as a solution to school problems. Implicit in it are a number of assumptions. a] *The ends justify the means.* Means are in fact not to be considered except in terms of evidence that they do indeed work. Validity, soundness of basic premises, theoretical assumptions, consistency with research, all are to be left to the contractor. b] *Any unplanned, incidental effects on learners are not of importance.* As long as the ends are spelled out as behavioral goals and the contractor promises to achieve those goals; never mind the bed-wetting, self-esteem, anti-social acts, or effects on other areas of learning. Such concerns are "fuzzy-minded." c] *Besides it's easier to stipulate end products than a program to achieve them.* d] *Educators have no input worth considering* (other than choosing whose promises to believe) and teachers in particular, by virtue of past failures, have forfeited the right to make educational decisions. They are to become efficient technicians, trained just enough to carry through the contractor's program but not enough

---

Reprinted with permission of Kenneth S. Goodman and the International Reading Association.

to interfere with it. In fact a pep rally might be better than in-service training since the main thing is that teachers have faith in and enthusiasm for the program.

Performance contracts in reading represent a fascinating exercise in logic. a] We do not know how to teach black children to read, likewise chicanos. b] Furthermore, nothing we have ever tried has been effective in substantially improving the reading achievement of black and chicano pupil populations. c] Therefore, we will seek bidders to accomplish this hitherto unaccomplished task. d] We will accept those bidders who make the most definite promises, stated most unequivocally. e] However, promises can be broken. Hence we will require them to agree that, if they cannot keep their promises, they are to forfeit part of their profit. f] A promise made, backed by a willingness to risk loss of payment is a promise kept. Note: if, however, the contractor will not agree to take the risk, we will accept his promises anyway. h] The unsolved problems of teaching black and chicano children to read will be resolved.

Since no new input is necessary, implicit in this logic are the assumptions that: a] Reading programs have been unsuccessful before because the publishers did not make promises (or at least sincere ones) b] Threats of loss of profit were absent in past relationships between publishers and educators and/or c] Speculators have been quietly sitting with the key to reading instruction waiting for the advent of performance contracting at which point they will surface, make promises, fulfill them and live profitably ever after and/or d] The solutions to problems in reading instruction are self-evident and all that is necessary is for a business organization to systematize the instruction. e] Non-profit agencies have not been able to provide funds sufficient to provide successful reading programs, but profit making agencies will do so, and make a profit besides, using the same revenue sources.

The possible applications of the performance contract to other human problems using this logic are limitless. For example: *Crime* – Government agencies sign performance contracts with private companies to eliminate, or alleviate to a specified level, the criminal behavior in a given community. The ends-means or input-output assumption may require that certain prior practices such as assumption of innocence, right to privacy, constitutional liberties be permanently or temporarily set aside. But after all, past efforts have certainly not reduced crime and no one would argue with the goals. *Health* – The applications of the performance contract to human health problems boggle the mind. A community could enter into contracts for cures to diseases such as cancer. One can also foresee a governmental agency or citizens group entering into a performance contract with a patent medicine supplier to halt an epidemic. If the contractor fails to meet the objectives he forfeits his profits. Even an individual might agree with his physician to a performance contract. For example if he is suffering from a heart condition the doctor might contract to keep him alive for X years. A sliding scale could be developed whereby the physician receives only part payment if the patient dies in less than X years. Quacks should not be excluded from bidding since out-put, not in-put is what matters. What could be more reassuring to a patient, as he goes into an operating room than that his doctor will receive no compensation if the operation is unsuccessful. That would surely be a prime example of accountability. *Space* – How much more secure those astronauts would have been at the time of the explosion in their space vehicle if that vehicle had been built under a performance contract. Furthermore, the expense of the huge NASA staff could be greatly reduced if input were no longer a concern and only output mattered. We could leave it to the contractor to deal with all input trivia secure in the knowledge that faced with a loss of his profits he would not promise what he could, in fact, not achieve. *War* – The Pentagon, the State Department and three administrations have not been able to achieve the goal of ending the Viet-Nam war. Performance contracts could be let which would end the war by a specific date with no more than X American casualties, no less than Y enemy casualties and no more than W new areas of military involvement. (Again outmoded considerations such as bans on the use of chemical and bacteriological warfare might be ignored as long as the end was achieved). In fact we might contract out all American involvement in international problems. To be fair we could give one company the Middle East, another the Soviet Union; still another could guarantee to cope with Red China. After that why not divorce, drugs, child raising. The Generation gap. And then, why not – why do we need elected officials? Why not a performance contract to run the country? Too complex? OK we will break it up. Separate performance contract to run each cabinet level department. Think of the savings on Congress alone which has demonstrated by its past performance its inability to handle the job.

The author prefers to bid on the treasury and promise a balanced budget, lower taxes, and a reduced national debt. He will get 2 per cent if he succeeds and 1 per cent if he does not. □

Kenneth Goodman is Director of Reading Miscue Research, Wayne State University, Detroit, Michigan.

Chapter Ten

HOW TO PERFORMANCE CONTRACT

I. A Guide to Performance Contracting
John W. Adams, Karen H. Kitchak
(Some down to earth specific suggestions for writing performance contracts.)

II. Performance Contracting: Making it Legal
Reed Martin
(A lawyer cautions that, without care, these contracts may easily be written illegally.)

I

A GUIDE TO PERFORMANCE CONTRACTING

by Dr. John W. Adams and Karen H. Kitchak
Minnesota Department of Education

"This publication. . .does not address the philosophical issues which local districts must resolve for themselves. Rather, it is intended to serve as a working guide for those who are considering, or have committed themselves to, performance contracts with public or private organizations."

Acknowledgements
The Minnesota State Department of Education wishes to acknowledge the assistance of a number of individuals who provided background information for this guide. A conference on the topic of performance contracting was hosted by Minnesota on January 26, 27, 28, 1971. It brought together persons with a wide range of experiences to discuss and present various points of view relative to the idea of guaranteed performance contracting. The ideas presented at this conference by the following participants have served as a basis from which this guide has been generated.

Mr. Albert Mayrhofer
U.S. Office of Education

Mr. Greg Mooney
Behavioral Research Labs

Dr. Walter Thomas
COMES

Dr. John Hayman
Council of Great Cities Schools

Dr. Donald Waldrip
Dallas Public Schools

Mr. Michael Keane
Philadelphia Public Schools

Mr. King Nelson
Institute for the Development
of Educational Auditing

Reprinted with permission by the Wisconsin Department of Public Instruction, 1971.

Foreword

Guaranteed performance contracting is one of the most widely discussed innovations which has arisen in public education during the past several years. This approach has broad implications for pupils, teachers, administrators and the general public as a dimension of educational accountability. Because of its many ramifications, the decision to use performance contracting must be made carefully and must be based on deliberate, sound reasoning.

This publication attempts to provide a framework for evaluating the use of performance contracting and does not address the philosophical issues which local districts must resolve for themselves. Rather, it is intended to serve as a working guide for those who are considering, or have committed themselves to, performance contracts with public or private organizations. At this early date not all of the issues, problems, and potential benefits of performance contracting have been understood or perhaps even recognized. As experience and knowledge is accumulated through its use in local board districts, however, we will be in a better position to evaluate this method as one of many to improve our public educational system.

William C. Kahl, State Superintendent
Wisconsin Department of Public Instruction

Theoretical Basis and Rationale

The idea of guaranteed performance contracting cannot be isolated from the larger, more-encompassing concept of educational accountability. Accountability means answerability for results, expressed in student performance, achieved from the expenditure of specified sums of money. Guaranteed performance contracting is not synonomous with accountability, although guaranteed performance contracting can be a part of the concept. Performance contracting is a technique that can be used to achieve accountability.

The contract process is not new to education. Schools for years have let bids fro a variety of products and services. Teachers have been contracted with to teach certain subjects without detailed discussion of student outcomes. Herein lies one of the new thrusts in education, a shift from the emphasis on *teaching* to an awareness that *learning* is what schools are expected to foster. A performance contract is an attempt by an educational institution to obtain improved *results* through a contractual arrangement, usually with an outside agency, with financial incentives related to specific performance standards. If these standards are not met, the school can withhold payment; however schools should be more interested in attaining results rather than in terminating the contract.

The results contracted for can be for such functions as planning, management, or improved student achievement. While most performance contracts to date deal with improved acquisition of basic skills (i.e., reading and math) some contracts involve specific vocational skills such as drafting and auto mechanics as well as achievement motivation.

While it is often difficult to specifically describe cause and effect relationships in social developments, it is apparent that guaranteed performance contracting is the outgrowth of the public's growing concern over the increased costs of education with little demonstrated effect on student outcomes. The rationale offered is that schools do not have the necessary management expertise to correct such alleged deficiencies as:

1) A large percentage of urban school children are reading well below grade level.
2) School costs are escalating without apparent increases in productivity.
3) The educational establishment is charged with being too conservative and resistant to change.
4) Schools have failed to demonstrate a great deal of success with compensatory education.

Those who propose the concept of guaranteed performance contracting, offer it as a catalyst for change and suggest that the public will be given the opportunity to place the blame for failure, or to give proper recognition for success. A number of advantages that could accrue from the concept of guaranteed performance contracting have been suggested. A representative sample includes the following:

1) It may work! Students may learn more than they presently are learning, and new ways of teaching may be found.
2) Performance contracting requires people to shift their attention to results and away from inputs.

3) It forces those concerned to define what education *is* – the objectives of instruction are spelled out in detail.
4) Performance contracting provides the opportunity to make available additional expertise to the district. New developments could be made available without large expenditures for research and development.
5) The potential for objectively defining the "good teacher" is available; the "good teacher" being the one that produces results in the classroom.
6) Lastly, the expectation of success may be a strong force in changing the climate in schools where failure has been an established pattern.

Potential disadvantages to a school district resulting from performance contracting include:

1) The school district will surrender some amount of its control and autonomy to the contractor.
2) Many potential difficulties may exist with the organized teaching profession, such as violation of teacher-pupil ratios agreed to in the contract as well as transfer of teacher clauses in the contract.
3) Performance contracting may end up costing more money, or may just be add-on-money if a district is not careful.
4) Performance contracting may prove to be nothing more than a "gimmick." Early over-exposure may negate any potential gains.
5) The students may suffer from the over-emphasis on results and the basic skills (i.e., reading, writing, and arithmetic). Some affective measures of student attitudes towards themselves should probably be included in the evaluation of the programs.
6) The whole problem of retention must be considered in writing the contract. Provisions for evaluation of long-term gains should be considered.
7) "Teaching the test" may be a temptation to the contractor. This term means that the contractor violates the random selection process in writing the programs and focuses on specific items included in the post-test. "Teaching to the test" differs in that the random

selection process is not violated, but that the program prepares students to do well on the post-test by including similar, but not identical times, in the program.

The Procurement Model and The Request For Proposal (RFP)
The school district's specifications, which will later be embodied in the contract, are initially spelled out in the Request for Proposal (RFP). Potential bidders are asked to respond to the conditions outlined in the RFP by submitting a proposal to the district. The steps leading to the development of the RFP are as follows:

Step No. 1

It is apparent that before a district decides to develop a performance contract several events should have occurred. First, the Local Education Agency (LEA) will have identified a problem area. This may be a problem in any of several areas such as instruction, staff capabilities, or administrative procedures. After becoming aware that a need exists, the district must identify the proper local personnel to assist in problem analysis, to provide programming ideas, to assess the relevancy of the ideas presented and of activities implied in the approaches outlined and to ascertain the concerns of various publics. This group might include representatives from all levels of school personnel, students, parents, teacher organizations, local colleges and universities, and the business community and local government. This group should then select a project director.

Step No. 2

At this point the district may wish to contract for the services of a management support group (MSG) which could provide any or all of the following services: (1) assisting with the specific needs assessments, (2) developing a number of alternatives (3) helping with selection and implementation of the selected alternative. The functions of the MSG and a discussion of the feasibility of purchasing these services will be developed in depth in another section of this paper. Suffice it to say that for the purposes of this procurement model the district may wish to examine the possibility of such a service at this time.

Step No. 3

The third important step involves the clarification of the target population. This identification must be as detailed as possible, especially if the alternative of guaranteed performance contracting is chosen so that the contractor can make the most intelligent bid. Beyond a general statement of present deficiencies and future projections, student profiles should be determined including educational deficiencies, socio-economic and racial composition, and attitudinal and motivational data, if possible. The target area should also be defined by educational resources, political variables, indices of community participation and effect of the program on vested interests. If it has not been done to this point the sources of funding should be specifically defined, including funds from government agencies at all levels and from non-profit organizations.

Step No. 4

The next important consideration regards the development of performance specifications. Essentially this means (a) stating the performance objectives to be achieved and (b) defining the general scope of work involved. Obviously the objectives must be directed at solving or strengthening the defined problem areas. This statement must include the following: (1) the performance objectives in terms which can be reliably, validly, and objectively measured; (2) the parameters of the work involved; and (3) the facilities and services to be provided by the district.

Step No. 5

Concurrently, while the specified group is developing a detailed Request For Proposal (RFP) the district may wish to prepare an announcement to invite bids. This letter may include the following: (1) an announcement of plans to invite bids, indicating the name of the superintendent and the name, address and telephone number of the Local Education Agency (LEA); (2) a summary of the problem and the performance to be contracted; (3) an address at which copies of the RFP can be obtained; (4) a statement of the type of contract (fixed price, cost plus, fixed fee, etc.); (5) a request for a letter of intent to submit proposal and the deadline date; (6) an indication of where and to whom to refer questions; and (7) a statement that the invitation to bid should not be construed as a contract or commitment of any kind.

Step No. 6

The heart of a successful contract is the adequacy of the request for proposal. It must have enough information so the contractor can make an appropriate bid but avoid undue restrictions which may cripple the capacity of qualified bidders to provide an innovative program. If the letter of intent suggestion is used, it may be helpful to have some informal input from contractors before the RFP is finalized. School districts should use discretion in using only those portions of significance to them, or it may be decided to include some of the standard clauses only in the final contract. Following is a detailed outline of what an RFP might include.

A. **Definition of the problem area.**
   1. The target population (specifically defined as discussed above)
   2. The number of participants.

B. **The scope of the work.**
   1. The performance objectives in measurable terms.
   2. The parameters of the work involved.
   3. The facilities and services provided by the LEA.
   4. The relationship of the contracted work with other school problems.
   5. The degree of labor intensity in the instructional program.

C. **The calendar.**
   1. The period of contractual performance.
   2. The location and date of the pre-bidders conference.
   3. The deadline date for receipt of bids.
   4. The date funding is available or approval expected.
   5. The date a decision will be made on a bid.
   6. The start-up time.

D. **Definition of parties.**
   1. The relationship between school administration and project administration.
      a. Identification of the local project director.
   2. Identification of a planning advisory group and/or MSG.
   3. Identification of an arbitrator for disputes, if known.

E. **Financial arrangements.**
1. A statement about independent price determination.
2. Dollar parameters (maximum dollar amounts).
3. Type of contract (cost plus, fixed price, etc.).
4. Method of payment (keyed to receipt of reports).
5. A standardized itemized budget form or schedule indicating major line items.
6. The manner in which budgets are to be submitted.
7. The salary schedule of the district.

F. **Policy guidelines and assurances.**
1. District eccentricities; e.g., attendance requirements, specific racial mandates, etc.
2. Assurances for subcontracts.
3. Applicable state and federal guidelines and laws, e.g., equal employment opportunity clause.
4. A statement that school officials cannot benefit from the contract.
5. A convenant against contingent fees clause.

G. **Evaluation procedures.**
1. Identify the evaluating agency.
2. Identify the auditor, if known.
3. Specify local instructional materials and testing instruments that will be made available, if any.
4. Specify when the evaluation will be done.
5. Provide the baseline data.

H. **Reporting procedures.**
1. Specify the documents to be provided by the LEA for the contractor. (type, number of copies, etc.)
2. Specify reports to be made by the contractor:
   a. format
   b. frequency
   c. topics to be covered
   d. person responsible for preparing and certifying the reports.
3. Provide a systematic process for review and revision of the contract.

I. **The format for the proposal (for ease of comparability in reviewing bids) and criteria to be used in evaluating proposals.**

Step No. 7

A. **Choosing a contractor**: If it has not been done at this time, the district and/or MSG should now identify the appropriate bidders and send them the announcement, and the RFP. There are a large number of potential bidders and it is difficult to present a legitimate list because it is a new business and a large number of firms are being developed. Once the requests for proposal have been sent the district should call a bidders conference to provide an opportunity for interested contractors to discuss the RFP with the district prior to developing a proposal.

B. **Alternative strategies in selecting a contractor**: There are alternative strategies available in selecting a contractor. The first alternative is one in which the district solicits a number of competitive bids from companies whose general characteristics best fit the district's needs. There will probably be little question of legality in this instance and the district may have the additional benefit of innovative input from which they might draw to improve the final contract. However, replying to a request is a lengthy and expensive procedure for a contractor and if there seems to be little chance of winning the contract in open competition, many smaller reputable companies may decline to bid. In addition the district should consider the time and staff necessary for careful review of the proposals received.

An alternative to the competitive model is the sole source model wherein the district chooses at an early data a single company which it feels can meet its needs. In this procedure the company can serve a useful role in the development of the specific performance requirements, however the district should carefully investigate the legality of this method.

A third procedure incorporates some features of each of the preceding. Here, three or four firms are contacted and asked to submit proposals. The district then evaluates these bids and calls a conference where the contracting firms are permitted to bid against each other. One result of this method might be that the district chooses more than one of the contractors, divides the target group proportionately, and conducts research as to the feasibility of each method for the turnkey phase.

C. **Criteria in choosing a contractor:** Obviously the first factor to consider in choosing a contractor is how well the proposal matches the RFP. This decision and recommendation can come from the MSG but to avoid collusion of interests the final selection must be made by the district. A useful procedure might be the designation of an evaluation team and a checklist by which they might compare and rate proposals. The guidelines used in Dallas, Texas, include many of the elements the reviewers might consider. There should be a detailed examination of these factors: 1) presentation and organization; 2) style; 3) the technical soundness of the approach; 4) socio-political ratings; 5) subjective judgements on the philosophy of the approach; 6) pricing arrangements; 7) the past performance and ability of the company; 8) the level of organizational commitment; 9) the ability to provide all services; and 10) the quality of the equipment. These considerations and a more detailed discussion of cost analysis are developed in the section entitled, "Considerations in Selecting a Contractor."

Step No. 8

Following the selection of the contractor and prior to the implementation of the process, the same procedure must be followed in selecting an independent auditor if the district chooses to validate the contract by that method. The role of the auditor and features of the audit contract are discussed in the section of this paper entitled "Third Party Functions."

Step No. 9

Finally, all of the involved parties must perform the necessary activities to put the contract into operation. These activities might include special construction, training of district personnel, pretesting of students, public relations, and other problems of "lead-time" significance.

Considerations In Selecting A Contractor

The program and staff capabilities of a contractor are one of the first considerations in selecting a contractor. Who are the members of the staff? What has been their past involvement and experience? What is the reputation or "character" of the firm? What is their "track record?" What other projects have they been involved in and what were the results? Is their program a multiple- or single-linear system? There should be alternatives available so if a student fails in the method provided by the contractor they can provide alternate routes for him to follow to accomplish the objectives.

The financial capability and status of the contractor should be explained. The district should consider who is to pay the start-up costs. While there may be advantages to the district to pay the start-up costs it must be realized that with this "front-end" load the district will assume major financial responsibility if the contractor fails to deliver. The ratio of start-up costs to total cost must be considered to avoid a project which is too expensive to replicate in the district. It is also a wise idea for the district to get a Dunn and Bradstreet rating on the firm. A performance bond may also be required if there is question as to the ability of the contractor to finance the project.

Particular attention should be paid to the system for turn-key outlined by the contractor. "Turnkey" refers to the process by which the contractor turns over operation of the project to the school district. Careful thought and consideration should be used to determine if the system outlined is operable. Turn-key is essentially a performance contract for *teacher* behavior. Will the contractor guarantee some percentage of cost effectiveness one year after the project has ended?

An understanding of the motivational system used by the contractor should be gained to see if it is consistent with district philosophy. Such questions as whether the rewards are intrinsic or extrinsic should be covered. Do the incentives apply to both staff and students? How would the PTA and other groups feel about giving students "green stamps" or other rewards for achievement? The kinds of management support (such as PPBS) to determine the cost effectiveness the contractor proposes to use should be spelled out. Is the contractor himself on a PPBS operation? Or does he at least have a program which appears to be operable? If he intends to write objectives for the program has his organization written out objectives for their own operation?

The way in which the contractor handles his research and

development (R&D) costs bears close examination. R&D can be either capitalized or expensed. If it is capitalized it is amortized over a period of years. If it is expensed it is charged to the period in which the costs were incurred. From the district's point of view it is preferable to have R&D costs expensed so that the district is being charged only for the actual costs involved in their project and not paying for R&D done on previous projects. If capitalized, a rationale should be offered as to how the previous R&D costs relate to the present project.

The school district should have a clear understanding of proposed subcontracting and the necessity for it. If a large portion of the contractor's work has to be subcontracted there may be waste in high consulting fees and over-all lack of continuity in the project.

An assessment must be made as to the potential "economies of scale" involved in the project. "Economies of scale" refers to the forces causing the long-run average cost of servicing students to decrease as the contractor (or district), increases the number of students. Two important economies of scale are (1) increasing possibilities of division and specialization of labor, and (2) increasing possiblities of using advanced technological development and/or machines.

Division and specialization of labor can be achieved through application of a differentiated staffing model utilizing teacher aides and para-professionals to conduct much of the routine and clerical work and reserving the teacher's time for more professional type activities. Districts should have the contractor reveal his staffing plan in advance so that student-teacher ratios, adult-student ratios and other factors are acceptable to the school board, administrators, teachers, parents, and other relevant groups. State staffing requirements and legislated ratios must also be considered.

Economies from using technological advancements such as teaching machines and other instructional hardware offers potential for cost savings. Economists speak of education as being a "labor intensive" industry because the input of labor resources is largest relative to other resources (land, labor, capital, and management). Many writers forecast that education will become increasingly a "capital-intensive" industry with the introduction of modern technological devices. "Capital" as it is used in this sense refers to any man-made aid to production.

The potential for cost savings by moving to the use of capital resources exists because of the possibility for use of the item by additional students. The same kinds of savings are realized when class size is increased, however, this is generally not a widely-supported option.

Additional terms coming into the educational vocabulary are "consumables" and "non-consumables". These terms obviously refer to the life expectancy of items purchased. Roughly, a consumable item is one whose useful life is less than one year, and a non-consumable item's useful life is of greater duration than one year. Care should be taken by the district to see that in a highly consumable system some guarantee is made that the contractor will not increase the price of the items after the turn-key phase, and that there is some assurance that the consumable items will remain compatible with the hardware over an extended period of time.

School districts should also refrain from purchasing non-consumable materials from the contractor during the first year of the project. If the project fails, the school district is still committed to pay for the materials. A preferred way would be for the contractor to lease the equipment or materials for the first year, and allow the district to apply the leased costs toward the purchase price if the system proves to be successful.

Contractors speak of the "critical mass" needed to make a project cost-effective. The term refers to the number of students that must be involved in order for the contractor to use his system most effectively. Systems designed with a low critical mass may not offer economies of scale that could be realized from a project whose costs could be spread over a large number of students.

Of paramount importance, but often overlooked, is the involvement of the community in the planning stages. A program offered by a contractor which is unacceptable to the consumers of the service has slight chance for success.

The Contract

This section of the paper covers the content of the contract. While every contract differs in content and style, most of them have a number of common essential elements. Districts are well advised to use the services of an attorney in drawing up this legal document to safeguard the district's interests. In addition, the district personnel and/or the MSG should be aware of the specific problems which must be clarified in their contract. The following should not be interpreted as a complete or model contract but rather should be regarded as a summary of items commonly found in contracts. The format of this section will be as follows: (1) a description of what the clause contains and (2) an illustrative mock-up clause.

1. **Definition of parties**: This should include specification of the fiscal agent, the residency requirements, director and manager names, and any subcontractors.

Contractor – Educational Learning Services Incorporated. Brownsville Independent School District No. 333 – the entity awarding this contract.

Project Director – Mr. George Allen (or his successor designated by the district) to reside in the Brownsville district.

Project Manager – Mrs. Jean Smith (or her successor, designated by the contractor) to reside in the district.

Management Support Group – Management for Education, Incorporated, to provide the agreed upon number of on-site days.

Auditing Contractor – Testing for Reliability, Incorporated, to provide the agreed upon number of on-site days.

2. **The establishment and description of responsibilities within school and within contractor:**

a) The district will appoint a Project Director and Management Support Group. The district will appoint a Project Director to oversee the project activities of the Contractors. He will be a full-time, paid employee of the district. The Project Director as the authorized representative of the district shall have general responsibilities for coorination and administration of the program with regard to the district, the contractor, the Management Support Group, the Auditing Contractor, the local community, project personnel, parents, and student participants. The Project Director, with assistance from the Management Support

Group, shall have specific responsibility for contract management; detailed record keeping; public relations, development of baseline data and continued monitoring; monitoring of the contractor costs and cost-effectiveness; initial and follow-up purchases, rental, maintenance, and replacement of equipment. The district or its designee shall provide the Project Director with all forms and procedures by which the above information is to be collected and reported. The Management Support Group will provide necessary training, development, and requisite project management assistance to the Project Director and his staff.

b) The contractor shall appoint the Project Manager subject to the prior approval of the Project Director. The Project Manager will report directly to the Project Director. He will be responsible for classroom scheduling and other administrative functions and decisions and will decide all routine matters concerning administration of the project. He will communicate his decisions to the contractor who may appeal such decision directly to the Project Director. All progress reports, position papers and other communications will be made individually by the contractor to the Project Director.

3. **Definition of personnel including hiring agency, certification requirements, provision of paraprofessionals, jurisdiction of local salary schedules or fringe benefits:**

The contractor shall control its curriculum, teaching aids, materials, and conduct of the Reading and Mathematics programs in accordance with the conditions of this agreement, and shall hire, train and fire its own employees, agents, or independent contractors, directly or indirectly paid by the contractor except for the Project Director and his secretary.

Teachers used in the Reading and Mathematics programs will be employed by the contractor unless the district deems it necessary to employ these teachers as regular district personnel. Upon notification by the district to the contractor, the teachers used in the Reading and Mathematics programs will be employees of and paid by the district. They will be placed in the Reading and Mathematics programs only after the contractor has signified its acceptance of these teachers in these programs. Upon notice by the contractor to the district that it desires the removal of a teacher from these programs at the contractor's sole discretion, the district shall authorize the contractor to interview potential replacements supplied by the district and to place an acceptable teacher into the Reading or Mathematics programs. The contractor agrees to reimburse the district the salary determined by the district plus the benefit costs for all teachers used in the Reading and Mathematics programs within ______ days after the receipt of interim payments from the district.

4. **Definition of proprietory concerns such as copyrights, distribution agreements and franchises.** In addition guarantees should be established for materials and prices at the time of turn-key. For example, a contractor with emphasis on non-consumables could offer the district a lower than market price, but at the cessation of his involvement could raise the price of the materials to which the district had been committed. It should be noted that materials developed by either the district or the contractor should be protected by the same type of clause. Precautions must also be taken regarding the dissemination of information pertinent to status of the project.

The contractor agrees to hold the district harmless of all lost costs and expenses because of any infringement of copyright on instructional materials, equipment and supplies used by the contractor in the performance of this Contract.

The contractor shall give advance notice to and shall seek and obtain approval of the Project Manager prior to publishing, permitting to be published, or distributing for public consumption, any information, oral or written, concerning the objectives, results, or conclusions made pursuant to the performance of this Contract. Only the district through the Project Director shall authorize the release of any test results to the public. Such results shall be group scores or individual scores, but the names of individual students shall not be made public.

5. **Specification of funds:** including the amount and source of funding:

In this project the district will provide funds for the following:
1) Physical plant facilities.
2) Maintenance and custodial services in Project Schools.
All other costs will be funded uncer ESEA, Title I.

6. **The schedule of fee payment**: This provision could become very complex covering such issues as:

1) The extent of the guarantee.
2) The nature of the reimbursement, e.g., mean gain versus individual gain.
3) Cost-plus or performance units only.
4) Reflection of incentives and penalties, and
5) Adjustment schedules.

The performance incentive measurement for establishing the unit price to be paid by the district for each student in the Reading and Mathematics programs shall be based on the results of pre- and post-test gains as measured by the standardized tests and interim performance tests established for each program. The average fixed maximum unit price based on gains in achievement level and interim performance tests shall not exceed an average of $189.75 per each student in the Reading and Mathematics programs. The total maximum incentive price for this contract for five hundred and fifty students in each year of the Reading and Mathematics programs shall not exceed $220,438.50.

Not withstanding any other provisions of this contract, the contractor shall receive interim provisional cash payments equivalent to sixty percent (60%) of the estimated total maximum contract price of $220,438.50. Provisional payments shall be separated into five (5) installment payments payable within ten (10) days following the administration of each interim test. Each payment will be the product of $28.70 times the total number of students taking the interim tests in mathematics and reading.

Within fifty (50) days after the final post-test results are established and reported to the contractor by the auditing contractor, the contractor shall submit an adjusted final voucher stipulating the final unit price for each student in the

Reading and Mathematics programs with detailed supporting information. The voucher shall state the total amounts which may be refundable to the district or additionally payable to the contractor in each program.

7. **A description of the instructional program, without necessarily divulging proprietory concerns of either the district or the contractor:**

The terminal performance objective is to increase, by the specific amount, the academic achievement and skills of fifth grade pupils in reading and mathematics. To meet this objective, the teaching material will predominantly use the inquiry approach, defined for the purposes of this project as scientific heuristics. It is assumed that intensive use of hardware will be inappropriate to the purpose and approach of this project.

8. **Provision for changes in the program, for example, new materials which are developed:**

If, during the contract period, the contractor wishes to change substantially the instructional system, materials, or equipment used, it will notify the Project Director of any such change. In no event shall the district be liable for the costs of a change to more costly instructional systems, materials, and equipment.

9. **Assurances agreed upon by both parties such as non-discrimination, equality of employment, bonding, rights of students, integration mandates, the corporate status of the contractor, the state permission for the contractor:** Such clauses may read as the two following standard clauses:

Recent decisions in a variety of jurisdictions, including the Supreme Court, have established student constitutional rights as against school districts, their agents, and administrative and instructional personnel. The contractor shall assume that the same constitutional prohibitions apply to it. All of the contractors actions in regard to participants in the Reading and Mathematics programs, particularily in the event of expulsion from a program, must meet constitutional requirements, especially those of procedural and substantive due process.

In connection with the performance of this contract, the contractor agrees not to discriminate against any person on the ground of race, color, religion, sex or national origin.

10. Covenant against contingent fees. This is a standard clause to guard against any third party profiting by the selection fo a particular contractor.

The contractor warrants that no person or selling agency has been employed or retained to solicit or secure this contract upon an agreement or understanding of commission, percentage, brokerage, or contingent fees excepting bonafide employees or bonafide established commercial or selling agencies maintained by the contractor for the purpose of securing business. For breach in violation of this warranty, the district shall have the right to annul this contract with liability or, at its discretion, to deduct from the contract price or otherwise recover, the full amount of such commission, percentage, brokerage or contingent fee.

11. Condition for termination: The contract should define the means for concluding the contract.

All obligations of the district undertaken hereunder are wholly subject to federal funds being made available to the district and committed for the purpose of this Contract, and the actual receipt of such funds by the district. In the event the funding from Federal sources is not received by the district as anticipated during the contract performance period, this Contract shall be terminated immediately upon written notice by the district to the contractor. The district shall have no further liability for costs accrued or fees earned by the contractor after the giving of such notice. Payment to the contractor for such costs accrued up to the date of termination shall be calculated on actual documented costs and payable to the contractor: (a) by applying all provisional and advance payments theretofore made to the contractor, and if there be an excess remaining, such excess will be refunded to the district; (b) if there be any balance remaining unpaid on said actual documented costs after applying such provisional and advance payments the balance shall be payable only to the extent that the district may have any remaining balance of Federal funds committed to this project, on hand, unpledged and unspent. The district reserves the right to first pay directly out of such balance of funds, if any, any obligation owing by the contractor to teachers and other personnel who were used by the contractor and assigned to the performance of the program covered by this contract.

12. **Provisions for the contractor's reporting and record keeping**: This clause should specify the format of reports, topics to be covered, frequency, and the person responsible for preparing and certifying the reports.

The contractor shall maintain records to reflect all actual start-up and operating costs in accordance with reasonable reporting forms and procedures established by the Management Support Group, and at specific intervals required by the Project Director for the reporting system and for such reasonable intent and purposes of the overall project as are stated in this agreement.

The contractor agrees to provide a full-time, on-site program manager who, in addition to operations for the contractor, will also be responsible to obtain such data information. The contractor further agrees to maintain the level of effort required on-site over the full contract period to assure the maximum possible educational development for each student in the Reading and Mathematics programs.

The contractor agrees to maintain books, records, documents and other evidence pertaining to the costs and expenses of this Contract (hereinafter collectively called the "records") to the extent and in such detail as will properly reflect costs, direct and indirect, of labor, materials, equipment, supplies and services, and other costs and expenses of whatever nature for which reimbursement is claimed under the provision of this contract. The contractor: accounting procedures and practices shall be subject to the approval of the Project Director.

13. **Provisions for the settlement of grievances and disputes and the agency which will handle appeals**: This example provides for

settlement of disputes within the district. Other alternatives, however, might include outside agencies such as the National Arbitration Board.

> Except as otherwise provided in this contract, any dispute concerning a question of fact arising under this contract which is not disposed of by agreement shall be decided by the Project Director who shall reduce his decision to writing and furnish a copy thereof to the contractor. The decision of the Project Director shall be final and conclusive unless, within thirty (30) days from the receipt of such copy, the contractor furnishes to the Project Director a written appeal addressed to the district General Superintendent. The decision of the Superintendent or his duly authorized representative for the determination of such appeal shall be final and conclusive unless determined by a court of competent jurisdiction to have been fraudulent, or capricious or arbitrary, or so grossly erroneous as necessarily to imply bad faith, or not supported by substantial evidence. In connection with any appeal proceeding under this clause, the contractor shall be afforded an opportunity to be heard and to offer evidence in support of its appeal. Pending final decision of a dispute, hereunder, the contractor shall proceed diligently with the performance of the contract in accordance with the requirements of the Project Director.

14. **Liquidated damages and delays and defaults**: This clause should cover the contingencies of both excusable delays and defaults and preventable delays and defaults.

> The contractor shall not be in default by reason of any failure in performance of this contract in accordance with its terms if such failure arises out of causes beyond the control and without the fault or negligence of the contractor. Such causes may include, but are not restricted to: acts of God or of the public enemy, acts of the Government in either its sovereign or contractual capacity, fires, floods, epidemics, riots, quarantine restrictions, strikes, freight embargoes, and unusually severe weather, but in every case the failure to perform must be beyond the control and without the fault or negligence of the contractor. If the failure to perform or make progress is a

> result of the failure of the contractor's subcontractor to perform or make progress, and if such failure arises out of causes beyond the control of both the contractor and his subcontractor, and without the fault or negligence of either of them, the contractor and his subcontractor shall not be deemed to be in default, unless the supplies or services to be furnished by the subcontractor were obtainable from other sources.

15. **Definition of the target population**: This should be a detailed clause including how the students are selected, what data are used, what type of students are included (e.g., drop-outs, shut-outs or special students in which case the contractor might be paid extra), and conditions for the student's retention. It should include all of the data in the RFP plus individual testing results if that was not included in the RFP. These may be specified in an appendix or attested by the independent auditor as valid.

> All students in the Reading and Mathematics programs will have grade level deficiencies in Reading and Mathematics as determined by a standardized, commercially-available, achievement test to be selected and administered by the district or its designee. Students will be selected for participation by the district through random assignment from a target population pool of 1,600 students in grade 5. The district shall obtain written parental consent for students to participate in the project. No students shall be placed in the Reading or Mathematics programs who would not be eligible and accepted for instruction in regular district classes by virtue of mental or emotional deficiencies. If, during the first thirty (30) days of the program the contractor determines that a student is not qualified to participate in the program because of emotional or mental deficiencies, it may request the student's removal in writing to the Project Director. Upon the Project Director's determination, an individual test will be administered by a certified psychologist under the aegis of the Auditing Contractor. In all cases, the Project Director's decision on student particiaption shall then be final and binding.
>
> Those students remaining in the Reading and Mathematics programs after the first thirty (30) day period shall remain in

such programs for the full number of class days normally scheduled by the school for all students. Any student who does not remain in a program shall be the subject of inquiry and certification by the Auditing Contractor, and the reason for students leaving the programs shall be stated by the Auditing Contractor in an evaluation report. For the purpose of this contract, the following are the only bonafide reasons for a student leaving the program:

a. The student is retained in institutional care, such as in a hospital, or confined before or after trial for law violation.
b. The family moves out of the metropolitan area.
c. The student dies or is incapacitated by illness or otherwise for either a continuous period of eleven (11) days or for intermittent periods totaling twenty (20) days in any three month period.
d. The student is removed upon request of parent or guardian.

In all these cases, the contractor shall give written notice to the Project Director when in its opinion a student's absences warrant removal from the program. The Project Director shall obtain a written statement from the parent, and the validity of the stated cause shall be certified by the Auditing Contractor.

The contractor shall, daily furnish the names of any absent students to the Project Director, and the district shall use the same efforts and procedures as are used for all other students in the school district to ensure continued attendance at future sessions and at any make-up sessions which may be required. If the student transfers to another school in the district, the district shall not be responsible for replacing such students in accordance with procedures determined by the Project Director. If regular school schedules are changed, the district will ensure that time will be provided for students in the Reading and Mathematics programs to continue to participate in these programs.

A student shall not remain in the Contractor's classes if receiving disciplinary punishment, including temporary expulsion from regular classes. The district shall inform the Project Director whenever a student receives disciplinary punishment or temporary expulsion necessitating removal from the

Contractor's classes. The contractor may request the district to initiate such action for particular students based on their behavior in the Reading Mathematics programs.

16. **Provision for turn-key**: (defined in an earlier section of this paper).

The contractor agrees that, upon request of the Project Director, the contractor will expend a reasonable amount of effort in training local personnel in the maintenance and servicing of the contractor's proprietory equipment used in the Reading and Mathematics programs.

The contractor agrees to train or orient project management staff selected by the Project Director and the Management Support Group in the use of management techniques and approaches involved in the contractor's instructional systems.

The contractor agrees to submit in writing to the Management Support Group and the Project Director, for their use in monitoring the overall project, a management plan with specific task assignments, activities, and planning charts not later than thirty (30) days after the beginning of instruction. The contractor agrees to make available to the district on a confidential basis all internal planning and operational documents related to the conduct of the Reading and Mathematics programs, as may be deemed necessary by the district to fulfill the intent and purpose of the overall project.

17. **Schedule of penalties for non-compliance, for example, penalties for teaching the test by either contractor or district personnel.**

Within thirty (30) days of the commencement of the Project, the Auditing Contractor will examine the programs that constitute the contractor's curricula in Reading and Mathematics. If the Auditing Contractor finds within the materials test questions from the standardized examination being used to evaluate the contractor, it will identify these items in a written report to the contractor, in like manner, the contractor will present additional materials that it introduces for use in the project to the Auditing Contractor at least ten (10) days

> prior to their utilization in the project and the Auditing Contractor will identify items that are unacceptable, for the reason that such are contained in the standardized test being used for evaluation of the contractor, and report to the contractor within ten (10) days.
>
> If, upon presentation of the instances of "teaching the test," the contractor agrees with the Auditing Contractor, then the items in question will be deleted from the curriculum. If the contractor disagreed with Auditing Contractor, the contractor will be permitted to present its case directly to the district. Should the district agree that the materials or items in question should not be used, the contractor will immediately remove them from their materials. If the contractor fails to do so promptly, the district may consider the contractor's inaction as a breach of this Agreement.

Other provisions which may be necessary in contracts are: The term of the contract, a statement of local philosophy, a statement of the evaluation design and/or specification of test instruments; a statement of district monitoring policies; conditions for all testing; and provisions for research and development being carried on in the school.

Third Party Functions

The Independent Audit:

If performance contracting is a technique which can provide accountability, the involvement of an independent third party seems mandatory. While most districts tend to choose an independent auditor, it should be pointed out that objective accounting can be provided in at least two ways. In the first situation a district may beel that it is not capable of providing a sophisticated evaluation. In this case the district may choose to conduct the activities of an MSG itself and hire an independent evaluator whose reports furnish independent validity. A modification of this plan provided for hiring two different parties to function as the MSG and the auditor. Here, presumably the interests of the evaluator are as objective as those of the auditor but carried out on the total population rather than a sample. A third alternative is the instance where the district serves as its own MSG-evaluator, but hires measurement experts who certify the validity and appropriateness of the instruments; who may assist in the testing procedure; and who may work to develop more appropriate criterion referenced tests for the project. The district should consider these alternatives before deciding to retain an independent auditor.

Basically, the independent third party role should be designed to assure the lay board and the community that the school leaders and contractors are doing their work not just in the area of administering funds, but in terms of demonstrated results from the investment. Dr. Leon Lessinger has outlined four advantages which may accrue from the involvement of an independent auditor. They may be summarized as follows: 1) The research of the auditors amy lead to more sophisticated knowledge of the relationship between inputs and outputs, i.e., the demonstrated product in terms of fiscal-human resources allocated; 2) The independent audit can form the basis for the discovery and improvement of good practice in education; 3) auditing highlights the need for work in the areas of basic academic and vocational skills; and finally, 4) it can "renew credibility in the educational process."

At this time the concept of the independent audit is encouraged by the U.S. Office of Education (U.S.O.E.). ESEA Titles VII and VIII mandate the use of an auditor and it is strongly suggested in Title III. There is an unfortunate lack of both personnel and understanding regarding the audit. Some attempts are being made to remedy this situation. For example, a non-profit organization known as the Institute for the Development of Educational Auditing (IDEA) represents an effort to advance the theory and practice of educational auditing. U.S.O.E. provides a training course leading to the certification of educational auditors. In addition a number of private agencies will contract for the position of independent auditor.

In selecting the type of independent involvement appropriate for its needs the district must be aware first of the limited number of certified auditors and second, of the lack of an official position documenting the requirements of auditors. However, IDEA states that the independent auditor must draw on a wide range of skills, including evaluation design, testing, operations research, systems analysis, information processing, performance budgeting and the various educational specialties dictated by specific projects.

Other criteria the district might use in selecting the auditor could include independence from the program, proximity to the site, and an acceptable performance record, or experience. Even though the audit contract will represent only a small percentage of the total funds, the contracting agent must make every effort to find a qualified party to assume this essential function.

W. Stanley Kruger of the U.S. Office of Education has defined the auditor's activities in terms of two stages, the developmental period and the operational period. During the first phase the auditor can first review U.S.O.E. guidelines, the preliminary proposal and draft the formal proposal. Second, the auditor should critique the proposed evaluation design. This might include determining the baseline data, the types of instruments, and the adequacy of the evaluation data to be collected. The auditor should also be sure that the evaluation will provide data on both product and process in operational and management areas. At this time the auditor may recommend revisions if he notes discrepancies between the objectives and the proposed evaluation. Third, the auditor and district should develop the audit plan and contract. Care should be taken that the contract is situation specific, clear as to purpose and types of staff services, and that the audit products are specified (e.g., reports, conferences, etc.).

The operational period can be divided into three activity phases: pre-visit, on-site visit, and post-visit. Prior to visits (which should be scheduled appropriately in terms of key evaluation activities) the auditor should have received and analyzed the evaluation documents from the local educational agency (LEA). On the basis of this information the auditor can determine the specific sampling activities and questions to be conducted during the on-site visit. The auditor should then develop the visitation schedule in coordination with the LEA.

During the on-site visit the auditor may perform any or all of the following functions. First, he will conduct sampling to verify the results of specific evaluation. This may include observation of evaluation procedures such as testing, observation of the program operation, interviewing students, parents, and staff, spotchecking tests, questionnaires, etc. and reviewing material products. Based on these findings the auditor will review evaluation data for any portion of the evaluation which has revealed discrepancies. Finally, he should determine procedures for handling the major discrepancy findings.

Post visit activities are as follows: First, preparing audit report. This report might cover these items: general comments on the quality of project evaluation, a detailed critique of the product and process evaluation, a description of the visit findings with a summary and interpretation of consistencies and discrepancies, recommendations for revisions in the evaluation design and confirmation or questioning of the need for program modifications which have been proposed as a result of project evaluation. This written document will probably then be presented to and discussed with the LEA. Finally, th auditor must prepare a final report summarizing the entire project which will then be submitted to the appropriate LEA personnel.

The Management Support Group:

The role of the MSG has been alluded to in this paper a number of times. The purpose of this section is to discuss the role of the MSG and second to present the possible functions an MSG may perform.

Discussion with a number of private firms and government agencies may lead the LEA to conclude that the retention of a management support group is integral to the use of performance contracting. As was stated in the section on the independent audit, it does seem most important to involve at least one outside group to lend credence and objectivity to the project. In the case of the first alternative suggested on p. 28 the MSG might perform this function in its capacity as an evaluator. However, if this is the position of the MSG, care must be taken to insure their objectivity in terms of the project. In this instance the district would probably either hire an additional firm for some of the MSG activities or conduct these function itself. Before hiring an MSG the district must first analyze carefully the functions for which they may contract. Secondly, they should review the capabilities of the district to perfrom these activities with its own staff, and finally, come to a decision based on time and cost considerations as to whether it is more feasible to spend the money on a private firm or conduct these functions on their own. It should not be taken for granted that a full-time MSG is necessary. Alternatives might include 1) contracting with an MSG for specific, limited activities (e.g., evaluation); 2) contracting with an MSG for a number of on-site days at crucial times; or 3) contracting with an MSG for in-service training designed to develop the necessary capabilities in the district staff.

Given these alternatives, the activities of the MSG may include any, all or none of the following:

1. Conducting a detailed needs assessment prior to or during initial planning.
2. Assisting in the development of goals and objectives. These statements will form the basis of the project and should be considered very carefully. Following the needs assessment the district generally states a limited number of board goals to meet the needs. Each goal should then be broken down into both product and process objectives. The latter refer to the task analysis of the work structure along with a time line as to when these tasks must be performed to get the project operational.
3. The development of a management system. Here the district and MSG determine who is responsible for which activities.
4. The MSG can be very helpful in developing the RFP (discussed in an earlier section) and providing a list of qualified bidders. It may also be helpful to use MSG assistance in negotiations at the pre-bidders conference, the analysis of bids, and as advisors in the selection of a contractor. In the negotiations with the contractor the MSG can be used as an outside party protecting the district's interest.
5. The MSG can be helpful in monitoring the performance of the contract. This is a sophisticated endeavor which should monitor procedures, develop a pupil data file, provide cost figures and perform both process and product evaluation. The evaluation is a complicated procedure doing for the entire population what the auditor does on a sample basis. Basically, it must 1) provide information as to whether the objectives of the proposal are being met; 2) provide enough data so that the program can be replicated with turn-key and 3) ascertain how much is being accomplished so that the instructional contractor might be paid accordingly. It is obvious that the evaluator must be skilled in the areas of measurement, programming, data analysis and reporting procedures.
6. Finally, the MSG can be of assistance in helping the district to decide whether to assume the program at the conclusion of the contract and assisting the district and the instructional contractor in turn-key procedures.

Dr. Lessinger suggests a number of advantages to the district in contracting for management support services. First, the MSG can serve as a communication link and/or buffer between the vested interests of the community and the school system which is developing program proposals. Second, the MSG has access to new developments in the field and can assist the LEA in developing the RFP to assure that the conditions and constraints in the RFP do not preclude but encourage the opportunity for these new developments to be demonstrated. Third, the MSG can serve as a buffer between the LEA and potential bidders. Finally, the MSG can provide technical assistance during the operational stages, perhaps on an "as-needed" basis.

Legal Considerations

As the concept of performance contracting in education is articulated, and more and more school districts undertake performance contracting projects, many legal constraints and questions will arise. The purpose of this section is to provide school personnel with some of the questions and answers regarding the legal considerations in educational performance contracting. This section should not be construed as an exhaustive study of the legal aspects of performance contracting in education, rather, it should be viewed as an outline which provides several parameters within which different school districts and states must respond individually.

The first major consideration is the way in which the state education agency and/or The State Attorney General's Office view the concept of performance contracting and its many ramifications. Following is a list of questions the answers to which are specific to the individual state in which a proposed project is to be initiated.

1. If an outside contractor is utilized by the school district for the provision of instruction and/or services for pupils, will the school district's statutory obligation for said instruction and services be fully met?

2. Are there state or federal limitations regarding the use of State, Local, and Federal funds to support all or part of a performance contracting project?

3. Do existing state plans for various federal programs, that may be potential funding sources for the project, permit utilization of outside contractors who will provide all or part of the instruction and/or services include in the project?
4. Will the State Education Agency authorize credit for instruction provided by the contractor in reading or mathematics?
5. Will the State Education Agency permit paraprofessional staff members employed by the contractor to perform certain teaching tasks under the direct supervision of a certificated teacher?
6. Will the State Education Agency permit the teachers in the contractors program to be contractor's employees?
7. Will an outside contractor's instructional personnel stand in *loco parentis* to the student?
8. Are the contractor-employed teachers required to be certificated?
9. Does a local district have authority to contract with or enter into agreements with an agency of the federal government?
10. Does a local district have authority to contract with or to enter into agreement with private concerns for the provision of instruction?
11. Does a local district have authority to expend state/local maintenance funds to pay for part or all of the cost of instruction provided by a private concern under contract with the district?

Experience indicates that the most effective way to have these questions answered is to prepare a brief to be sent to the State Attorney General via the State Education Agency. This brief should include a description of the proposed project and a delineation of the roles of the oustide contractor and the school district.

The remainder of this section outlines some of the legal aspects of performance contracting as they effect the local districts regulations and policies. Potential considerations can be grouped into the following areas:

1. Personnel
2. Funding
3. Liability
4. Facilities
5. Students
6. Copyrights

Each of the above areas will be considered independently.

1. Personnel

The primary question in this area is whether project personnel (e.g., teachers and paraprofessionals) are considered employees of the education contractor or the local school district.

If personnel are considered contractor employees, and have been previously employed by the local district, certain benefits such as retirement, teacher association insurance, etc. would be either lost or discontinued. Another related question is whether the contractor should be required to provide an equal level of benefits to personnel in the program as a comparable district employee receives. One possible solution to this dilemma is for district personnel selected for inclusion in the project to take a leave of absence thus retaining the option to return to the district without losing tenure or other accrued benefits.

Existing district employment compensation rates, particularly where established through union negotiations, will be a constraint on the education contractor who may wish to use an incentive—penalty compensation scale based upon student achievement. This problem must be negotiated with the teacher union and/or the education contractor.

The majority of states have not yet set accreditation standards for instructional aides and paraprofessionals. As a guide, education contractors should be required to follow the regulations concerning salary, educational background and experience requirements already in existence within the district.

Some minimum requirements must be met in most instances regardless of whether the project personnel are employed by the education contractor or the local district. These are (1) employees must be selected without discrimination pursuant to Executive Order No. 11246, September 24, 1965, and (2) the education contractor or local district meet all requirements under the act including minimum wage standards and (3) all health certificates, X-rays, vaccinations, etc. required by the district should also be required of the education contractor.

2. Funding

The district should consider what allocations are allowable in a special learning facility for instructional managers and aides.

Federal funds are available for performance contracts with outside private education contractors under the Elementary and Secondary Act (P.L. 89-10) Titles I, and VII, and Executive interest in the general area has been recently expressed (see President Nixon's March 3, 1970, message on education). The only qualification regarding the use of federal funds is that ultimate control of the project must remain in the hands of the local education agency.

One possible constraint to the continued use of Title I funds involves recently issued guidelines for ESEA Title I. Basically, these guidelines require that state and local funds must be spent to provide comparable services among all schools. Only then can Title I funds be used to provide supplementary services in schools qualified for Title I projects. The question arises whether State and Local funds spent on a learning facility which does not have comparable resources, (higher pupil-teacher ratio, more instructional hardware, longer hours of facility utilization) will violate those guidelines. This question will require decisions at several levels; which so far have not been forthcoming.

3. Liability

There are three general areas of liability other than the general contractual liability of both parties: (a) facilities use during "regular" and "after" school hours; (b) student travel to and from the learning center facility and (c) liability of the district, the education contractors, and instructional personnel. Following are some suggestions regarding these three areas:

a) Careful consideration should be given the area of liability during contract negotiations between the local district and the education contractor. Agreements should be reached on such variables as insurance, policy dollar amounts, and responsibility for payment of premiums.

b) The educational contractor and his personnel should owe the same duty and obligations as does the regular local district personnel. During after hours use of facilities there should probably be a joint liability to both personnel and students.

c) Within the confines of the learning center, the education contractor should assume the liability. Travel to and from the learning centers should be a joint responsibility of district and education contractor.

d) As mentioned, liability should be negotiated, and should be stipulated in the contract. Although instructional personnel may be full-time education contractor employees, the local district should consider assumption of liability for the employees. This appears to be more desirable from both a political and legal vantage point.

4. Facilities

The most important consideration in this area is whether or not the facility or classroom which houses the education contractor's program should be considered a school facility. Many education contractors need extensive electrical wiring for their technology; sometimes requiring a separate facility (mobile learning units) designed to meet their specific needs. The question remains as to whether outside facilities utilized by the contractor should be viewed as school facilities. A suggestion is that all contractor facilities regardless of the acquisition arrangement (e.g., lease, buy, etc.) be designated as local school facilities and that these facilities be accorded the same benefits (e.g., insurance) as other school facilities.

The local district and the education contractor should agree on general maintenance charges, facility code requirements and safety requirements. All equipment installation and classroom modifications should be made in accordance with district policy.

It should be anticipated that the facility will be utilized during "other hours"; this "other hours" clause includes before and after school use of facilities for student make-up work. Other hour utilization is desirable for both parties, however, a definition should be drafted stipulating the nature and responsibilities of such use.

5. Students

Selection of target student participants and instructional personnel cannot be made on the basis of race, nor can assignment to facilities be made on the basis of race. Since in most projects, students will be in regular district classes the majority of each day, the structure of these classes should be the controlling factor, presuming the classes are within desegregation guidelines. Within the contractor operated learning center, if the racial composition of classes deviates substantially from the average racial composition of the local district schools, there may be some problem under current court decisions and federal guidelines. However, the fact that accelerated upgrading hastens the process of effective desegregation should counter arguments as to the intent and consequences of the project.

A special and fast evolving area of concern involves the local district codes for student conduct, penalties for violation, and responsibility for enforcement. An agreement should be reached between the education contractor and the local district as to student rights within contractor operated facilities. The question, in essence, is who dictates policy within the contractors operated facility, the school district or the contractor.

It should also be understood that state or federal laws or con stitutional provisions may restrict the extent to which such things as tort liability, rights of students, and other legal obligations may be negotiated at all. It is possible, for example, that an agreement that the contractor assume liability for certain torts, or responsibility for administering penalties for violations of rules of student conduct, might be invalidated by a statute or court decision which prohibits the school district from contracting away such obligations.

The local district and the contractor should also negotiate the authority to remove a student for disruptive conduct. A related area is the relationship between the contractor's project director and the principal of the school in which the project is housed. This is a particularly sensitive area and the obligations and authority of each should be enumerated in the contract document.

6. Copyrights

After the selection of the education contractor, the district should be able to ascertain which materials are developed and copyrighted and which materials will be developed during the operation of the project. The district should then negotiate with the contractor over the copyrighting of materials, the production and testing of which would be underwritten by the local district.

The local district should be able to share in the royalties or benefits accruing from a developmental effort in which they in part fund. This concept is analogous to Leon Lessinger's concept of "Developmental Capital" in which a school district through developing needed educational products can share them with other districts and receive some compensation; this concept indeed inspires innovation.

The legal and policy constraints in education performance contracting are many and varied. The success of performance contracing in fostering innovative practices in education rests on the integrity between business and education. Realizing this fact increases the need for careful consideration of the legal and policy ramifications.

Summary of National Performance Contracting Activities

With the number of schools and school districts engaging in performance contracting growing daily it is beyond the scope of this report to attempt a complete listing of all of the performance contracting activities. The Rand Corporation was awarded a $300,000 contract by the U.S. Office of Education to do a comprehensive study of performance contracting activities. An interim report due in mid-1971 should provide a comprehensive listing of activities which has not been available to date.

A valuable resource person at the Office of Education is Mr. Albert Mayrhofer, in the Bureau of Elementary and Secondary Education. He has had extensive experience in helping school districts who are contemplating entering into a performance contract.

A list of the Office of Economic Opportunity performance contracts follows:

Office of Economic Opportunity Contracts

School District	Contract Value	Contractor
Portland, Maine	$ 308,184	Singer/Graflex Corporation
Rockland, Maine	299,211	Quality Education Development
Hartford, Connecticut	320,573	Alpha Systems, Incorporated
Philadelphia, Pennsylvania	296,291	Westinghouse Learning Corp.
McNairy County (Selmer,) Tennessee	286,991	Plan Education Centers, Inc.
McComb, Mississippi	263,085	Singer/Graflex

School District	Contract Value	Contractor
Duval County (Jacksonville) Florida	342,300	Learning Foundations, Inc.
Dallas Texas	299,417	QED
Taft, Texas	243,751	Alpha
Hammond, Indiana	342,528	Learning Foundations
Grand Rapids, Michigan	322,464	Alpha
Fresno, California	299,015	Westinghouse
Seattle, Washington	343,800	Singer/Graflex
New York (Bronx), New York	341,796	Learning Foundations
Clarke County (Athens), Georgia	301,770	Plan Education
Las Vegas, Nevada	298,744	Westinghouse
Witchita, Kansas	294,700	Plan Education
Anchorage, Alaska	44,632	QED
TOTAL	$5,649,252	

II

PERFORMANCE CONTRACTING: MAKING IT LEGAL

by Reed Martin

If your district is considering performance contracting, watch how much power you delegate.

The history of performance contracting in education has shown that, when this process is planned and executed carefully, it can show positive results, but when improperly planned, it can be a terrible mistake. A large part of the planning of a performance contract involves legal considerations.

Authority to contract: The first consideration is the ability of a local school district to contract with private organizations to perform instructional tasks. Local education agencies, as creations of the state, are given very limited powers to contract, and any contract in excess of that power is void, even though both parties agree to it.

Most schools may contract with outside parties to provide certain services, but those are generally services not imposed upon the school by constitutional declaration or by state delegation. Where the school is under a duty to perform a task, then an outside contract for its performance may be null.

Although there are as yet no judicial decisions directly on educational performance contracting, cases on the general problem indicate that a controlling factor may be that a school cannot contract to employ private individuals when public employes have been retained to perform a comparable job.

Thus, having a private company take over the full operation

Reprinted with permission from *Nation's Schools*, January, 1971.

of a school, even with the purpose of doing a "better" job than an employe already retained on the public payroll, may raise a legal barrier. A contract for more limited services which the school cannot provide may come closer to meeting legal requirements.

Delegation of powers: Assume that a school has the authority to contract for the type of services it desires. A second legal obstacle may then arise: improper delegation of powers. States delegate certain educational policy-making functions to the local school and these powers cannot be delegated to a private group. That would be an abdication of responsibility on the part of the local school.

Cases seem to indicate that courts will examine a school's policy-making role even more closely than its authority to contract. It is not clear where a court might draw the line in regard to the various educational tasks a school might ask a company to perform, but policy roles *must* be controlled by the school.

Three factors are important in determining whether a school is retaining control under a performance contract. First, properly drafted program specifications, contained in a Request for Proposals, can indicate the school's intent to remain in charge. If the specifications are incomplete or vague, and subject to the bidder's own interpretation, then the school may be delegating too much authority to the bidder. The outside agency might thus be making decisions tantamount to policy-making.

A second area is staff expertise. The school must provide a monitoring function during the program in order to retain authority and protect policy-making prerogatives. If staff does not have the expertise to do this, the company will in reality be in control and the school would have abdicated its responsibility. Many schools secure outside management support not only to increase their capability in planning but also to assure their ability to retain control over the program.

The third area for consideration is the basic purpose of the contract. Some schools unfortunately perceive performance contracting as a way to contract out their problem students, foisting responsibility for failure onto an outside party that guarantees success. One cannot really blame overburdened schools for finding such a notion so attractive, but contracting out as an end in itself may be a delegation of too much authority. If a program were to be conducted for a specified period of time, evaluated and then either abandoned or absorbed by the school, the school would obviously be retaining full authority. If a program might be extended indefinitely, always under contract to an outside agency, then effective control of decisions with policy implications may have passed to the contractor.

The state commissioner of education in Texas, which has four performance projects underway, drew that line clearly in posing this question recently to the state's attorney general: May a school district enter into performance contracts with private corporations where the program is primarily proposed for a study of the capability of the private sector to facilitate desirable educational reforms, as distinguished from any general plan or movement to contract with private corporations for actual instructional services? The attorney general answered in the affirmative.

One may assume that a school is on safest legal ground when it specifies in the original contract the procedures for taking over the operation of a successfully demonstrated instructional program. This process has come to be called the *turnkey* phase – when the contractor turns the "keys" over to the school so the school can run the program thereafter. Where the purpose of the contract is not "to facilitate desirable educational reforms," and the contractor insists on keeping the keys rather than turning them over, the state may insist that the school change its lock.

Assuming that the school has the legal authority to contract for instructional services, and that it is clearly retaining its policy-making role, the next step is developing the contract. (The delegation question, however, must constantly be kept in mind.) At this point, the school may choose one of two courses of action: 1) it may develop a Request for Proposals (RFP), a set of educational specifications to be contracted for, which is the subject of open competitive bids, or 2) it may skip this step and contract with a company on a "sole source" basis. Most schools choose competitive bidding.

Developing the RFP: Assuming that the school will seek open bids, the RFP becomes important because it will be the basis of all that follows. It specifies the type of programs the school wants proposed in terms of time, cost, levels of performance, guarantees and conditions, such as training local personnel.

Consistent with the turnkey process, the RFP should ensure that the program being developed specifically for that school, if successfully demonstrated, would be a program that could be expanded throughout the entire school system and acceptable to all parties concerned.

The major legal consideration should be the conduct of the bidding process, according to cases involving housing turnkey problems. The delegation problem inherent in program specificity has already been noted. In addition, the proposals must be evaluated in a way that is fair to bidders and serves the public interest in selecting the best proposal. Evaluation standards and procedures should be stated in the RFP and scrupulously followed by the school decision-makers. Unless the RFP requires bidders to supply all the information needed for evaluation, in a consistent format that allows proposals to be contrasted, then the award of a contract may be susceptible to challenge.

"Sole source" contracts: The school may choose to award the contract on a sole source basis. In this type of contract, there is usually no public goal setting, no community participation in decision-making, and no accountability for the decision-making process. Experience of several school systems in recent months has shown that the cost of these contracts is usually higher, the performance guarantee lower, and the public interest less likely to be served.

This last consideration raises a possible legal problem. A court might find it strange that the purchase of many goods and services by schools is required to be on open bid but the service most related to the constitutionally mandated educational function can be purchased behind closed doors. Such a practice might be found not to be in the public interest.

A sole source arrangement raises the further legal problem of how much authority is being given to the company. Where a company initiates the contract with the school (rather than the school seeking out companies), proposes an approach which includes curricular contents and the scope of the program, and the school signs the contract, the company may have in fact assumed too much responsibility in the area of educational policy formulation. Courts might feel that program specifications (the RFP) initiated by the school, with the school choosing among competing bidders, better demonstrates the school's control over policy questions.

Drafting the contract: A contract can be drawn up which incorporates the necessary terms and conditions of the RFP and the successful bidder's response. Two areas that are the most difficult, and also the most controversial, are testing and payment.

The whole question of testing is one of the most complicated in developing a workable contract. Testing instruments must be specified in the contract, and the responsibilities for administering and scoring tests should be stipulated. Procedures for testing students before and after the program, testing replacement students when they enter the program, and testing students who are dropping out of the program should all be considered. The school should be protected against the contractor's including test items in his curriculum. Testing instruments should also be developed to measure interim as well as final performance. As an indication of the complexity of these provisions, they require about ten pages in most performance contracts currently in use in the education field.

The next most difficult area in the contract is spelling out the payment provisions. Payment schedules should reward performance above the minimum guaranteed level and penalize the failure to perform. In addition to final payment, the school will probably want a schedule of payment for meeting interim performance objectives. There will have to be a different schedule of payment for students, depending on when they entered and when they left the program and, whether they were pretested or post-tested adequately. There may be a dollar ceiling on the total contract so the payment schedule must reflect a graduated scale which cannot exceed a certain amount. And of course the contract must stipulate the conditions under which no payment will be made to the contractor.

It is vital that payment schedules provide real incentives for the contractor to maximize the performance of each child and to continue the program at a full level of effort all year long. Some "performance" contracts allow a contractor to ignore slower students or push them out of school, maximize the performance of a few individuals, and cut back the level of effort as maximums are achieved. Other contracts provide little or no penalty for failure.

Virtually all of the legal questions raised by the involvement of the private sector in public education revolve around the public interest. That interest cannot be served by schools' seeking easy solutions to educational problems, or comapnies' seeking quick profits. The public interest will best be served if performance contracing is used as a legal tool for institutional reform so that schools can increase their ability to meet their responsibilities to their state, their students, and themselves. □

Mr. Martin, an attorney, is an officer of Education Turnkey Systems, Washington, D.C., which is providing management support to performance contracts in 30 cities this fall.